Thomas F. De Voe

The market Assistant

Containing a brief description of every article of human food sold in the public markets of the cities of New York, Boston, Philadelphia, and Brooklyn

Thomas F. De Voe

The market Assistant

Containing a brief description of every article of human food sold in the public markets of the cities of New York, Boston, Philadelphia, and Brooklyn

ISBN/EAN: 9783744736442

Printed in Europe, USA, Canada, Australia, Japan

Cover: Foto ©Suzi / pixelio.de

More available books at **www.hansebooks.com**

THE MARKET ASSISTANT,

CONTAINING A BRIEF DESCRIPTION OF

EVERY ARTICLE OF HUMAN FOOD

SOLD IN THE PUBLIC MARKETS

OF THE CITIES OF

NEW YORK, BOSTON, PHILADELPHIA, AND BROOKLYN;

INCLUDING THE VARIOUS

DOMESTIC AND WILD ANIMALS, POULTRY, GAME,
FISH, VEGETABLES, FRUITS, &c., &c.

WITH

MANY CURIOUS INCIDENTS AND ANECDOTES.

BY

THOMAS F. DE VOE,

AUTHOR OF "THE MARKET-BOOK," ETC.

"What we eat."

NEW YORK:
PUBLISHED BY HURD AND HOUGHTON.
1867.

Entered according to Act of Congress, in the year 1866, by
Thomas F. De Voe,
in the Clerk's Office of the District Court for the Southern District of New York.

PREFACE.

I have introduced myself to the public in the first volume of "The Market Book," by giving them a history of the Public Market-places in the city of New York from the earliest settlement, with numerous and curious incidents, more particularly relating to the local history of that city. It was also my intention to have included in the second volume of that work much of the matter which I have placed in this. The dreadful Rebellion, however, commenced with the attack on Fort Sumter the day after I had arranged for the publishing of ("The Market Book") the first volume, and I concluded to wait for the suppression of the Rebellion before entering upon the second. In the mean time my gathering notes had accumulated to such formidable dimensions that I was compelled to divide the *useful* from the *historical;* the first of which is presented in this volume, called "The Market Assistant;" and the latter will soon appear in the second volume of "The Market Book."

The object of this volume is to present that which may be found practically useful as well as interesting. It aims at bringing together, in as small compass as possible and in a form easy of reference, those items of information which many would desire to possess when called upon to cater for the household. In order fully to carry out the practical views here indicated, this work is divided into several headings; all of which, however, harmonize into one connecting form, "*What we eat:*" Domestic, or Tame Animals; Wild Animals, or Animal Game; Poultry; Wild Fowl and Birds, or Bird Game; Fish; Vegetables; Pot and Medicinal Herbs; Fruits and Nuts; Dairy and Household Products, etc.

The desire to present such a work, has lead me—pleasantly—to employ many of the leisure hours from my professional duties in placing together the thoughts and experience of thirty-five years' observation.

What I deem the *useful* is gleaned from the daily wants, and the common expressions of the day—something to eat!—"What shall we have to-day for dinner? What is there in our Markets fit to eat? What kinds of meats, poultry, game, fish, vegetables, and fruits are in season? What names are given to the different joints of meats, and what dishes are they severally and generally used for? We have had roasts, steaks, and chops; and chops, steaks, and roasts, until we are tired of them! Now, do say, what shall we have for dinner?" These, with many other exclamations, are daily discussed, and no one to answer. We, however, claim for this Book a comprehensive answer to all questions of this nature.

More fully to carry out the views I have entertained in relation to the various articles of food of our citizens, I have thought proper to illustrate with outlined diagram figures of such animals usually portioned out and sold by the public-market butchers, with the various names, as illustrated by the accompanying engraved cuts of the principal joints; which are intended to assist in their recognition when called for, as well as to aid in rendering perfect the dishes commonly made from them.

I may here remark, that many of these engravings were sketched by me from nature, and, although some of them may not represent what I would wish from them, if so, it is proper here to state that the faulty drawing of such must not rest on the engraver (Stephen Weekes, Esq.), as his reputation in this beautiful art must not be impaired by my inexperience as the draughtsman.

After the Butchers' Meats will follow a brief description of other articles of food, with the periods of their season or when considered best; how to judge and select them in the various public market-places.

In obtaining a more thorough knowledge of many of these articles of food noticed, I have been greatly assisted by the experience of many of the intelligent dealers and others, who have on all occasions evinced a communicative and friendly feeling to my oft-repeated visits and numerous inquiries. To enumerate or name all—with the many and various and useful works, and especially the newspaper press—from which I have derived much interesting matter, would now be impossible, as a long period has elapsed since the commencement of my *gatherings* took place; and I can only say, that my indebtedness is hereby acknowledged, with a sincere return of my warmest thanks to each and all for their great assistance.

Many of the various articles of food are often found in the private markets, or "meat-shops," but never the variety, quantity, or with the same chance for cheapness, or choice, as are to be found in our established public markets.

Having had practical experience in both public and private markets, I am free to say, that citizens and others can be best protected and accommodated in public markets—the larger the better—and more especially when the products are obtained from first hands.

"The market-place" was originally designed, simply to accommodate the producer and consumer; a *mart* where all might meet at certain times—the one to sell and the other to purchase or trade. Eaton, in his review of New York in 1814, gives the reader some idea of "the market-place" at that period, which he presents to us in the following lines:

"The place where no distinctions are,
All sects and colors mingle there,

PREFACE.

Long folks and short, black folks and gray
With common bawds, and folks that pray,
Rich folks and poor, both old and young,
And good, and bad, and weak, and strong,
The wise and simple, red and white,
With those that play and those that fight
The high, the low, the proud the meek.
And all one common object seek;
For lady, belle, and buck, and lass,
Here mingle in one common mass,
Contending all which shall be first,
To buy the cheapest, best, or worst.
In fact their object is to get
Such things as they can 'ford to eat—
Some *beef*, some *pork*, some *lamb* or *veal*,
And those who cannot buy must steal—
Nothing more clear, I'll tell you why,
All kinds of folks must *eat* or *die*.
Objects of honor or disgrace,
Are all seen at the *market-place*.
Do you a slothful debtor seek?
Go there, and you may with him speak;
Seek there a fool, a friend, a foe,
For all together there will go.
Are you a painter, and would trace,
The features of one in distress?
Go there, for there you're sure to find,
An object suited to your mind.
And do you seek a beauteous form,
A well-shaped leg or handsome arm?
Go seek it there, for there are all,
Of every person since the fall:
The virgin, matron, husband, child,
Upon this place have often smiled;
Whate'er you want, you'll find it there,
There's every thing, and every where
But those who are on killing bent,
Alone shall feel my chastisement;
In *Boston* these, 'tis said have not,
Or common sense or feelings got;
And therefore they are not allowed,
The common jurors' seat to crowd;
But butchers here, like other men,
Have common sense and sense of pain;
These weigh the *meat*, and you must know,

The *meat* side of the scale is low,
And wants your care to balance it,
If you would have your proper weight,
Or else *two pounds* of *beef*, you'll see,
Will just *two pounds odd ounces be*
The *rich*, who buy a stately piece,
Will scarcely know their *meats* decrease;
But 'tis the *poor*, who little buy,
That miss their *meat*, and wonder why.
'Tis thus with some—but not with all—
For many, from the loaded *stall*,
With balance even, weigh the meat,
Too honest to defraud or cheat."

Now, we find, "the market-place" assumes another aspect—a change which time and circumstances have created. The producer is often hundreds of miles in one direction, while the consumer may be as many hundred in another, from the *mart* at which the productions were sold and purchased. Through the course of the year, the products of the North, South, East, and West, are to be found in our large public market-places; from which great quantities are disposed of, to be consumed in other cities, towns, or villages, or on the many ocean or river steamers or other vessels, as well as in foreign countries.

A great trade has imperceptibly grown upon us (particularly in New York), which I have sometimes thought, would have been more profitable to both producer and consumer, if proper laws, and practical, honest heads, had been placed over these vast interests, which so much affect the general health and comfort, as well as the *pockets* of our over-taxed citizens; and I cannot avoid the conclusion, that if our public markets were properly conducted, they would be highly advantageous, not only to the city and citizens, but to all who have occasion to obtain supplies, as they facilitate the voluntary inspection, as well as the comparison of every article offered for sale in them, and they also concentrate the trade by which the people are protected from imposition.

This great metropolis should have her public markets as objects of our city's pride, by having proper and substantial buildings, kept orderly, cleanly, well-arranged and *officered*, when they could be visited by strangers in safety and comfort, as well as by all her citizens, who would find pleasure and exercise in the performance of a necessary and agreeable duty.

THOMAS F. DE VOE,

Butcher.

JEFFERSON MARKET,

City of New York, 1864.

WHAT WE EAT.

THE first natural demand of man is food to nourish his wasting system, and for this purpose he has been bountifully provided for with an extensive choice, furnished by the various productions of both land and water. Man in his natural state, like the wild beasts of the forest, consumes food naturally and spontaneoüsly obtained; but civilized man, luxuriously trained and educated, obtains his principal support from artificial food, or that which has been produced by his skill and labor; and thus we find that the wild and cultivated animals, as well as the natural and cultivated plants, is the proper and sole food for cultivated man.

> "Man is a carnivorous production,
> And must have meals at least once a day·
> He cannot live, like *woodcocks*, upon suction,
> But, like the *shark* and tiger, must have prey."

The various fruits, grain, roots, and herbs, with flesh, fish, and fowl, all contribute to the sustenance of man, or rather, to furnish the daily wants, and to supply the wear and tear of his body. The perfect conformation of man's organization is capable of converting into nourishment every peculiarity of food, and separating the nutritive portions of every variety from each production.

Authors agree that animal food is found to be strongly nourishing, and, when extensively used, it is too heating and stimulating, and, withal, overworks the digestive organs, which, after a time, exhausts and debilitates the body; while, on the other hand, a pure vegetable diet seems insufficient to secure to the human system all the strength and vigor of which it is capable, although thousands of individuals live almost entirely on the latter, but it is found they are seldom so robust, so active, or so brave. Physiologists, therefore, are of opinion that a mixed diet of animal and vegetable food is best suited to the nature and constitution of man. In warm climates, however, meat is found less desirable than any other kind of food.

"All animals, with but few exceptions, are used as food by various nations of men, although that which is selected as a delicacy by one country is refused as unfit and loathsome by another. The Englishman refuses to dine on *Snails* with an Italian, on *Frogs* with a Frenchman, on *Horseflesh* with the Tartars, or on the *Crocodile, Toad,* or *Locust* with the African.

"A traveller, in the last century, remarked to certain Arabs that he wondered at their eating insects so disgusting as *Locusts ;* to which they replied, with some show of reason, that it savored of affectation in a person who could swallow an *Oyster* to be startled by any thing in the way of eating."

"The Americans will not eat *horses, asses, dogs,* cats, rats, or mice, but they are all used as food, and some as great luxuries, in other countries."

In Africa the natives eat *Ants* stewed in Palm Oil, and the large *Termites,* or *White Ants,* are roasted in iron pots and eaten by handfuls, as sugar-plums ; and as for *Locusts,* Dr. Phipson says they are far from dreading their invasions, but look upon a dense cloud of *Locusts* as we would look upon a miracle of *Bread* and *Butter* floating in the air. They smoke them, or salt them, or boil them, or stew them, or grind them down as *Corn,* and get fat on them.

"Lo ! the poor Indian, who untutored feeds
On *Locusts, Beetles, Frogs,* and *Centipedes !*
His taste keen hunger never taught to sigh
For Beef, Veal, Mutton, Pork, or *Pumpkin Pie ;*
But thinks, admitted to that equal feast,
All things are good for man as well as beast."

It is also found that *Horseflesh* is not an uncommon article of food, either in Denmark, Sweden, Norway, and other places, where it is publicly exposed for sale in their public markets. It is upon record that about the year 1810, in the town of Christiana, Norway, four hundred horses had been killed for the consumption of that town for a period of a little over two years. We also find it asserted by M. Duchatelet that a very large quantity is consumed in Paris. The *Knackers* (Horse-slayers) and their families, who live principally on it, have a remarkably robust and healthy appearance. Surgeon Larrey also states that the French armies, during many campaigns under Napoleon I., were greatly indebted to *Horseflesh* for the means of subsistence. A correspondent from Vienna to the "New York Times," 1855, gives a favorable account of its use in that city, as follows: "The consumption of Horseflesh by the poorest classes, which for the past two years has been more and more resorted to, tends to check any rapid rise in Beef and the common meats. While good *roasts* and bake-pieces cost fifteen kreutzers the pound—not even so high as in New York—Horseflesh is bought for five kreutzers. An acquaintance who has eaten *beef-steak* from this meat—would it do to call it *horse-steak?*—assures me that it does not taste at all bad—that it is indeed a delicacy—and argues from the nature of the food of the two, that horseflesh is a much choicer diet than fried chicken. It may seem to show how well the poorer classes like it, to state that within the past few weeks, in Hamburg, if I remember rightly, the price of this article of food has risen to almost its former rate, owing to the increased demand."

Mule-meat has also been spoken of as being excellent eating; although its trial took place under peculiar circumstances, yet it was compared with horseflesh and such beef as was in the possession of the besieged rebels while *caged* in Port Hudson. A Confederate officer who has, or is, preparing a detailed account of what took place inside of this fortification during its beleaguerment, says that when (29th of June, 1863) "the last quarter-ration of beef had been given out to the troops, on the 1st of July, at the request of many officers, a wounded mule was killed and cut up for experimental eating. All those who partook of it spoke highly of the dish: the flesh of mules being of a darker color than beef, of a finer grain, quite tender and juicy, and as having a flavor between that of beef and venison. There was an immediate demand for this kind of food, and the number of mules killed by the commissariat daily increased. Some horses were also slaughtered, and their flesh was found to be very good eating, but *not equal* to the mule. Rats, of which there were plenty about the deserted camps, were also caught by many officers and men, and were found to be quite a luxury—superior, in the opinion of those who ate them, to spring-chicken."

The ancients appear to have been rather singular in their choice of diet, as Dick, in his "Diet and Regime," says—"They used neither buckwheat, nor *French Beans*, nor *Spinach*, nor *Sage, Tapioca, Saless, Arrowroot*, nor *Potato* or its varieties, nor even the common, but a sort of marsh-grown *Bean*, nor many of our fruits, as the *Orange, Tamarinds*, nor American *Maize*. On the other hand, they ate substances which we now neglect: the *Mallow*, the herb *Ox Tongue*, the sweet *Acorn*, the *Lupin*. They used greatly *Radish, Lettuce, Sorrel;* they liked the flesh of wild *Asses*, of little *Dogs*, of the *Dormouse*, of the *Fox*, of the *Bear*. They ate the flesh of *Parroquets*, and other rare birds, and of *Lizards*. They were fond of a great many fish and shell-fish which we now hold in no esteem. They employed as seasoning *Rue* and Assafœtida."

An amusing article on diet, written above one hundred years ago, is found in a London paper called "St. James' Chronicle," dated November 6, 1762, and thus reads:—"There is no affectation more ridiculous than the antipathies which many whimsical people entertain with respect to diet. One will swoon at a *Breast of Veal;* another can't bear the sight of a *Sucking-pig;* and another owes as great a grudge to a *Shoulder of Mutton* as Petruchio, in the farce.

How often does it happen in company that we are debarred of a necessary ingredient in a salad because somebody, forsooth, cannot touch oil! And what a rout is made, whisking away the *cheese* off the table, without our being suffered to have a morsel of this grand digester, if any one should happen to declare his dislike to it!

"There are others of an equally fantastic disposition, who, as we may say, choose to quarrel with their bread and butter. These are eternally suspicious that their food is not sweet. They bring their plates up to their noses, or their noses down to their plates, at every thing that is put upon them. Their stomachs are so delicately nice that they descry a fault in all they eat. The *fish* is stale, the *mutton* is rank, or the *suet* in the pudding is musty. I have an aunt who almost starves herself on account of her squeamishness in this particular. At one time she is sure the *sheep* died of the rot; at another the *pork* is measly; and she would not touch a bit of *beef* all the time of the distemper among the horned cattle. *Veal* she detests, because, she says, it is well known the Butchers blow it up with their nasty breath; besides, the *Calves* have brine given them to make their flesh white. She used to declare *House-Lamb* to be the only wholesome food, because the innocent creatures were fed with nothing but their mother's milk; but she has lately taken disgust to this likewise, since she has been told that some rascally butchers keep large mastiff-bitches on purpose for their *Lambs* to suck.

"I dined with her yesterday, when she made an apology for the *Beef* not being salt enough, saying that she was under a necessity of boiling it too soon, as she did not think it safe to buy any meat yet awhile, on account of the late inundations; for she was apprehensive that the drowned carcasses of *hogs*, *sheep*, and other cattle would make their way up to the London shambles. I was surprised that a suspicion of this sort should have entered her head, but more surprised still to find it hinted at afterwards by the following advertisement in the 'Public Advertiser' of Monday:

"'The Master and Wardens of the Butchers' Company do hereby acquaint the public that they have not been able (notwithstanding the utmost care and assiduity has been used by them) to find that any of the hogs or sheep that were drowned in the late unhappy floods, have been exposed to sale within this city or the suburbs thereof.

"'☞ Any person that sends notice to the Company, at their hall in Pudding Lane, of any *casualty* or unwholesome flesh of any sort that is exposed for sale, so that the same may be seized, will receive the thanks of the Company, and be a friend to the public in general, the Company being determined to prosecute all persons selling *casualty* or unwholesome flesh.'

"'I cannot help observing that it seems odd the butchers themselves should sound the alarm about *casualty flesh*, which many people otherwise might never have thought of. The fishmongers would never cry stinking *fish*, and the bakers would be unwilling to have it even supposed that any made use of alum in their bread. I remember, for a great while after the affair of Elizabeth Tofts, the Rabbit-woman, the owners and renters of warrens were all ruined, for persons would as soon eat a *cat* as a *rabbit*. Should the like disgust prevail against flesh, from the fear of its being *casualty flesh*, what would become of Smithfield and Leadenhall Markets? There is, indeed, some danger that people will conceive an antipathy against barrelled beef, pickled pork, and all kinds of soused meat, on this occasion; and it is to be hoped that the contractors for victualling His Majesty's Navy will not buy up any of the drowned cattle, to turn the stomachs of our sailors. The unwholesomeness, however, of *casualty flesh* I have heard denied by a gentleman, who had been in Italy, and declared that he himself had eaten heartily (without any ill effects) of a *hog* that was casually barbecued, and an *ox* that was roasted whole in the eruptions from Mount Vesuvius."

The mode of living adopted by some, especially among the rich, who, by their late dinner-hours and sumptuous

feasts, no doubt prepare themselves for early
an old author says, "Some stop their breath
and *carpe;* some poison themselves with soups a
and others stifle nature with cheese-cakes and t
—Divers worthy citizens make custard their
And who would think it? even beef and puddi
lic-spirited victuals and good protestants as the
are frequently guilty of man-slaughter; and ma
squire, when he escapes drowning in a sea of (
up the springs of life with a rump of beef.

"Harmless mutton itself does frequent miscl
So that the butchers, as well as the 'pothecε
licensed poisoners of a commonwealth. It 1
seem strange that the sacrifices of oxen should
of men too, and that ignorant butchers should i
the learned of *Warwick-lane,* and yet the facu
it; for though butchers are tolerably *illiterat*
yet, as their profession is the killing of brute l
do not see why the college should permit suc
Brethren. Alas! a butcher has but one instrun
and that is his knife: and what is that in (
Dr. Carlyon also tells us that "Mixtures, an
wines are the ruin of half the stomachs in the
see: You take, at a dinner-party, soup, a gl
wine-punch perhaps; turbot and rich lobster
may be, an oyster *paté,* or a sweet-bread, to a
with while the host is cutting you a slice of t
haunch; this, with jelly and French beans, is
with a couple of glasses of hock or sauterne a
wing of a partridge or the back of a leveret, s
little red hermitage, succeeds; then you at or
and chill your heated stomach with a piece of
which you preposterously proceed to warm
glass of noyeau or some other liquor: if yo
posed to roguet with a spoonful of jelly in add
sure to try a bit of stilton and a piquant sala
of port therewith. At dessert, port, sherry,

ıre. This is about the routine of the majority of 'es. Such a dinner is, in fact, a hospitable at- ur life."

·, we find, will not eat the flesh of any animal d by them without it has been killed and ex- ›ne of their own persuasion, called a *shoket* (Jew ao is appointed by their synagogue, or some ·siastical authority, as they retain the opinions n from "olden times," concerning the killing the table. They also will not eat *guinea fowls*, other *ducks*, having fleshy crests, besides bears, ırrels, etc.; but such game as *deer*, *partridges*, vhen trapped, or otherwise caught alive, and *ioket*, their flesh is then accepted.

icular manner of slaughtering a bullock is by ıind legs *slung*, and hoisted high enough to its fore-feet. The shoket, or "cutter," as he is ·own among butchers, stands ready with his ·d, keen knife, waiting to have the animal's upwards, which is done by those who *dress* the with one hand, the left, pinches up the skin ;, and, with the knife in the other hand, lays · to the point, on the throat. He then, with a thrust forward, and a sudden draw back, with- e knife, divides the flesh and the jugular veins. ›ubt, the best mode of more fully clearing the lood: the Jews believing that the *blood* is the Mosaic law, which forbids the destruction of

rocess of skinning has commenced, the *shoket* domen, and with his hand examines, by feel- s, liver, etc.; and, if found in a sound and 'tion, he places *seals*, stamped with Hebrew *ıly* on the fore-quarters,. which particularly ·y of the month when slaughtered; and the is then termed *cosher*, or good Jew or Hebrew or their use. Twenty years ago, these *seals*, which were then used, were made of lead, but, since that period, they have used thick paper and wax.

If, however, the animal is found defective, either with lungs grown fast to the side, liver diseased, or any other abnormal or unhealthy indications of disease (which is seldom the case with a thriving fat young animal), the *shoket* pronounces it *trifa*, or unfit to be used by them; then it is not sealed, but resold to those whose religious scruples may be no bar to its use.

The *gut-fat* of the *cosher* animal is also sealed, and used in the place of *suet* (which is never used by the strict Jews) for all cooking purposes.

The *hind-quarters* of the animals thus slaughtered are not *sealed*, and therefore not eaten in this country by the strict Jews, although their laws allow of their being eaten when operated upon by the professional *porcher;* but as there are none known or recognized by them in the United States, this choice part is left without seals. The operation of the *porcher* is in the difficult performance of extracting the blood, fat, veins, and sinews, numbering above fifty, recognized by them in the *hind-quarters;* and I am told they count *one hundred and eleven* in the whole body, but those from the *fore-quarter* are more easily removed.

They point to the cause of their refusal to eat the flesh from the *hind-quarters* (and, in fact, to all their different laws, customs, and belief), to the *Old Testament,* more particularly, on this point, to Genesis xxxii. 32: "Therefore the children of Israel eat not of the *sinew* which shrank, which is upon the hollow of the *thigh,* unto this day, because he touched the hollow of *Jacob's thigh* in the *sinew* that shrank."

This *shoket* is paid by the society in which he worships, an annual salary, and, in addition, a perquisite from the owners of the animals which he slaughters.

The edible productions of the present day, considered fit for human food, are very numerous, some of which are the greatest delicacies, while others of them the simplest food, with prices to correspond with their scarcity, rarity, or plentifulness. Many, of course, are unseasonable and unnatural to this climate; but by artificial means, and the swift steam-engine, they have become and are looked for as "things in season." In fact, the public market-place in the various cities under consideration, furnishes us with a "Bill of Fare" which includes almost every article known; among which we have from the *North*, the moose and bear meat, salmon, mascalonge, white-fish, pike, and drawn poultry; the sea-shore—*East*—furnishes us with shore-birds, fowl, sea-fish, oysters, and lobsters; from the *South* comes the early and fine Bermuda potatoes, onions, peas, oranges, bananas, and early shad, with the excellent wild duck from the Potomac; while the *West* pours in her wild-fowl, venison, poultry, butter, all of which comes by the millions of pounds weight, through the course of the year.

In order to arrange these various productions, and other subjects treated of, I have placed them under the following different heads, viz.: *Going to Market; Domestic or Tame Animals; Beef; Veal; Mutton; Lamb; Pigs, Hogs, and Pork; Goats' Flesh; The Parts we use from Domestic Animals; Wild Animals, called Game; Poultry; Wild-Fowl and Birds called Game; Fish; Fish, Large and Abundant; Fish, Small and Abundant; Fish, Large and Scarce; Fish, Small and Scarce; Shell-Fish; Vegetables; Pot Herbs, Medicinal, and other Plants; Fruit; Nuts; Dairy and Household Products; Pot Plants, Roots, and Bouquets; Economy in the use of Meats; Hung Meats; Bleeding Animals;* and *Cooks and Cookery.*

The first in the above arrangement appears somewhat important, as well as necessary, to assist the young housekeeper in purchasing the market supplies wanted, and perhaps a few hints on the subject will be acceptable to her or any others interested. They will appear under the head—

GOING TO MARKET.

Some fifty years ago it was the common custom for the thrifty "old New Yorker," when going to market, to start with the break of day, and carry along with him the large "market-basket," then considered a very necessary appendage for this occasion. His early visit gave him the desired opportunity to select the *cuts* of meat wanted from the best animals; to meet the farmer's choice productions, either poultry, vegetables, or fruit, and *catch* the lively, jumping fish, which, ten minutes before, were swimming in the fish-cars.

Soon after followed the "good housewife," who would not trust anybody but herself to select a fine young turkey, or a pair of chickens or ducks, which she kept hold of until the bargain allowed her to place the coveted articles in her capacious basket, that was being carried by a stout servant, who also carried a bright tin, covered kettle, ready to receive several nice rolls of *butter*, so cleanly and neatly covered with white linen cloths.

The modern "marketer" will still occasionally observe some "relics of the past," who cling to the old custom taught them in their youth, perhaps, by an honored *sire*, who was not too proud to carry home a well-filled market-basket, containing his morning purchase, which his purse or taste prompted him to select. These old-fashioned ideas, alas! are all *lived down*, and we reluctantly turn from them, as we would from an interesting but worn-out book to peruse the pages of modern composition.

We now find many heads of families who never visit the public markets, who are either supplied through the butcher or other dealers in our markets, or by their stewards or other servants, or by some that may be termed *go-between-speculators*, who take orders for marketing, groceries, etc., on their own *hook;* and, of course, they purchase the various articles of those who will give them the largest percentages. I am sorry, however, to be compelled to state that there are but few of this species of help, or *market assistants*, who can lay claim to the title of trustworthy.

It is, therefore, as necessary for our health as it is to our interest to obtain the knowledge of what we desire to purchase, that the articles shall be what they are represented to be, and that they are furnished at the regular market price.

To market well, then, requires much experience, although many rules might be introduced, but they would be seldom successfully followed. Practice gives the looks, smell, feeling, and many signs that are almost indescribable, and which are formed from close observation.

Many dealers know too well how to disguise an inferior article, so as to deceive those who have but little knowledge of marketing; although a lower price may be demanded, such provisions are dear from the fact of their inferior quality, and when prepared are neither relished nor half consumed—perchance they are wholly wasted.

Another class of dealers, while they furnish good articles, they do not fail to obtain exorbitant prices, of such a character as to come under the name of extortion. To succeed in such extortions, different modes of misrepresentation are adopted, which, in our plain vernacular, might be termed absolute lying—"business lying," white or black lying, or any other lying the reader may choose to designate the system.

Their articles are represented as being—"The very best that were ever produced!"—"The finest and largest you ever saw!"—"Could not be better!"—"First-rate!"—"Excellent!" — "Elegant!"— "Beautiful!"—"Splendid!"—"Can't be beat!"—"As cheap as dirt!" and "Can't be got elsewhere!"

One day I heard a military hero say to a person who was extolling a good common goose, and enlarging on the numerous splendid accessories surrounding it—"Why, your *geese* are all *swans*—I do not want any of them. I merely want a good young *goose*, about that size."

The numerous falsehoods sometimes told, are expressed with such appearance of innocence, that many really feel that what they say must be "the truth, the whole truth, and nothing but the truth," and so accede to their extortionate demands. This class of dealers effect more business and succeed better than the honest, conscientious dealer, who, when asked, "Is this article the best I can get?" will answer, "I should not like to say it is, but I think it is as good." Such an answer is not always a satisfactory one to the questioner, as he would require one of certainty, or—"It is the very best that comes to the markets, and you cannot get it elsewhere so good, nor so cheap." This appears to be a great fault with many purchasers, that to induce them to buy the dealers must bespatter their articles with a dozen falsehoods, and sometimes fifteen or twenty per cent. above the market price, before the purchasers are fully satisfied with their bargains.

This wretched system or custom, we find, generally pervades everywhere, and in every business, where goods and other property are exposed to sale; both men and women, merchants and mechanics, tradesmen and salesmen, in fact all kinds, are afflicted with this prevailing *tongue-disease* of exaggeration.

This dishonest custom gives the honest salesman or purveyor but little satisfaction while doing business, as they are often subjected to many petty annoyances, which usually come from those whose education should teach them better. There are others who are deficient of this desideratum, who claim from the lack of educated honesty some charity and excuse for their acts. We occasionally find among purchasers some who are known as "shoppers" and "runners," who make no difference where they trade, so long as it shall be the best article at a low price; and to make a sale to such the market-price must generally be reduced; and when that is done, suspicion steps into the "shopper's" mind, who examines and re-examines, with question after question, whether "perfectly good, tender, and sweet;" and upon being answered in the affirmative, the "shopper" often turns from the dealer with a supercilious gesticulation, as if they placed no confidence in the recommendation. We recur to an instance where a *lady* had several times treated a butcher to this negative treatment to his recommended meat, when she was, by him, impressed with this well-merited retort: "My previous answers, in relation to the quality of meat which you several times before selected, have not received such attention as was expected from you; hereafter you will be obliged to judge for yourself." She was not a purchaser on that occasion, but afterwards she gave no further trouble in this respect.

There are other dealers, again, who use much of what may be termed outside deceit—that is, by placing some attractive mark or emblem, in the way of flags, ribbons, signs, etc., to represent the articles so dressed and decorated as being either premium or prize or superior, or some extraordinary quality about them, from the good or general average of what they should represent; and this is done for the purpose of procuring a higher price for an inferior article. In fact, I have heard it said: "I put ribbons and flags on my meat to make it sell for a good price, as I am bound to make money some way or another." This method this class adopt as a "legitimate manner of doing business."

The safest plan for the inexperienced is to select respectable dealers, on whom they can rely. They may charge higher prices for that which they furnish; in the end, however, more satisfaction is afforded, by less risk, and more saving and relish—in fact, cheaper in every way, because all good articles are with profit used—that, while the best articles may cost more money in the purchase thereof, they will be found to be the most economical in the end.

On the other view, unprincipled dealers are always ready for what they term *chances*, either by giving short weight, short measure, or short change; and, if they are detected, "Why, it's a mistake!" or, if he (or she) think that blustering, or loud and harsh words, will frighten the wronged purchaser, this mode of tactics is brought to bear.

Many respectable purchasers, not having the time to go to the public markets, will sometimes purchase of the "cheap shops," or street-pedlers, many of whom are still worse than those we have already spoken of, especially street-pedlers, who cannot be found when their fraud or deceit is too late discovered.

A few years ago, one of the city sealers of weights and measures, in one of the districts of our (New York) city, collected fifty-four measures, from grocers and wagon-pedlers, that fell short of the standard. A half-bushel fell short three and a half quarts; twenty-one half-peck measures fell short about one quart each; fifteen two-quart measures were short six quarts in the aggregate; and sixteen one-quart measures were short, in the aggregate, six quarts.

An old law, as well as a long-standing custom, makes it incumbent upon the seller that all articles subject to be sold by the measure—such as apples, peaches, potatoes, and others of a round, oval, or flat conformation—shall be heaped up above the even line of the measures, to make up for the interspaces between the irregularities of such articles of food, etc.

The fish, fruit, vegetables, etc., which are usually peddled about the streets in carts and wagons, are seldom found so good as those offered for sale in the public markets, they being either the refuse of the markets, unfit to be offered by the respectable dealer, or it happens to be a glut, or very large quantities offered; and, even then, their selections are generally of those which sell at the lowest price; then, in their sales through the streets, their false-bottomed measures, short weights, or their stale or unfit articles, are detected by examination; they are off, and not to be found, until the frauds and their persons are forgotten.

When the purchaser desires to be served through orders

by the butcher, or others, it is best that they should have such latitude or choice of sending the purchaser that which they may have in the best condition for immediate use. If it be for a *roast*, it should be either a rib, sirloin, or other piece of beef; or leg, loin, saddle, or shoulder of mutton; or fore or hind quarter of lamb; or fillet, loin, shoulder, or breast of veal; or turkey, capons, chickens, venison, partridges, or grouse, etc. If for a boil, a leg of mutton, rump or round, plate, navel, or brisket of corned beef; and the same, in fact, with all the various dishes.

Without particular joints, or other articles, are ordered for an arranged or "dinner-party," it is then best, as well as proper, to give notice a day or two before, that the butcher, or other, may prepare a particular, prime, or choice article, such as may not only please the purchaser, but will give the butcher, or other dealer, some satisfaction—as it is gratifying to the conscientious dealer to hear that his joints or other articles were praised, as it is to those who pay for that which is acceptable and pleasing to them.

DOMESTIC OR TAME ANIMALS.

The domestic or tame animals which are usually prepared by the butchers into meat, produce one of the chief articles of food in our daily supplies; and the first among these animals stands the ox, one of the richest gifts to man, being useful to the farmer as a faithful worker, a great assistant in enriching his land, and then as a mill to grind his surplus fodder into *beef*, while every thing about him, from his hoofs to his horns, is profitable for some purpose or other.

Nearly all of these animals, while living, are known by the names given to them by our Anglo-Saxon fathers; but, when slaughtered and dressed, their flesh assumes another name, as the *ox*, with its varieties—the bullock, steer, cow, heifer, stag, and bull—are changed to *beef; sheep*, consisting of the wether, ewe, stag, buck or ram, are changed to *mutton; calf*, to that of *veal; hog, i. e.*, pig, shoat, barrow, sow, stag, hog, and boar, to that of *pork*. The same changes will also apply to some species of wild animals.

Beef, mutton, lamb, veal, and pork, are usually found throughout the year, in its various seasonable preparations, in all the public markets, and they may be reasonably considered "always in season;" but there are certain months in the year when each are found in greater perfection than at other periods of the year, although, when a sound, healthy animal has been properly fed and prepared, the flesh will be found to be excellent eating in any part of the year. The additional advantage of a cool atmosphere (not freezing the flesh), permitting it to hang for several days, or even weeks, such flesh as beef, mutton, lamb, venison, etc., will render them not only tender, but also add much to the richness of their flavor. I may here also add, that the flesh of all animals, poultry, and game (drawn), is much better in the warm weather, when it can be placed in a cool cellar; a deep well (tied in a linen bag, and hung by a rope near the water), a refrigerator, or an ice-house, for a day or two, will render the flesh cool and firm enough for good eating.

When it is necessary to send or carry any kind of fresh provisions great distances—such as butcher-meat, poultry, game, or fish—either article should first be kept in a refrigerator, or other cold place, until thoroughly cooled, then wrapped in a coarse linen cloth, around which should be placed cabbage-leaves (or other green leaves), and the whole again wrapped and tied up in a coarse cloth, and placed in a basket, when the articles may be carried from six to ten hours without the danger of becoming sour or tainted. Poultry, game, or fish should be drawn, and a piece of charcoal, wrapped in a thin linen rag, be inserted into the drawn parts; as the intestines, when left in, are apt to give the flesh a disagreeable flavor.

Beef and mutton are usually found best from November

to May, from the fact that those animals producing this flesh are then generally "grain or stall fed," although those fed, or which are fattened, on roots, pumpkins, or grass, produce good, sweet, and tender meats; but it has not the weight, substance, or heart that is found in "stall-fed" meat. From a letter written to B. P. Johnson, Esq., Secretary of the New York State Agricultural Society, found in their "Transactions" (1852, vol. xii., p. 282), the following extract refers to this subject: "You are aware, no doubt, that the greatest quantity of 'barrelled beef' sent to foreign markets is packed in the West. Great portions are of young cattle, fattened on grass, principally of a quick and large growth, and are what we New York butchers call 'grass-fed beef.'" The beef when fresh will eat soft, tender, juicy, and sweet, but will not have the delicious flavor, solidity, firmness, weight, or the heart or nourishment that the stall-fed (with grain) beef has. It appears to me, as soon as the salt touches "grass-fed beef" it draws back, shrinks into a smaller compass, and changes to a dark color, as if there was not firmness or solidity to resist the action of the salt; and when boiled, especially if salted a long time, will shrink very much, leaving it tasteless, juiceless, without heart or substance, and, when cut, of a dark color. "Stall-fed beef," on the contrary, is like corn-fed pork, which has the appearance (when properly cured) of being firmer, brighter, plumper, or has a swelled look, as if the well-mixed fat protected the lean parts of the flesh. We seldom hear of farmers, or others, salting down "grass or milk fed pork." They pen them up, and feed as much corn, generally, as the animal will take, for sometimes months before slaughtering; and when they are salted—I quote an old saying—"Put one pound of corn-fed pork in the pot, it comes out two," which will apply to "stall-fed beef."

Animals in sound health, which have been fairly fed, will have a layer of fat between the skin and the flesh or muscles. This may be termed the outside fat or *back fat.*

The fat will also be mixed in and through the muscles themselves, according to the quantity and quality of the feeding. When highly fed the flesh increases, the back fat thickens, the muscles become marbled with small particles of fat throughout the body, and a large collection of fat around the kidneys, which butchers call suet, to designate it from the common meat or flesh fat.

I may here observe, that it is artificial or over-feeding that produces the prize, choice, and extra-large fine cattle, sheep, etc., sometimes exhibited at our fairs and cattle-markets.

BEEF.

In relation to the best cattle for beef, the question may properly be asked, Which among the varieties of neat-cattle will generally produce the best or choicest eating beef?

This point, I am well aware, many of our most respectable butchers, epicures, and others, will honestly differ in. I, however, shall present the experience which has brought me in contact with all sorts and sizes, shades and colors, and not only by hundreds, but by thousands, from the poorest, toughest "old bull," used for jerked-beef, to feed the slaves of the West Indies, to that of the choicest—the winners of many *first-prizes*—which have been so elaborately prepared, both to tickle the palates of the many epicures and lovers of good beef, and also to gain the admiration of thousands. Notwithstanding this, my observations may not be correct; they, however, are my convictions. I therefore proceed to place them in the order as they appear, as follows:

First—Spayed Heifer, from four to seven years old.

Second—Steer or bullock (never worked), from four to six years old.

Third—Free Martin (or barren heifer), not over eight years old.

Fourth—Ox, from five to eight years old.
Fifth—Heifer, " three to four "
Sixth—Cow, " " to eight "
Seventh—Stag, " " to " "
Eighth—Bull, " two to six "

In the above arrangement I have placed the Spayed Heifer first—from four to seven years old—as generally affording the best and choicest beef. I mean, of course, with the same breed, care, and partaking of the same feeding. My reasons for this are: that she is more docile and quiet, a gentler disposition, not apt to roam or run so much as the common heifer or steer, and therefore she will naturally flesh and thrive faster, while her nerves, muscles, or flesh and fat, are rendered more tender from her general quietude. I do not pretend to assert that this quiet manner of growing beef will produce that which shall be the most nutritious and wholesome, because this question must be left to scientific research; my wish here is to show that which shall prove the most profitable, tender, and well-tasted beef.

The usual appearance of the above-described *Spayed Heifer*, or fine steer, beef, when first cut with a knife, or afterwards, when it has laid together against or on marble, a dish, etc., it will be found to be quite a dark red color; but the action of the air, on being exposed to it, in five minutes after will change its color to a clear cherry red.

This beef will also have a juicy or sappy appearance, with a fine smooth grain to the touch, and in cold weather (or if it has been thoroughly cooled by the aid of ice) it should present a well-mixed or marbled appearance. The fat, both outside and through the muscles, presents a clear, straw-colored appearance, and that on the outside should entirely cover the back of the loin and ribs, in some parts not less than half an inch. The kidney-fat, or suet, should be so large, or so well filled up under or inside the loin, especially the thin end, that the whole sirloin (when cut up), suet, or kidney-fat, down, will lay nearly on a level; or, in other words, the thin end should appear nearly as thick as the thick or rump end when laid on a bench or block to be cut up.

The suet should be of a brighter shade than the meat or muscle fat, dry and hard, break or crumble easily, and at the same time show but little fibre through it. When greasy or oily, or tough and full of tough fibre, small in quantity, is a certain indication that the animal has been improperly fed, overdriven, or brought from a great distance, and therefore the quality of the beef is deteriorated by rendering it more tough, dry, and tasteless.

Ox and cow beef, when in good condition, will show their flesh and fat of a darker color; that of the ox, more particularly, will have an open and a coarser grain, as well as hard, tough cartilages, sinews, ligaments, and muscle, less flesh according to the quantity of bone, and if the animal has been always kept in a good fat condition, the flesh will not be, or eat so tender nor so juicy or fine-flavored as one (not too old) which has been worked down in flesh, then turned into fine pasture with a "summer's run," taken up and stall-fed for two, three or four months, when all the newly made, or growth of flesh, will be a much more tender, a rich cutting, and also well-flavored beef, than the preceding; but still the old nerves and muscle is not replaced, but left behind, and show themselves, more particularly in the pieces which are called plate, navel, and brisket pieces. If, however, the animals (old or young) are poor, then when slaughtered their flesh will show little or no fat on the back and through the muscles, and will also be of a darker color, quite dry looking, very little kidney-fat or suet, and the kidney itself not well covered; and this kind of beef will be usually quite hard, dry, and not well-flavored eating.

Stag-beef is usually found more fleshy than the ox or steer: of a dusky red, close-grained; and unless the animal has been well fed the flesh will be quite tough and somewhat strongly flavored. If, however, the stag has been altered when quite young, it will much improve the quality of the flesh. Their horns are generally thicker and shorter than those of the steer or ox.

Bull-beef is the poorest eating of all beef, especially an old, poor, worn-out bull. They are always heavy-fleshed, especially in the neck and buttock. The color of the flesh is sometimes almost black, usually tough, with a strong rank scent or flavor, especially when it is fresh killed; although some months in the year a fine, fat young bull will keep hunger off, but will never be choice eating.

All animals should be killed when they are in the coolest state, or when respiration is the least active. Their flesh then will keep much longer fresh, and be more beautiful, sweet, and healthful; but when killed in a heated condition, or immediately after a hard drive, the flesh will take longer to cool through, spoil sooner, and the flesh and fat will have a feverish, dark look (caused from its being full of blood), and of course it will not be so inviting or considered so healthy.

The animal for beef, after having been killed and dressed, is called a *carcass of beef;* the one-half (a hind and fore quarter), a *side of beef;* and the separate quarters, a *hind-quarter of beef* and a *fore-quarter of beef.* The same terms will also apply to mutton, lamb, veal, pork, or, in fact, to almost all animals.

The whole carcass, before being "split down," or divided through the back, has been occasionally roasted whole, here, as well as many other places, usually to celebrate some great event. I have witnessed several public occasions in this city when the roasting of an ox was one of the great features, which, of course, took place on some public ground, and, five times out of six, part of the carcass would be invariably spoiled or tainted, as it appeared almost impossible to apply the heat so as to roast the inside of the thick parts; and the consequence was, that it would be about half-roasted—some portions burnt, and the greater part heated just enough to make it turn sour or spoiled, and, of course, unfit to be eaten. No doubt, large iron spits or skewers could be introduced or forced through the thick parts, which, when properly heated, would produce the desired object.

The first account of an "Ox-Roasting," which has come under my notice, would now seem a very curious and expensive affair, as it happened in the latter part of the year 1727, on the "King's Birthday," in the then fashionable city of Bath, England. This account is found in the *New York Gazette* (January 29, 1728), which ushers the day in as follows:

"At four o'clock in the Morning, the Bells struck out; a Bonfire was lighted, and a whole Ox set a roasting, with a Quantity of Liquor, and Huzzas to his Majesty's Health. At 6 the Drums beat the young Gentleman Volunteers to arms; by 8, an Hundred and Sixty assembled themselves together at the Colonel's House; by 10, they were ready to march, but first every Man drank a Glass of Brandy to his Majesty's Health. The Officers were extremely rich in their Apparel—Velvet, Embroidery, Gold and Silver Laces; the Men with fine Caps, Cockades, Holland Shirts, Silver and Gold Ribbons, Shoulder-knots, fine Scarlet Cloth Breeches, richly laced white Stockings, red Tops to their Shoes; the Slings to their Pieces had this Motto: '*God save King George the Second.*' By 12, they marched through the best part of the town, with two Sword-Bearers, a sett of Morris-Dancers, and Martial Musick before them; then came to the *Market-place*, where they drew up in Order for Fire. Wine was brought, and every Officer charged his Glass; the King, Queen, and Royal Family went round distinct, with a Volley at each Health; the Glasses were thrown over their Heads; and in other parts of the town they did the same. Then Captain Goulding repeated this Verse, *extempore:*

'In spite of Legions of Infernal Devils below,
To ye Powers above, supream Divine.
Let George in the Center our Standard be,
And his Queen the great Caroline

"One Colonel Edward Collins, that keeps the *White-Hart Inn*, and Captain Thomas Goulding, *Jeweller* in the Walks, Captain James Warriner, *Bookseller* in the Walks, Lieutenant Collins, *Woolen-Draper* in the Churchyard, Lieutenant Taylor, *Sword-Cutter* in the Churchyard, and three more young Gentlemen of the Town-Officers, which makes 8 in Number, that gave the Ox and all the charges thereto. They drew to the Beef when roasting, with Handfuls of Silver, each Officer, and obliged the Cook to stuff it into the Shoulders and Neck; and Captain Goulding, *Jeweller*, stuffed above an Hundred true stones into the Buttocks of the Ox, several Diamonds, Rubies, Saphires, Emeralds, Garnets, Amethists, and Topasses. At two, the Ox was ready, brought to the Table, put into a Dish 12 Foot long and 6 wide, made on purpose. They dined in the *Public Market-House;* but the stuffing made the Mob so furious that they flung themselves over the Heads of the Officers, into the Dish, and stood over their Shoes in Gravy; and one was stuffed into the Belly of the Ox, and almost stifled with Heat and Fat. The Grease flew about to that Degree which made the Officers quit the Table, or all their Cloaths must have been Spoiled. They stopt and looked on their Proceedings till three; then they all Marched to the Colonels, and staid till four. They went out again on their Procession. At five, the candles begun to light; at 6, the town was illuminated. They went into the Colonel's Quarters, near Seven, with Huzzas—'*King George for ever!*'—where there was great Quantities of Wine and Beer drank to his Majesty's Health, and all his loving Subjects in his extended Dominions. At Eleven, the Drums beat '*Go to bed, Tom!*' and all departed in Peace after Pleasure."

The following figure represents the form of a *Spayed Heifer*, which is found marked with lines, numbers, and letters, showing where the several joints or parts of the animal for beef are taken from, and how to cut the quarters up in the common manner—as cut in the city of New York. Those marked with the letter S are commonly used for steaks of the best, middling, and poorest kinds. The numbers on the top of the back denote the number of ribs in each "roasting-piece;" while those numerically numbered

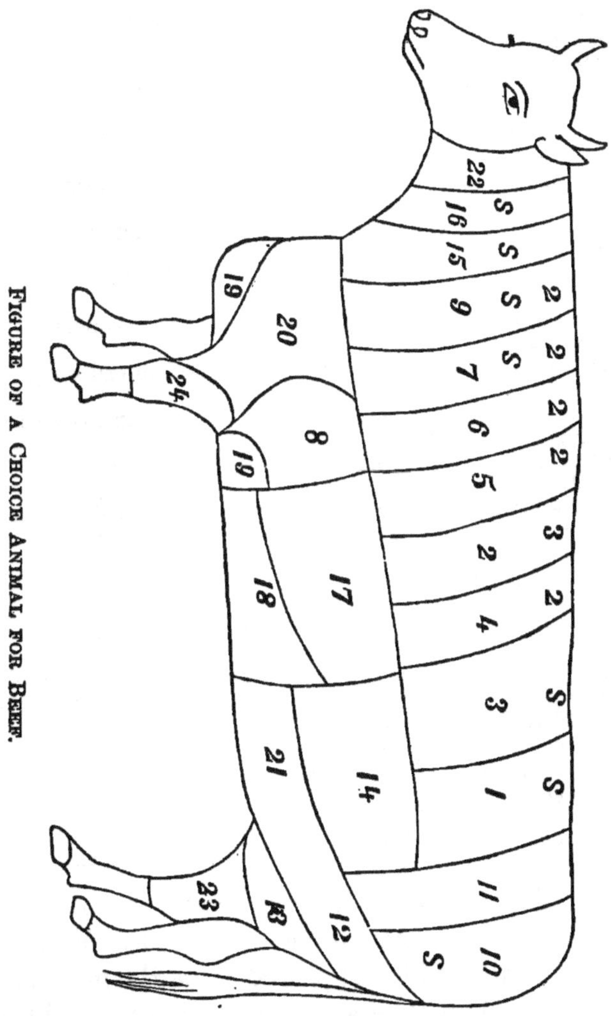

FIGURE OF A CHOICE ANIMAL FOR BEEF.

designate the common name of each part, as used in the cities of New York and Brooklyn, followed by those of Boston and Philadelphia—the two latter, however, as near as can be given, from the marked joints in the foregoing figure.

New York and Brooklyn.	Boston.	Philadelphia.
1 S Hip sirloin or thick sirloin.	Part of the rump or hook bone.	Pinbone sirloin.
2. Second-cut ribs or middle ribs.	Second prime-ribs.	Middle-rib cut.
3. S. Small end sirloin.	Sirloin.	Sirloin.
4. First-cut rib or first rib-piece.	Fore-rib or first prime-rib.	First-rib cut.
5. Third-cut ribs or thick ribs.	Third prime-rib.	Third-rib cut.
6. First-cut chuck ribs.	First chuck-rib.	Best chuck-rib
7. S. Second-cut chuck rib.	Second chuck-rib.	Chuck-rib cut.
8. S. Cross rib.	Leg or shoulder-of-mutton piece.	Boler-piece.
9. S. Third-cut chuck rib or chuck-piece.	Chuck-piece.	Chuck-piece.
10. S. Rump of beef.	Aitch or edgebone (part of).	Tail end rump.
11. Socket or face rump.	Rump (part of).	Rump-piece (part of).
12. First-cut round.	Round.	Round.
13. Second-cut round.	Leg-ran.	Round (part of).
14. Top of sirloin.	Thick flank.	Cut with Sirloin Steaks
15. S. First-cut neck or neck-piece.	Neck-piece.	Neck-cut
16. S. Second-cut neck or neck-piece.	"	"
17. Plate-piece.	Rattle-Ran or Runner piece.	Plate-piece.
18. Navel-piece.	Navel end of brisket.	Thin end of brisket.
19. Brisket-piece.	Butt end of brisket.	Thick end of brisket.
20. Shoulder clod.	Clod (part of).	Clod (part of).
21. Flank-piece.	Thin flank.	Flank.
22. Third cut neck or neck-piece.	Neck-piece.	Neck.
23. Leg of beef or leg.	Shank.	Leg.
24. Shin of beef or shin.	Shin.	Shank.

In presenting the above names, as it were, belonging to each city, I was somewhat puzzled to procure, from numerous inquiries, those which appeared to be the most common ones; although there were some which all appeared to agree upon, then again, no two were alike; some had been always used to one name, while others had another, and if I had given all it would have been quite difficult for the buyer, or even the seller to have become reconciled to the large number, so I concluded to adopt those which appeared to have the most intelligent friends. I also found that many foreign butchers had not only brought their countries' customs of cutting up meats, but also their names of the joints; and then, again, there were others in the same markets who have different ways of cutting, and they also have adopted names which appeared to have been known only to themselves. I have, however, a hope that the following woodcuts may assist the eye to distinguish the most prominent of the above-named joints, and also to know how to use them, or, rather, what dishes they are severally and generally used for; and, therefore, we will proceed to cut up, first, the different quarters of beef.

The **hind-quarters** are usually considered the choice quarters, as from them are cut or taken the large and famous "*Baron of Beef*," which the English hold in the highest estimation as the crowning dish for the Christmas dinner. This joint is seldom prepared in this country, but it is cut much like a saddle of mutton; that is, by leaving the two sirloins together; when being dressed, the hind-quarters of the animal are not separated, but cut so as to saddle or *baronize* them, by taking off the buttocks, rumps, sockets, tops of sirloins, and a part of the suet, which leaves almost a square-looking piece, first known in England as the baron of beef; and this enormous piece is roasted whole.

The principal dish, from time immemorial, for the sovereigns of England at their Christmas dinner is the "Royal Baron of Beef." In an English print I read that "it was this year (1854) cut from a fine Highland ox, fed by Prince Albert, and weighed eight hundred and forty pounds. It was put down before an enormous fire on Saturday afternoon, and for fourteen hours was watched and basted by relays of assistants under the head cook, after which it was trimmed and decorated, with the holly and mistletoe apparently sprouting from the outside fat of the meat."

I also find the following advertisement for the Christmas festivities: "A Baron of Beef will be roasted on Wednesday next at the Merchants' Dining Rooms, Lancaster Buildings, Exchange-street, East Liverpool. Will be placed on the table at one o'clock," etc.

In this city I have found several instances where this great dish was prepared and served, and a few of these evidences of the fact are now in my possession in the shape of old bills of fare. About the first found on my list was given by William Sykes, who kept one of the best public houses at the period of which this "baron of beef" was given, then called the "New York Coffee House," and located at the corner of William-street and Slote-lane (Beaver-street.)

This took place on the 8th of October, 1823, in honor of the union of the Erie Canal waters with the Hudson River, on which occasion he served up "a 'baron of beef' measuring nearly four feet in length, and weighing one hundred and twelve pounds. It was placed upon a marble slab and surmounted with a white silk flag, bearing the arms of the State, and painted for the occasion." Then at the Agricultural Society's dinner, which took place on Friday, the 31st inst. following, at a place called "Mount Vernon," located on the East River, just above the (Youle's) shot-tower. Another "baron of beef," weighing but one hundred and nine pounds, was furnished by Thomas Gibbons, No. 60 Fulton Market.

The year following (1824), the corporation gave a dinner, on Monday, the 5th of July, in the City-Hall, when a large baron of beef was on the table; and the next year they gave another, quite as large as the previous one, on Monday, the 4th of July. I am also much indebted to Charles H. Webb, Esq., the almoner of St. George Society, who informs me that this Society has had several barons of beef served up at their Anniversary dinners, which were principally prepared by Mr. and Mrs. William Niblo. The following incident will show one of the mistakes which occurred with perhaps the largest and finest baron of beef ever prepared for, or attempted to be roasted in New York, or elsewhere. This, no doubt, occurred from the anxiety of Mrs. Niblo to outdo all former efforts of giving this choice piece in the greatest perfection. She gave the order and her instructions to Mr. Andrew C. Wheeler (butcher, No. 19 Fulton Market), that it should be the *largest* and *finest* that he could procure. It was taken from a very choice animal, and, when trimmed, weighed some two hundred and eighty pounds then sent to Niblo—who then kept his famous garden and hotel corner of Broadway and Prince-street—the day before the grand dinner of the St. George Society was to take place. The same night, late, Mrs. Niblo was about to put it down to roast. She found it so large and unwieldy that she could not spit it, let alone roast it; so, about midnight, she sent for Mr. Wheeler, who came, and, after cutting some one hundred pounds or more off of it, they were enabled to get it spitted, and near enough to the fire to commence this great roast for the next afternoon's dinner. They had, however, almost given it up in despair before they succeeded; but it was said that it was superbly cooked and served up, as every thing else was with which Mrs. Niblo had to do.

Dividing the baron of beef exactly through the centre of the loins, or back-bone, produces two *sirloins*—a name which has become extensively known and commonly associated with this choice part of the carcass. It is said that the name originated with Charles II., who jocularly knighted that part of the animal *Sir-Loin*.

We will again turn to the different quarters of beef, and show the most prominent joints marked on the figure separately; but perhaps a brief explanation, showing how and where to obtain these joints, which to cut off first, and how to handle or lay the different quarters in the most convenient way to separate or cut them up, is first in order.

The hind-quarter is first laid down on a strong table, back down; the buttock and flank, together, are first separated, the other part turned over on the other (suet) side, when the knife divides the rump-piece from the sirloin. These two pieces—rump-piece and buttock—will be subdivided hereafter; in the mean time, we will show that, if the sirloin-piece is wanted or sold for the use of hotels or steamers, it is either sent whole or cut into roasts or steaks, as desired.

The Boston and Philadelphia butchers, after cutting off the buttock and thin-end sirloin, are prepared to cut their fine rump-steaks, which are much the same as our sirloin-steak, only cut more across the hip (or pin) bone. Many of them remove part of the bone.

We will now divide the sirloin-piece into portions suitable for families who want roasting-pieces, which are cut of all

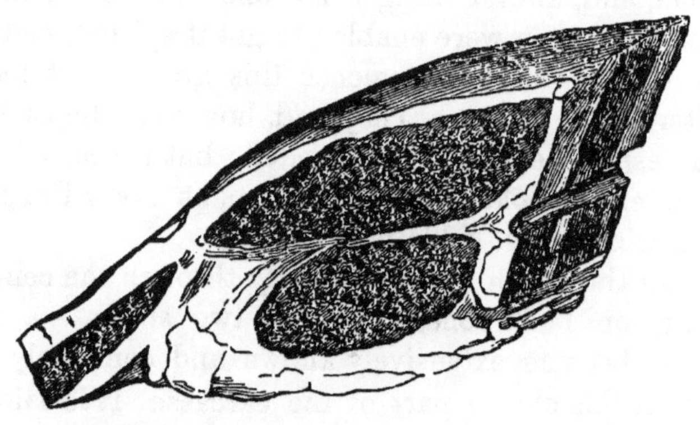

MIDDLE-CUT SIRLOIN.

sizes: the thick part, containing the hip-bone, will give the largest piece, while the small end cuts two small pieces, say from eight to twelve pounds each. The best of these is shown in the above figure, and usually called the "middle-cut sirloin."

The other part, adjoining the ribs, is usually known as the *thin-end sirloin*, being much like the middle-cut sirloin, but with less tenderloin, and is sometimes preferred for a small family, or those who seek it for its close proximity to the prime ribs. It is also cut up into small-loin or porter-house steaks.

The thick part of the sirloin, by cutting off a few round-bone steaks adjoining the rump side, contains the largest part of the tenderloin, or *filet-de-bœuf*, which forms a large and choice piece for roasting, from twelve to twenty-five pounds in weight. This piece is shown in the figure below, and usually known as the "hip-sirloin."

This choice part of the beef is sometimes termed the *thick-end sirloin;* and, when it is not used for roasting, it is cut into three kinds of the finest dinner-steaks, all commonly called sirloin steaks, but separately. The first and

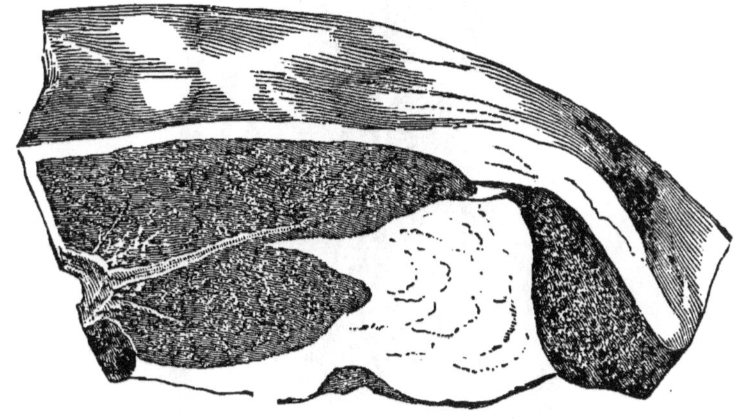

HIP-SIRLOIN.

best, containing the largest quantity of tenderloin, is shown in the figure on following page, and known as the "hip sirloin-steak," of which there are but two or three in one sirloin.

Next in order is the "flat-bone sirloin-steak" (shown in figure on page 43), of which there are about the same number as the "hip sirloin-steak." This is followed by the same number of the "round-bone sirloin-steak" (shown in figure on page 44), which is cut up to the socket-bone or socket-piece. This latter steak makes an excellent beef-steak-pie, beef-tea, minced collops, etc., as it contains more lean than either of the preceding-named steaks.

I am much indebted to Henry W. Dunshee, Esq., for the following "Origin of Beefsteak:"

"The discovery of the chief sources of human enjoyment has all been attributed to some fabulous origin in the ancient world. The story of that important feature of dinner, the beefsteak, was thus given in the middle ages :—Lucius Plaucus, a Roman of rank, was ordered by the Emperor Trajan, for some offence, to act as one of the menial sacrificers to Jupiter; he resisted, but was at length dragged to

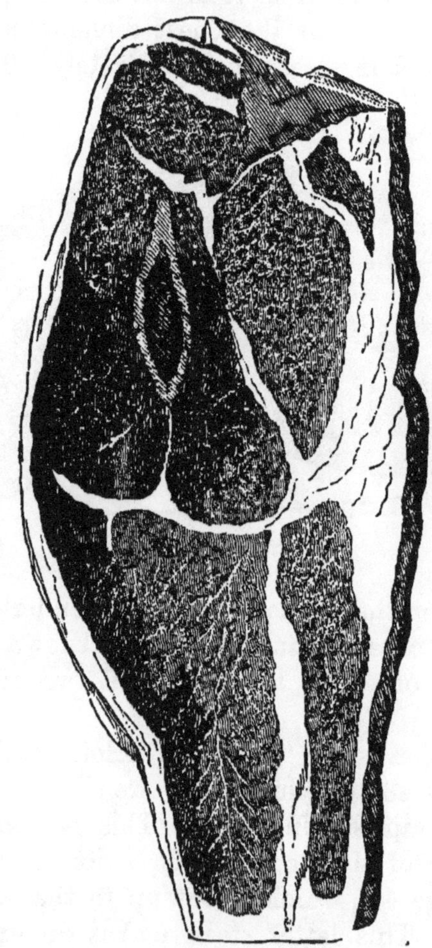

HIP SIRLOIN-STEAK.

the altar. There the fragments of the victim were laid upon the fire, and the unfortunate senator was forcibly compelled to turn them. In the process of roasting, one of the slices slipped off the coals and was caught by Plaucus in its fall. It burned his fingers, and he instinctively thrust them into his mouth. In that moment he had made the grand discovery that the taste of a slice thus carbonaded was infinitely beyond all the old sodden cookery of Rome. A new expedient to save his dignity was suggested at the

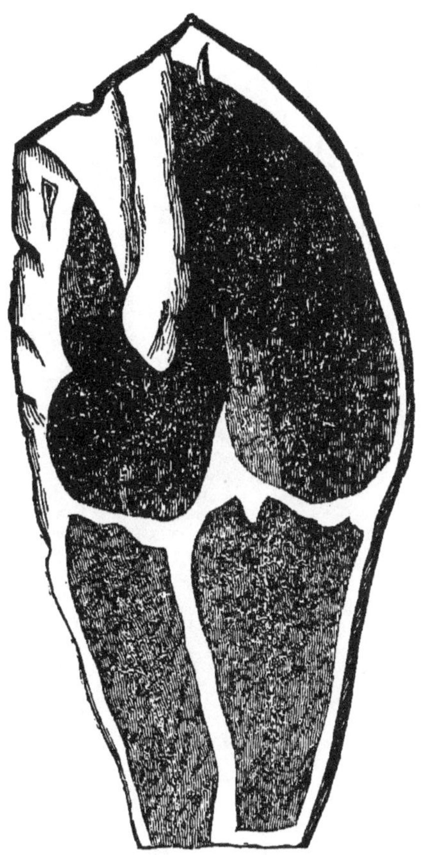

FLAT-BONE SIRLOIN-STEAK.

same time, and he at once evinced his obedience to the emperor by seeming to go through the sacrifices with due regularity, and his scorn of the employment by turning the whole ceremony into a matter of appetite. He swallowed every slice, deluded Trajan, defrauded Jupiter, and invented the *beefsteak!* A discovery of this magnitude could not be long concealed; the sacrifices began to disappear with a rapidity and satisfaction to the parties too extraordinary to be unnoticed. The priests of Jupiter adopted the practice with delight, and the king of Olympus must have been soon starved if he depended on any share of the good things of Rome."

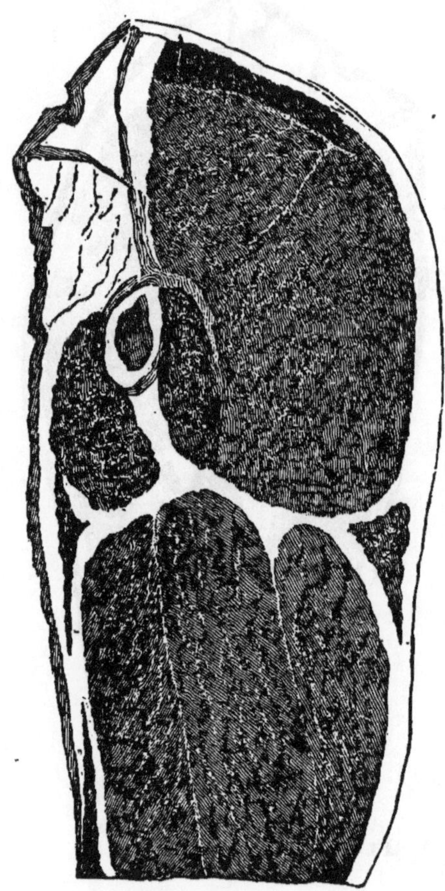

ROUND-BONE SIRLOIN-STEAK.

Broiling Steaks.—In the early part of the nineteenth century, when travelling by the stage-coaches was the fashion, Mr. Southmayd, my neighbor, says: "Travellers going to the eastern cities and towns—Boston, New Haven, etc.—and those who travelled much, were always anxious to reach New Haven, to enjoy a good broiled *beefsteak.* A man, by the name of Butler, kept a public house in that town, in Chapel-street, and, about that time, was famous for his delicious steaks, which he always cooked or attended to himself. You would find him, with his white cap and apron on, before a heap of live hickory coals, in front of the great wide old-fashioned chimney, having a long handle attached to a large double (hinged) gridiron, and a fine steak fastened up in it, so that he could keep the steak turning, first on the one side then on the other, that not a drop of the fine gravy should drip off. When done, it was dished up, and placed steaming hot before the hungry travellers, who never failed to do ample justice to the efforts of the cook, who, by these means, built a reputation, as well as a fortune, by the knowledge of *broiling* a beefsteak."

The rules adopted by the celebrated "Beefsteak Club," organized in England, in 1734, were thus represented:

"HOW TO COOK A BEEFSTEAK.

"Pound well your meat until the fibres break;
Be sure that next you have, to broil the steak,
Good coal in plenty; nor a moment leave,
But turn it over this way and then that.
The lean should be quite rare—not so the fat:
The platter now and then the juice receive.
Put on your butter—place it on your meat—
Salt, pepper; turn it over, serve and eat."

The *small-end sirloin,* when not called for roasting, is cut into "small loin steaks," vulgarly known as "porterhouse steaks," which are represented in the following wood-cut under the head of "small loin steaks."

The origin of the name of "porter-house steaks" took place about the year 1814, in the following manner:

Martin Morrison was the proprietor of a long-established and well-kept "porter-house," located and known at that period at No. 327 Pearl-street (New York), near the "old Walton House." We introduce him in 1803, where we find

Small Loin, or Porter-House Steaks.

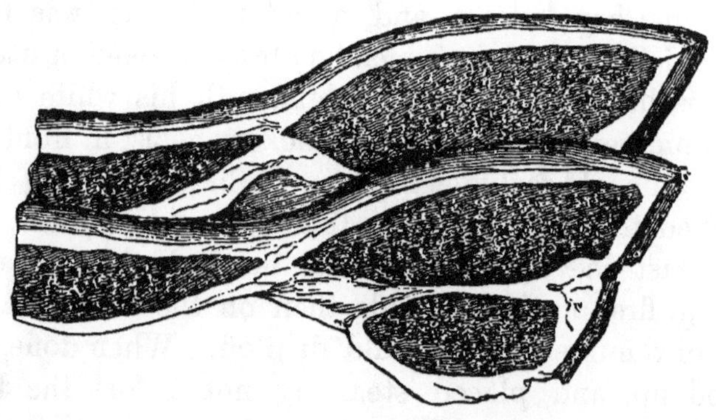

he opens a "porter-house" at No. 43 Cherry-street, which became a popular resort with many of the New York pilots for his prepared hot meals, at any hour, at their call, they being occasionally detained on shipboard until their vessels were safely moored.

The "porter-houses" in those days were not so devoted to tippling, dram-drinking, and the common nests for the loafing, or the manufacturing of politicians and corrupt officials as at the present day, but rather to accommodate the hungry and thirsty travellers, old and young bachelors, seamen, and others with a cold lunch after the English custom —"a pot of ale [or porter] and a bite of something." Some "porter-houses" prepared a hot meal of one or two dishes, among which was Morrison's, who must have been quite famous for his excellent broiled beefsteaks, which were universally called for at his place.

On one occasion (at the above period, 1814), Morrison having had an unusual call for steaks, he had cooked his last steak, and, as fortune would have it for all future partakers of beefsteaks, an old favorite but a rough pilot, made him a late visit, both hungry and thirsty, having been several hours without food. Not caring for the salt junk aboard the vessel which he had piloted in, he concluded to wait until he got on shore, that he might cast his anchor at Morrison's, where he could enjoy his "hot steak and mug of porter."

In his honest language the pilot gave his usual order. Morrison had nothing but his family dinner for the next day, which consisted of a sirloin roasting-piece, of which he offered to cut from if the old pilot would have it. "Yes, my hearty, any thing—so long as it is a beefsteak—for I am as empty as a gull!" exclaimed the pilot. Morrisan cut off a good-sized slice, had it dressed and served, which the pilot ravenously devoured, and turning to the host (who had been expecting a blast from the old tarpaulin, but who, to his astonishment, received the order): "Messmate, another steak just like that—do you hear?" Having finished his steaks and the second mug of porter, the old pilot squared himself towards his host, loudly vociferating, "Look ye here, messmate, after this I want my steaks off the roasting-piece!—do ye hear that?—so mind your weather-eye, old boy!"

It was not long after this when the old pilot's companions insisted upon having these "small loin steaks" served to them. Morrison soon discovered that these steaks were more suitable in size to dish up for single individuals, and he ever after purchased the sirloin roasting-pieces, from which he cut off these small steaks as they were called for, the large sirloin-steaks becoming less in demand.

Morrison's butcher—Thomas Gibbons—in the Fly Market, one morning put the question, after he (Morrison) had selected several sirloin pieces, "Why he had ceased purchasing the usual quantity of sirloin steaks?" Says Morrison, "I will tell you the reason: I cut off from the sirloin roasting-pieces a small steak which serves my pilots and single patrons best; but as it is now cold weather, I wish to have these roasting-pieces cut up as I shall direct every morning." After this, Morrison's sirloins were daily cut up by Mr. Gibbons, with his order to "cut steaks for the porter-house;" hence the sirloin was changed into "cut the *porter-house steaks.*" Their appearance attracted the attention of other butchers and keepers of porter-houses, who admired their appearance and convenient size; in a few years their name and character became quite common to the butchers of the Fly Market, from which the name has spread to the several principal cities of the United States, and I doubt not that the name, *porter-house steak*, has reached across the Atlantic.

Tender-loin (or *filet de bœuf*). This most tender portion of the beef is taken from the under or kidney side of the whole sirloin, behind the suet, stretching along the inner loin or backbone. It commences at, and connects with the round-bone steak, extending to the thin-end sirloin, and seldom weighs above ten pounds when all taken out. It is much thicker and broader at one end, gradually tapering to the other, and measuring from sixteen to twenty inches in length. It is considered the most tender, and by many the choicest part of the animal, and therefore always commands an extra price.

The reason of the tenderness of this choice bit is, that it is so situated in the animal while living, that the uses of this flesh or muscle is little called into action, and lies well warmed and protected by the fat on one side, and on the other by the backbone. It is found that those parts of the animal's flesh are tender which are not brought into wear and tear by the ordinary movements of the animal, of which it would seem the back, the loin, and the rump appear to have the least straining, and therefore in those parts is found the tenderest flesh; on the contrary, the neck, legs, sides, and buttocks are brought into violent action by the physical efforts in walking, eating, lying down, stretching, rubbing, and other muscular movements.

The *tenderloin* is not recognized by the epicure as either being the sweetest or best-flavored meat. The cause of this will be readily understood when it is known, as already stated, that this muscle is not used as much as are the other sweeter portions of the beef; hence, the blood flows more sluggishly through its substance, with the consequent less nervous force brought to bear upon it. We therefore find, while the tenderloin possesses the attribute of tenderness, it must be recognized as being flabby, or soft, or deficient in tone or firmness compared with the glowing life-giving essentials observable in the meat of ribs, rumps, and the top side of the sirloin, and other outside portions of slaughtered animals.

The animal which is kept housed, especially in a small dark pen, often breathing an impure atmosphere while fat-

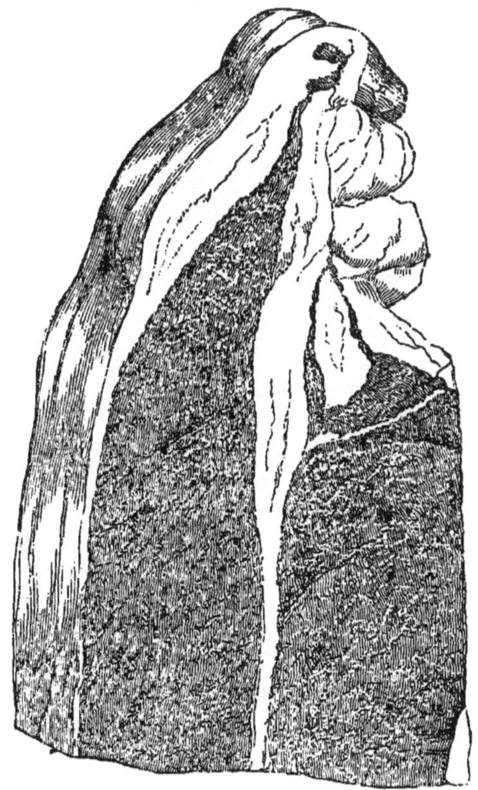

SOCKET-PIECE.

tening, will not produce well-flavored flesh; but it certainly will be more tender (in consequence of the inaction, from being penned up and forced into quietness) than that which is taken from the animals fattened and exercised in the free open air, upon the same food. In fact, wild animals, which range and fatten upon the hills and mountains, always produce flesh the sweetest, as well as of the highest flavor, and

Rump of Beef.

certainly the most healthy for human food. It would appear that the genial warmth of the sun, the pure mountain air, and the short sweet mountain-grasses, produce their influences in perfecting and sweetening living things, whether animal or vegetable, intended for our sustenance.

The whole rump-piece is usually divided into two or more pieces. The first, or that which joins on the sirloin, is called the *face-rump*, or "socket-piece" (shown in the figure on preceding page). The other part is known by the common name, "rump of beef" (shown in the above figure).

When this piece is divided through the centre streak of

fat, cutting about half-way across the dark bone, on the left side of the fat, the smallest piece on the left side is called the *edge-bone* (aitch, H, itch, or adze bone), and the other side the *tail-end-rump*, or "rump-piece." From the rump of beef are also cut pieces for doube, bouilli, stewing, potted beef, fricandeau, etc., and, when left whole, is one of the best joints of corned beef.

The buttock, cut large or full, by cutting off the flank and fat, forms three pieces for smoking, viz., *inside piece*, *outside piece*, and *veiny piece;* the first is generally preferred, although the latter is the most tender. This leaves a large *leg of beef.* Or the buttock can be cut into two rounds of beef—the first and second cuts. The second cut is usually smaller and not so good as the first cut. They are used for *à-la-mode, à-la-doube,* bouilli, stewing, and for corning.

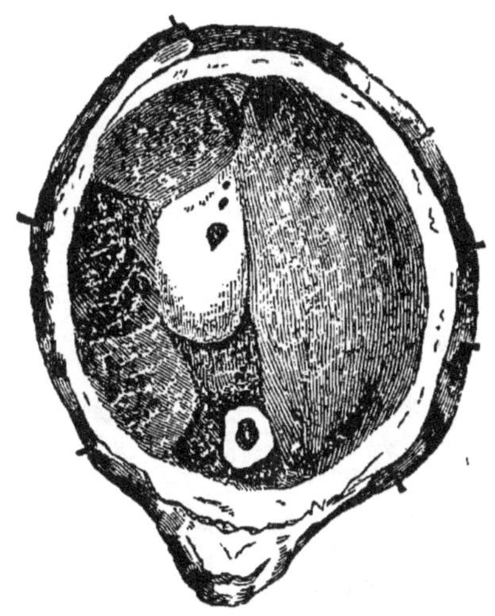

ROUND OF BEEF.

The parts remaining, being a small veiny piece and the thick part of the leg of beef, are used for soups, etc., after having been cut into pieces across the marrow or leg-bone.

The buttock is often prepared by some "old-country men" for a *Scotch ham,* by taking off the flank, the veiny piece, and removing the whole of the leg-bone; it is then cured in a sugar and spice pickle, after which it is bound hard with cord, when it is either hung to dry or lightly smoked, and is then generally used as smoked beef.

If the buttock is cut for a Scotch ham or smokers, the leg, when taken out, will have the marrow-bone attached, and assume the appearance of the following figure.

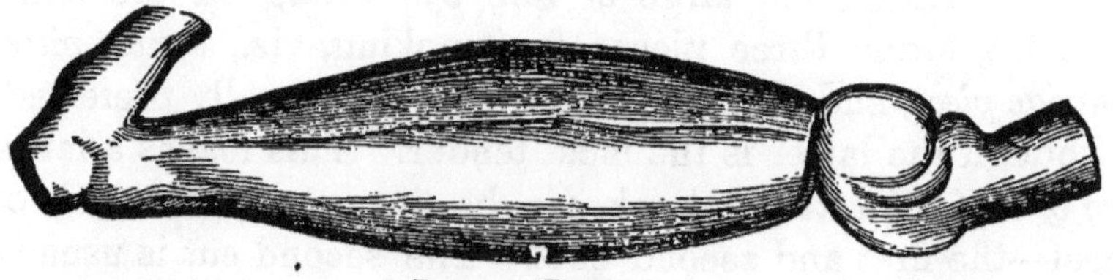

Leg of Beef.

Top of Sirloin.—This piece is known by some as the "thick flank," being a connection with the flank and the sirloin—a piece without bone, quite tender, and well mixed with fat; used for corning, stewing, etc. The flank is either turned on the round of beef, or the fat trimmed off, when the lean parts are excellent for stewing, etc.

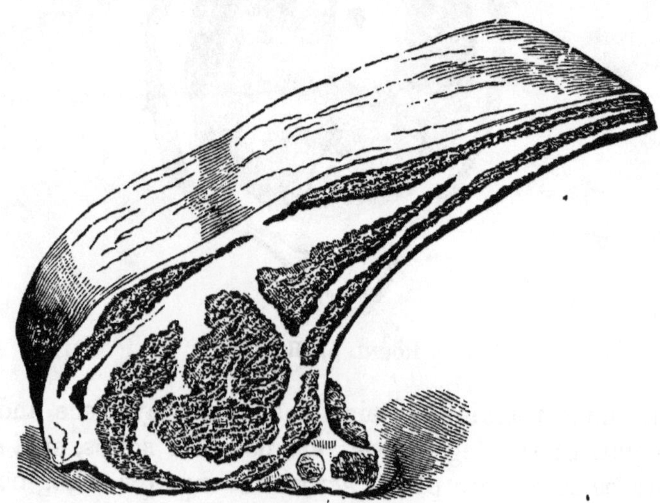

Middle Ribs.

The fore-quarter being now ready, is laid upon a bench or block, ribs or inside down. It is then cut down on the chuck side, close against the large prominent shoulder-bone, which is sawed through, and the shoulder-clod is cut off. The other part of the quarter is then divided, leaving the ribs and chuck in one piece, and the plate, navel, cross-rib, and brisket in the other. We next separate the two latter from the plate and navel (after counting four ribs under the cross-rib), and follow on by cutting off the brisket, and separating the navel from the plate-piece They are then ready for *cuisine*.

There are thirteen ribs in this quarter, nine of which are cut off from the *chuck:* the first seven of which are called prime ribs, and are cut into the choicest roasting-pieces, by

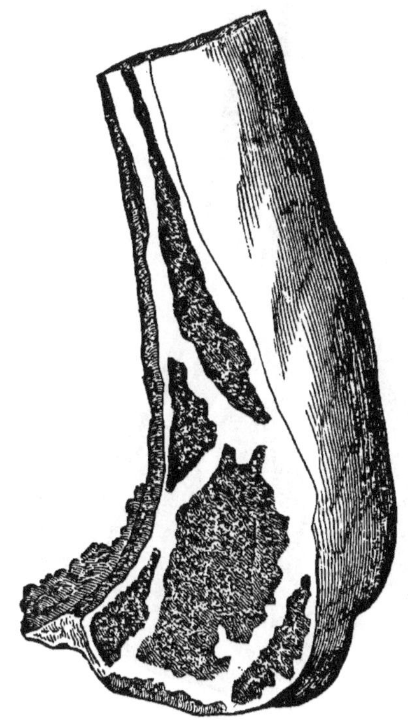

FIRST-CUT RIBS.

subdividing (if not sold whole) into three or more pieces. The first ribs begin from the thin-end sirloin, and are always the smallest and most suitable for a small family; which, when required, it is usual to cut two ribs—first and second (or first, second, and third)—which are called the "first-cut ribs," a representation of which can be seen on the preceding page.

The next ribs—third and fourth—or representing the third, fourth, and fifth as the "middle-cut ribs," or "second-cut ribs," are illustrated on page fifty-two.

And the last two (sixth and seventh), the thickest part of the prime ribs, are called

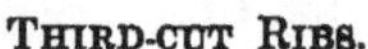

THIRD-CUT RIBS.

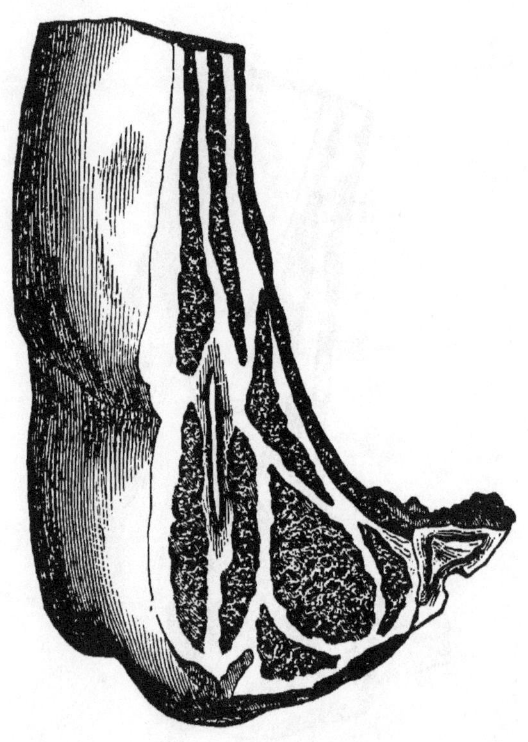

Each of these prime ribs is considered by many epicures to be the finest and best-flavored pieces of the animal, not

excepting the sirloin. These choice pieces are usually roasted, although the first and second cuts are sometimes used for rolled beef, having all the bone taken out and skewered into a round form, when it is used for *à la mode*, or occasionally roasted in this form.

The last of the nine ribs (eighth and ninth) are known as the

FIRST-CUT CHUCK RIB.

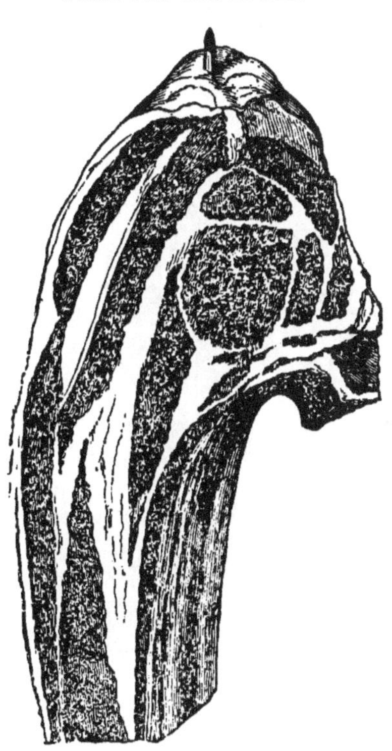

Although it has a thin point of the shoulder-blade through it, yet it is supplied with more flesh, according with the bone, which makes it a profitable and good piece, both as to price and quality.

The *chuck* contains the last four ribs (making thirteen in all) running under the shoulder-blade, and the neck-piece makes up the balance of the chuck.

These chuck ribs are usually divided into pieces of one or

two ribs each. The first two—tenth and eleventh—are called

SECOND-CUT CHUCK RIB.

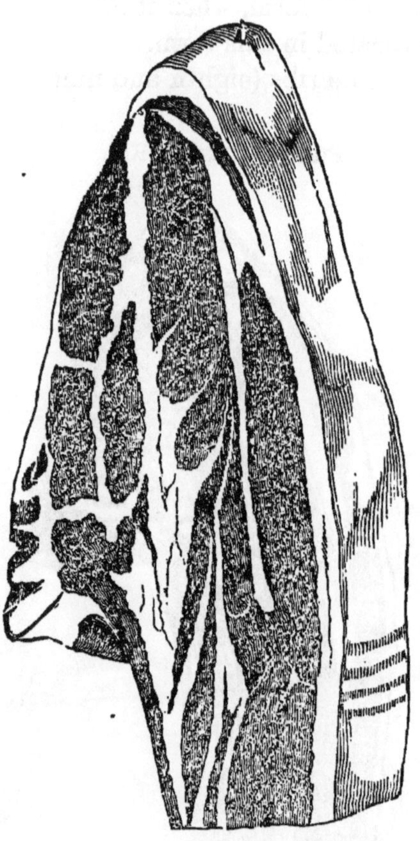

A very sweet, juicy eating-piece of beef, not quite so tender as the first-cut chuck rib, but as well flavored. This joint sells at a much less price per pound. The next cut, being the twelfth and thirteenth, or both ribs together, is usually known as a "chuck piece," or chuck rib. These pieces are not quite so good, but having the blade taken out (as all others should be that have it in), and a piece of nice fat or suet placed or skewered in, makes an excellent piece to "roast in the pot," *à la mode*, potted beef, bouille, for mince pies, soups, etc.

When four of these chuck ribs, with the neck end, are left together, it is known as a chuck, and ofttimes this whole piece is cut into and sold as *chuck steaks*; the first of them, when from a choice animal, are next in quality to the sirloin steaks, being as well mixed or marbled with fat, and are equally sweet and juicy.

The balance of the chuck, or rather neck-piece, is usually divided into three or more pieces. The first, next to the chuck, is called *first-cut neck-piece*, and so on. These pieces are excellent for a sweet, strengthening soup, or mince pies, bolognas, etc.

The **cross-rib** (which the English call *leg-of-mutton piece*), is a profitable and good piece, very fair for a plain roast, one of the best for stewing, *à la mode*, bouille, and for what some of our "old-fashioned folks" call "roast in the pot."

The **brisket-piece** is much used by the French for bouille, soup, and a very good piece corned or salted.

The **plate-piece** (in Boston called *rattle-ran*) is commonly used for corned or salted beef, and the best for pressing. Many butchers roll it—after taking all the bones out—with sugar, spice, etc., then tie or skewer it up in a round form. After being well cured it is known as Scotch roll, a name given it by the author. It is an excellent dish when cold.

The **navel-piece** (or *thin-end brisket*) is much used for the same purposes as the plate and brisket pieces. These three pieces are used principally for salting, packing, exportation, and shipping uses.

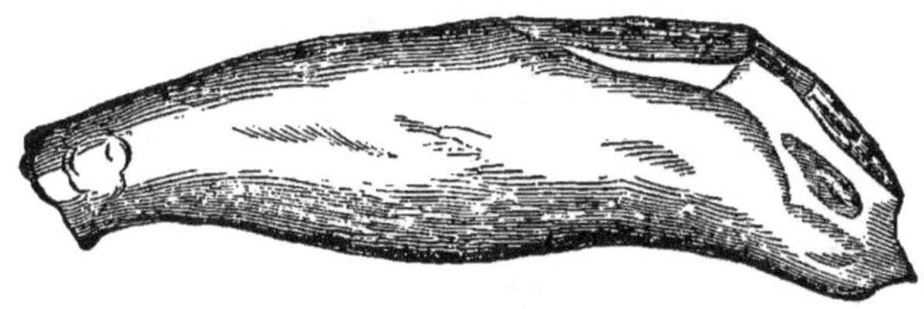

SHIN OF BEEF.

The **shoulder-clod**, or **clod**, when cut in pieces, is principally used in soups, bouille, etc. The meat is juicy and tender, with a nice marrow-bone in each piece, except the thick end, sometimes known as "Old Tom," although it contains a large bone, which, though hidden from view, is excellent for a rich soup.

The **shin of beef,** which is represented on the preceding page, is taken from off the clod; it is fit for nothing but stock for soup. When well and properly boiled, it makes a rich, gelatinous soup.

The **sticking-piece** is also taken from the clod, but of late years is seldom taken off. It is used principally for mince-pies, stews, soups, etc.

Half-bison (or *buffalo*) **heifer**.—An animal of the half-breed, or cross of the bison bull and Durham cow, was slaughtered by me in the month of October, 1855, and for further particulars the following extract is taken from the

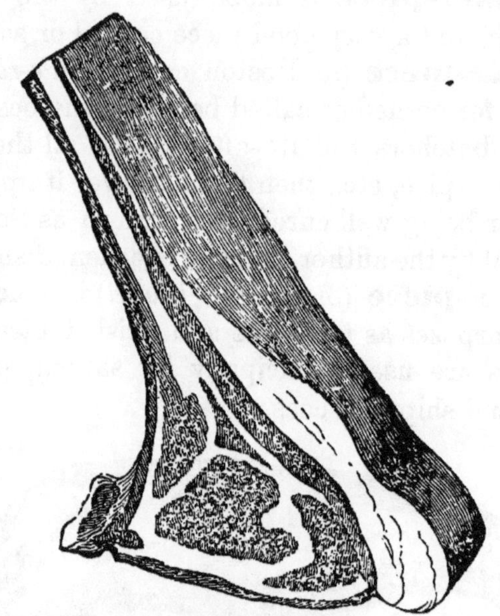

FIFTH AND SIXTH RIBS.

"Transactions of the American Institute," page two hundred and nineteen of the volume for 1855.

"This animal's age was between three and four years

—live weight nearly one thousand seven hundred pounds. The four quarters (dead) weighed nine hundred and forty pounds (rough fat one hundred and twelve pounds—hide seventy-five pounds). On the hump the fat measured three and one-half inches, on the loin two inches, and cut beautifully marbled. (See figure of the fifth and sixth ribs.)

"Her color almost black, with tan-colored long hair on her shoulders, and also long hair under her chin and at the fetlocks; with the turn-up horns, round nose, and the wild flashing eye of the bison. When fastened up in a large pen she was so cross and vicious that no person dare go in the pen with her, and when a red object presented itself, whether a shawl on a lady or the red shirt of a workman, she would become very much excited and pitch directly at the object, or as far as she could go.

"Colonel De Voe reported that he had sold all her 'beef,' without giving an opinion either in favor or against the eating qualities, but wished those to whom he sold cuts to report on this point after having partaken. There were but two who reported unfavorably, some ten or twelve who thought 'they never eat finer flavored or more tender beef,' and a very large number, among whom was Lieutenant-General Scott, reported that the 'beef' was very high-flavored, with a taste of game, but not so juicy as our first-quality beef."

VEAL.

The **calf**, after it is slaughtered and dressed, is called *veal;* but, unlike the ox or steer, in the dressing, our regular butchers seldom take off its skin until the day it is to be placed on their stalls for sale. It is retained on the carcass for the purpose of keeping the flesh moist, bright, and clean.

Selecting the various calves to produce the best veal, I have placed them in the following order:

1. Heifer-calf, from 4 to 6 weeks old, fed wholly on milk.
2. Bull-calf, " " "
3. Steer-calf, from 6 to 10 weeks old, fed partially on milk and meal.
4. Heifer-calf, " " "
5. Bull-calf, " " "
6. Steer-calf, from 10 months up to yearling, fed as above.
7. Heifer-calf, " " "
8. Bull-calf, " " "

The age of the calf not being less than four nor more than six weeks, produces the best veal, if properly fed and in a healthy condition. At a less age veal is not fit for food, as the flesh is flaccid, gelatinous, and watery. When calves are wholly fed from the cow, and range between the age of

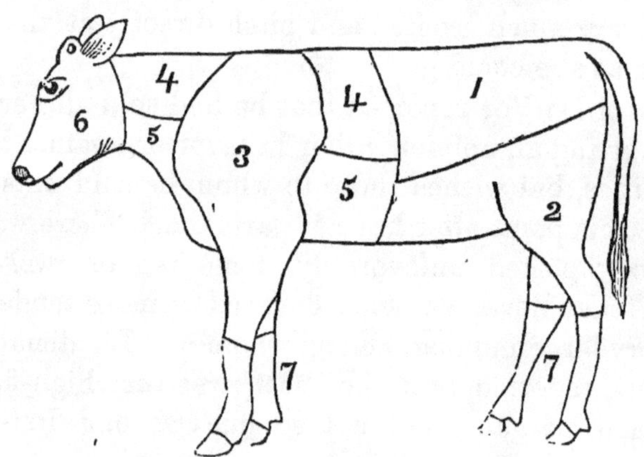

1. Loin of veal.
2. Leg of veal.
3. Shoulder of veal.
4. Neck of veal.
5. Breast of veal.
6. Calf's head.
7. Calf's feet.

four to six weeks, they produce what may be called *milk veal*, being the most white, tender, and delicate, and considered the choicest eating of all other veal. After six weeks the calf requires more food than the mother can produce: the milk of another cow, or a little meal, grass, or hay, is also given. This change of food, with advance of its age, of course, materially alters the character of the flesh, both in quality and color, which becomes darker, while the fat is more yellow and the meat less juicy. When turned out and wholly fed on grass *(grass calves)*, the flesh is rendered poor, dry, tasteless, and usually dark-colored.

Good veal should be finely grained, tender, and juicy, the fat firm and of a whitish color. If too white, the veal will show that the calf has been bled before being slaughtered—a process which may add to its appearance, but which deprives the meat of much of its juiciness as well as its sweet flavor.

The figure on preceding page represents a calf about six weeks old, and is marked out with lines and numbers, showing the different joints and their several names.

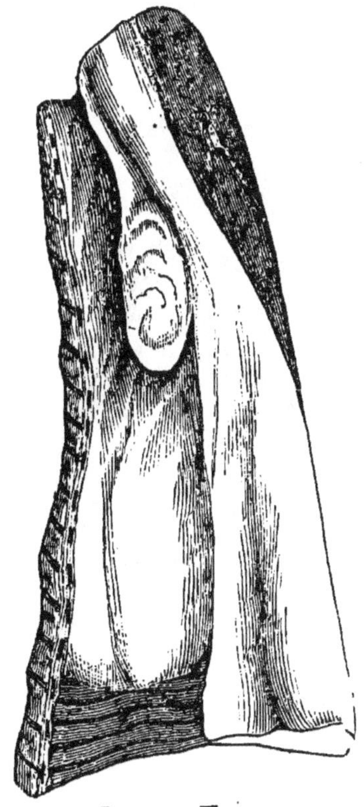

LOIN OF VEAL.

The **hind-quarter of veal** is the choice, and always commands the highest price. It is usually divided into two parts when found on the butcher's stall, which are commonly called the *loin* and *leg of veal.* The figure on preceding page represents a loin of veal, which is the choicest portion for roasting, either whole or divided. It also makes fine veal chops, either for broiling, frying, or stewing, etc. When the loin is too large, it is divided into two small joints; the thin end is called "kidney-end," and the other "thick-end," and, by foreigners, the "chump-end."

We now turn to the

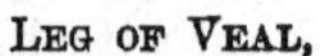

LEG OF VEAL,

which is sometimes used whole for roasting, or from it is cut the "fillet of veal," "veal cutlets," for fricandeau, forcemeats, collops, etc. The fillet of veal is boned by the butcher, and is used generally for roasting, stewing, etc. The "knuckle of veal," being a part of the leg of veal after the fillet or cutlets are taken from it, makes a good light soup, a stew, or boil, etc.

The **fore-quarter of veal** comprises the shoulder, the neck, and the breast. The following figure represents a

SHOULDER OF VEAL,

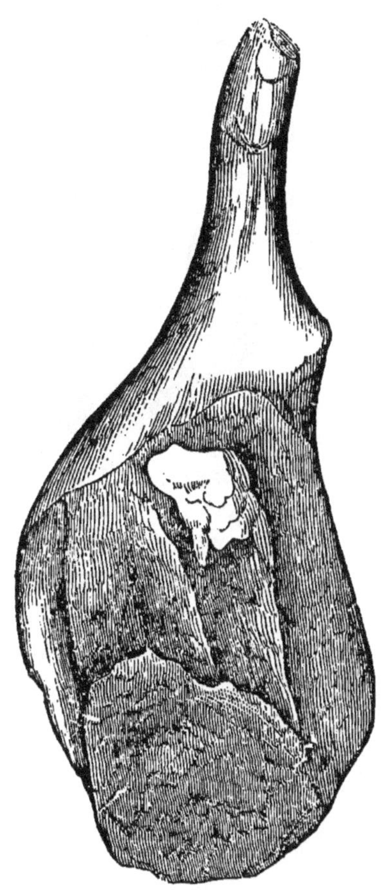

with all the bone, or blade, taken out. It is a good joint for being stuffed to roast, and will answer for that purpose without boning. A small family can make two dishes from it, by having the blade taken from the thin end, for roasting, stewing, etc. The "knuckle," or hock-end, left with the flesh on, with the blade-bone, will make a good soup or stew, at a slight cost.

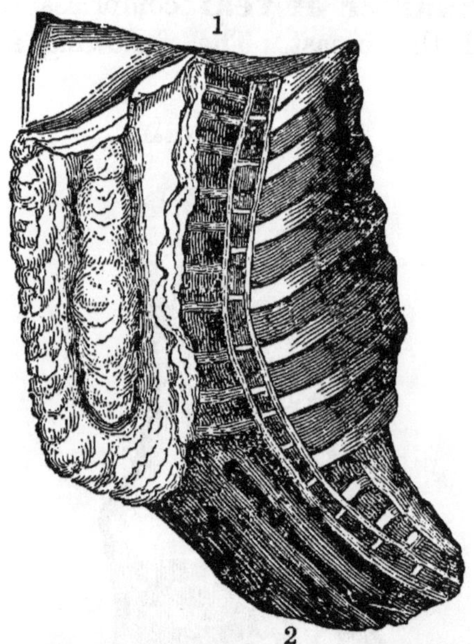

NECK AND BREAST OF VEAL.

The **breast of veal** is shown, on the left of the above engraving, connected with the "neck of veal," running from figure 1, directly down across the inside ribs, to figure 2. The breast is seen with the fat and throat sweet-bread attached, as it is usually dressed by the market-butcher. The sweet-breads are, however, sold separately.

Many persons prefer the breast of veal for roasting, stewing, veal-pie, and ragout; and it is sometimes boned, so as to roll, or a large hole is cut into it for the reception of stuffing, etc.

The **neck of veal** is used for stewing, fricassee, veal-pie (either pot or oven); and the best or rib end is preferred by the French and Germans for "rib chops" or "veal cotelettes"—(not "veal cutlets.")

The head, feet, haslet, sweet-breads, and other parts of the calf, are noticed under another head.

MUTTON.

THE flesh of sheep, when slaughtered and dressed, is known by the name of mutton: a single one whole, a carcass of mutton; many together, mutton carcasses.

The various kinds, ages, and sex of sheep producing the best mutton, are placed in the following order:

1. Wether (cosset),	from 3 to 5 years old.		
2. Wether,	" " "		
3. Wether,	" 1 to 3 "		
4. Ewe (cosset),	" 3 to 5 "	never having had lambs.	
5. Ewe,	" " "	"	"
6. Ewe,	" 1 to 3 "	"	"
7. Ewe (young, breeding, but dry).			
8. Ewe, of any age.			
9. Stag sheep, of any age—young best.			
10. Buck or ram,	" "		

The age of the animal producing the best mutton appears to be between three and five years old. They are then better interlarded, or mixed with fat, through the flesh, when full fed, and if not driven too far will have a large kidney fat. The cosset wether is selected as producing the best mutton, because we find its temper and habits are more docile and gentle. It is usually better fed than other sheep, and it is rarely worried in or out of the fields, but rather treated as a pet around the house or barnyard; therefore we find its flesh generally in the best condition.

Young wether mutton, although usually tender, has not so much rich flavor and sweetness as the same kind when older or fully developed by proper feeding and age.

It is asserted by some that mutton is best immediately after being killed, or before the animal heat has parted from it. If so, I have not discovered it, and I have eaten from the same animal on several different occasions—when fresh and long killed—and have always found the fresh-killed mutton taste much as it smells when dressing the animal, that is, what butchers call "woolly," or "sheepy," and never so sweet or tender as the long-killed, or that which has hung the longest in clear, cool air, where the flesh has not been permitted to dry too much or become tainted; the fibre then has become tender, yields easily to the powers of mastication, and, while much of the fresh, thin, tasteless juices or water are dried out, experience shows that the thick, sweet juices are left.

The different breeds and feeding have also a great deal to do in producing the best qualities. A large-framed, coarse-woolled, fat sheep produces a coarse-grained, dry, and but indifferent-flavored mutton; while the middle-woolled, round, plump, thick sheep—generally found in the Southdown, Leicester, Cotswold, etc., breeds—produces the close-grained, tender, juicy, and high-flavored mutton, especially when they are allowed to feed upon the short, sweet grass of the hills and mountains, with the addition of proper stall-feeding afterwards.

A great deal of the mutton brought to New York City by the steamers from England, and paraded so ostentatiously at many of our first-class restaurants, hotels, etc., is generally no better than our best mutton, which can be procured from any of our first-class butchers, and more especially when it has been "hung." The principal advantage of the English mutton is on account of its being long-killed when it arrives here. I will not, however, say that we produce as much fine mutton, because I know we do not. The climate of England is more favorable, it never being so cold but that the sheep can be left out all winter, without being housed at all: in fact, I am told that these animals can eat the turnips out of the ground, where they are left for that purpose, while ours, to keep them improving, must be housed and well cared for, to produce this excellent meat in perfection.

Many travellers say that mutton is the favorite meat of the English people of all classes; it, however, is not so in this country yet; but its consumption is gradually increasing, and, I think, quite as fast as the improvement and increase of the fine breeds of sheep.

General opinion confirms the fact that good mutton is one of the most wholesome, as well as the most easily digested, of all the meat kind, and therefore best calculated for invalids.

In choosing the best mutton, perhaps a few remarks may assist the unpractised buyer. The fat should be white, clear, and hard, the scored skin on the fore-quarters nearly red, the lean firm, succulent, and juicy, rather of a darkish red color, and the leg-bones clear and nearly or quite white.

Indifferent and poor mutton is seldom fat; but if so, the fat will have a yellowish appearance: and if the animal has been driven a long way, or diseased, the flesh will be flabby, the kidney-fat small, with a stringy appearance, and the lean seen through the skin on the back of a dark bluish shade.

The flesh of **ram-mutton** is usually found to be dark,

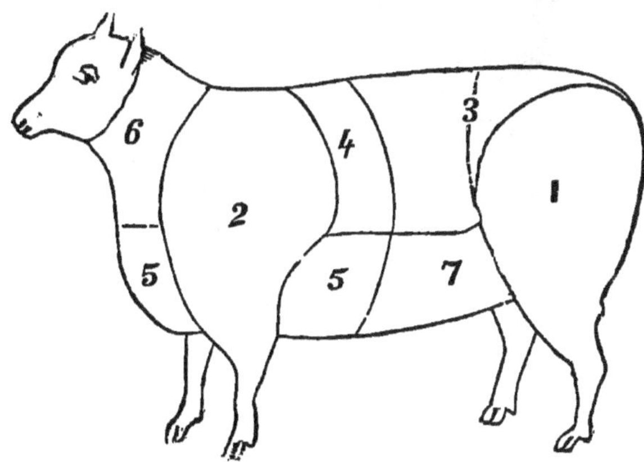

1. Leg of Mutton.
2. Shoulder of "
3. Loin of "
4. & 6. Neck of "
5. Breast of Mutton.
6. Scrag " (end of the neck).
7. Flank "

close, and coarse-grained; the fat is of a darker (and some times of a yellowish) shade than that found in good mutton, while the flesh is softer and spongy, and rank in its flavor.

In dividing or cutting up a "carcass of mutton," it is usual, first, to split it through the backbone into two sides, and if the weather should be unfavorable for hanging them any length of time, it will be best to hang them separately, without quartering them. "In some parts of England," says the Westmoreland Gazette, "it is usual at Christmas for the farmers to kill each a sheep for their own use, on

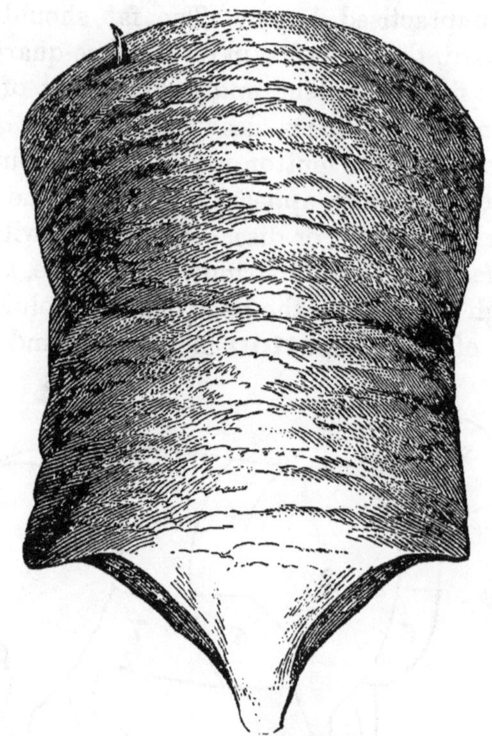

SADDLE OF MUTTON.

which occasion, when the butcher inquires if they want any meat against Christmas, the usual reply is, 'Nay, I think not; I think o' killing myself.' Last Christmas a butcher called on a farmer of his acquaintance in the usual manner, saying, 'Will ye want a bit of meat, or ye'll kill yerself this Christmas?' 'I nae not,' replied the farmer, 'whether I'se kill myself or take a side o' me father.'"

In the figure on page sixty-seven is shown the various prominent pieces, designated by the number of each piece.

The carcass is also often cut with the two hind-quarters together, and so hung up on the stalls, sometimes for weeks, if in weather fit for keeping it, or long enough to ripen it. This hanging of meats is a great loss to the butcher, from the effect of drying out the juices, thereby lessening the weight. An animal of eighty pounds weight, hung up for two weeks, will lose from eight to twelve pounds, according to the state of the weather, which loss, with the risk of sudden changes of either close, damp, warm, or muggy weather, should demand an increased price, or a proper allowance made for the loss on the original weight. There are some families, however, who have proper places, and buy their mutton fresh, when it is used as it is required.

When two connected hind-quarters, which I have designated hind-saddle, are ready to be used or cut for a saddle, they are hung by the right leg: then cut a part through the aitch-bone; and again, cut off the legs, either ham (as seen on the preceding page) or haunch fashion, which leaves the two loins together, and are known as a "saddle of mutton."

This being the finest and choicest part of the mutton for roasting, it should always, if the weather will admit, be well hung, and then, before use, have the outside fleshy skin taken off. An excellent large chop which I have called *saddle-chop*, is cut off from the rib end of a saddle of mutton. When in a frozen state, it should be sawed off like venison, which adds much to its tenderness.

The two **fore-quarters**, when left together, I have designated with the name of *fore-saddle*, although usually called fore-quarters; and this name is usually given them when separated; but fore-quarter will properly apply to one, as it is usually known.

When the **fore-saddle** is wanted for a large roast, or to corn, the two breasts and shanks are taken off, with a piece or scrag end of the neck; which leaves a good thick piece I have named *chines of mutton*, but when separated, each one a *chine of mutton.* By taking out the shoulder-blade it leaves less labor for the carver. For a small family, the latter piece makes a profitable and good piece, either to roast, corn, or it may be cut into lean chops.

If, however, the carcass is split and quartered, either one of the four quarters can be used whole for roasting, etc., or the

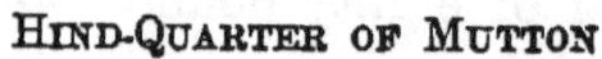

HIND-QUARTER OF MUTTON

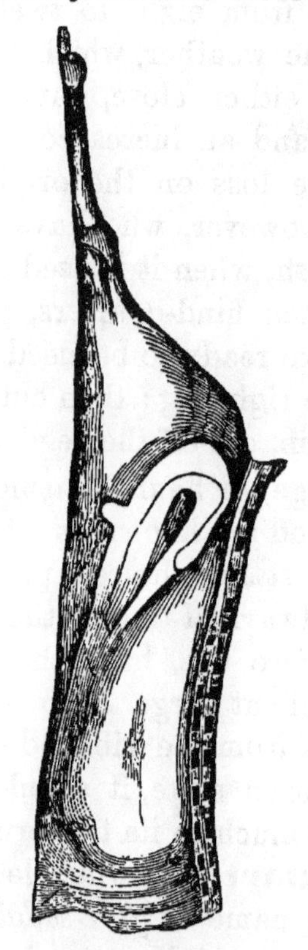

can be divided by taking off, ham fashion or haunch fashion, as shown in **leg of mutton** on opposite page.

One of the most useful, it commands the highest price of any joint of the carcass. It is a choice part for boiling, soup, corned, etc., and when well hung it is best for a roast. The part left of the hind-quarter is called the *loin of mutton.*

LEG OF MUTTON.

which is generally used for chops (sometimes called English chops), or for roasting, haricot, etc. The loin of mutton being one-half of the saddle, should also have the light tough skin taken off the back fat before use. The following anecdote was created by a gentleman who was carving this joint, when he said: "Shall I cut this loin of mutton saddle-wise?" "No," said his friend. "Cut it bridle-wise, for then we may have a chance to get a *bit* in our mouths."

THE FORE-QUARTER OF MUTTON,

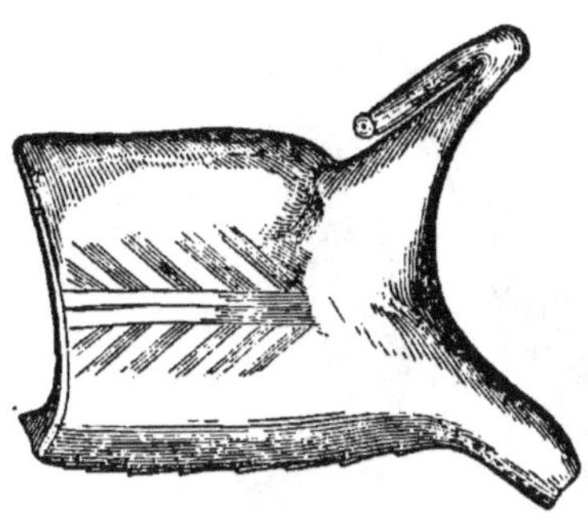

if small, not too fat, and cracked like lamb, or it has the shoulder-blade taken out, makes an excellent piece to roast, or corned whole ; but when wanted in pieces, the shoulder should be first taken off, which will appear as follows—

SHOULDER OF MUTTON,

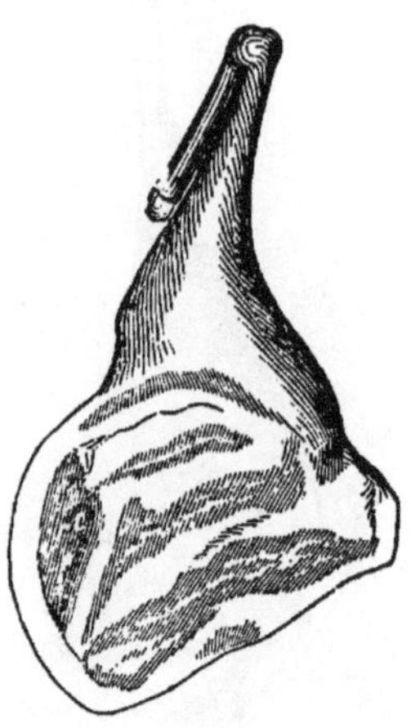

used for roasting, soup, stewing, etc. A London paper of 1804 says : "Yesterday a journeyman blacksmith, of the name of Sattle, a noted gormandizer, undertook, for a trifling wager, to eat a shoulder of mutton of six pounds weight, with a proportionate quantity of vegetables, and a threepenny loaf, and to drink a quart of ale, at a public house in the neighborhood of Golden Lane. He was to perform the task in an hour ; but he completed it in fifty minutes, and actually bespoke a supper of bread and bacon." We

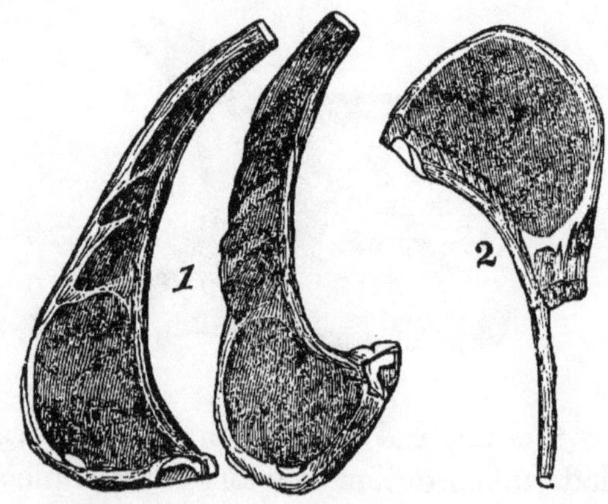

turn and chop off the neck of mutton from the breast, which is fit for a stew, haricot, etc., or from which are cut ribs singly (Fig. 1), the French cotelette, or rib chops (the one on the right, Fig. 2, is ready trimmed for use), which leaves the scrag end of the neck—a piece much used for broth for the sick; or the whole neck, cut up, is used for haricot, stew, pies, etc.

The **breast**—the lowest-priced joint of the carcass—is used for stewing, pies, etc. Other parts of the sheep are described under another head.

LAMB.

Lamb is accepted by its name after it is slaughtered and dressed. The same terms and names apply to the similar named joints of mutton, by using the word lamb in place of mutton.

This young animal is usually known among butchers as lamb until it arrives at the age of about twelve months, when it is termed *yearling*, although at this period the yearling is often dressed "lamb fashion."

The size, fatness, condition, age, and sex are considered best in the order as follows:

1. Spring (or house) lamb (ewe), from six weeks to three months old.
2. Spring lamb (buck) " " " "
3. Wether lamb " " three months to eight months old.
4. Ewe lamb " " " " "
5. Wether lamb, or yearling, eight months to twelve months old.
6. Ewe lamb, " " "

The spring lamb, occasionally called house lamb, especially by some foreigners, it is presumed from the circumstance of its being born during the winter months, when its tender life, if not carefully housed, fed, and kept warm, would perish, remain dwarfish, or become sickly. Its flesh is prized for its unseasonable character, and, although delicate and tender, is quite insipid and no way nourishing.

The old-country fashion of preparing house lambs was, many years ago: "As soon as the lambs are born they are put into a warm outhouse. Some white peas and bran are mixed together and placed near them, with a little fine hay and a chalk-stone to lick. The dams are turned into good grass, and brought to their lambs four times a day. Every lamb is suffered to suck as much as it will. By this process they become extremely delicate." But in this country it usually lacks the pleasant flavor that grass imparts to the flesh.

Lamb occasionally is sold in our markets as early as the month of March; after which it slowly increases in size and numbers, and in the months of June, July, and August it is in full season, and of fine quality. When first brought to market lamb is not sold in less quantity than a quarter, its weight being seldom above five or six pounds. As it increases in size by age, and amply fed by the grass-fed ewe —aided by the warm sun—the lamb speedily increases in weight, the quarters from eight to twelve pounds each. Later in the season, the animal with age and forced feed, the quarters will weigh as much as twenty-five pounds.

To choose lamb, first examine the fat on the back and then that of the kidneys, both of which should be white, hard, and of the same color. Lambs are tender creatures. Rough handling, cold, stormy weather, kept without food, and being long driven, produce a feverish state, which causes the flesh and fat to be veiny and of a dark red color, and also renders it dry, tough, and tasteless.

The **kidney fat** of a fine (or inferior) lamb should not be raised, stuffed, or blowed; but merely its own caul or fat laid on its legs and flanks (see Fig.), to prevent them from drying or burning when roasting. Beware of two or three colors of fat found about the dressing of the hind-quarters, which in all probability is here appropriated from some other animal, which gives it a different flavor when cooked. This caution applies to all kinds of meat of blown or spongy appearance, this being frequently produced by human breath. It is needless to observe that the breath of the human lungs (even from those of the most healthy and sweet condition), in this manner blown into meats, is neither calculated to add to its sweetness nor to render it palatable to delicately-educated people.

The **carcass of lamb** is first split down the centre of the back and neck into two sides, which are quartered by leaving two or three ribs on the following

HIND-QUARTER OF LAMB.

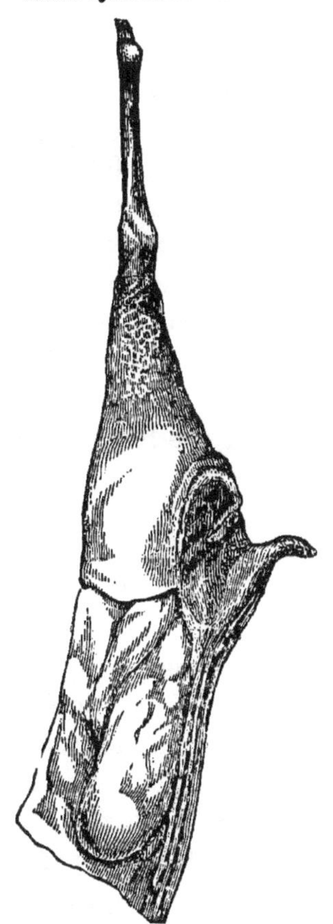

When large enough, and it is desired by the purchaser to be cut or divided, the leg is first cut off and prepared for roasting, boiling, or cut into chops, etc.

The **loin of lamb** is usually cut into chops, or cracked for roasting, etc.

The **fore-quarter of lamb** (see fore-quarter of mutton) is smaller than the same joint of mutton; the bones are of a more reddish color. The fore-leg is broken off immediately above the joint of the foot, at the point where the fore-foot or hooflock joint is cut from the mutton, which connects with the white joint bone. Some call it lamb as long as the foot breaks off with the hand at this place; this, however, often occurs in old sheep.

Small old sheep, very poor and thin in flesh, are often dressed up "lamb fashion" by irresponsible butchers and others, who sell it under the name of lamb, and many years ago such was known as "Staten Island Lamb." This meat is usually sold at exceedingly low prices.

By many the fore-quarter of lamb is preferred for the delicacy of the ribs and breast when roasted. Removing the blade-bone from the quarter greatly assists the carver. Separated from the shoulder, the neck and breast broiled make a choice dish.

Other parts of the lamb are found noticed under another head.

PIGS, HOGS, AND PORK.

The young pig, termed "roasting-pig," is not changed in name, like the full-grown animal, by the fact of slaughtering. Living or dead, it is named a pig, a roaster, or a roasting-pig. When dressed for choice eating, it should not be less than three nor more than six weeks old. The skin of the roaster should be white (unless it has been a spotted or black-haired pig), plump, hard, and well cleaned. The flanks, where it is opened, should be thick and fat, and it ought to weigh from eight to fourteen pounds. Its season is best in the fall and winter months.

The half or full grown shoat, or hog, and its varieties,

when prepared for the stall, is changed to the name of *pork*. When living, and of different ages and sexes, they are known by several distinct names: those under one year are either called pigs, shoats, or porkers. If the female within one year have pigs, she is known as a "young sow," and no longer by the name of shoat, etc. When spayed, the animal is then known as a "spayed sow." Above one year, the male is named a "young boar;" when aged, an "old boar;" and, when altered, a "barrow," or "barrow-hog," or "hog;" and, when altered late or aged, it is called a "stag-hog." The female is similarly named "sow," "sow-hog," or "hog." These terms are mostly applied to the living animals.

Experience and information, in relation to the varieties which will produce the best pork, may be placed in the following order. The first are those which are fed with corn:

1. Barrow-pigs or shoats, from three months to one year old.
2. Sow-pigs or shoats, from three months to six months old.
3. Barrow-pigs, etc. (milk and grass fed), from three months to one year old.
4. Sow-pigs, from three to four months old.
5. Barrow-hogs and spayed sows, when found over one year old, corn-fed, selected usually for bacon-hogs.
6. Sow-hogs, do., do., selected usually for bacon-hogs.
7. Stag-hog.
8. Boar-hog or boar—youngest best.

The general appearance of the most choice pork is from an animal the carcass of which will not weigh less than fifty and not more than one hundred and twenty pounds. The skin should present a semi-transparent appearance, approaching white in color; the fat on the back should not be less than half an inch thick, white and firm, and the lean of a pale reddish color, and sappy. The skin of the older animals, or bacon-hogs, is thicker and coarser, while the lean is of a darker color, but equally sweet, juicy, and tender.

Hogs selected for bacon, clear pork, hams, shoulders, back fat, or for salted or barrelling pork, are usually from one hundred and fifty to five hundred pounds in weight —some, indeed, have weighed above one thousand two hundred pounds.

By many, fresh pork is considered to be exceedingly unwholesome during the months of the year of high temperature. This, no doubt, to a great extent, is true: the fatty, gross character of the flesh not being easily assimilated when the animal economy of the human system requires less heating nourishment to the blood, and therefore requires less irritating food to the digestive organs. The instincts of experience no doubt lessen the demand for fresh pork during the heat of the summer trade.

Animals procured from those who properly feed them (the food producing a great influence on the quality of the flesh) must prove good, sweet, and wholesome, although it may be soft; but if the animals are allowed to run at large, which is generally the case with shoats and hogs in the spring and summer, eating whatever they can pick up—their uncleanly character is too well known, both as to habit and the filth or animal substances they select for food—there can be no doubt that pork, from such animals, offers unfit and unwholesome food.

Shoats or hogs selected for slaughter, after they have been properly fed, are penned two or three months, first giving them swills, vegetables, or grain, which afterwards is increased in quality and quantity, such as Indian-corn, by which the character and quality of the flesh is much improved. The tenderness is also increased by the hanging of the carcass of the slaughtered animal for several days before being cut into the various pieces for use.

The **carcass of pork**, being intended for immediate use while in its fresh state, is hung by the foot of its right hind leg; then cut down, through the skin of the centre of the back, from the tail to the neck, followed with the splitting down of the backbone through the line of the incision, dividing it into halves or sides. These are again divided, after taking off the head, into quarters.

SHOAT-PORK.

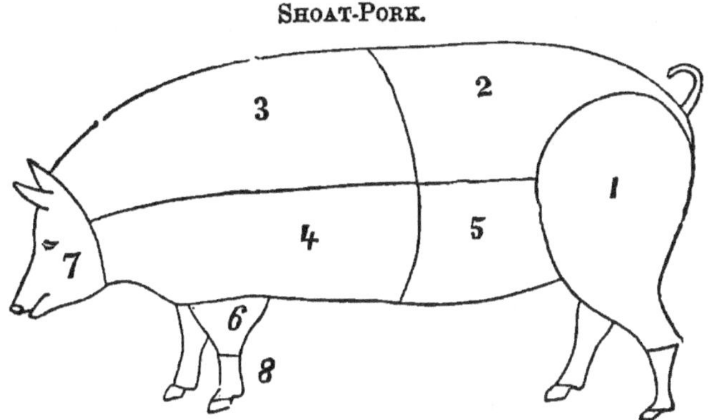

1. Leg of pork.
2. Loin of pork. } often cut
3. Chine of pork. } together.
4. Brisket of pork.
5. Flank of pork.
6. Hocks.
7. Pig's-head.
8. Pig's feet.

The **hind-quarter** (represented in the preceding figure, including Nos. 1, 2, and 5) is first divided by taking off the leg of pork, which is generally used fresh for roasting, after having the bone neatly taken out and finely scored; but when intended for corning, it should be kept in pickle ten or twelve days before use.

The **loin of pork** being left, if not too fat, presents the finest piece for roasting; it should also be finely and evenly scored, as all pork ought to be when intended for roasting; the scoring should be a quarter of an inch in width, to prevent its blistering, and render the joint more readily carved. The loin also furnishes fine pork chops, and small delicate corning pieces.

The **fore-quarter of pork,** if small, is often roasted whole, after having the blade-bone removed; if large, it is divided across the ribs (see figure between 3 and 4), using the thin part, or brisket of pork, for corning, after taking off the hocks and feet.

The **chine of pork** (figure 3) is used for roasting, or the ribs are used for rib-chops, up as far as the blade-bone, and the remaining part for pork-steaks.

The carcass being very large and fat, and the lean portions intended to be used fresh, the two following figures (furnished me by the kindness of the *American Agriculturist*) will assist this explanation, in the cutting of it up.

The figure 1 appears lying on a block or table. We must

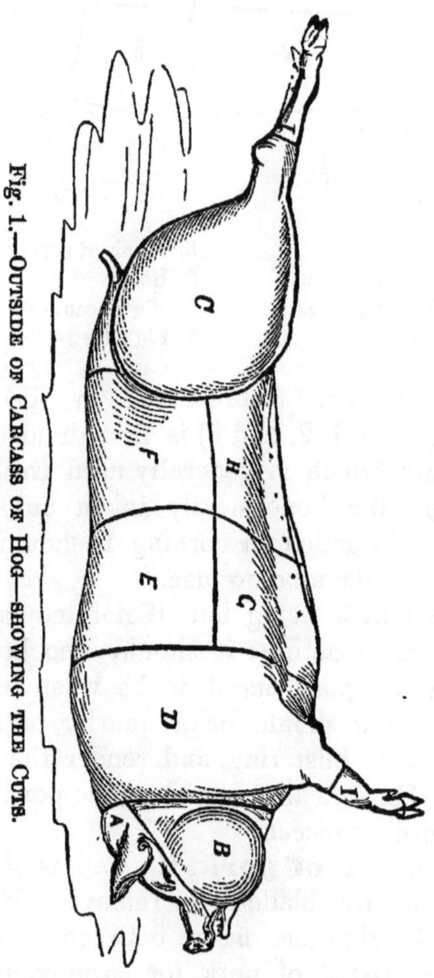

Fig. 1.—Outside of Carcass of Hog—showing the Cuts.

first separate the head from the carcass; then split (or saw, if frozen) the carcass through the back-bone with a chopper. Each side will then appear as represented by the figure on opposite page. This done, with a sharp knife loosen the leaf and kidney fat (near the letters N and K, figure 2), and tear it away towards the leg, or fresh ham; the kidney is brought away with it. Each side is then divided into its fore and hind quarters, by leaving two ribs on each of the latter. The next cut loosens the tenderloin

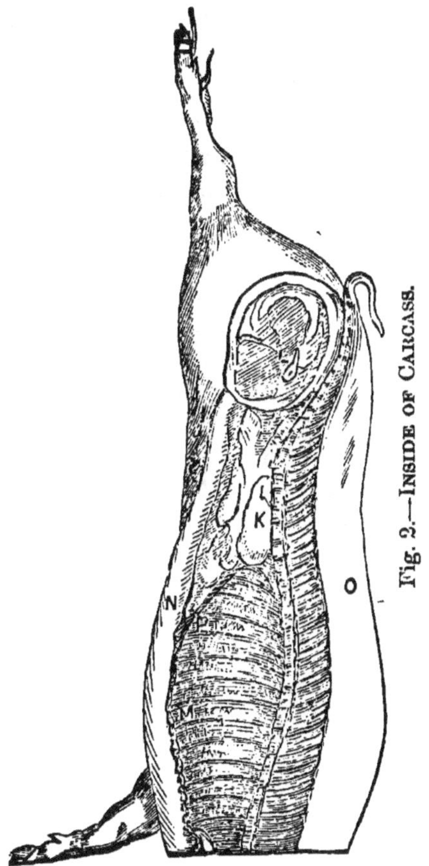

Fig. 2.—INSIDE OF CARCASS.

from where it is connected with the fresh ham, when it is torn out upwards towards the ribs or head. The fresh hams are then removed, beginning at the tail-side, and cut circularly to the flank (figure 1, C), after sawing the small bone about half-way, and chopping or sawing off the feet (figure 1, I, I).

Next, cut the **brisket of pork** off (see first figure, No. 4, p. 79), which is usually corned; the chine piece turn over, that the thick clear fat (fig. 2, O) can be easily cut off close to the lean. This fat is usually salted, and is known as back fat; it is used for various purposes in cookery, and also by many butchers in the dressing of calves. Sometimes a very thin slice will be observed on a fat-appearing loin of veal—this deceit is called *plating*, although, in fact, it may be considered an addition to the veal, by aiding its cooking and its flavor; it is usually done, however, with the intention of hiding the uncovered kidney of a poor young veal, which too often is not fit to be eaten.

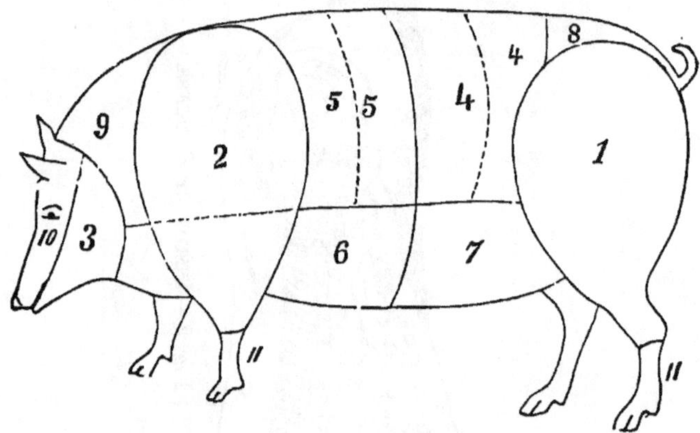

1. Leg, or fresh ham.
2. Shoulder (after being trimmed).
3. Chops or cheeks.
4, 4. Loin-pieces.
5, 5. Rib, or chine-pieces.
6. Brisket.
7. Flank.
8. Tail-piece.
9. Neck-piece.
10. Pate or skull.
11. Feet.

The **chine of pork,** without the back fat, is much used for chops, steaks, or roasting: while some prefer this part (after taking out all the bones) for sausage-meat.

The **back-fat,** on the loin, is also taken off in the same manner, when the loin is prepared for either chops or roasting.

This kind of pork is now usually preferred, instead of the small quarters, or that which has the skin usually left on it; the flesh being considered more luscious from having been better fed and cared for, while it is leaner and thicker.

The hog intended for bacon is always large and fat, especially that intended for English and "Irish-singed bacon;" these, however, will be found noticed under the proper head of bacon.

The figure of the hog on the preceding page represents by the numbers the mode of cutting the carcass for barreling.

The same mode of cutting is adapted by separating the head from the carcass, then splitting the carcass, cutting off the fresh hams and feet, tearing out the leaf and kidney fat, taking out the tenderloin—as previously shown. Then the head (Nos. 10 and 3) is divided by cutting off the cheeks, beginning from the corner of the mouth, following the line towards No. 9 (see fig. 1, A B,) and saw off the jaw-bone, which separates the cheeks from the pate; then crack the bone of the under jaw, between the front teeth, and the cheeks are held together to hang up by. Next take off the shoulder by cutting straight across the side, as shown fig. 1 (B); then trim off the spare-ribs, by cutting under the breast-bone, and so follow the ribs as far as the chine-bone, when the knife is continued on directly to the end of the long bones in the back, which leaves the shoulder about one thickness, and the spare-ribs (not too spare), with meat enough left on under them to make a roast. Then trim the shoulder round (see No. 2), saw off the feet, which forms the shoulder similar to a ham. The brisket and flanks are now cut off; the ribs (5, 5) and loin (4, 4) pieces are cut in suitable sizes, when all are ready to salt, except that the trimmings and some other pieces can be used for sausages. The leaf-fat and pieces of fat, rendered into lard; and the pate, etc. for head-cheese.

The **pork tenderloins**, when cut out of pork, are usually sold separately at a higher price than the other parts. Their ordinary weight is from half to one pound each. Many consider them the choicest part of the pork; but, as already observed, they are usually found tender, but dry and tasteless.

Measly pork.—The flesh of the hog, with this disease, when slaughtered, is exceedingly unwholesome, and is not fit to be used for any purpose. It may be known by the many yellowish lumps or kernels seen through the fat and lean, as well as the flesh having a heavy, dull appearance.

GOAT'S FLESH.

These animals are sometimes found in our markets dressed for sale, but their flesh is considered inferior to that of mutton. Although that from a young wether goat or kid is very tender and sweet, but has not so agreeable a flavor as mutton or lamb, nor is it so easily digested—the flavor partaking the character of venison.

A very fine, fat goat, killed after the fashion of the Jews, by Bernheim & Sons, Jefferson Market, May 9, 1856, weighed, when alive, ninety-six pounds, and after being dressed, including the head and haslet, weighed sixty-four pounds, exclusive of sixteen pounds of rough fat.

The flesh had much the appearance of stag or ram mutton, the fat being of a reddish color, soft and oily; the lean was dark in color, but juicy and tender. Those who partook of it were well satisfied, though no doubt the flavor

NOTE.—Some curious market laws of the Island of Antigua, West India Islands, are found noticed in the New Haven Gazette, October 26, 1786, which parts of, refer to the pig and hog. One of which says:

"Be it enacted, that all choate (pigs) exceeding nine pounds a quarter, be esteemed hog, and so sold, and that no flesh be esteemed veal, except the clerk of the market really approve it as such.

"And, whereas, the office of clerk of the market is very troublesome and of small advantage; be it therefore enacted, that the offices of "common crier,' and 'common whipper,' in the respective towns of this island, be added thereto, with all the fees, perquisites, and advantages belonging, or which shall belong to the same.

"And be it enacted, for the encouragement of poor people, who for the most part do raise stock to supply the markets of this island, all rumps, sirloins, and buttocks of beef, be esteemed choice pieces, and sold at eight pence per pound."

would have been much improved had a few days longer keeping of the carcass been allowed by the Jewish laws—the Jews not being permitted to eat flesh killed over three days, without it goes through a cleansing process by a shoket, or unless none other is to be had.

THE PARTS WE USE FROM DOMESTIC ANIMALS.

There are many choice dishes prepared from various parts of the domestic animals used for food, which in former times were either sold for a mere trifle or thrown away. The increase of domestic animals has, by no means, been pro-rata with the rapid and vast increase of our population, hence prices have increased to double what they were in the "olden time;" the consequence of which is, we find, a gradual increased demand for such portions of the animal as were once altogether refused, or considered unfit to be eaten, or too troublesome to repay for the time consumed in preparing them into proper food. These considerations—of high prices, professional cooks, or "artists"—with cookery books and foreign cookery notions, have introduced a system of knowledge as to the preparation of excellent and cheap dishes from the various and numerous parts of the domestic animals.

In presenting these remarks to notice, I ask attention particularly to the choosing and judging which are the best, with the general uses of the different parts which follow, commencing with those taken from

NEAT CATTLE.

Beeves' tongue. This part of the animal has always been considered a delicacy. When purchasing, choose those which are thick, firm, and with plenty of fat on the under side. They are used, when fresh, for mince pies, stews, etc., and, when pickled or smoked, for boiling, and, when cold, are excellent eating. In the living animal's mouth, the tongue is very rough, being almost a compact bed of spines, which nature has furnished to draw the grass or other food into the mouth, as well as to scratch or lick its body; these spines, however, come off of the tongue with the skin when boiled.

Beeves' liver. The best liver presents a clear, bright, yellowish-red color, although that which is of a clear, dark color is good; and mashing easily under the pressure of the finger, is a sure sign of tenderness. But those affected with dark, "sedgy" streaks, sandy spots and abscesses, are unwholesome and unfit to be eaten. These are known as "sedgy livers," which, no doubt, is caused by the animal drinking from the Western pools of water and swallowing a small leech, or bloodsucker, as boys used to call them. I have frequently taken them from the liver in a perfect state, and again, on an examination, I have found these leeches filled with blood, and a gritty substance like sand; others, again, present their contents as if in a dissolving condition, which we find in darkish streaks scattered through the substance of the liver. When in the course of the natural healing of these parts, we find numerous sinewy, tough, light streaks, or scars, through them, which would always remain, like the healing up of an old sore.

Thirty or forty years ago, almost all our Western cattle would have these bad livers, when they were compelled to be driven on foot through to our (New York) city; but since the rail-cars, steamboats, etc., have carried them, we do not so often find bad livers.

A remarkably fine, large liver was sold in Jefferson Market, in December, 1860, taken from a small, Kentucky heifer. It was very yellow, tender, and fine, and weighed twenty-eight and one-half pounds. The cause of this being so large —from so small an animal—was conjectured to be, that the animal had been fed upon hot or cooked food, and kept in a very warm place. The distillery, or "swill-fed" cows generally have large, handsome livers, but not well-flavored.

Beeves' heart. Those with a large quantity of nice, clear fat around the top part are the best. They are usually stuffed and roasted, or stewed, and make a good, wholesome, and nutritious meal, and one of the cheapest in the animal.

Beeves' kidney. There are two kidneys in each animal; the best are without dark spots, or water bladders, but of a clear, dark, reddish color. Used for stewing, broiling, etc.

Beeves' suet. This untried fat is taken from around the kidney, and is much drier, shorter, more tender, and firmer than the common meat or flesh fat. It should also be white, clear (not bloody), and easily break or crumble into very small pieces; it is much used in mince pies, puddings, candles, etc.

Beeves' gut fat is much like suet, but has more fibre through it. The Jews use this in cooking in the place of lard, which, by their laws, they discard; but it must be from animals slaughtered and regularly sealed by their *shoket*, or Jew butcher.

Some people imagine that beeves' fat or suet is the same as tallow, and I once read of a case where a tallow-chandler by the name of Webb charged a prisoner with stealing his *tallow* (instead of *fat*). The prisoner having no counsel, the judge became his advocate, and asked the prosecutor:

Judge.—"How do you know, Webb, that you lost just eighty-nine pounds of tallow?"

Webb.—"I am sure of it, my lord."

Judge.—"I want to be sure of it, too. Do you keep an account of what you receive or what you use?"

Webb.—"No, my lord."

Judge.—"What, no book in which you minute down your goods?"

Webb.—"Yes, my lord, I keep a day-book."

Judge.—"Well, that is what I wanted: and did you, in this book, make an entry of the tallow received, or taken from it, for the purpose of making candles?"

Webb.—"No, my lord, for it was not fit to make candles of."

Judge.—"Why, then, man, it was not tallow."

Webb.—"Yes it was, my lord."

Judge.—"Then why not fit to make candles?"

Webb.—"Because, my lord, it was not run into tallow."

Judge.—"Not run into tallow?"

Webb.—"No, my lord."

Judge.—"Why, then, it must be *fat*, and not *tallow*."

Webb.—"Yes, my lord."

Judge.—"Ah! that's very well. Gentlemen of the Jury: You find, by the prosecutor's own evidence, that you must acquit the prisoner. This man charges the prisoner with stealing *tallow*. The prosecutor is a tallow-chandler, and yet you hear from his own mouth that he does not know the difference between *tallow* and *fat*."

The prisoner was acquitted.

Beeves' or cows' udder. An udder from a young, dry cow, when nicely corned and boiled, is very good eating. Some parboil and roast it.

Beeves' head. From the sides of the head the ox-cheek is cut, which makes an excellent soup: or, the head is broken or cracked with an axe, the brains taken out and then boiled, so that the meat can be taken off easily from the bones. For making mince pies, meat puddings, etc.

The Germans cut off the nose, and prepare a dish called **ox mow**. It is sawed off through the nostril bones, leaving on the grisly skin, then boiled until all the bones can be removed easily, when it is usually fried or soused, etc. Said to be good eating.

Beeves' or ox marrow is taken from the marrow bones, principally from the hind-quarter. It should smell sweet, look clear, and be of quite a straw-color. Sold by the pound, and used for pomatums and cookery.

Marrow bones. These are cut from three to five inches long, and, when for the table, should be quite fresh. Either for roasting or boiled, after being covered with a floured cloth; to be used on toast instead of butter, etc.

Tripe. This article of food is always found cleaned,

and generally boiled ready for use. In selecting tripe, choose that which is white, thick, and fat. Many prefer the part called the night-cap or honeycomb; others again the thick seam; and some again the thin part. In the spring and summer seasons it is apt to have a greenish look on the inner side, in consequence of the animal feeding on grass. However, when dark and quite thin, it is either from eating or drinking distillery swill, or is from an animal diseased, and becomes dangerous food.

Ox tails. The word ox is more particularly used with this article. These are seldom found ready for sale, but when ordered are furnished by the "help." They are generally sold attached to the hides. An excellent and savory soup is made from them. Three tails will make a common tureen of soup. Prior to 1685 the butchers of London, in disposing of the bullocks' hides to the felt-mongers, were accustomed to leave on the tails. The French refugees, however, bought them up, and introduced into use that nutritive dish called "ox-tail soup."

Sweet breads and skirts. These were known many years ago by many of the poor inhabitants near slaughter-houses. They consisted of two strips of thin, skinny meat attached to the ribs and plate-pieces. These were cut out, and, with the (coarse) sweet-breads (more particularly noticed under the head of "Sweet-Breads from Calves"), were tied in a bunch with a rope-yarn, and generally sold from the slaughter-houses. These were a part of the perquisites given to apprentice boys above twenty years ago; but since that time the perquisite system has been changed, and in lieu more wages are paid.

Beeves' palates. These palates, which lay at the roof of the mouth, I have lately learned through "one of the great generals of the age" (Scott), who had enjoyed the eating of them prepared at the South, and who pronounced them excellent eating.

Ox feet, or cow heels. These are principally used by foreigners in making fricassee, stews, bake, jellies, etc., after having been scalded and dressed as the calves' feet. They require five or six hours' boiling. The fat skimmings of ox feet or cow heels is called "neat's foot oil."

Beeves' brains. These are used in many of the dishes, as those prepared from calves' or sheep's brains, but are not so delicate.

Beeves' or ox gall. These greenish bladders, or the contents, are used for various purposes, such as cleaning cloths, carpets, removing oil-stains, for liniments, salves, and also the mixing of paints. Buy it in the original bladder; and that which is quite thick, of a darkish green, and feels like glue, is the oldest and best. When scarce and in demand, some boys, to enlarge their perquisites as well as the size of the gall, adopt the plan of a dishonest milkman.

Ox eyes. These are called for sometimes by the medical student for examination and study; and I have known them to have been prepared in sauces for the table.

Ox or cows' teeth. Thirty years ago the teeth from an old ox or cow, when about half worn out, were used by dentists. In that state they are tough and solid. Many a set, cut off with a small piece of the jaw, have I sold for twenty-five and fifty cents, within the above time, to one whose reputation has always stood at the head of his profession (Dr. Eleazer Parmly), then residing at No. 11 Park Place, mineral teeth being then unknown.

Beeves' casins. When the animal is slaughtered the small gut is stripped for the sausage-maker. They clean and prepare them, when they are then known as beeves' casins. Those from lambs and hogs are also used. Another part is called bung-gut, the largest portion and an end of the larger intestines, which is generally used, when cleaned, for head-cheese.

Cattle's feet. These are usually sold by the butchers for one year (from "new-year" to "new-year" again). The present price (1858) is about six dollars per hundred feet. Their principal use is in making glue, and the bones and hoofs are afterwards used in making buttons and Prussian blue. Mr. Peter Cooper is the heaviest purchaser for the last forty years, and has them gathered daily from the slaughter-houses in our city.

Bones. Those which are daily collected by being taken from the various parts of the different animals when cut up, and from "cracking" or taking off shanks. Blade, socket, chine, and other bones, are collected together and sold, usually by the boys (as a perquisite), to the bone-gatherers at about forty cents per bushel. Some of them are used by the turners for handles, buttons—some for bone-black, etc., after they have been well boiled, that the marrow and fat may all be extracted.

From Calves.

Sweet breads. These, no doubt, are the greatest delicacy of the meat kind. There are but two in a calf, one from the neck or throat, called "throat sweet-bread;" the other from or near the heart, which is known as the "heart sweet-bread." The largest are the best, and the latter, or heart sweet-bread, the most delicate. Their color should be clear, and a shade darker than the fat of the same animal.

Calves' heads. These are usually found with hair scalded and shaved cleanly off, and, when fresh, the eyes have a bright, full look, while the skin seems firmly fastened to the head. There should also be a prominent rise or appearance of the young horn, to denote that the animal was old enough. If the head should be small and no signs of horns, it shows that the animal was too young to be wholesome food. Never purchase either calves' head or feet if they have a yellowish look, or a slippery or slimy feeling. The nose (yours) will detect a bad smell in the brains, more particularly when the head is cracked or split open. The head makes the mock-turtle soup, or a plain boil, etc. The head is sometimes found skinned, when it is not so valuable, or only fit for a plain soup or boil, etc.

Calves' feet.—Although these and the preceding are usually sold together, yet their uses are generally different. Very small feet are not generally good, in consequence of the risk that they are from too young a calf. Their uses are principally for the excellent jelly, or they are cooked in with the head.

Calves' tongues are sometimes taken out and used separately for stewing, or salted, boiled, pickled, etc.

Calves' brains.—With some preparation, very nice, delicate sauces and other dishes are made, but it requires the skill of a cook. They are taken out when the calf's head is cracked open.

Calves' eyes are also used separately by many foreigners, in sauces, etc.

Calves' haslet.—This comprises the heart, liver, and lights (sometimes also the melt), connected together; but when separated they appear with the names of calves' liver, calves' heart, and calves' lights. This liver is the best of all the animal livers, and I do not except the famous *paté de fois* or goose liver. Both the heart and liver are used for frying, boiling, roasting, etc., but when for a hash, the lights can be used.

Calves' kidneys.—These are usually found in the loins of veal, but are sometimes taken out and sold separately. They are the best of all kidneys.

Calves' entrails and **fat** or **chitterlings.**—This part of the calf, prepared by the Germans and French, is made into an excellent dish, which I have eaten with a good relish. They are taken from the calf while warm, then the entire gut is slit or cut open, well cleaned and soaked, and they are ready for use.

Calves' melt.—This small, dark piece, attached to the lights, is seldom used in this country, but it is said to make a very good dish when prepared by the English cook. I give one receipt for cooking it: After soaking three or four hours in a little salt and water, and also a little vinegar, wipe dry, pepper it well, and boil it.

FROM SHEEP AND LAMBS.

Lambs' frys and **sweet-breads** are generally found in our markets in the spring and summer months, on dishes, nicely cleaned, and prepared ready for use. Some sprinkle a little parsley to decorate them. They are considered, and certainly are, delicious eating, known as mountain oysters.

Lambs' and **sheep's tongues.**—These can be had, fresh or salted, from the boys, being one of their perquisites. They generally want some trimming before they are read for use. These small pickled tongues are an excellent lunc when nicely prepared. The best are from the lambs.

Lambs' and **sheep's haslet,** or **pluck.**—These consist of the heart, liver, and lights of the lamb or sheep. Sold at low prices. The lamb's haslet is better flavored, more tender, and not so dry eating as the sheep's. In some parts of England the name *pluck* designates only the lights, or lungs, and thirty years ago it was a common name for all haslets in New York.

Lambs' and **sheep's kidneys.**—A great many kidneys are taken out of the loin suet, and are sold and used separately. The French are particularly fond of them. Used for stews, broils, etc. Those from lambs are the best.

Lambs' and **sheep's heads.**—Many foreigners use them, after having the brains and tongue taken out, the wool or hair singed or shaved off, which leaves a considerable quantity of flesh on the head. They make an excellent broth, for a very small sum and little trouble. The "Tup's Head Dinner," about Michaelmas, was once held in high repute.

Lambs' and **sheep's brains** and **eyes.**—The brains are the most called for, and are used in sauces and other delicate dishes. The eyes are sometimes used with them: occasionally they are used for study by the student.

Sheep's suet.—A great deal of this suet is used in making salves for chapped hands, etc.

Lambs' or sheep's trotters.—Prepared like calves' feet, then soaked in water until quite white, when they are ready for use. They are best stewed.

Lambs' or sheep's melt.—Prepared in the same manner as the calves' melt, but not quite so good eating.

Lambs' guts or casins are cleaned and prepared by the sausage-makers to fill for sausages. Those that you find of the small size are the caseins from the lambs. The sheep caseins cannot be used here for that purpose; but I am informed by Professor Thurber that they are used in South America: after having been cleaned they are rolled up into a ball and roasted in the earth, and he found them good eating.

Sheep's paunch, or stomach.—An excellent dish is made of this article by the Scotch, called "Scotch haggis." The following was furnished to me by Mrs. John Duncan:

"Procure the large stomach-bag (paunch) of a sheep, also one of the smaller bags, called the king's hood, together with the pluck, which is the lights, the liver, and the heart.

"The bags must be well washed, first in cold water, then plunged in boiling water, and scraped. Great care must be taken of the large bag; let it lie and soak in cold water, with a little salt, all night. Wash also the pluck. You will now boil the small bag along with the pluck; in boiling leave the windpipe attached, and let the end of it hang over the edge of the pot, so that impurities may pass freely out. Boil for an hour and a half, and take the whole from the pot. When cold, cut away the windpipe, and any bits of skin or gristle that seem improper. Grate the quarter of the liver (not using the remainder of the haggis), and mince the heart, lights, and small bag very small, along with half a pound of beef suet. Mix all this mince with two small teacupfuls of oatmeal—previously dried before the fire—black and Jamaica pepper and salt; also add half a pint of the liquor in which the pluck was boiled, or beef gravy. Stir all together into a consistency. Then take the large bag, which has been thoroughly cleaned, and put the mince into it. Fill it only a little more than half full, in order to leave room for the meal and meat to expand. If crammed too full it will burst in boiling. Sew up the bag with a needle and thread. The haggis is now complete. Put it in a pot with boiling water, and prick it occasionally with a large needle, as it swells, to allow the air to escape. If the bag appears thin, tie a cloth outside the skin. There should be a plate placed beneath it to prevent its sticking to the bottom of the pot. Boil it for three hours. It is served on a dish without garnish, and requires no gravy, as it is sufficiently rich in itself."

Another way. Procure a good thick sheep's paunch, without holes or thin parts, and have it well cleaned. Clean a sheep's pluck, or haslet, thoroughly, make incisions in the heart and liver to allow the blood to flow out, and parboil the whole, letting the windpipe lie over the side of the pot to permit the phlegm and blood to disgorge from the lungs: the water may be changed after a few minutes' boiling for fresh water. A half hour's boiling will be sufficient; but throw back the half of the liver, to boil until it will grate easily; take the heart, the half of the liver, and part of the lights, trimming away all skins and black-looking parts, and mince them together. Mince also a pound of good beef suet, and four or more onions. Grate the other half of the liver. Half a dozen of small onions, peeled and scalded in two waters, to mix with this mince. Have ready some finely-ground oatmeal, toasted slowly before the fire for four hours, till it is of a light brown color and perfectly dry. Less than two teacupfuls of meal will do for this quantity of meat. Spread the mince on a board and strew the meal lightly over it, with a high seasoning of pepper, salt, and a little cayenne, first well mixed. Put in tho meat with a half-pint of good beef gravy, or as much strong broth as will make it a very thick stew. Be careful not to fill the bag too full, but allow the meat room to swell; add the juice of a lemon, or a little good vinegar; press out the air and sew up the bag; prick it with a large needle when it first swells in the pot, to prevent bursting; let it boil slowly for three hours, if large.

FROM SHOATS AND HOGS.

Pig's head and **tongue** are applied to many uses. Some are sold either fresh for roasting, head-cheese, etc., or corned, for a plain boil; others have their chops or cheeks taken off, salted and smoked, with or without the tongue and the balance.

Pig's pate, or **skull**, is either made into head-cheese, fresh, or plain boiled when corned and salted, after having been properly cracked and cleansed.

Pig's tongue.—This is excellent eating when prepared as the sheep's tongue. There are a few persons who use them fresh.

Pig's hocks.—The top part of the fore-leg, from the knee up to the shoulder, is usually called the hock. In very small animals the foot is left with it, and sold together as pig's feet. The hocks are generally corned or salted for boiling, etc.

Pig's ears are sometimes used for a boil or souse, or put in head-cheese.

Pig's feet.—A great many are sold in the fresh state, for stewing, boiling, or sousing, but are usually preferred corned for the latter purpose or a plain boil. They should be well cleaned of hair, and the hoofs taken off.

Pig's kidneys.—Very good dishes are made from these kidneys, especially from the shoats, either stewed, fricasseed, fried, or broiled.

Pig's haslets.—These are seldom found in our markets. They are generally sold at the slaughter-houses, or made into meat-puddings, etc. This is one of the poorest domestic animal's haslets or livers.

Leaf-fat, or **leaf-lard**.—The fat taken from the inside, which adheres to the ribs and belly, is called leaf-fat. In this untried state it is used for many purposes in cookery.

MEATS USED AS CORNED, SALTED, SMOKED, AND OTHERWISE PREPARED, ETC.

There are so many different ways of corning, salting, or curing, and other preparations of meat, that a person might question all those they may meet engaged in it—"How do you cure or prepare (certain) meats? Their answers would seldom be two alike; and each would recommend his receipt as the best. Many have also a little variation in the manner of cutting up the various animals in their different joints, and also in the preparation of their flesh.

Some of the Western packers use nearly the whole animal to "barrel." Some, again, put certain of the choice pieces together, and the other qualities divided, making sometimes three or four grades, with names to correspond. But our public-market butchers, and those who deal in prepared meats, select certain pieces from the various animals for their different and numerous uses, some of which I have noticed elsewhere.

Time for salting meat.—Meat should be salted in cool weather, as soon as it shall stiffen or become rigid. If in warm or hot weather, the animal should be killed in the afternoon, and the next morning salted, and placed in an ice-house. If in freezing weather, it should be salted before freezing, as I have known frozen beef to lay in strong pickle two weeks, and then salted only on the surface—the inside being still frozen and fresh.

Corned and salted beef.—The pieces generally used for this purpose are the plate, navel, brisket, top of sirloin, etc., which have the fat mixed through them. Many, however, prefer the rumps, sockets (or face-rump), edge-bones, and rounds, on account of their leanness and the delicacy of the outside fat. The kernels, or pope's-eye, in the rounds (centre-fat), flanks, necks, and shoulder-clods, if to be corned or salted, or even kept for any length of time, should be extracted, as it is the first part or thing to spoil.

Jerked beef.—This name was early given to the following process of curing beef: first, all the bones are taken out; then the flesh is cut into sheets, or thin pieces, put into a strong pickle, or rubbed with dry salt, and packed away for two or three days, when it is thoroughly salted; then spread out in the sun to dry hard, gathered together, and dry packed in boxes of two and three hundred pounds each, and generally sent to some of the West India islands.

About the year 1825, there were large quantities put up in this city, made from all the low-priced fleshy animals, such as bulls, stags, and any coarse, thin cattle that had the least flesh on their bones, with sometimes the coarse parts of other beef-cattle. I recollect one instance, about this time, of having to assist in slaughtering one hundred bulls, that were bought and sent in one drove to my employer for this purpose. It was the principal source of disposing of the poor, often *diseased*, and the unmarketable fleshy cattle, the flesh of which could not be sold in our public markets, in consequence of the stringency of the market laws. The making of jerked beef, in large quantities, continued until about fifteen years ago (1840), when I believe it failed to be profitable.

Corned mutton.—The legs, chine, and shoulders, are sometimes corned, and are excellent eating when boiled.

Corned and salted pork.—For family use, the carcass is cut up for salting, or parts are reserved fresh for sausages, steaks, etc. For market purposes, the loin and chine, or shoulder and ribs, of shoats are usually kept fresh, and the legs, brisket, and flanks for the above purpose; if the animal is quite small, the loins and chine are also used. If the hogs are large and fat, the back-fat is taken off clear and salted; when cured it is used for various purposes. When the rib-bones are taken out of the thick side-pork, it is generally called "clear pork;" this is also corned or salted. The brisket of pork is usually the part which takes in the leg-half of the shoulder. The brisket and flank together are an excellent piece when corned.

Cured and smoked meats.—In beef, three pieces are taken from the buttock (for particulars see *buttock*)—the inside, outside, and veiny pieces. These are generally used for smoking after having been salted from three to four weeks. The plates, navels, briskets, and tongues (see *tongues*), are also excellent, when prepared in the above manner, to boil with greens.

In mutton, the legs are sometimes cured and smoked, but seldom thus prepared in our cities, as the demand for these parts is greater than for any others.

In pork: the hams, bacon, shoulders, chops or cheeks; and the prepared meats—bologna and smoked sausages, etc. The best hams, whether corned or cured and smoked, are from eight to fourteen pounds weight, having a thin skin, fat solid (white, if corned), and a small, short, tapering leg or shank. Try with a skewer (if buying of a stranger), running from the flesh-side towards the shank; the skewer, when drawn, should smell sweet and agreeable.

Bacon.—The part of the shoat or hog commonly used here for bacon is the thin part of the ribs and belly, salted, and either dried or slightly smoked; some also use spices, sugar, etc. If it be not too thick and fat, it is generally preferred. The regular bacon of England, however, is differently prepared; and there it is usually called "flitch of bacon," when cured in the following manner. The hog having been slaughtered, instead of scalding the hair off, it is burned off with straw, then shaven clean with cold water, and dressed. When cooled through, it is divided, the hams and head taken off, and the bloody veins carefully removed. The spare-ribs and other bones are then taken out, and the whole covered with fine salt and a small quantity of saltpetre, with also a little brown sugar, which gives a pleasant flavor to the bacon. The flitches are laid down upon one another and re-salted daily, when the top one is put under, for about three weeks. They are then hung up to dry, or very slightly and slowly smoked. The Irish singed bacon is cured here, by some of our large packers, in pretty much the same manner.

A curious custom originated at a very early period, of presenting a flitch of bacon to all married couples upon certain conditions, which are fully explained in the following. The New York *Gazette and Post Boy*, September 30, 1751, shows that, "On the 20th of last month (June), John Shakeshanks, wool-comber, and Anne his wife, of the parish of Weathersfield, in Essex, appeared at the customary court of the manor of Dunmow-park, in that county, and claimed the bacon, according to the custom of that manor, which was delivered to them with the usual formalities—this is the only claim that has been made since the year 1701."

"The famous old story is as follows, viz.: one Robert Fitzwalter, a powerful baron in this country, in the reign of Henry III., instituted a custom in the priory there, that, 'Whatever married man did not repent of being married, or differ and dispute with his wife, within a year and a day after his marriage, if he and his wife would swear to the truth of it, kneeling upon two stones in the priory churchyard, set up for that purpose, in presence of the prior and convent, should have a gammon of bacon.' This custom is still kept up, notwithstanding the dissolution of the monasteries, only instead of the prior and convent, the business is now transacted at a court-baron, held before the steward of the lord of the manor. It may be some amusement to our readers to see the words of the oath on this occasion, which are to the following purpose, viz.:

"You do swear by custom of confession,
That you ne'er made nuptial transgression;
Nor since you were married man and wife,
By household brawls, or contentious strife,
Or otherwise, in bed or at board,
Offended each other in deed or in word;
Or in a twelvemonth's time and a day,
Repented not in thought any way;
Or since the church-clerk said Amen,

Wished yourselves unmarried again,
But continue true, and in desire,
As when you joined hands in holy choir."

The sentence pronounced for their receiving the bacon is in words to the effect following, viz.:

"Since to the conditions, without any fear,
Of your own accord you do freely swear,
A whole gammon of bacon you do receive,
And bear it away with love and good leave,
For this is the custom of Dunmow well-known;
Tho' the pleasure be ours, the bacon's your own."

Then, twenty-six years afterwards, the New York *Journal*, of 1767, notices the flitch of bacon claimed again. Among the London news, dated June 9th, was—"A certain Irish nobleman and his lady went last Thursday to Dunmow, in Essex, in order to claim the flitch of bacon, which, according to the custom of the manor, is given to those who swear that they repented not of their marriage within a year and a day after the celebration thereof. This is the first time that persons of their rank have laid claim to it." The same paper, a few years after—"We have an account from Dunmow, in Essex, that there were computed to be five thousand people there from all parts to see the ceremony of delivering the bacon to the couple who had not repented of their marriage. The man was examined by a jury of men, and the woman by a jury of women: she declared that she never repented but once, and that was, that she had not married sooner. We have it from undoubted authority that the happy couple made upwards of fifty pounds by selling slices of it to several gentlemen and ladies present, who were whimsically merry on the occasion."

Shoulders.—The same process of curing hams will also apply to shoulders; and when purchasing either—in a cured state—should they have a white or dried salt appearance over them, you may conclude they will be very salt, and of course a great deal of the sweetness extracted by having been kept in a strong, harsh pickle a long time; or they have been cured by those who do not understand the business. To be good, they should be bright, clean, and firm.

Cheeks or Chops.—These are cured with the hams and shoulders, and are very fine when boiled with greens in the spring of the year. Select those which have the most flesh on.

Bologna Sausages.—There are many receipts for making these fine sausages, of which there appears to be two different kinds—the fresh bologna and dried bologna sausages.

Fresh bologna sausages are prepared usually for immediate use. They are sometimes made of fresh lean beef and pork, having all the fat and sinews extracted and finely chopped; after which, thin strips of cured back fat are interspersed through, and nicely seasoned. This is forced into cleansed beef casins of different lengths. Smoked (say one night), and boiled, or rather simmered, from one to two hours. When pork is high it is sometimes left out, but retaining the back fat to relieve the lean look, and also to add to their flavor. The other kind,

Dried bologna sausages, are made for long keeping. They are prepared with salt pork or ham, with the lean fresh beef, and more highly seasoned; instead of being smoked, they are hung up and dried. But otherwise prepared as the fresh bolognas.

Rolliches (from the Dutch word *rolletje*).—This peculiar meat preparation was once a famous dish among the ancient Dutch settlers of New Amsterdam, and although the making of it has almost been discontinued in our (New York) State, yet there are many old families in New Jersey and other places, who continue on from year to year, in preparing this as one of their principal dishes, to be used throughout the winter months, especially where fresh meat is only occasionally to be procured. It is found to be a wholesome article of food when properly prepared, and for the following receipt I am indebted to Mrs. Ann Hill, who has prepared and assisted in its preparation for about twenty years. She says: "Take the fresh, uncooked, but well-cleaned tripe, cut it into eight or ten as near square pieces as possible; then cut up the flanks and tops of sirloin pieces of beef, in strips, about as large as a good-sized finger, and lay them so as fat and lean will mix throughout, and enough to fill each piece of the tripe; pepper and salt should be well sprinkled between each layer of meat (some also add herbs to give peculiar flavors); then sew them up tightly and put them into a large pot, and boil slowly, until a broom-wisk or rye-straw can be pushed into them without breaking; they are then taken out, put under a weight, and left so all night; next morning the fat is skimmed off from the liquor, when the rolliches are put into a tight tub or pot, and a mixture of half vinegar and half pot-liquor is poured over, and enough to cover them; then a weight placed on top to keep them under. When wanted, one or more is taken out, cut up into thin slices, and warmed up in the liquor in a frying-pan, when they are found to be excellent eating."

They are occasionally found in our markets, having been brought in by the Jersey Dutchmen, who sold them in ordinary times for about twenty-five cents per pound.

Lard.—Among the many preparations made, no doubt lard is one of the most important in the culinary art. The fat cut from the various parts of the hog—consisting of the leaf fat and the meat fat—is cut into very small pieces, then boiled until quite rendered, that the pieces begin to look quite brown, when it is taken out, and the pieces or scraps heavily pressed. The melted fat, after having passed through a strainer into pots, etc., becomes lard when cool. The best should be white, without a disagreeable smell.

Sausages.—The best sausages are prepared altogether from pork, chopped small, seasoned, and run or stuffed into casins. Those made in the city are usually quite small in size, as the meat is run into the lamb casins.

Country sausages.—Those sausages usually made in

the neighboring country towns are prepared in the same way, but run into beeves' or hogs' casins. Some of the latter are cleanly and well made, and some again are almost as dangerous as some of our city sausages. One plan of deceit is to add a large percentage of water in mixing the meat; some will add one-eighth or more before it is pressed into the casins, which gives them a very moist, soft, and flabby appearance, while good sausages are firm, and also quite dry on the outside. There is danger, also, in the kind and quality of the flesh which some use, it being almost impossible to tell, from outward appearance, of what animal or in what condition the flesh was, when hid in those skins; and the only protection for the buyer is to purchase of those dealers who are certainly known to you, or else to buy the meat and prepare it yourself.

Sausage meat.—This meat is prepared as that for sausages, but not put into casins, and, of course, more open for inspection. Both this and sausages are excellent eating when you feel satisfied that they have been cleanly and properly made; if not, you had better have nothing to do with them. In fact, the same will apply to all of the prepared meats.

Head-cheese.—This article is made usually of pork, or rather from the meat off of the pig's head, skins, and coarse trimmings. After having been well boiled, the meat is cut up in pieces, seasoned well with sage, salt, and pepper, and pressed a little, so as to drive out the extra fat and water. Some add the meat from off a cow or ox head, to make it lean, or not so luscious.

Spiced puddings.—These puddings are made somewhat like head-cheese, and generally prepared by the German dealers, some of whom make large quantities. They are also made of the meat from the pig's chops or cheeks, etc., well spiced and boiled. Some smoke them.

Blood puddings are usually made from the hog's blood with chopped pork, and seasoned, then put in casins and cooked. Some make them with beef's blood, adding a little milk ; but the former is the best, as it is thought to be the richest.

Common puddings.—These puddings are made of the pork skins, beeves' head meat, pigs' liver, etc., seasoned and stuffed into beef's casins, and cooked. Sold at low prices. These puddings, like the preceding, were more generally used many (forty) years ago by the poorer classes, and especially the hungry laborer, who would take a pair of these puddings (which then weighed one pound) at the cost of three or four cents, and the same amount spent in butter-crackers (nearly or quite as much weight), which would give him a cheap, wholesome, and hearty meal. But of late years the character and reputation of many of these prepared meats have been, except in some instances, any thing but "first rate."

Brawn.—I have no knowledge of brawn being used in this country, although prepared from pork, or, properly, from the wild-boar. The old-country method of making it appears in Willich's Dom. Ency., and is as follows :

"The bones being taken out of the flitches (sides) or other parts, the flesh is sprinkled with salt and laid on a tray, that the blood may drain off, after which it is salted a little and rolled up as hard as possible. The length of the collar of brawn should be as much as one side of the boar will bear ; so that when rolled up it may be nine or ten inches in diameter. After being thus rolled up, it is boiled in a copper or large kettle, till it is so tender that you may run a stiff straw through it ; when it is set by till it is thoroughly cold, and then put into a pickle composed of water, salt, and wheat-bran, in the proportion of two handfuls of each of the latter to every gallon of water, which, after being well boiled together, is strained off as clear as possible from the bran, and, when quite cold, the brawn is put into it."

Pemmican.—One of the most useful applications of buffalo meat consists in the preparation of pemmican, an article of food of the greatest importance, from its portability and nutritious qualities. This is prepared by cutting the lean meat into thin slices, exposing it to the heat of the sun or fire, and, when dry, pounding it to a powder. It is then mixed with an equal weight of buffalo suet, and stuffed into bladders. Sometimes venison is used instead of buffalo beef. Sir John Richardson, while preparing for his Arctic Expedition, found it necessary to carry with him pemmican from England. This he prepared by taking a round or buttock of beef cut into thin steaks, from which the fat and membranous parts were pared away, and dried in a kiln until the fibres of the meat became friable. It was then ground in a malt-mill, and mixed with nearly an equal weight of beef suet or lard. This completed the preparation of the plain pemmican; but to a portion raisins were added, and another portion was sweetened with sugar. These latter changes were subsequently highly approved of by the voyagers. The pemmican was then placed in tin canisters and well rammed down, and after the cooling and contraction of the mass, these were filled up with melted lard through a small hole left in the end, which was then covered with a piece of tin and soldered up."

Meat biscuit.—A valuable preparation for long voyages, etc., prepared by Mr. G. Borden, jr., was introduced here a few years ago. He says: "The meat biscuit contains, in a concentrated and portable form, all the nutriment of meat combined with flour . . . . by drying or baking the mixture in an oven, in the form of a biscuit or cracker."

Rennet.—To prepare this article for use, take the stomach of an unweaned calf, lamb, kid, or pig (the calf's preferred), empty it of its contents (some preserve the contents, curds, for use, but they are generally somewhat offensive), wash it slightly with cold water, let it lie ten days in salt, spread it out, and dry it quite hard. To prepare it for use take one quart of soft water, and add salt enough to make a strong pickle; boil, and let it stand until cold; break your dry rennet in small pieces, put it in a jar with this pickle; in three days it will be fit for use. Strain, bottle, and cork it, and set it in a cool place.

A quick mode of curing meats.—The meat to be cured is placed in a strong iron vessel connected by a pipe and stop-cock with the brine-tub, also with an exhausting-pump. The cover having been screwed down on the iron vessel, the air is extracted and a vacuum established; whereupon the stop-cock being turned, the brine rushes in and takes the place of the air, filling the pores and penetrating the meat.

If some of the parts should not be impregnated with the pickle, more is pumped in by a small condensing engine (connected with the iron vessel), until a pressure of from one hundred and fifty to two hundred pounds on the square inch be attained. It is then allowed to remain ten or fifteen minutes under pressure, when the meat will be found to be fully salted or well cured.

Preserving meat in a fresh state.—A Doctor Londe, of France, a few years ago, presented a plan for keeping meats in a fresh state for a long period. The process, is to "bone the meat, as far as practicable, plunge it into a kettle of gelatine, at about the temperature of boiling water, where it is held about six minutes, and then hung up to dry. Forty-eight hours later, it is again plunged, with its gelatinous envelope, into a solution of water, and then hung up to dry."

Several specimens of this kind of preserved meats (which I suppose were the best) were shown by Mr. Marle, as samples, at the fair of the American Institute, held at the Crystal Palace, 1856. One piece of beef, representing five ribs, which appeared to be from a small, thin animal, and would not weigh over seven or eight pounds (not so much as two of our ordinary ribs), appeared to be dry and hard, looking like a piece of varnished wood, with a smell any thing but agreeable. A leg of mutton, also, that appeared to have been hung up in the sun and dried (as the Indians cure meat, without salt), and then several coats of varnish dried on it.

Curing hams and shoulders.—Rub the meat well with fine salt, when perfectly cool; lay it in a sweet cask for two days. Then, to every hundred pounds of meat, take eight pounds of ground rock-salt, two ounces of saltpetre, two pounds of sugar, one and a half ounces of potash, and four gallons of water. Mix these well together until quite dissolved; skim it and pour it over the meat, when it should be kept under this brine about six weeks (some boil this pickle, and, when cool, pour it over the meat); after which, take out the meat, soak it in cool water for about four to five hours, string the several pieces and hang them up to dry for two days, when they are ready for the smoke-house.

In the *Chelmsford Chronicle* (1836), "an ancient ham" is thus spoken of: "Mrs. Hyam, who died on the 19th ult., aged eighty years, received, on the day of her marriage, a present of a ham, with a request that it should not be cut until the birth of her first child. The lady never attained to maternal dignity, and the ham was kept until the funeral —sixty-four years—when it was dressed, and, to the surprise of all present, was perfectly good and tender."

Tainted meat or **game** may be restored as follows: wrap it up in a fine linen cloth, closely, so as to prevent dust or cinders getting in; have ready a pail, or larger vessel of cold water; take a shovelful, or larger quantity of live wood-coals, and throw in; then put the meat or game in, and let it lie under the water for five or ten minutes (according to the size). After taking it out, all the offensive smell will be removed; but it must be immediately cooked.

Fly-blown meats.—The fly which usually blows the meat is known as the green or meat fly. They are always, in the warm weather, found wherever there is fish or flesh, slaughter-houses, markets, larders, pantries, etc., which they frequent for the purpose of "blowing," or leaving their eggs in some moist crevice in the meat. These eggs will hatch in a few hours, so that live maggots are seen to creep.

Many housekeepers imagine that meats in this state are spoiled, and unfit to be used; but such is not the fact, as a little vinegar or salt and water will wash all signs away. Some also think the fly will not blow the newly-killed meats. I have known them to blow in fifteen minutes after the animal has been dressed, and in four hours afterwards found them creeping.

Frozen meat and poultry.—Meat and poultry, of all kinds, should never be frozen, if it is possible to avoid it; it changes the flavor of the flesh, as well as the juices, as it does vegetables and fruit. Nor will meats ripen, or, rather, grow tender, in that state. But, if frozen, it should not be thawed until ready for use, and then not in a warm room gradually, as that will make it flabby and very soon become putrid or spoiled, and, when cooked, be deficient in its flavor. The proper way is to place it in a vessel, cover it with cold water, and there keep until the ice is thawed out, which will be found to form around it.

To make beef tender.—If the weather is cool enough to keep the beef over-night, it should be cut into slices (about two inches thick); then rub over each piece a small quantity of carbonate of soda, and lay it down on dishes until just before cooking, when it should be washed off, and cut into pieces or steaks of suitable thickness, and cooked as wanted. This process will answer for any kind of flesh or fowl. In some of the Southern States, where little else than poor, tough beef is seen, this "tendering" method is adopted, but at the expense of the natural sweetness of the beef.

WILD ANIMALS, CALLED GAME.

THE wild animals found in our States and Territories, hunted by the white and red man, for food or for pleasure, are accepted under the general title of "game." Professional sportsmen, and even zoölogists, particularize the character of these animals. Some animals there are—the squirrel, raccoon, opossum, etc.—which, although not strictly game, yet are sought after with a zeal by the hunter, as if they boasted of the high character; while others—the fox, the otter, etc.—are mostly hunted for the excitement arising from this manly pursuit.

All animals, whether tame or wild, whose flesh is not strong and tough, more especially when killed in season, are, no doubt, fit for human food; and those which feed principally upon vegetation are to be preferred. There are, however, but few of those which subsist wholly upon flesh or fish that are much sought after for the table. Those with which I am most familiar, both at table and from information, as to their edible qualities, have been introduced in the following pages.

The various wild animals which formerly inhabited this and the adjoining States, in large numbers, have gradually diminished and disappeared at the rapid improvement of agriculture. Before steamboats and railroads came into existence, some species of game were scarce, or only found in our markets during the winter season. They were brought great distances; and when any thing unusual appeared, it was generally noticed in the press, as from the following will appear, in the *Commercial Advertiser*, February 1, 1823:

"Wild Meats.—Our markets are not only well supplied with every variety of domestic meat and fowls, but there is a great variety of wild meats and wild game. Mr. Sykes (who kept the New York Coffee-house) has a fine bear* (weighing two hundred pounds), which he is soon to serve up to his friends; and we yesterday saw, at Fulton-market, two wagons, from Sullivan County, N. Y., the one filled with white hares and partridges, and the other with venison. On the top of the bucks, which were stowed closely, stood a fierce-looking panther, almost eight feet long, as if to guard

* The bear was purchased by Sykes from the owners of these wagons when they arrived.

the buck-tailed tribe. The panther was killed in Sullivan County, about two weeks since."

Six years after, in the same paper (January 30, 1829), we also find—"Good venison has been a scarce article in this market during the last few weeks; and that of an ordinary quality was sold this morning at eighteen cents per pound. A little after nine o'clock, however, a wagon drove up to the Bank Coffee-house, with a noble load of deer, topped off by a panther of some eight or nine feet in length. They were taken in the town of Liberty, in Sullivan County, upon the Delaware."

Since that period, the employment of steam facilities have been greatly increased, both on land and water, by which the most distant uncultivated States and Territories have been reached, which tended not only to increase the variety of game, but also to enable the importation of large numbers into our numerous towns and cities. No doubt, in the course of future seasons, we shall have our markets supplied with many of the most choice and rare species of game found inhabiting the distant climates and regions, and placed before our citizens as articles of food. At the same time, the advance of agriculture will be the extermination of these animals from the face of our continent.

In New York State, a game-law was passed, on the 6th of April, 1860, in which it is found that moose and deer are protected from being killed during certain months, of which the following is an extract: "No person or persons shall kill, or pursue with intent to kill, any moose, wild deer, or fawn, during the months of January, February, March, April, May, June, and July; or shall expose to sale, or have in his or her possession, any green moose, deer, or fawn skin, or fresh venison, at any time during the months of February, after the 15th day thereof, March, April, May, June, and July, under a fine of twenty-five dollars for each deer so killed, and for each green moose, deer, or fawn skin, or fresh venison, so exposed for sale or had in his possession."

Bison, commonly called **buffalo.**—The flesh of this large animal is very seldom found in the markets of the eastern cities; but it does occasionally appear, however, in the winter season, and sometimes in excellent condition. I have several times heard of its being in New York, Chicago, etc., and this year (1865), in the month of January, I was enabled to purchase one hind-quarter (with the skin on) and part of another, which was brought here by Mr. J. R. Cook, of Council Grove, Kansas, who had some two or three thousand pounds of nothing but hind-quarters of cow and heifer bison meat. I cut, sold, and presented a large portion of my purchase, so that it might be thoroughly tested as to its qualifications for the table; and I also tried different parts of it roasted, broiled, etc. The general answer returned to me was—it was excellent eating, being very tender, juicy, and fine-flavored, with a slight "gamey" taste: while some described it as being like the breast of the quail, others something like long-killed, sweet, juicy venison. Perhaps, however, this meat was eaten under the most favorable circumstances: in the first place, the animal was fat, having been killed then about two months, and at the same time it was kept in good condition, and thus it was made as perfect for choice eating as it could well be.

In comparing the flesh or meat with that of beef, it appears somewhat darker, both flesh and fat, the latter much redder—in fact, the whole appearance was like that of an overheated animal, when killed in that state, and I found it much more juicy than I expected.

As to the meat when fresh-killed, we must take the evidence of the travellers and hunters, who generally consider it very savory food; and no doubt it is, especially when the animal is a heifer or young cow; or if, like our domestic cattle, a young, fat bull is selected, in some months of the year the meat may be enjoyed by many, and more especially by the hungry traveller. Mr. John G. Bell, the well-known taxidermist, of our city, who travelled with "Audubon," informs me that he had killed many buffaloes, and that the meat which had been cut off from the cow buffalo, when fat, he always found excellent eating. He compared the flesh of one with that of beef from a domestic cow, and thought the choice was in favor of the bison beef. He also says they always selected these (cow and heifer) for their best eating. In certain seasons, when very dry, and especially in the spring of the year, the buffaloes are all found poor and thin, and unfit to be eaten.

When the Indians hunt them for food, they look among the herd for the extraordinary large animals, feeling sure that they have been castrated when calves, which are often taken in their hunting expeditions, the operation performed, and then let go.

"Audubon," in a letter to Dr. Gideon B. Smith, of Baltimore, in the spring of 1843, says: "Our folks have shot buffaloes, but I have not done so, simply because they were worthless, through poverty, and when killed only display a mass of bones and skin, with a very thin portion of flesh; and if you shoot a bull, the rankness of its better parts is quite enough to revolt the stomachs of all but starving men."

A common true saying is, that "Hunger is an excellent sauce:" I would add that Starvation is a most terrible one! Imagine the dreadful condition of the living, emaciated, starving frames of Truxton, Maury, and others of the Darien Exploring Expedition, when one of the party (Truxton) saw a toad, which he instantly snatched up, bit off the head, spat it away, and then devoured the quivering body! Another (Maury) picked up the rejected head and said to the other (Truxton), "You are getting quite particular! something of an epicure, eh! to throw away the head!" He then quietly swallowed it, although he said afterwards "it was d—sh bitter." The idea that a human being could be in such a necessitous condition as to eat and enjoy the body of such a revolting, loathsome, and disgusting reptile is a most dreadful one.

The hump of a fine fat buffalo is composed, nearly or all,

of a sort of meat,—rather fat, somewhat like the udder of a spayed heifer, with the addition of the peculiar wild or gamey flavor, and is said to be very fine, but rather luscious eating. The tongue will also partake of this flavor, and I should think would be very acceptable, especially if it was properly cured. Hunters say the liver is well-tasted, and the brains are often eaten without undergoing the process of cooking. The marrow-bones are also highly esteemed, especially when roasted, and are often used as a substitute for butter, as the marrow-bones of all animals are filled with a short, buttery fat.

Venison.—The flesh of all the deer species is called venison, although there is but one kind plentiful in our public markets in its season. As commonly spoken of, it means the flesh of the *common deer, or Virginia deer*. This animal is not now found plenty in our State, although many are killed, or, rather, a gradual extermination has been going on for several years past, and more especially in the event of a severe winter and deep snows, when they are slaughtered by hundreds, in an unfit state. Large numbers are also brought from the Western States as well as the Canadas. Prior to 1830, a great many were yearly killed—as well as grouse, or prairie hen—on the Hempstead plains and other parts of Long Island, which brought high prices in our markets.

Buck venison, is best when killed from the 1st of August to the 1st of November, but it is quite difficult to have it fresh in our markets at this early date. After the 1st of November the *doe venison* is preferred, and it continues good until the 1st of January, after which these animals should not be killed. Venison first begins to make its appearance in small quantities in our markets in the latter part of September, and is sometimes found as late as the 1st of March, the next spring, having been kept for months in a frozen state, for the purpose of obtaining the usual high prices which prevail at this late period. It cannot be too fat, and if it have no fat on the back it is of a very poor quality, and will always eat dry and tasteless, without the skill of the cook is considerably taxed.

> "Thanks, my lord, for your venison, for finer or fatter,
> Never ranged in a forest, or smoked on a platter;
> The haunch was a picture for painters to study,
> The fat was so white and the lean was so ruddy."—*Dr. Goldsmith.*

Very large portions of venison is found in (hind) saddles only, and principally with all the skin on, which keeps it in good condition. It is cut and sold by the saddle, haunch, leg, loin, fore-quarter, or in steaks: the latter, however, should not be cut until ready for use. It is considered highly nutritious and very wholesome food. The skins furnish the buckskin of commerce. The Boston *News Letter*, December 7, 1732, says: "A buck was lately killed in the Narraganset country, which weighed sixty-nine pounds a quarter, and is reckoned the largest deer that has been killed in these parts for some years past."

The Bethany, Wayne County, Pennsylvania, *Enquirer*, says: "The largest buck within the recollection of our oldest hunters, was shot on the 10th inst. (November, 1831), in Lebanon township. He has attracted the attention of hunters in that neighborhood for about five years past, on account of extraordinary size, and has been repeatedly shot at, but has hitherto escaped *shot-free*. He was started on the run-way, and was greeted with a fire from two of the hunters; but (to use the language of Big Hunter), Mr. William J. Shields, of Philadelphia, did the job. The deer weighed, before he was dressed, three hundred and sixty-five pounds!!! When dressed, his meat weighed two hundred and ten pounds; tallow (fat), ten pounds; hide, twenty-three pounds six ounces."

The Cornwall *Freeholder*, 1855 (Canada), relates the following hunting incident as an absolute fact. "As two hunters were hunting on the banks of the river Nacion, near Crysler's Mills, their dogs pressed close on a deer, which took to the river, where the hunters pursued it in a canoe.

On approaching the animal they were surprised to perceive it struggling desperately, being every now and then jerked under water. The hunters immediately approached, and with the aid of others at hand, dragged the deer into the canoe, when, to the astonishment of all present, a large turtle (snapper, no doubt), weighing forty pounds, was found firmly fastened to the tail of the deer, which would have undoubtedly been shortly drowned by its amphibious assailant. The turtle sustained its grip for upwards of two hours after the deer was killed. This extraordinary circumstance is attested to by several witnesses."

In the *News* from Charleston, December 21, 1815, "A gentleman, resident of John's Island, hunting there a few days since, discovered the bodies of three dead deer, who had been engaged in fighting, and their horns were so entangled that they cannot be disengaged without breaking them."—*Commercial Advertiser*, Dec. 30, 1815.

The same paper, November 6, 1821, also notices a hunt near Boston, as follows:

"*Deer Hunting.*—A party of gentlemen left Charlestown, with fox-hounds, to hunt deer in the woods of Sandwich. They arrived at Swift's, in Sandwich, and early next morning started a fine buck, which, after a smart run of twelve to fifteen miles, closely followed by the famous cry, and the huntsmen at full speed, took to the water, was pursued by boats and shot. Another buck was soon after uncovered, and after a short but smart chase, was also killed. The parties returned, bringing with them the carcasses of the venison, which are in fine order, and are in Faneuil-hall Market."

Elk or **Wapiti.**—Elk venison, both from the wild and tame animal, are occasionally found in our city: two of the former, which had been killed in Iowa, I saw near the Washington Market, in Fulton-street, in 1856 (see Moose), and several since.

Several tame specimens were exhibited at the Fair of the American Institute Cattle Show, on Hamilton Square, in

1854; and on the 16th of June, 1858, a very fine female was brought with a drove of cattle from Iowa, and sold at the Bull's Head yards. About one week after it dropped a young one, which soon after died.

We find the Cleveland *Leader* (1859), "announcing the arrival in that city of Mr. George Raymond, all the way from Salt Lake City, via Cherry Creek Mines and Kansas, having come the entire distance driving a span of elk before a wagon. The elk in question are only three years old, an age at which horses are not at all fit for use, yet Mr. Raymond assures us that he actually travelled as far as one hundred miles in a single day. He was on his way to Vermont with his novel team. The elk have now upon them horns three feet in length, which have been only six weeks in growing."

The venison from a well-fed animal, in certain seasons, is very good eating, but not so good as from the common deer. But a buck elk, killed out of season, is very poor and strong eating. The horns, in their soft state, are prepared and eaten, and by some considered a delicacy.

The New York *Gazette*, June 6, 1763, says: Last Tuesday two uncommon animals were seen in Milford, which being pursued betook themselves to the water, and were followed by a number of people in a small vessel, and were taken. The he one was strangled in the water by a rope being made too fast about his neck. The she one is now alive, is big with young, and is about fourteen and a half hands high. They are much the same color as a deer, and are extremely nimble; they have a neck about the length of a common horse's, and short mane, and have little short knobs of horns. The he one was about sixteen and a half hands high; and those that ate of his flesh say it tasted a good deal like venison.

"They were thought to have been elks when they were first taken, but they don't at all answer the description we have had of those animals, which are said to be about the size of a mule, and to have a large horn."

Caribou, or American Reindeer.—This animal appears to be yet found in Maine, and along the borders of the St. Lawrence. Although the flesh of this animal has been brought to our city, I have not yet been able to eat of it. However, it is said, when the animal is in good condition, its flesh is excellent food, being very tender, and the flavor superior to any other venison; but when poor and lean it is quite insipid eating, which "fills the stomach but never satisfies the appetite."

Since writing the above I have eaten of the venison from two different animals, and found both equal to the above description. The sinews and ligaments, however, were very tough and wiry, showing great strength and power of endurance possessed by the animal. It certainly was the best-flavored venison I ever ate.

Black-tailed Deer, or Mule-deer.—Perhaps this animal, or rather its flesh, should not be noticed by me, it being so scarce and far away; but considerable difference of opinion appears among the naturalists about its quality. I have thought proper to introduce what little knowledge I have obtained in my inquiries in relation to it. From one source it is said to be "insipid and inferior to that of the common deer." Another says, "that it is far superior to any of the deer species." Audubon, however, who has killed many of them, describes it as being tender and good flavored; and Mr. Bell (his companion) says "that he had often killed them and eaten their flesh, under ordinary circumstances, and found it quite as good as that of the common deer."

Moose.—The flesh of this scarce animal may be properly termed moose venison; the appearance of all I have ever seen was not so inviting as the common venison, it being a coarse, dry, dark, and tough-looking meat, although the Indians and some hunters say it is excellent food, and they can stand more fatigue while eating it than when using the flesh of any other. Others again say, that it is apt to produce dysentery with persons unaccustomed to use it.

There is no doubt but the flesh of the tame male, either moose or elk, when castrated, could be converted into a dish which the epicure could not resist. The tongue is considered a delicacy, as is also his *moufle* (the large gristly extremity of its large nose), when properly prepared and cooked. The skins are much used by the hunters for snow-shoes and moccasins: for these purposes they are best when taken in the month of October.

Mr. Wm. Paul had, when I saw him on the 7th of February, 1856, in Fulton-street, New York, near the Washington Market, nine moose and two elk, which he had brought from Iowa. They were in good condition, although killed some five weeks before.

Sibley, in his interesting history of the town of Union, Maine, says of this animal: "Probably there is no part of the United States in which moose were so numerous as in Maine. It is said that as recently as 1849 more than fourteen hundred were killed in one year by the Indians, chiefly for the value of the skins."

The N. Y. *Mercury*, January 11, 1768, says: "We hear from Deerfield, in the province of New Hampshire, that on the 26th day of November last one Josiah Prescot, of that town, being out a hunting about three miles from his house, he spied a large moose at about a hundred yards' distance. He immediately fired at her, and shot her down dead: upon that there arose up two more at a small distance from the first. He immediately charged his gun again and shot down the second; and while the other was smelling of his mate, he charged again, and shot down the third; and while he was charging his gun again, a fourth came up towards the others, and he shot her dead also. Two of them were old ones, the other two young ones. One of the old ones was ten feet high and ten feet long, the other eight feet high and ten feet long; the other two were about six feet high and eight feet long. After this extraordinary exploit was over, he was joined by a partner, who, being within hearing of the guns, came up to his assistance, and on going home, he got help to dress the moose: a wild-cat they also killed on their return. This is a fact."

One other curious incident I wish to put on record before I part with it. About the year 1840 a gentleman informed me that while living near Syracuse, New York, a Mr. Nathaniel Dickinson, farmer, who lived between that place and Lake Oneida, had a young heifer stray away and was gone all winter, and when found the next spring she had a half-moose calf by her side, about four weeks old. He did not know whether it grew up or not, as he left the place. At that period a great many moose were found there.

American antelope, or **prong-horn**.—This scarce animal is said to inhabit the great Western prairies in Upper Missouri, Oregon, etc. Lieut. Wilkes (U. S. Expl. Expd.) says that the flavor of the meat was thought to be superior to that of the common deer; and Mr. Horace Greeley, in his interesting letters while travelling to Pike's Peak, etc., in one dated June 2, 1859, says: "The flesh is tender and delicate—the choicest eating I have found in Kansas. Sly and fleet as he is, he is the chief sustenance, at this season, of the Indians out of the present buffalo ranges."

In the same year a remarkable shot was made by Dr. Irwin of the United States Army, of Fort Buchanan, "who killed two antelopes at a single shot with a Colt's carbine, the distance being over three hundred yards. The ball passed through the heart of one animal and the liver of the other."

Big-horn, or **mountain sheep**.—The big-horn is said, by travellers, to be much larger than the common sheep. The male (full grown) often weighs two hundred to three hundred pounds, and upwards. When fat, the flesh is considered excellent when in season, resembling the finest mutton, and even exceeding it in flavor. If so, there seems no reason, except scarcity and distance, why this animal could not be domesticated, as it is asserted that the scantiest vegetation is sufficient to support it. The gray or brown wool or hair may be too coarse to be profitably used, which appears the only drawback, except that it may not bear confinement and artificial feeding in winter.

In the month of July, 1817, a skin of this animal, then called "white wild sheep," was presented by John Jacob Astor, Esq., to Dr. Samuel L. Mitchell, who exhibited it at a meeting of the Lyceum of Natural History, and then deposited it in their cabinet. It was brought, among other skins, from Missouri, by the way of Lake Superior.

Rocky Mountain goat.—As this animal's name denotes, the Rocky Mountains claim its principal habitation. I read and believe what travellers assert, that its flesh is not much valued, it being hard, dry, and unpleasant; but there is no doubt it could be domesticated and treated like our common goats, when its flesh would no doubt be well flavored, as well as having the advantage of very fine glossy hair or fleece.

Northern hare.—This animal is found in greater numbers in our markets now than ten years ago. They are nearly one third larger than the common rabbit, the fur much finer, nearly the same color, except in winter, when they are found almost white. The flesh of an old hare is tough, dry, and insipid; but the leveret, or young one, when in good condition, is very fair eating, not however so good as the rabbit. They are generally in our markets in the months of November, December, and January, but are good until March.

This hare was originally introduced into Canada by several English officers during the time of the French war, and from there brought into the States, where they have spread. Several gentlemen sportsmen, in 1827, collected about fifty hares, transported them to Long Island, and turned them loose near the Hempstead plains. I believe, however, that they have been all exterminated many years ago.

A curious incident relating to one of these animals is found in the St. James *Chronicle*, January 12, 1764, as follows: "A person of veracity from Lincolnshire (England) says that a few days ago the water suddenly overflowed a field where sheep were grazing, and the poor things being up to their bellies in it, the owner went to get them out, when lo! upon the back of one of them he found a hare sitting, which he laid hold of and brought home, and has it now alive."

Rabbit, or **gray hare.**—The flesh of this plentiful animal, when over one year old, is quite dark, dry, and tough eating, without considerable aid from the cook. The young, when nearly full grown and fat, are tender and rather delicate eating. When old, their claws are long and rough. They do not change their color like the hare, but always remain gray. Generally found in our markets from September to January, after which they should not be purchased. In the best condition in November, they are brought in large quantities from every quarter, and if they were not so reproductive they would be soon exterminated, as great numbers are shot by the pot hunters before they are half grown: many are destroyed by animals, hawks, owls, etc. In 1850, I went out one morning about daybreak to shoot gray-squirrels. In getting over a fence I discovered a large barred or hooting owl on the ground with a full-grown rabbit, minus the head, which he had devoured. The owl was so busy with his breakfast, and no doubt was quite hungry, that he allowed me to get within ten yards of him, when he started on the wing, carrying the rabbit in his claws. I shot it down, but he clung to his prey until nearly dead.

Domestic or **fancy rabbits.**—They are often found in our markets (both alive and dead), sometimes ready dressed, generally very fat and fine, and much superior to the wild rabbit, being more juicy, tender, and better flavored. Poulterers keep them alive, for sale, of various colors. The young, for the table, are best from twelve weeks to twelve months old. "In England, the rabbit formerly held the rank of 'farm stock,' and thousands of acres were exclusively devoted to its production. Families were supported, and rents, rates, and taxes were paid from its increase and sale. The 'gray skins' went to tne hatter, the 'silver skins' were shipped to China,' and were dressed as furs, while the flesh was a favorite dish at home."

Guinea pig or **cavy.**—This restless little animal looks much like a small pig with a fur skin: is a native of South America, but has been domesticated here. They are found in numbers in our markets, alive in cages, for sale. Many keep them as pet animals, although their flesh is eatable, but not much thought of by those who have eaten of it.

Squirrels.—Among the varieties of squirrel found in our markets are the fox, cat, gray, black, and red. I have also seen the ground, or striped, and the flying squirrels alive, but never dead, for sale; they are all, however, edible, and much better eating than the rabbit. The gray and black are found sometimes in plenty along in the months of September, October, November, and December. The fox and cat squirrels are somewhat larger than the gray, and occasionally seen here, having been brought from the Western States. I have shot the gray, black, and red (and might have shot the striped) in the same wood, in one of my hunting excursions in Cayuga County, New York. At another I found the gray and black travelling, or, rather, migrating, which they sometimes do, when their food is scarce. It is said they always travel to the east, often hundreds of miles, and when necessary to cross a river or lake they enter the water like dogs, if it is quite smooth. In the month of September, 1851, I arrived at Lake George where I found the gray and black squirrels had been travelling for several days and were still moving. Early one morning I discovered three or four at several distances, swimming from the western to the eastern shore of the lake, which at that time was as smooth as glass. I watched them as long as I could see the ripples which they made, and supposed they succeeded in crossing the lake, which at this point was more than a mile wide. They will not enter the water when there is a ripple, as they swim very deep and of course drown easily; sometimes they are caught out in the rivers or lakes with a sudden breeze, just enough to agitate the water, when it drowns them, without they are lucky enough to catch a floating piece of bark or wood to mount upon, and with their tails curled up they are blown or wafted ashore. In this situation, I suppose, some writers have found them who assert that "when it becomes necessary to pass a lake or river, they lay hold of a piece of larch or fir, and mounting it, abandon themselves to the waves; they erect their tails to catch the wind." All squirrels, when sitting, curl their tails up against their backs. I found many of both black and gray squirrels floating or lying along the shores of the lake drowned. Persons frequently went after them in boats, and on putting down the oar before them they would run up into the boat almost exhausted, when they were secured alive. I saw several that had been so taken at Lake George.

The gray squirrel is easily tamed, and soon becomes acquainted with those who feed or treat him kindly. I had one which ran around the house, out into the yard, and at times would sit on my knee or shoulder to feed.

In Boston (and Philadelphia also) I have seen them in the large parks, or public grounds, running up and down the large trees and over the ground. I found they had nests in small wooden houses which were fastened up into the trees, and when some little school-children came along and called them, the squirrels would come down and receive a nut or a piece of cake from their hands. I am told they breed every season in those parks.

Black bear.—The flesh of this animal is the only species I ever knew to be brought to our markets for sale. Bear, or b'ar-meat, is the common name used to designate its flesh (when spoken of), and it is rather luscious but savory eating; that from a young bear, when nearly full-grown and fat, is considered best. Generally found in our large markets in the late fall or winter months, and some years in great plenty. The dealers in its flesh cut it to suit purchasers, for roasting, steaks, etc.

The taking of one of these animals in swimming across the Hudson River, about the period of the Revolution, and exposing its body for sale in an old market, then known as Hudson-market, which stood on Greenwich-street, east (one block) of the present Washington-market, changed its name to that of the once well-known Bear-market. (See history of the Bear-market, in "The Market-book," vol. i.)

The following will give some idea of their plentifulness in our State, and especially along the Hudson River, at an early period. The New York *Gazette*, October 8, 1759, has recorded—"A gentleman, who came down in one of the last sloops from Albany, says that he was ashore at several places on each side of the North River, and that at every place he landed there were great complaints made of the damage done by bears. Some complain of the loss of their sheep, hogs, and calves; others, of their devouring their fields of Indian-corn, and adding that they are more numerous than has been known in the memory of man. And, particularly, he was at a tavern on the post-road, near Poughkeepsie, when the landlord counted to him thirty-six, that had been killed within three weeks of that time, in the compass of four or five miles. Whilst this gentlemen and the captain were ashore at this tavern, two bears came out of the bushes where the captain and himself landed, and swam across the river, passing very near the head of the sloop; but the battoe being ashore, it was not in the power of the people of the sloop to pursue them."

The same paper, January 3d, 1763, notices a very large *bair*, as follows: "Last week, a bair was shot in Connecticut River, at Saybrook, which weighed seven score and seven pounds. About forty men dined on it."

The *Commercial Advertiser*, November 10, 1824, thus notices the taking of a *white bear:* "On Monday, the 18th ult., a white bear was killed on the west branch of the River Susquehanna, four miles below Youngwomanstown, by Mr.

John Graham. The fur is thicker, and appears to be softer than that of the black bear, and its ears much larger. It was in company with a black bear at the time it was killed; and Mr. Graham is of opinion that, if he had had assistance, he could have taken it alive. This is the first quadruped of this species that has been seen or taken in this part of the world by any of the oldest inhabitants."

In the same paper (December 1, 1838) will be found a marvellous incident and escape, in a letter dated "Linneus, Me., November, 19, 1838—"About seven o'clock in the evening, Mr. Isaac Saunders' son James, who is about eight years of age, was sent to the barn to feed the cattle, and, while returning therefrom to the house (the distance from the barn to the house is about forty rods), had his attention arrested by the appearance of a black object directly ahead of him. He stood still a moment, not knowing whether to advance or retreat. At length he concluded to go ahead, when the bear rose up on his hind legs, and put himself in an attitude to receive the youngster with his fore paws. The boy, perceiving the attitude of the bear, and his apparent determination to maintain his ground, gave a loud screech, and turned and ran towards the barn. At this the bear started in pursuit, and came up with the boy, who was still screeching. Just as the men in the house, who had heard the alarm, were approaching the theatre of action, the bear seized the boy with his fore paws, raised himself again upon his hind legs, and started with his prey, with all possible dispatch, for the woods. The men hotly pursued him for some three-quarters of a mile, when the bear, finding himself but a few feet ahead of his pursuers, turned around and stood face to face with them, when the men, each of whom was armed with an axe, made a motion to give him a gentle tap on the head; but his left paw was ready for a fend-off, while he held the boy tightly with his right one. The men finding it was useless to fight with axes, one of them started for the house for a gun, which he loaded with buckshot, and returned to the woods. On his arrival at the scene of battle, the bear, in attempting to turn and try leg-bail again, was shot through the left side of the body, which brought him to the ground, and caused him to relinquish his hold of the boy, who scampered home, more frightened than hurt, having received no other harm than a most unconscionable hugging. The bear weighed, when dressed, three hundred and sixty-two pounds, and is said to be the largest ever caught in this town."

Raccoon.—These animals are occasionally seen in our markets for sale, both alive and dead—usually more plentiful in the fall months. The full-grown or old raccoon will weigh from seven to twelve pounds, the flesh of which is quite rank and strong. The young are better; but I think them inferior eating, and must confess that I was not in a situation to give them a fair trial when I ate of them.

I had the pleasure, or rather, as it turned out afterwards, a punishment of several days' confinement to my room with excessive hoarseness obtained from the enjoyment of a "raccoon-hunt," some twelve or fifteen years ago (1846), away from the United States, in the dominions of New Jersey, with a few friends. On a cool, clear, autumnal evening, we took our departure, travelling some three or four hours before our hound-dogs started the game—a raccoon; which, however, proved to be double game—two raccoons leading our party. We followed their trails for several miles, through the drear wood and underbrush, until we brought up under a large-sized tree, where the dogs gave tongue "right merrily." The darkness of the woods, rendered more dense, if possible, by night, prevented us seeing each other or any thing bearing shape, save now and then a twinkling star peeping through the vast roof of leaves. One of the party, of keener vision, thought he perceived, pendent from a bough, a peculiar-looking bunch, which his imagination left him at a loss to speculate upon. I being the only one in possession of a gun, I proposed taking a shot at it. This being agreed to, I pointed as near as the darkness would permit, and fired. The discharge caused the black bundle to change its position, which gave life to our party. Here was something. I charged again—this time with buckshot—and popped away at the black bunch. To our amazement, down tumbled a fine young raccoon. The dogs were not satisfied to leave the tree yet. All raccoon-hunters have what they term a "climber"—a boy or man that can quickly mount to the top of a tree; so one of our party enacted this character for this time, and proceeded to ascend the tree. His keen eye soon espied another gentlemanly raccoon, lying well out on an extended limb. With a few shakes, his raccoonship either sprang or fell to the ground, when he instantly fell a prey to the attentions of the dogs. This species of hunting continued throughout the night, varied, however, with the distant and dismal owl-hooting of cat or barred owls, and the scent of several dog-worried skunks, whose occasional proximity was any thing but agreeable. This sport to the dogs, as well as to ourselves, was painfully interrupted now and then by a scratch on the face or lacerated eyes from limbs or bushes, or otherwise stumbling into the depth of some mudhole, or swamp measured, or by becoming a regular "stick in the mud." Finally, before the morning light, one of the hunters discovers a feeling within that a little to eat and drink would be more than agreeable, situated as the party was, but finds to his horror that the noise of the dogs added to the party a most hungry and thirsty addition of hunters, which originally were not "counted in" nor even thought of from the start, who had managed to take particular great care of all the eatables, etc.—we will not refer to the drinkables, which our man "Friday" had the special care of, but who, on getting *tired* and sleepy, as a person naturally will, who over-eats and over-drinks himself, when their legs get weary and their heads become so heavy that they will insist, nay, almost swear, that in their hats they carried a "brick." To wind up this hunter's experience is a violent cold, with hoarseness,—no doubt, from the exposure of the throat in looking through the tree-tops for mares or raccoons. The fruits of three days' hunting were the carrying of two well-filled game-pockets, consisting of a couple of raccoons, as many rabbits, several quails and partridges, and a plump nine-pound double-gun; hungry, thirsty, tired, hoarse, and used-up generally, unable to speak aloud for several days, with divers other disagreeables, the result of my experience, and of my first and last "coon-hunt."

Wild-cat, or **bay lynx.**—This savage little animal, as well as the Canada lynx, is occasionally hunted in this and the neighboring States. The hunters are usually satisfied with their beautiful skins, except in case of short provisions, when they partake of their flesh with much satisfaction—it appearing much like white veal. Audubon says of its flesh—"We have seen it cooked, when it appears savory, and the persons who partook of it pronounced it delicious."

Opossum.—This animal is occasionally found in the markets for sale, in the fall and winter months. The full-grown is about as large as a ten-pound pig (but its flesh is not equal for the table), of a grayish-white face, and under nearly white, and a long rat-looking tail, with a part of it, next to the body, covered with hair.

They are considered by many country-people, and others, who have partaken of their flesh (especially those that have been feeding on the persimmons, and then, above all, well dressed and well cooked), as being tender, luscious, and well-flavored (one man told me it was better than any pig ever roasted). These, and, in fact, all animals, should be dressed as soon after having been killed as possible, and never purchased in any other manner. The skin of this animal is sometimes found on sale, but they are usually scalded like a pig.

Wood-chuck, or **ground-hog.**—This small, stout, brown-colored animal is only occasionally seen in our markets, although often killed within twenty miles of the city of New York. In the fall months they are very fat, when the flesh of the young is quite palatable, somewhat like a pig, and is considered wholesome. The old ones are tolerably good, but much better after having been frozen some time. They usually weigh from eight to twelve pounds. A fine fat young one, weighing six and a quarter pounds, dressed like a roasting-pig (hair scalded off), and much resembling that animal, was shown in Jefferson Market, August 17, 1860; it was shot at Throg's Neck, West-chester County, New York. In the *Deerfield News*, June 4, 1820 (Hampshire County, Mass.), is noticed—"Our famous woodchuck-hunt terminated, on Wednesday, in favor of the party under Mr. E. Nims, who destroyed one thousand one hundred and fifty-four. Those under Mr. J. C. Hoyt destroyed eight hundred and seventy-three—making a total of two thousand and twenty-seven!"

Porcupine.—These slow but harmless animals are found quite plentifully in the western parts of our State, where they are often killed, and their bodies left to decay. Their armor, or the great number of little defensive thorns which cover and protect them from their foes when alive, render them very troublesome to skin after death; but I am told their flesh, after having been nicely cleaned, is very tender, luscious, and wholesome eating. The Indians esteem its flesh. It weighs from ten to fifteen pounds.

Skunk.—The flesh of this most detestable animal is, I am told, when properly prepared, as good as raccoon. I have heard those who have eaten it say it was very sweet and savory after it had been dressed. I never saw it for sale in our markets, although I have heard of its being dressed and sold under another name.*

Professor Kalm says of this animal: "I have spoken with both Englishmen and Frenchmen, who assured me they had eaten of it, and found it very good meat, and not much unlike the flesh of a pig. When the Indians kill them they always eat its flesh, but are very careful in dressing or skinning it."

This animal's soft, black, or mottled skin or fur would

* The skins of the striped and black skunks are often on sale here, the latter being the most valuable.

be quite as valuable as many other small animals' skins, if it was not for their unpleasant smell. Usual weight, seven to eight pounds.

Beaver.—This animal was once a native here, but civilization and the beaver's valued skin have almost exterminated the family, although now and then a specimen is taken in our State. It is said "the flesh of this animal is greatly prized by hunters and voyageurs, especially when roasted in the skin after the fur is singed off." This, of course, is an expensive luxury, and is frowned upon by the fur-traders. "Care must be taken, however, to examine the herbage on which the animals feed, or mischief may follow an unwary repast. Mr. Ross's party were once poisoned by feasting heartily on beaver, and some of them had a very narrow escape. The Indians eat this kind of beaver, but they roast it; boiled, they say, it is pernicious."

Professor Kalm, in his "Travels in America," in 1748, says: "Beaver flesh is eaten, not only by the Indians, but likewise by the Europeans, and especially by the French on their fasting days; for his Holiness, in his system, has ranged the beaver among the fish. The flesh is reckoned best if the beaver has lived upon vegetables. The tail is likewise eaten, after it has been well boiled and roasted afterwards."

Doctor Goodman also, in his "Natural History," says: "During the winter season the beaver becomes very fat, and its flesh is esteemed by the hunters to be excellent food. But those occasionally caught in the summer are very thin, and unfit for the table."

Otter.—This now scarce animal is seldom seen in our city, although it is brought here occasionally, but more for the taxidermist than for the quality of its flesh for the table. I am told, however, that the flesh is quite good eating, except being of a fishy flavor. I saw a fine specimen in 1857, taken in one of the streams in New Jersey, and I find in the "New York Sun," May 17, 1856: "An otter, weighing eighteen pounds, and three feet six inches long, was caught in

Paramus, Bergen County, N. J., on Thursday last, in a net, drowned. The skin weighed two pounds." The skins are occasionally found in our markets.

A remarkable shot is recorded in the "Commercial Advertiser," March 20, 1838, as follows: "There have been exhibited in our town (Williamsport, Pa.) to-day, three large otters, killed by Mr. Isaac Dodd, about two miles from this place, on the canal, at a single shot, with a musket loaded with small squirrel-shot, the largest (otter) of which weighed twenty-five pounds and the smallest twenty pounds."

Badger.—These animals are sometimes taken, but more for their skin than their flesh, although by some they are considered good eating. They are little larger than a raccoon, with a thick fur coated with long hair of a reddish, brindle color, except underneath, which is white. They are very intelligent-looking in the face, with sharp teeth and long claws. An occasional skin is found in our cities for sale.

Musk-rat or **Musquash.**—This animal is among the many kinds that are seldom or never seen in our markets, yet they are often killed for their fur skin, and their flesh would be (more) eaten if it was thought eatable. The name it bears would almost condemn its flesh from being used as food; but I know several persons who, having dressed and eaten them, say its flesh is tender and very well flavored, when young and in good condition. If its flesh can be hung and frozen a few days it is considered still better. A large number of their skins are brought to our (New York) city and sold.

POULTRY.

UNDER this head we place all kinds of domesticated fowls, tame pigeons, etc. These are received from Long Island, and other parts of our State, Connecticut, Rhode Island, Massachusetts, Vermont, New Jersey, and Pennsylvania. Large numbers arrive here from the latter State, of the choicest quality, all ready dressed, put up in various packages in the cold seasons. During the hot weather numbers are sent here alive in "coops;" but many of our large dealers prepare boxes, in which poultry, carefully dressed, are packed in ice, by which means they arrive here in good condition. In the dressing, care should be taken in the "picking" not to tear the skin, nor should the wings be cut off, but picked to the end, and the necks tied up, so that the bodies should not get bloody. Large numbers go through the process of scalding, that the feathers may be taken off more readily; these are not so much liked as dry-picked fowls. This mode of dressing appears to us an unnecessarily cruel one: the fowl is usually stuck in the mouth up through the upper jaw into the brain, and then, while slowly bleeding and struggling, they are picked; if laid until the fowl is quiet and dead the feathers become set, and then, of course, the skin is torn in plucking them off.

Poultry would be more delicate eating, better flavored, and command higher prices if all the useless offal, such as the head, feathers, and intestines, were removed, and the blood washed out with cold water. This would remove the injury often done to the flesh by the flavor of the excrements, when having been killed some time. The caponed fowl may be left with the head on, that the purchaser may judge whether he be a capon or not, by the withered comb and gills. The common fashion now to prepare poultry for our markets is to stick them through the jugular vein, then either to scald and pick them, or dry-pick them (as above), often leaving attached the tail, neck, and wing feathers, with the addition of the head, and sometimes a piece of bloody rag around the neck; all this useless waste is then to be weighed, they being generally sold by the pound, thus adding over half a pound to each fowl above its proper weight.

The food given to poultry produces great influence on the character and flavor of the flesh. Fowls cooped up for a few weeks before killing, and fed upon cereal grain, have a delicate, tender, and sweet flesh; whilst, on the contrary, those that are allowed to run, pick up rancid meats, fat, fish, scraps, or other unfit substances, have a corresponding taint or taste, and, at the same time, the flesh is less tender and less fine-flavored. The conclusion is, the cleaner the diet the more delicate the flavor.

To judge fresh poultry.—The eyes should be full and bright, feet moist, soft, and limber. When stale, the eyes will be dry and sunken, the feet and legs dry and stiff, and if too stale, the body, or some parts of it, will be dark-colored, and sometimes green. The "New York Tribune" of December 16, 1853, speaks of a lot of chickens, of about eight thousand pounds, which had arrived here in a damaged state, and after remaining on the dock two days, was bought up by a speculator for fifty dollars, or six-tenths of a cent per pound, for the lot. The poultry, on being unpacked, was found in a slimy, tainted condition, on the verge of putrefaction. Before being exposed for sale it underwent a process of being "manufactured over," a process well known to the knowing ones. This is accomplished by soaking the poultry in alum-water, which relieves it of the slime and appearance of decay, and restores it to an apparently fresh state. "In three days the entire lot was disposed of, from the sale of which the speculator realized a profit of over eight hundred dollars. Poultry that has undergone this process turns black (when the skin has been torn off) after having been exposed a short time to the air." In several of our large public markets nearly all kinds of the various species of poultry, of the choice, rare, and fancy kinds, as well as many species of fancy, curious, and table birds, both large and small, are often to be had alive. With these few remarks on poultry, I will proceed with the different species.

Caponed fowls.—There is no doubt that the caponed fowls stand at the head of all the poultry kind, and they always command the highest market price. They are considered the greatest delicacies, preserving the tenderness of the chicken with the fine juicy flavor of maturity. The breed of fowls the most profitable for making capons appears to be the Bucks County fowl, although the Dorkings, Cochin-China, and other large breeds, are by some preferred. The object, however, appears to be to get large, square, heavy-bodied fowls (cockerells are generally used, as the hen chickens are smaller and seldom used for that purpose) that have a rapid growth.

One of the largest young capons I ever saw was sold by Hedden & Sons, Jefferson Market, March 18, 1859, which weighed twelve pounds, and when laid out measured above three feet. I have seen heavier, but they were older. They also had a pair of nine months old capons, on the 4th of April, 1863, which weighed twenty-four pounds, and they were not coarse-made, but plump, fat, and fine.

To judge the capon.—Generally the head is small (for the size of the body, compared with the uncaponed fowl), the comb is quite pale, short, and withered, the feathers on the neck, if left on, are longer, and, if quite young, they will have smooth legs, and short, thick, soft spurs. The body is larger, fatter, more plump and round than the common fowl, in proportion, and generally they have a fat vein on each side of the breast, running into the hard, fat stomach and rump, which is the most unprofitable portion of this fine fowl. In some instances the performance of caponizing is not complete, when the head and large comb will show themselves more like the uncaponed fowl, which gives them the appearance of having large bones and less flesh. In this state they are called

Slips, or **slip-capons**—which are of course inferior to the capon, but are generally dressed like them, and very often sold for them by the dishonest dealer.

Chickens.—Many of the poulterers term all under a year old "chickens;" but long before that period arrives many hen chickens commence laying, and then they are properly called, by many persons, "pullets." The cockerell is also considered fully matured when from five to eight months old, and begins to enjoy all the rights and privileges of the poultry-yard. It certainly cannot be expected that the flesh of these matured birds will be as delicate as the young, growing chicken, which is daily making a new and tender flesh. Therefore, to designate the young, growing chicken, it will not be improper to place them under the head of

Spring-chicken or **broilers.**—This name is not an uncommon one among some of our best dealers, who deal largely in broilers varying from the size of a quail to two or three pounds per pair. Although we have them of all sizes in almost all the months of the year, yet the greatest portion is hatched in February, March, and April, and brought to our markets in the spring months.

In choosing, never select the coarse, long-legged, thin-breasted chicken because they are the heaviest, but take the plump, full-breasted, partridge-shaped, for juiciness, fine grain, and well-flavored eating, besides having plenty of the breast-meat and less bone.

To judge a chicken from a fowl. It is nearly the same as judging a young turkey. The lower end of the breast-bone is always soft, like the gristle in a person's ear. The spurs of a young cockerel are soft, loose, and short. When old, the comb and legs are rough, spurs hard and firmly fixed, and both cock and hen have a hard breast-bone. There are few species of the bird kind more tender than a young chicken, and very few tougher than an old cock or hen.

Mr. Samuel Hazard, of Philadelphia, informs me that while he was travelling in the Island of Malta, in the Mediterranean, it was the custom for small families to buy at the markets parts of a chicken—the half or a quarter is sold, as the purchasers wish. Another curious custom he also noticed: there being no cows kept for milk, goats are used, and the milk-women drive the goats to the customers' doors, and there milk from them the quantity desired. Pity we could not have our cows' milk obtained in some such manner, or, rather, as pure.

Fowls.—This name is generally applied to both the cock and hen of the common dunghill fowls, by our dealers generally, after having passed the age of one year When seeking for the best fowls select those which are the youngest, plump, fleshy, and fat, and that flesh nearly white. When the flesh on the breast will mash under the pressure of the thumb, it is best. Among the many breeds producing the best fowls are the Dorkings, Polands, Black Spanish, Dominiques, etc. The coarse, long-legged, big-boned breeds (among which the Shanghais are the poorest), have very small breasts according to their size and quantity of bone; their flesh is also coarse and not well flavored.

Live fowls of all the various kinds, breeds, and conditions, are always to be found in our public markets, and large numbers are sold to shipping vessels, steamers, etc. This business has now become so large, that one firm (Messrs. Tilton) in Franklin Market (N. Y.), keep many thousand ready for that purpose, and some days their sales and receipts of live fowls have been enormous. One of the firm told me, that in the month of April, 1862, they received one lot, from Indiana, which numbered above 8,000 fowls and chickens, which came through on railroad and steamboats, in coops, and were daily fed and watered throughout the passage. A large business from the Western States has grown up since the rebellion commenced, which closed the Mississippi River; and hereafter, no doubt, we will receive their surplus stock.

A (*fowl*) curiosity is noticed in the *New York Journal*, December, 1797. "Captain Bradford, of this town (Boston), last week purchased a fowl in the market, of about four pounds weight, which on opening for the purpose of cooking, was discovered to be entirely filled with liver, to the exclusion of almost every other kind of entrails. The liver commenced its growth in the common place; but had increased so enormously as to occupy almost the whole interior cavity,—a small *intestinum* passing by its side to convey and void the food after digestion. The liver weighed upwards of a pound. Several gentlemen of the faculty, and many respectable private citizens have viewed and been astonished at this phenomenon."

In the month of January, 1858, I purchased a young cockerel, in Jefferson Market, which appeared with a double vent and a false rump. I opened it and found the vent connected after its entrance into the body about half of an inch. Both were perfect, and appeared to have been used alike. Since that period I obtained another curious specimen—a chicken full grown, with three legs—the third leg was fast in an immmovable socket, about one inch to the rear of the socket of the left leg. The joints of this extra leg were immovable, and without toes. A curious freak of nature.

Bantam fowls.—These very small and generally feather-legged fowls, are, I believe, seldom raised for the table, but rather as a fancy fowl or curiosity. When found "dressed" in our markets, their bodies are not much larger than a partridge; their flesh, however, is finely grained and of a superior quality, if the young and fat are chosen.

Guinea-fowls, or **pintada.**—The flesh of the Guinea-fowl is dark, like that of the grouse, and many consider it more delicate and savory than the common fowl, but not so juicy. They are generally found unpicked in our markets, and by raising the feathers on the breast you will easily perceive if they are fat and plump. A good fowl will weigh from three and a half to five pounds. They are considered best in the winter months, when they take the place of partridges after they are out of season. When alive they make a harsh, grating noise, very much like the sharpening or filing of an old saw, and in a flock this noise is almost continuous.

Turkeys.—These splendid birds are almost the year through found in our markets, but the best season for them is in the fall and winter months, when the young ones are in perfection. To judge young turkeys from the old:—the young has smooth, and most of them black legs (the young "Tom" has, also, short, loose spurs), and a soft, gristly breast-bone, at the thin end, where it joins the stomach. Some have a very crooked breast-bone, caused from their roosting on a narrow perch, which they at night rest upon, but it does not injure their flesh, except to lessen the quantity, on the one side or the other, when very crooked or deformed. When the legs are rough, the spur of the "cock" long and hard, and the breast-bone hard, covered with a soft, tough-looking fat skin, these signs are generally those of age.

The *young hen*, for a small family, is preferred, as they are smaller, plump, and generally fatter. But for a large family, a fine young "Tom," when well roasted, is a dish that can hardly be surpassed.

The *old turkey* is best for boning, and generally preferred for a plain boil. In March and April, the flesh of all turkeys begins to get soft, dry, spongy, and not well flavored, although I have eaten, and seen for sale, turkeys that were killed, dressed, and drawn, in their proper season, kept frozen for nearly five months. On the 10th of May, 1858, I purchased one, and found the flesh tender, juicy, and firm, but not quite so well flavored as a fresh-killed turkey in its season. It has become a large and profitable business (in Vermont especially) to prepare them in this manner. They are sold in the spring months, and realize one hundred per cent. more than the usual price in the fall months.

Occasionally, very large turkeys are exposed for sale in our markets, one of which I saw, January 23, 1852, on the stand of Messrs. Packer & Knapp, Washington Market, which weighed, dressed, thirty-three pounds six ounces. In 1859, Chester K. Crook, No. 55 Bowery, is said to have had on exhibition a turkey which was reported to have weighed forty-one pounds three ounces, for which he paid forty dollars. On the last day of December, 1858, I saw a young (spring) turkey, which weighed twenty-one and a half pounds, on a stand in Jefferson Market. A still larger one, hatched in the month of May, 1864, which came from Charles Norton, Esq., near Bristol, Connecticut, who sent it to his brother, H. G. Norton, Esq., for his Christmas dinner, weighed twenty-five and a half pounds. He also informed me, that his brother, in the spring of 1863, sold a gobbler turkey, about four years old, which weighed forty-two pounds.

Ralph H. Avery, Esq., of Wampsville, Madison County, New York, writes me, on the 24th of June, 1858, and says: "I have on hand now a turkey gobbler two years old, that weighs thirty-two pounds, and is thin; also a hen turkey weighing twenty-one pounds. I sold a gobbler in February, 1856, that was two years and eight months old, that weighed thirty-four pounds, for one dollar per pound. He was purchased by J. M. Matthews, Esq., of the firm of Matthews, Hunt & Co., of your city, and presented to President Buchanan at his inauguration, and I learn he can now be seen in the gardens of the Presidential mansion. He acts, I suppose, as a member of the 'kitchen cabinet.'"

The largest turkey, perhaps, ever grown, was owned and raised by Widow Lounesberry, Stamford, Connecticut, and sold by her to the Union Club of that town for twenty-five dollars, and by them sent to President Johnson as a present for New Year's Day, 1866. This turkey was not quite two years old, yet it weighed, alive, forty-seven pounds!"

Turkey poults, or half-grown turkeys, are seldom brought to our markets; they are considered very delicate and tender, but not much flavor, and rather insipid eating.

Capon Turkey.—The Capon turkey is occasionally found in our markets. It is said they are more difficult to raise than the Capon fowl, and more destructive to the young poultry of all kinds in the yards. When found, they are the most delicious eating of all the turkey kind, being more tender, juicy, and fine-flavored.

Pea-fowls.—These beautiful birds are generally kept for ornament, but when young its flesh is almost or quite equal to the turkey. I had a fine young pea-hen, weighing just six pounds, roasted, which my family thought quite as good as turkey, and I must admit, the dark flesh was quite as good, if not superior, to any turkey I ever eat, being more tender and sweet. I therefore disagree with an old adage, in relation to this bird, as not having a single redeeming quality, which says: "It has the plumage of an angel, the voice of the devil, and the stomach of a thief." "In ancient times," says Martin, "no great feast in the baron's hall was served up without this bird to grace it; well cooked, served on a large dish, but rearranged in its gorgeous plumage."

Tame pigeons.—These beautiful birds, when used as food, are found to be dry eating, but well flavored; if, however, they are young, then cooped up and strongly fed a few days, their flesh will be more delicate and tender. They are only fit to fricassee, stew, or for a pie, etc.

Many varieties are found for sale alive in our large markets, of all kinds and colors, some of which are very beautiful. They are known as "fancy pigeons," among which are the carriers, pouters, or croppers, ruff-heads, tumblers, topknots, duffers, fantails, baldpates, magpies, etc. Among these the ruff-heads wear a frilled or fanciful cap on their heads, and ruffles around their necks, which give them some of the appearance of the ladies' ruffles of Queen Elizabeth's time. These ruffles are raised feathers, which commence behind the head, proceed down their neck, and join on the breast. The colored ruffs with white heads are the most beautiful.

The pouters have the power to distend the crop or breast with wind, so that it is almost half as large as itself; then the tumbler, which turns over and over while on the wing; and the useful and curious carrier, which has a peculiar-looking fleshy tubercle growing on the sides of the eyes and bill. They are very strong and swift on the wing, quick-sighted, and possess great attachment for the place of their birth, which causes them, when carried away from their home, even hundreds of miles, to find their way back when let loose. In olden times, or until the telegraph had commenced its operations, they were much used to convey messages, news, etc.

Tame squabs, the young of tame pigeons, are usually

found the year round in our markets. Their flesh is very tender, delicate, and light food, and well adapted for the sick.

Domesticated swan.—There are several persons in this country that have these beautiful and graceful birds domesticated, and keep them more as an ornament than for the table. In the waters of Central Park large numbers are to be seen daily.

In England, swan-feasts are common in the months of September and November, and often as late as Christmas.

The young, or cygnet, is considered a capital dish, very highly esteemed, and never better than in the month of November. Yarrell says: "The town-clerk of Norwich sends a note from the town-hall to the public swanherd, the corporation, and others who have swans and swan-rights, on the second Monday in August. They are collected in a small stream or pond, the numbers varying from fifty to seventy, and many of them belonging to private individuals. They begin to feed immediately, being provided with as much barley as they can eat, and are usually ready for killing early in November. They vary in weight, some reaching to twenty-eight pounds. They are all cygnets. If kept beyond November, they begin to fall off, losing both flesh and fat, and the meat becomes darker in color and stronger in flavor."

Ducks.—There are many breeds of ducks which are very fine for the table, among which are the Muscovy, topknot, Cayuga black, etc. A cross between the common and Muscovy produces a very large bird at an early age, and is considered by many the choicest duck.

The young, or spring-duck, is always the best; but sometimes to select is rather difficult for the uninitiated, as it requires the experienced eye and hand to judge both the young duck and goose. There are, however, some general signs which are found correct. The joints in the legs will break by their own weight; the windpipe will also break easily under the pressure of the fingers. The lower end of the flat breast-bone should be soft, and, above all, the should be plump and fat.

Geese.—Among the best breeds of geese for the table are the Bremen, Chinese, African, etc. Hybrids are also highly prized for their superior size and flesh.

To choose the young goose, the same signs as the duck will also apply. Usually the bill and feet are yellow (but red if old). If the goose has been scalded when dressed, the pressure of the thumb and fingers behind and under the wing will break the ribs ; a pressure also on the wind-pipe will snap or mash like a stiff straw, and a pin's head will break through the skin easily.

The flesh of an old goose is very poor eating, and more especially when thin and very old, they are one of the worst in the family of poultry. I have known them to live above thirty years, and read remarkable stories of their being above one hundred years old ; but the following goose story, or hoax, must convince all of this fact. Among the articles exhibited at the New Jersey State Fair, 1859, was an antiquated goose, which attracted much attention. Its history was posted on the coop which contained the venerable bird, and read as follows : "Madame Goose is now owned by Robert Schomp, of Reading, Hunterdon County, N. J. She has been in his possession twenty-five years, and was given to him by his grandfather, Major H. G. Schomp. Robert's father is now in his eighty-fifth year, and this goose was a gift to his mother as a part of her marriage outfit. The mate of Madame Goose was killed in the Revolutionary War, being rode over by a troop of cavalry. She enjoys general good health, is not so active as she once was, but moves about among her descendants with dignity and considerable activity. In the spring of 1857 she laid six eggs, three of which were hatched, and the goslings raised. In 1858 she made seven nests and laid but two eggs, evidence perhaps of failing faculties. Her eyes are becoming dim, one having almost entirely failed. The year of her birth cannot be known, but she remains a representative of the olden time,' and is worthy the respect which honorable age should ever command."

When purchasing, if possible, select those geese which are fresh and fat, the head and giblets cut off, and nicely drawn, as it will make a saving of nearly two pounds in their weight. They are always best in the fall and winter months.

A novel mode of bringing live geese to market was performed by "a Mr. Downing, formerly a sheep-broker, at Browning's (Bull's Head, Sixth-street), who brought to market four hundred and seventy-five geese and turkeys, and four hundred and fifty chickens. They came in cars, were driven like sheep twenty-five miles to Columbus, Ohio, and there shipped by Erie Railroad, and sold here same as cattle, by pound, live weight—the geese at nine cents per pound, and turkeys at ten and a half cents. Eight hundred and fifty more are expected on Friday." They, however, did not give satisfaction for the table, as their flesh was generally tough and dry eating.

The origin of eating goose on Michaelmas-day is thus handed down to us: "Queen Elizabeth, on her way to Tilbury Fort, on the 29th of September, 1598, dined at the ancient seat of Sir Neville Umfreville, near that place; and, as British Bess had much rather dine off a high-seasoned and substantial dish than a flimsy fricassee or a rascally ragout, the knight thought proper to provide a brace of fine geese to suit the palate of his royal guest. After the queen had dined very heartily, she asked for a half-pint bumper of burgundy, and drank *destruction to the Spanish Armada.* She had but that moment returned the glass to the knight, who had done the honors of the table, when the news came (as if the queen had been possessed of the spirit of prophecy) that the Spanish fleet had been destroyed by a storm. She immediately took another bumper, in order to digest the geese and good news, and was so much pleased with the event, that she, every year after, on that day, had the above excellent dish served up. The court made it a custom, and the people have followed the fashion ever since."—*Commercial Advertiser*, Dec. 5, 1806.

Green geese.—This name is applied to the gosling that is about three parts grown—say from two to three months old, when they have been generously fed and allowed to run on fine pasture. Many are prepared for our summer tables, and they are considered very fine eating.

In some parts of Europe they cram their geese to such an extent, as, with the addition of heat, to cause their livers to increase to one and two pounds weight, which are considered a great delicacy. They are sent here in packages, and often found on the tables of our foreign epicures.

Giblets.—Thirty years ago it was quite common to find tied up in bunches the necks and wings of geese, ducks, turkeys, and fowls, for sale under the name of "giblets;" but the cook now adds the heads, gizzards, and livers of all kinds of poultry or game-birds to the name. They are used for stewing, fricassee, pot-pie, etc.

WILD-FOWL AND BIRDS, CALLED GAME.

The variety, quantity, and quality of wild-fowl and birds, called game, and others not placed under this head, received in the public markets, especially of the city of New York, is not surpassed in any other city in the world. The prairies of the West, the forest-regions of the North, the gulfs and coasts of the Northern and Southern States, and even European cities, all contribute to keep well supplied the wants of our citizen epicures, in every month or season of the year. No doubt new and rare varieties of game will be added to our already numerous species, as the facilities for transportation increase.

We avail ourselves of a passage from "Frank Forrester's Field Sports," which says—"Within a few years, there is but little doubt that the Western species (of all game) will be exposed for sale in our markets; and, should Whitney's

Oregon Railroad go into effect in our day, who knows but we may live to shoot 'cocks of the plains' ourselves, and bring them home the next day to dinner at Delmonico's," so says the late Henry William Herbert.

In naming the numerous species of game and other birds, I am anxious merely to show those which it is proper to take, kill, or destroy, as well as those which directly or indirectly affect our tables or are found in our public markets. In doing so, I do not wish to encourage the destruction of a single life that would be more useful to the economy of nature than its dead body for the table. In fact, I would go so far as to wish the passage of a United States general law that would especially protect all birds smaller than the quail, except a few shore-birds, or those which are considered and known to be injurious.

Thousands of birds of the small species are wantonly killed merely for the sport, or a few pence. These slaughtered birds, when alive, destroy millions of insects, flies, worms, slugs, etc., penetrating every nook and corner of hedge, thicket, or field; bush and tree, they clear limb after limb, while every passing, folded, or withered leaf is carefully examined and deprived of its concealed but destructive tenant. Without these useful and beautiful little "trespassers," the many destructive insects would increase so rapidly as to become almost a plague, by destroying all fruit and vegetation; while the loss of a little fruit or seed for their subsistence for a short period would amply repay the cultivator for the great services they render him.

It has been particularly noticed that they do not often touch the sound fruit when they can find those that have worms in them. From this fact, they should not be driven from the fruit-trees: they are friends and benefactors, not only to the cultivator but to mankind at large, and to all who have a sentiment for all that is beautiful, poetic, and most musical of nature's productions.

Since writing the above, I find game-laws were passed on the 6th of April, 1860, which at least protect some of the useful birds, and others called game-birds, for certain periods or months. It says, no person or persons shall kill or expose for sale "any woodcock between the first day of January and the fourth day of July, in each year; or any partridge or ruffed grouse, between the fifteenth day of January and the fifteenth day of October; or any wood, black, or teal duck, between the first day of February and the first day of August, in each year, under the fine of two dollars for each and every of said birds so killed or had in possession.

"No person or persons shall kill any prairie-fowl or pinnated grouse, in the State of New York, within five years from the passage of this act, under a fine of ten dollars for each bird so killed.

"No person or persons shall, at any time, within this State, catch any quail (sometimes called Virginia partridge) or ruffed grouse, with any trap or snare, under a fine of two dollars for each bird so caught." Nor "kill, cage, or trap any nightingale, night-hawk, blue-bird, yellow-bird, Baltimore oriole, finch, thrush, lark, sparrow, wren, martin, swallow, or any bird of the species of woodpecker, or other harmless bird; nor shall any person or persons kill, cage, or trap any bobolink or robin, between the first day of February and the first day of October, in each year, under a fine of fifty cents for each bird so killed, caged, or entrapped."

WILD-FOWL.

Wild swan or **whistling swan**.—This is a scarce bird in our markets, although occasionally seen. The cygnets (young) are very fine eating, but should not be above a year or two old. They require five or six years to reach maturity. The third year the bill becomes black. Very old birds have a hard protuberance on the bend of the last joint of the wing. Their season here ranges from November to January.

The "Brooklyn Star," in the winter of 1846, notices that

"a flock of white swans made their appearance in Hempstead Bay, and one of them was shot, weighing seventeen pounds." Mr. George T. Sammis, of the Seaside House, Rockaway, Long Island, on the 25th of February, 1866, found a pair of swans in Jamaica Bay and bagged them both,—their wings measuring eight feet extended, and weighing twenty-five pounds.

Trumpeter swan.—This species is not so scarce in our markets as the whistling swan; in fact, nearly all brought here are of this species, generally shot in the Chesapeake. The young are pretty good eating, but the old are very dry and tough. In season from November to January.

The most remarkable feature of this bird is, when dissected, you will find a very lengthy windpipe encased in the breast-bone, which, no doubt, is the cause of the loud trumpeting sound it makes.

Wild goose, or **Canada goose**. This bird is plenty here, in its season, and to designate them you will find the head and greater part of the neck is black, cheek and throat white. The young are very fine eating, and are considered superior to the common goose. They are best in October, November, and December: although there are not many killed in the latter month, yet they are found in our markets as late as January.

This goose is not an uncommon inhabitant of the poultry yard, having been domesticated and even bred from. I recollect, some forty years ago, Mr. McComb, at Kingsbridge, had, for many years, a large flock around his house; but most of their time they spent in the Spuyten Duyvil Creek.

When breeding with the common, the Chinese, or the Bremen, this goose produces a hybrid, or mongrel, which grows rapidly, and acquires a larger size than either of its parents. Their flesh is also of a finer flavor, and commands a higher price in our markets.

Snow-goose or **white brant.**—Occasionally the young of this fine white bird is seen exposed for sale in our markets, and it is said they are superior to the former (Canada goose), both in juiciness and flavor. When found here it is generally in the month of May, and again in November.

Mud or **Hutchins' goose**.—This species is not an uncommon one in our markets. In size smaller than the Canada goose, but appears much like that bird. It is said that its flesh is strong and fishy.

Brant or **brent goose**.—The flesh of this bird is considered fine eating, although, at times, it is a little sedgy, which, no doubt, is caused by its "feeding-grounds." The adult has entirely black wings, while the young has them tipped with grayish white. A good bird will weigh about four pounds. Large numbers are found in our markets in their season, which appears to be in April and May, when some consider them best; then again, it appears in October, November, and December.

Canvas-back duck.—This, no doubt, is the finest and choicest wild-duck known for the table, when in season, which generally appears to be in the latter part of November and through December; and then, provided they have been killed in the Susquehanna, Chesapeake, Potomac, and Delaware Rivers, feeding on what is commonly called wild celery, they are very fat, fine, tender, and with that delicious flavor so much admired. If taken at any other season and place they are but little better than some of the common sea-ducks. To judge a fine wild-duck, is in their superior weight; and by feeling behind their legs they will be plump and full, and of course fat and always good.

Canvas-back duck received its name from the fact that a portion of the back of the drake resembles a piece of canvas. The bill of this duck is black, and higher at the base than the red-heads, and nearly in a straight line with the head, about three inches long.

They are found in our markets earlier and later than the above months, but usually in smaller quantities. Large numbers are sent by our swift steamers to Europe, where they command high prices. The question may be properly asked—"Where are all the wild ducks taken that are brought and sold in our large cities?" The wild-duck trade is a large business, especially on our southern waters. The "Norfolk Herald," of January 8, 1857, will give some idea as answer to the above question:

"Edward Burroughs, Esq., a substantial farmer of Princess Anne, Long Island, Back Bay, from time immemorial famous as the resort of wild-ducks and geese, has had twenty men employed constantly since the commencement of the season; and up to the 20th of December, 1856, they had consumed in their vocation twenty-three kegs of gunpowder, with shot in proportion. The ducks which they killed were brought to Norfolk once a week, and piled up in the warehouse of Kemp & Buskey, on Roanoke Square, where, on every Wednesday, they were packed in barrels and shipped for New York by the steamship Jamestown. The number of barrels thus sent off weekly have, up to this time, averaged from fifteen to twenty-five barrels, and one week the number reached as high as thirty-one. They consist of all the varieties of the duck species known in our latitude, such as canvas-back, red-heads, mallard, black ducks, sprig-tails, bull-necks, bald-faces (or widgeons), shovellers, etc., to which may be added a good proportion of wild geese."

Prior to 1820 there were but few canvas-back ducks brought to our public markets; in fact, those that were brought either to New York or Boston were shot by sportsmen from those cities, who made annual visits down to the Chesapeake and Susquehanna, and brought these and other game home; when a few friends, or those celebrated caterers, Niblo and Sykes, were sure to receive all that could be spared, as they were generous in the prices paid for them, which, no doubt, soon led to their more general demand and introduction. The "Commercial Advertiser," December 13, 1822, thus notices canvas-back ducks: "We have had an unusual supply this season of this delicious species of the wild-duck from Havre de Grace. At no former season do we recollect to have seen them so abundant, and at the same time so fine. A single pair out of the lot sent to Mr. Niblo the other day weighed twelve pounds. We are informed that both he and Mr. Sykes have made arrangements for receiving regular supplies of them from the Susquehanna and Chesapeake, during the winter." And for many years they received principally all the canvas-backs sent to this city for sale.

About fifty years ago this dainty bird was found to frequent the Hudson River. This fact was noticed at that period as follows: "The principal feeding-place is in the neighborhood of Pollepel's Island and Fishkill Landing, where they sometimes overspread acres of water. There the *valisneria* grows plentifully a little above the reach of the salt water: and these diving ducks resort there to feed on it in great numbers. When the ice prevents their obtaining their favorite food, they take their departure, and return in the spring as soon as the river opens."

Until very lately, the gunners used to confound these birds with broad-bills, red-heads, and other ducks, and sell them all together. There was then no difference in the price. Twenty-five cents would purchase a canvas-back as readily as an ordinary duck. But now the distinction is well understood by the fowlers. They bring them to market, and offer them for sale as true and real canvas-back ducks. The lovers of good eating buy them eagerly, and the price of a pair of these rare birds has risen to two and three dollars. Good preparations of the New York male and female were made by Mr. De la Coste, and are now in the collection of ornithology in Princeton College; and another pair from the Hudson, in fine preservation, is in the possession of P. A. Schenck, Esq., the Surveyor of the Port of New York.—*Med. Repos.*, vol. x.

Red-head, or Pochard.—This is also an excellent duck, and frequently sold for the canvas-back to those who do not know the difference, as it is much like that bird. The bill is of a bluish color, and towards the end it is black, and about two and a quarter inches long, a little curved from the head. This duck commands a high price, but not so high as the preceding. Their season commences in November, and they are found sometimes very plenty all the winter long, and then again in straggling numbers; but their flesh is best for the table in the two first months.

Mallard.—This beautiful and very fine duck is second to none, except the canvas-back and red-head, for the table. The color of the head and upper part of the neck is of a deep green, with a white ring about the middle of the neck. Its flesh is considered best in the autumn months, but the bird is found scattering along through the winter months.

Black duck, or **dusky duck.**—This duck is very fine eating when fat and taken from the fresh water; but when the lakes and ponds are covered with ice, they betake themselves to the salt waters, when their flesh assumes a fishy flavor, and becomes rather dry eating. They appear in our markets in the months of September, October, November, and December. In the two latter months they are frequently found in the best condition, and are highly esteemed. I have seen them scattering along until May.

Wood duck, or **summer duck.**—This most beautiful species of the wild duck confines itself entirely to the fresh water, where it is more or less shaded by trees and bushes, although sometimes it will alight on trees (the only species of duck that do so), generally on the limbs that are quite bare or dead. Its principal food are insects, seeds, and plants, which render its flesh excellent eating, without the fishy flavor so objectionable to many. They are not so large as the black duck. Many are taken alive in nets, and often sent to Europe to be kept either for breed or ornament. In season in the months of August, September, October, and a few stragglers in November.

A beautiful male duck of this species was shown at the Horticultural and Agricultural Fair held by the American Institute in September, 1860. Some two or three were purchased at Boston by Mr. Simpson, of Westchester County,

N. Y., who tamed them so as to eat out of hand, and this one was exhibited at this Fair, where it attracted much attention.

Bald-pate, or **American widgeon**.—This duck, when taken feeding with the canvas-back, or rather stealing from them their food (wild celery), are excellent. When the canvas-back rises from the bottom, they snatch the delicious morsel, and then make off. Their flesh then is considered of an excellent flavor, and much esteemed. Found in season in the months of October, November, and December, but best in the two latter.

Broad-bill, blue-bill, or **scaup duck.**—This bird is common in our markets in their season, which commences about the 1st of October, and continues until the severe cold drives it further South. When fat, the flesh is much esteemed. Another called,

Creek broad-bill, or **lesser scaup duck,** is closely allied to the preceding, but inferior in size; about the same quality and season. And still another broad-bill, called

Bastard broad-bill, ring-necked, or **tufted duck**, is much like the broad-bill, except the slate-colored markings on the wings. They are not at all plenty, but found scattering in the spring and fall months. They are considered good eating when found fat in the fall months.

Blue-winged teal.—This small duck, it is said, is the first of its tribe that returns to us in the autumn from the North. Their flesh is excellent, as they feed chiefly on vegetable food, when they become very fat. They are here in season in September, October, and November.

Green-winged teal.—This little duck, like the two preceding, is a fresh-water duck, and feeds upon the same kinds of food. If there is any difference in the eating qualities of these two teal, I should give it in favor of this little duck. It is quite common in our markets in September, October, November, and December, and scattering in January.

"A good shot" is noticed in the *Philadelphia Gazette*, October, 1822, which states that "Mr. Hart of the Lazaretto Inn, opposite Tinicum Island, on Friday afternoon (4th inst.), started sixteen teal, and, with one shot, killed fifteen of the number—a circumstance which is, perhaps, unprecedented in this species of sport. They all proved to be very fine and fat."

Pintail duck, winter duck, sprig-tail duck.—This duck is found more plentifully at the West than here, although we have them some seasons in large numbers in the fall months, and scattering in the first winter months. Its flesh is very savory and quite tender.

Gray duck, Welsh drake, German duck, or **gadwall.**—This is a beautiful and rather scarce duck here, but, when found, its flesh will give the epicure perfect satisfaction. The sportsman finds it a difficult bird to kill, on account of its expertness in diving; it is said, however, that it has been successfully domesticated.

Shoveller, or **spoonbill.**—This handsome duck is by many highly prized for the table, as its flesh is tender, juicy, and delicate. The bill of this bird is peculiarly shaped and very large, being about three inches in length, of a black color, and much the widest towards the extremity, which gives it somewhat the appearance of a shovel, and is, no doubt, the origin or cause of its name. The whole bird is beautifully marked, and is in season in April, and again in the fall months, but rather scarce.

Weaser, buff-breasted merganser, or **goosander.**—Three of these beautiful ducks I had the pleasure of seeing in the possession of Mr. Abraham Snediker, a dealer in game-birds, Washington Market, on the 22d of January, 1856. He said they went by the name of "weasers." They were very fat and heavy. Its flesh is best in the fall and winter; in the spring it becomes oily and rancid.

Harlequin duck.—This handsomely-marked duck is rarely seen in our markets. It is known by some sportsmen as the "Lord" and "Brass-eyed Whistler." It is highly spoken of for the table by those who have partaken of its flesh. The only one I have ever seen was among the collections of Mr. John G. Bell, the noted taxidermist, of New York, to whom I am much indebted for information in relation to some birds and game animals.

Whistler, or **golden-eye duck.**—This duck is called by many "Great-head," from its beautiful, rich, and thickly-crested head. In the month of November its flesh is considered fine, and of an agreeable flavor, as it then generally feeds in fresh water. At other seasons its flesh is strong and fishy.

Salt-water teal, or **ruddy duck**.—This appears to be a scarce duck here; but they are sometimes found here in the months of September and October, when it is fat and its flesh very savory.

Dipper, butter-ball, or **buffel-headed duck**.—This duck is found very fat throughout the winter, when their flesh is quite savory, but somewhat fishy, as its food consists of small fish. In season from October to March.

Old wife, old squaw, long-tailed duck.—This is a plentiful bird in our markets in the winter and spring seasons. The general character of its flesh is tough, strong, and fishy; but the young bird, when fat and properly cooked, is very fine eating. It is usually sold at low prices.

Squaw duck, shoal duck, or **eider duck**.—This is a scarce species here, as it belongs to a more northern latitude; but it is sometimes taken here in severe winters. Its flesh is quite oily and fishy, but its down is of a superior quality, and valuable.

One of this species was shot in 1859, in the Miscomet Pond, Manchester, N. H., upon whose tongue a large muscle had fixed with a firm grasp. "The duck had probably seized upon the open muscle for a meal, and his muscleship, not liking such treatment, had closed his shell upon the tongue of the duck, and was thus torn from his bed. The instinct of the duck had probably led him to seek the fresh water, for the purpose of making him relax his are boat going over some seaweed, and would soon get clear again. It not doing so, however, he examined the cause of the stoppage when the boat arrived at New York. After taking off the injection valve and a portion of the pipe, he found in it, tight up against the guard of the valve, a large (loon) duck, weighing seven pounds, which had been drawn into it by the force of the vacuum created by the engine. Mr. Vanderbilt thinks that the duck must have dived when the boat approached it, as, when it was found, its head was downward, with its back towards the bow of the vessel."* The duck was stuffed as a curiosity, and afterwards presented to Barnum for his Museum, but was burnt up, with many thousands of curiosities, many of which can never be replaced.

BIRDS CALLED GAME,

And others, which are found in our markets.

WILD TURKEY.

Wild turkey. This fine bird is occasionally found in our markets, in its season—generally in the months of November, December, and January. They are chiefly sent from Pennsylvania, and sometimes further west; arriving here in a frozen state. The flesh of a fine young wild turkey is darker, and considered more delicate,

* *Commercial Advertiser*, April 30, 1847.

NOTE.—For the above representation of the wild turkey, and three other illustrations used in this work, I am much indebted to the editors of the "American Agriculturist," whose volumes teem with useful and interesting matter of all kinds.—EDITOR.

more succulent, and better, or more gamey tasted than that of the tame turkey. They are in the best condition in the month of November. When found in our markets they have all their feathers on. The bill is short and thick, head small in proportion to the body; half of the neck (especially of the male bird) is covered with a naked, bluish skin, on which are a number of red, wart-like lumps. On the lower part of the neck, near the breast, is a fleshy substance, full of long, black, coarse hair. The feathers are of a glossy dark color, almost black, with bronze spots on the wings and tail. Their usual weight is from nine to twenty pounds, but I have read of their weighing above forty pounds. The "Commercial Advertiser," September 9, 1801, notices—"A remarkable large wild turkey, weighing twenty-two pounds dressed, was shot, on the 1st inst., by G. L. Barret, within a short distance of Mr. Scriba's seat, Newark, N. J." We also find in Archdale's North Carolina, that in the year 1707, was purchased "a wild turkey of forty pounds, for the value of two-pence, English value."

Partridge, pheasant, or **ruffed grouse**.—These excellent birds are found in great plenty in our markets, from about the 1st of September to the 1st of January; but they are best, especially the chicken partridge, in October and November, although they are found earlier and later. They are smuggled in by "poachers" and "pot-hunters," to avoid the proper "game laws," who then sell them under the name of owls, or some other fictitious name, to others, who also regard no law where taste is consulted or money to be made. These wholesome "game laws" were made not only for the protection of birds, etc., but also for the protection of our citizens, when such birds were out of season, and known to be unfit, unwholesome, and even poisonous. In very cold winters, and particularly heavy snow-storms, the partridge should not be eaten, as they are then deprived of their ordinary food, become thin, poor, and starved, and are forced to feed upon the leaves of the poisonous evergreens. They have been found with their crops filled with the green laurel, and in that state their flesh is considered unfit to be eaten. There are many instances of persons having been poisoned by eating them in these improper seasons.

It is said that we have no partridge or pheasant in this country, that they are all grouse; the reason they give is that they are all feathered on the legs below the termination of the thigh, and some quite to the toe-nails. The partridge, or ruffed grouse, is feathered below the knee; and the prairie hen, or pinnated grouse, as also the Canada grouse, is feathered down to the ankles. The flesh of the partridge is tender, fine flavored, and generally much esteemed.

Prairie-hen, heath-hen, prairie-chicken, or **pinnated grouse.**—This fine game-bird is somewhat the color, form, and size of the partridge, but more regularly marked, or barred, on the breast. The tail feathers are fan-like, but quite short and thick, and the neck has on each side a feathery mane hanging down. Prior to 1830, this bird was quite plentiful on Long Island, as well as deer, but since that period the grouse have entirely disappeared, and the few deer left are protected by law.

The "Suffolk Gazette," March 25, 1805, gives us some facts in a few verses of poetry:

"Here on Smith's Point we take our stand,
When free from toil's gymnastics,
Where death and lead go hand in hand,
Among the fowl at Mastic.

"The grouse, the pheasant, and the quail,
In turn we take by changes,
Or hunt the buck with flippant tail,
As thro' the wood he ranges."

The "Gazette," of the 16th November, 1821, also says: "A very fine pair of grouse, from Long Island, were offered in our markets for five dollars."

A few years later, 1826, I have known these birds to bring eight and ten dollars per pair; and thirty-five years after—

1861—I bought them as low as thirty-eight cents, and several times at fifty cents per pair. About the year 1827, a few pairs were occasionally brought from Pennsylvania, which Niblo would generally purchase, and then announce that he had secured a few pairs, when the epicures either purchased from him or eat his "game dinners," which were duly announced.

Within the last fifteen year's they have been brought from the West—Illinois, Iowa, Wisconsin, etc.—in large numbers, in fact, so large as to create a glut in the winter and early spring months. They begin to arrive in October, and continue until the month of April; usually brought in barrels and other packages in a frozen state. Their flesh is quite dark, but from a young fat bird it is excellent eating; and when purchasing select the heaviest as the best, at the same time try the feathers around the vent; if they pull easily they are apt to be too stale; the nose must also be brought into use to detect the least unpleasant smell.

Sharp-tailed grouse.—This fine bird is sometimes found with the prairie hen, in the quantities sent here. The color is nearly the same, but the markings are not so regular on the breast, being scolloped-like; the tail feathers are shorter, except two or more in the centre, which are slim and about one inch longer; and all except these are tipped with white. The feathers on the legs are also shorter. They are also excellent eating.

Spruce partridge or **Canada grouse.**—This is a rare bird and seldom or never found in our markets; but they are, nevertheless, sent or brought to our city in small numbers from Maine, Massachusetts, the Canadas, etc. The back feathers are of a very dark gray color, with a fan-tail, tipped with light brown, and the breast has several black and white feathers mottled together. The flesh is dark, and only fit to be eaten when it feeds on berries. In winter it feeds on leaves and plants, when the flesh becomes bitter, and has sometimes a strong, disagreeable taste, as if cooked in turpentine.

Willow grouse, or **white grouse.**—At first sight this very rare bird appears like a white pigeon, with its winter plumage on. In summer it changes to quite a brownish red, and mottled in the spring and fall months, but always with a few dark or black feathers on the sides of the tail. About the size of the partridge, but not so fine eating.

Cock of the plains, or **sage cock.**—This is another rare bird, and a great deal larger than the preceding birds; it is said that the average weight of a full-grown bird is above ten pounds. Travellers give it the name of sage cock in consequence of the taste of its flesh, from the fact that it feeds principally upon a species of wormwood or artemisia, which grows plentifully on the great Western plains. It is a beautiful large-breasted gray bird, especially the cock, when in full plumage.

California quail.—We occasionally meet with this pretty and somewhat smaller-bodied bird than our common quail, but quite as good eating. It is covered with a dark blue, and gray or steel-looking feathers, with white-tipped feathers interspersed on the lower part of the breast. The male and female have black plumes on their heads; the male's plume bends gracefully over towards its bill: it has also a line of white feathers, which look like a wreath hanging around its neck, commencing from the back of the eye and running down on the breast about one and a half inches. While on the subject of scarce game, it would be well to introduce here several species of English game which are sometimes found here.

English pheasant.—These beautiful long, and sharp-tailed birds I have often seen for sale in the markets, and they are also occasionally sent to friends here from the other side. I saw a very fine pair of fresh-killed birds—both cocks—on sale, in Jefferson Market, which were raised on an island near Newport, Rhode Island, by Robert L. Maitland, Esq., of New York. He succeeded in raising the first birds from eggs, which were carefully brought from

England, and from these he has produced several broods. The price asked for this pair was ten dollars; and they weighed four and three-quarter pounds. The body of these beautiful birds are larger and longer than our partridge, and the flesh from a fine young one is considered its equal, although I must say, the conclusion from my experience was different. We eat them here under disadvantages: generally birds of the finest plumage, and of course "old birds," are sent to us, or they have been too long killed, and this cause may apply to all the English game. Best in September and October.

English partridge.—This bird somewhat resembles our quail, but about half as large again; and is considered for the table next only to the preceding.

Black cock, or black grouse.—This black game-bird of England is almost as large as our partridge, and its flesh stands next in quality to the English partridge.

Red grouse, or moor cock.—This bird is smaller and not so highly esteemed as the preceding, and is not found here so plenty, but in the "old country" it has many friends.

English woodcock.—This bird is much like our woodcock, but much larger, and seldom found here.

The above are all the "English game" brought here, except hares and rabbits, which are larger and somewhat inferior eating than these species of America.

Quail.—These fine game-birds (known at the South as partridge) are generally found in great plenty in our markets, in their season, except in cases where the preceding winters have been unusually stormy, cold, and the ground lay covered with snow a long time, by which many quail perish under snow-banks, or from starvation. Many in this frozen state are picked up and sent to our markets for sale. This, however, generally occurs late in such seasons, or when the game laws are against their use. The years following these severe seasons will sometimes show great scarcity, and very high prices are charged for these fine birds.

Many thousands are brought from the far West in a frozen state. As soon as the frosty weather sets in, the great slaughter of Western game takes place, and hundreds of boxes of quail and other game are sent from Wisconsin, Illinois, Iowa, etc., for the eastern cities, where they arrive generally in good condition; however, those which are killed near by are to be preferred.

The flesh of the quail is white, tender, and delicate. One of the best-flavored game birds. Their size is about one-third of the partridge or ruffed grouse.

Woodcock.—This highly prized bird is in season from the first of July to the first of November, and brings the highest price of any bird brought to our markets. Its flesh is no doubt the most delicate eating of all the birds known, and generally found best in the month of October. The head of the woodcock is large, and somewhat triangular, with the eye fixed high in the head, a great distance from its long bill, the body about the size of the quail, and a fine bird will weigh half a pound.

The largest woodcock found on record, was shot by Richard Tetley, in Washington township, New Jersey, in 1859. It measured in length from tail to beak, twelve and a quarter inches; width around the breast ten and a half inches; over the back three inches; height seven and three quarter inches; weight, one pound one ounce.

English snipe, common snipe, or **Wilson's snipe.**—These birds, though small, are excellent eating when in condition. The richness and delicacy of their flesh is considered second only to that of the woodcock. Their bills are about twice as long as their head, neck short, legs slender, feet bluish gray, feathers brownish black on the back, below grayish yellow, and a much smaller bird than the woodcock. They are found in our markets from about the 20th of March to the 20th of April; then again, in (small numbers), in October.

Mr. J. T. Brownwere while hunting for snipe in a swamp, about three-quarters of a mile from Bushwick Ferry, L. I., in the month of September, 1815, met with a Southern stranger, in the shape of an alligator. The press says: "While in the act of levelling his piece at a flock of snipes, he discovered the alligator within a few yards of the spot where he stood, making towards him, when he instantly lodged the contents of the piece in its throat and killed it."

Robin snipe, or **red-breasted sandpiper.**—This red-breasted snipe is well known, and its flesh highly prized by many of our epicures as a great delicacy. Their season commences in April and May, and again in August, September, and October. The latter month they are considered best, and are then often known as *white-robin snipe,* in consequence of the light change of their feathers.

Gray plover, grass, field, or **upland plover.**—The proper name of this much-esteemed game-bird appears to be Bartram's sandpiper. They are generally found in our markets in June, July, August, and September. It is considered best and most highly prized in the two latter months.

Frost plover, greenback or **golden plover.**—This delicious bird is known among many sportsmen and others as plover and frost-bird. They sometimes appear in numbers in the months of April and May, and then again in September and October, when they are in fine condition, their flesh well flavored, and sell quickly at high prices.

Ring plover, or **ring-neck.**—This small bird appears quite numerous some seasons in our markets. Many are killed in the fall months, especially in September and October, when they are considered best for the table.

Beach bird, or **piping plover.**—This bird is found scattering in season from April to October. In the months of September and October it gets very fat, when its flesh is excellent.

Brant bird, horse-foot snipe, or **turnstone.**—This fine bird is much sought after by gunners, and is often found in large numbers for sale. It makes its appearance early in the months of April and May, and again in September and October, when it is in fair condition and much esteemed.

Dowitcher, quail snipe, or **red-breasted snipe.**—This bird appears in our markets in large numbers when in their season. They begin to show themselves in April and May, and then again from the 15th to the 20th of July, and so continue until the end of October. It appears in the best condition in September and October, but its flesh is not considered a delicacy, although well flavored.

Bull-headed or **beetle-headed plover, black-bellied** or **whistling plover.**—This bird is generally quite plenty in our markets early in May, and then again in August and September. In the two latter months it is in a very fat condition, and its flesh quite well flavored.

Kildeer plover.—This bird is generally known as kildeer. It is sometimes found in our markets in the months of July, August, and September, and when in good condition its flesh is considered good eating.

Sanderling, or **ruddy plover.**—This small bird may be had in May, and then again in August, September, October, and November. It is generally fat and fine in the fall months, when it is much esteemed.

Marlin, or **great marbled godwit.**—This large bird also enjoys the name of red curlew by some gunners. The flesh is quite tender and juicy, when in good condition. In season in May, and again from August to November.

Ring-tailed marlin, or **Hudsonian godwit.**—This bird is not so plentiful as the preceding, but about the same quality for the table. The season the same.

Black-breasted snipe, winter snipe, or **red-backed sandpiper.**—This small bird is sometimes found in great plenty. It first appears in our markets in April and May, and then again in September and October, when some give it the name of winter snipe, dunlin, ox-bird, and purries. It is then usually very fat, and excellent eating.

Buff-breasted sandpiper.—This bird is rather

scarce, although a few are sometimes found tied up with the meadow snipe, for sale. Found in August and September, but more plenty, very fat and excellent, in October and November.

Long-legged sandpiper.—This long-legged bird is not at all common in our markets, although some seasons several little "bunches" appear in the months of July, August, and September.

Meadow snipe, or **pectoral sandpiper.**—This excellent bird is known by several different names in various places. Giraud says it is termed by bay-men *short-neck;* on the coast of New Jersey, *fat-bird;* and in Pennsylvania *jack-snipe.* A few are found in our markets in the month of May, but more plenty in August and September, and in a very fat condition in the months of October and November, when it is much sought after.

Yellow-legged snipe, or **yellow-shank tattler.**—This is a common snipe, and well known to our sportsmen. Some seasons they are quite plenty in April and May, and then again in August and September. I have shot them near Kingsbridge above thirty years ago, where they were occasionally found in large numbers. They are best in the fall months, but are not much esteemed for the table.

Greater yellow-legged snipe, or **tell-tale tattler.**—These birds are not so numerous as the preceding, but found generally earlier in the spring and later in the fall months. Their flesh is well flavored, and more esteemed in October and November.

Willet, or **semi-palmated tattler.**—This bird appears early in the month of May, when it is considered a very fair bird for the table, but a more pleasing game-bird to the sportsman in the month of October. Many of this and other species are brought from the South in the oyster and other sailing vessels.

Blue-stocking, or **American avocet.**—This blue-legged bird is also known on the Southern coast as the *law-*

yer, from whence it is occasionally brought by the coasting vessels. A few also are found here, brought from Long Island. They are not much esteemed for the table. In season early in May, and then again in October and November.

Lawyer, or **black-necked stilt.**—Although this is a scarce bird here, yet they are, as the preceding, brought here in the oyster and fishing vessels, and, like all other rare or scarce species, are quickly bought up, if at all in a good condition, for the taxidermist or others. The season same as preceding.

Long-billed curlew, or **sickle-billed curlew.**—This long arch-billed bird is often found in our markets in the spring and autumn months. But, like the short-billed, or jack curlew, their flesh is considered indifferent eating. In the fall months they are quite fat, but are not even then very well flavored.

In 1838 Daniel Fordham, of Southampton, Long Island, killed a curlew, which measured from the tip of the bill to the tip of the tail two feet three inches; from the tip of its wings, three feet five inches; length of the bill eight inches, and weighed one pound fourteen ounces.

Futes, or **Esquimaux curlew.**—This bird in the Eastern States is called the *doe-bird*. The flesh when in a fat condition is well flavored, and the best of all the curlews.

Flood gull, or **oyster catcher.**—This bird, although scarce, finds its way to our markets in the summer months. One of our oldest dealers (Snedicor) calls this bird *flat-foot snipe*, and also says that its flesh has not many admirers. Many agree with him on this point. Its flesh is dark-colored, and quite strong and unpalatable.

Seaside finch, or **gray shore-finch.**—"Giraud" says: "This species is familiar to all our sportsmen who practise bay-shooting." It is sometimes found in our markets in the summer months, but its flesh is quite indifferent eating, being somewhat fishy.

Shore lark, or **horned lark**.—This bird is also known by some as the sky-lark. "Wilson" says: "They are frequently brought to Philadelphia markets. They are generally very fat, and are considered excellent eating." In season, though scattering, nearly all the winter months, in some of our markets.

Brown lark.—This species of the lark is not quite so plenty here as the preceding. Generally found here in the months of March, April, and May, when their flesh is said to be equal to the shore lark.

Semi-palmated sandpiper.—These small birds generally appear in small quantities in our markets in the months of April and May, and then again quite plenty in September and October, when it is in fine condition and delicate eating.

Ox-eyes, little, or **Wilson's sandpiper**.—This is a still smaller bird than the preceding, but more plentiful, and much better in flavor and juiciness. They are also best in the months of September and October.

Schinz's sandpiper.—This bird, like many others, is no doubt scarce, but is occasionally found with others of its species in our markets along in the summer and autumn months.

Wood tattler, green-rump tattler, or **solitary tattler**.—This pretty, trim bird is sometimes found, but generally in small quantities, in our market. It is said to be delicate eating. In season in May, and again in August and September.

Teeter-tail, tilt-up, or **spotted sandpiper**.—These little birds are seldom brought to our markets in large quantities, although they remain on our shores and streams from April to November. They are a delicate morsel, when fat, which is in the fall months.

Sora, English, or **Carolina rail**.—This trim-looking bird is seldom seen for sale, although it is much sought after, and some seasons it is found quite plenty by sportsmen in New Jersey. Its flesh is of an exceedingly delicate flavor, and much enjoyed by epicures. In the best condition in September.

Meadow hen, or **clapper rail**.—This bird is sometimes found in plenty in our markets, but not much sought after, although when in good condition it is very well tasted and tender. In the month of May it is generally quite poor and not well flavored, but usually fine and fat in the months of September and October. Their eggs are more highly prized by some than their flesh, and thousands are found in the salt grass.

Virginia rail, **fresh-water marsh**, or **little mud-hen.** Occasionally this bird appears in our markets in the months of April and May, and then again in September and October; its flesh is not very delicate, but considered best in the fall months.

Blue water-hen—Virginia water-hen.—This water bird (it is said) is brought principally from Virginia to our markets. I have seen in Fulton Market (December 31st, 1855) several of these birds in very good condition, which were called Virginia water-hens. Their color was of a dirty blue, the tips of the centre feathers of the wings were white, as also the under side of the tail feathers; legs dark green, and about half web-footed; the head had the appearance of a young pullet.

American coot, **hen-bill**, **mud-hen.**—This bird is often killed by sportsmen, but seldom sent to market, as it is quite inferior eating. It is, however, sometimes seen there, in the fall months, for sale.

Black gull, or **black tern.**—This species, as well as many of its varieties, are occasionally found in our markets for sale: I should suppose not so much for the table as for the collectors. The flesh of the black tern is considered better tasted and more palatable than any of its species, in consequence of its food being collected near the fresh-water streams. "Giraud" says: "The flesh of the gulls and terns not being considered suitable for the table, they escape the torture to which birds of a more delicately-flavored flesh are subjected. Still, they are not entirely exempt from persecution, as there are those who fancy a gull's egg an exceedingly delicate morsel.

"The Florida Keys, which are the breeding-places for great numbers of gulls and terns of various species, are resorted to annually by 'eggers'—persons who make a business of collecting the eggs of these marine birds"—and those known to be fresh are taken to the West Indies, where they are by many highly esteemed. "The fishermen, I am told, make free use of the eggs; those of some species, they say, are exceedingly well tasted, affording palatable and nourishing fare."

Great blue heron or **crane.**—This long-legged, long-necked, and long-billed bird, I have often seen when brought to our markets, but presumed it was brought more for the curious than for the table. Although a large, awkward, coarse bird, it is said by some of my friends, that when young and in good condition its flesh is well flavored, and not coarse, as its appearance would indicate. Best in the fall months.

"SINGULAR PHENOMENON.—A gentleman residing at Hoboken, N. J., informs us that great numbers of woodcock have been destroyed by a flock of cranes, which have infested that neighborhood during the present week. For the veracity of the gentleman from whom this intelligence is derived, we will vouch."—"Commercial Advertiser," June 20, 1807.

Quawk, night heron, or **black-crowned heron.**—Although this bird is seldom seen in our markets, yet it is often shot and eaten, and I believe much better for the table than the preceding, as it feeds more upon frogs, mice, etc., or I may say, that it lives more upon "fresh meat than on salt." Many years ago, they appeared to be more plenty than they are at present.

White poke, snowy heron, or **white-crested heron.**—This also is a scarce bird in our markets, like many other beautiful, rare, or scarce birds, which are previously engaged and kept for those who are daily looking after them for their collections. The young are best when in condition, in the fall months.

Green heron, schyte-poke, or **fly-up-the-creek.**—This is a common bird in most of our creeks, and sometimes finds its way to our markets; its flesh, when in condition, is very well flavored, and considered best in the fall months.

A friend of mine on a hunting excursion in New Jersey, had shot several of these birds along the edge of one of the fresh-water streams, which he found were very fine and fat, and he *bagged* them; he, however, came suddenly upon one which did not take wing, but sat quite motionless: he advanced towards it with the expectation of finding it a dead bird, *set-up;* he saw it move and he shot it: when he picked it up, he found that it must have been in the act of swallowing a cat-fish, when its two sharp horns had got crossways in its throat, where the points had run through each side; which, no doubt, had closed its throat from all other food, and when thus found, it was so poor and exhausted that it could not fly. He informs me that the taste of their flesh is much like that of the meadow lark, Indian hen, American bittern, or look-up. This bird, though common, is not numerous. On the sea-coast of New Jersey, it is known by the name of *dunkadoo*, a word probably imitative of its common note. It is said to be excellent eating when fat, and is generally so in the fall months.

Wild pigeon, or **passenger pigeon,** and **wild squabs.**—These numerous birds are found in our markets, both alive and dead, very plenty, and generally cheap in the latter part of September and October; they are also found in less numbers through the winter months.

Great numbers are taken alive with nets, cooped up for several weeks, and fed with grain until fat, then brought to our markets as the prices advance; while those that are brought dead have been shot from off the "spar," and sent here at the time of their "flying," which takes place generally in the month of March, when they are going north, and then again in the fall, about the 15th to the 25th September, when they leave for the Southern climate. Large numbers of the old birds and squabs are sent here from the "West," where they are killed or taken alive at their "roosts." The wild squabs, when fat and fresh, are very delicate eating; the cooped bird is also good, the flesh being rather dry; but a poor wild-pigeon is very indifferent eating, even if well and properly cooked. They are found best in the months of September and October.

I have often enjoyed the sport of taking the wild pigeon, both with the "net" and shooting them from the "spar." A few days previous to their usual flight, a "bough-house" is made by placing cedar bushes in the ground, in a circle, large enough for one or two persons to go behind or out of sight. A "floor" is then prepared by levelling the ground about twenty feet square—say from fifteen to twenty yards from the "bough-house;" then, on the left side of this "floor," four crotched sticks are driven in the ground; the two nearest the "bough-house" are placed quite close together, or about one foot apart, and the other two some fifteen feet further off, and some three or four feet apart, ranging a little higher than the two first, on a line from the "bough-house," when two poles, of about twenty feet long, are placed on these crotched sticks. The further end of the poles should set high enough, that when the pigeons alight they can be all seen from the "bough-house." A pigeon-stool is then driven in the ground near the "floor," but so as not to be covered when the "net" is sprung. The "stool-pigeon," is blinded by drawing the under eyelids over the eyeballs, so that the bird cannot see, and his feet and legs tied with a woollen slip-noose fast to the stool, when he is ready for action. A "flyer-pigeon" (and sometimes two or three), are also blinded, and their legs tied to a fishing-line, sixty or one hundred feet long. The net being large enough to cover the "floor," is fastened to a strong rope, one end being fastened in the "bough-house," and the other end carried beyond the "floor," also firmly fastened to a stake. The net is drawn back from off the "floor," and fastened with a trap, when, by a strong pull on the rope in the "bough-house," the net flies quickly over, and covers the whole "floor." This ground-floor is covered with buckwheat or rye-grain.

As soon as a flock of pigeons is discovered at a distance of five or six hundred yards, the "flyer" is thrown up, and flies to the length of his line, then hovers down to the ground, as if in the act of alighting. By this time, the flock being within one hundred yards, the "stool-pigeon" is gently raised by means of a line leading into the "bough-house," then suddenly let down, which causes him to flutter as if also alighting. This is repeated until the flock is attracted, and begins to sail around the "bough-house," when the "stool-pigeon" is left quiet, and the flock discovers the grain.

If the flock pitches on the "floor," a strong pull and they are covered; then haste to the net, and, if a large flock, stones must be placed on the edges to keep them down, or they would raise it up and escape. They are then taken out as quickly as possible, ready for another flock, placed in large flat baskets prepared for this business. If, however, they are a small flock—say from thirty to fifty—and they alight on the spars, then the gun is brought to bear, which sometimes sweeps them all off. I have known fifty killed at *one shot*. I chanced to kill seventeen with one barrel, and thought I was doing considerable in that line.

The largest number taken in a net, I ever heard or read of, was noticed in one of the Detroit papers—the *Owosso American*—in the year 1858, which says: "Mr. Merritt Richardson, living a couple of miles south of this village, on Wednesday last, caught, at one haul of his net, *six hundred and forty-eight* wild-pigeons."

In the seasons of "great flights," thousands are brought to our markets; and, in "olden time," above one hundred years ago, they were sold very cheap. I find, from the

New York *Mercury*—"One day last week, upwards of seventy-five thousand pigeons were brought to the market, insomuch that fifty were sold for one shilling."

The *Boston Weekly Post-boy*, May 2, 1771, says: "The great numbers of pigeons that have been brought to our market within the fortnight past has greatly reduced the prices of all kinds of provisions. It is said that nearly fifty thousand were sold in one day."

Turtle-dove, or **Carolina pigeon**.—This bird is smaller, but much like the wild-pigeon in general appearance. Its flesh is much superior to that bird, and found best in the months of August and September. They are seldom found for sale in our markets, except in a living state.

Robin, or **red-breasted thrush**.—Large numbers of these well-known birds are found in our markets, and thousands are also shot by *all sorts* of sportsmen, in the months of September and October, when they are fat and delicate eating. Again, in the spring months, they return to the North, when some are guilty of shooting them, who ought not to be encouraged by any one purchasing them, as they are then "pairing off." I, however, think that these birds are more useful to man living than dead.

Meadow-larks, or **meadow-starlings**.—These yellow-breasted birds I have often shot in the neighborhood of the present Twenty-fourth street, New York (and, I believe, lower down), both on the North and East River sides of New York, many years ago. The white flesh of a young fat bird is almost as good as the quail, but not so plump or large. The feathers on the back and head are a sort of grayish-brown, while those on the breast and under are yellow, spotted with black. In the fall months they are in the best condition.

High-hole, **clape**, or **golden-winged woodpecker**.—This handsome bird is common in our markets in the fall months, when it is fat, and its flesh quite savory, but not so tender as the robin. Along in the month of

June, I have seen the squab high-hole in our markets, looking like a very small morsel of food, which perhaps a sick person might relish; but as for the nourishment, I should think there was a very small quantity. In fact, it is a cruelty to take such birds from their nests, without it was to save human life. These birds are fond of wild cherries, pepperage, or gumberries; from the trees which the latter grow on I have shot hundreds—sometimes as many as twenty to thirty from off one tree, in an afternoon.

Red headed woodpecker.—This is not a common bird, but is often killed in our State, and is quite as good eating as the golden-winged woodpecker, but smaller.

Oriole, or **Baltimore oriole**.—Although this beautiful bird is often seen on sale, yet they should never be purchased except for a collection. They are of so much value to the fruit-grower or farmer that they should never allow them to be shot on their premises, as I am told they are the only bird that eats the destructive curculio, besides many other fruit-destroyers. Their nests are very artistically formed, being somewhat like a pocket hanging down from the limbs of trees. They are beautiful as well as valuable.

White snow-bird, **ortolans**, or **snow bunting.**—Its season with us begins with December, but is much fatter and better in January and February, when its flesh is much admired by the epicure.

Lark and **lark bunting.**—Giraud, in his "Birds of Long Island," says: "In the winter of 1838, several specimens of this bird were observed in the New York markets, having been shot on Long Island." No doubt, its flesh is equal to the preceding, being of the same species and habits.

Blackbirds.—There appears to be four species of these birds which are occasionally found in our markets—the cow-bunting, crow, red-wing, and the rusty graole—all somewhat different in their colors and nature, but all are called blackbirds. One curious fact in relation to the cow-bunting is, that it never builds a nest or hatches its eggs. It lays its eggs in the nests of other birds, who hatch out the young and feed them. They are small, but sweet-fleshed. Many are found along about the first of April, then again in September, October, and November, when they come from the North in very large flocks, from which great numbers are killed at a single shot.

Reed-birds, rice-buntings, rice-birds, or **bob-alinks.**—These little fat birds, when brought dead and picked to market, are usually called reed-birds, of which large quantities are sold, tied up in bunches, like so many pieces of fat strung together. Large numbers are found in the Philadelphia markets, as it is quite near their feeding-places. They are commonly known in Philadelphia as reed-birds, in Charleston as rice-birds, and North, in the summer months, when alive, as the bobalink (see *bobalink*). For the table they are best in September and October, when they have many admirers among epicures.

King-fisher, or **belted king-fisher.**—This blue-crested bird I have seen in our markets occasionally, but it is not much thought of as human food. Its flesh is quite dry and tough, and generally strong, as it feeds principally on fish. The young birds are best. I think one of the fattest birds I ever saw was one of this species. They are more valued for collections.

Snow-birds.—These birds are generally found in our markets in October and November, and sometimes scattering later. When fat it is considered excellent eating.

Blue-jay.—This handsome blue-bird is often seen in the fall months, tied up with robins, etc., in strings, for sale. The head is tufted and quite large in proportion to its body. Flesh not so well flavored as the robin. It is found in our markets sometimes as late as December.

Bobalinks (see also reed or rice birds).—This bird, under the name of bobalink, is frequently exposed for sale, alive in cages, in our markets, but seldom killed for the table until they are found feeding on the "wild rice" at the

South, under a new coat and name, when they are fat and fine.

English robins, cedar-birds, yellow-tails, cherry-birds, chatterers, quaker-birds, top-knots, crown-birds, spider-birds, cedar wax-wings, etc.—These small birds are known by more names than any other birds in the country. They are occasionally found in large numbers in our markets. Their flesh is but a morsel of delicate eating, and only fit to eat in the fall months. But I think they should never be killed, as they destroy more destructive worms than perhaps any bird in existence. In fact, all such worm-destroyers should not only be protected by a stringent law, but every person should be so instructed that no law would be required for their protection. The few cherries they eat are generally wormy.

Night-hawk.—This common bird is often heard, with its harsh, jarring noise, over our city in the spring and summer months, flying and dashing through the air in chase after the winged insects, upon which it feeds. Its flesh is very delicate eating.

Cat-bird, or **black-capped thrush.**—This little bird is sometimes found, tied up with a string of small birds, in the summer and autumn months. Its body is very small, but the flesh is sweet and good.

Brown thrasher.—This small, brown-backed bird is not quite so large as the robin, and is often found tied up in strings with other birds and sold in the markets. Its flesh is delicate, what there is of it; but its live body is *larger* to the farmer, who ought to protect it.

Wood-robin or **hermit-thrush.**—This secluded little brown bird I have, when a boy, often shot, mistaking it for the female robin, in the wood, among the thickets. Its flesh is sweet, but not worth a charge of powder, even to a starving man.

Chewink, ground-robin or **towhie bunting.**—These birds are scarcely ever found in our markets, yet, when fat, its flesh is very delicate, and highly esteemed, so they say, in Louisiana, where it is called *grasset.*

Pine grosbeak or **bull-finch.**—These are rather scarce birds, but have been known very plenty some years. They are, when found here, in season in the months of December and January. Their flesh is very sweet, much like that of the robin, and about the same size.

Cuckoo or **cow-bird.**—There are two species of this bird—the *yellow-billed* and the *black-billed*—both of a brownish cast, with a long tail. They are sometimes found tied up with other small birds, for sale. Their flesh is quite sweet, but rather a small body to so large-looking a bird.

Purple finch, or **crested purple finch.**—These little birds are sometimes found in our markets. Although small, their flesh is very delicate when in good condition. Best in the fall and early winter months.

Yellow-birds — American goldfinch. — These beautiful little yellow-birds, with black head, wings, and tail, are often found alive, caged, and for sale, in our markets. The male bird is always the songster, and changes its color in winter to that similar to the female.

Eagles.—This noble bird is never seen in our markets for sale as eatable food, but I have seen them there for sale, caged alive. "Charlevoix" says that "his people threw down, near Oswego, an eagle's nest, which was composed of a cartload of wood, and that it contained two eaglets, which were not as yet feathered"—that "they were eaten, and made very good food." They are often killed on Long Island, both the gray and bald-head species, and brought to our markets for the taxidermist.

BIRDS WHICH ARE SELDOM OR NEVER USED HERE AS HUMAN FOOD.

The following are some of the birds which are seldom found here, being exceedingly rare or scarce, but are used for the table in other climates and regions; others, again, which are seldom or never eaten, except in extreme cases, either the flesh being too strong, tough, fishy, small, or otherwise considered unfit for human food :

Eagles, hawks, goshawks, falcons, harriers, vultures or buzzards, ravens, crows, gulls, terns, auks, puffins or shear-waters, jagers, guillenots, grebes, herons or egrets, cross-bills, cormorants, gannets, petrels, sea-doves, ibis, skimmers, grosbeaks, shrikes, gallinules, tonagus, orioles, mocking-birds, whip-poor-wills, blue-birds, martens, swallows, with several species of wild ducks, snipe, plover, sandpipers, buntings, larks, woodpeckers, thrushes, etc., etc.

An anecdote is found of Prince Achille Murat, when he resided in Florida (1847), where he often engaged in hunting, and it was said that nothing "that swims the water, flies the air, crawls or walks the earth, but that he served up on his table. Alligator steaks, frog shins, boiled owls, and roasted crows are found palatable ; but there is one animal that the Prince don't like. The buzzard is one too many for him. He says : 'I try him fried, I try him roasted, I try him stewed, and I make soup of him, but the buzzard is not goot. I have no prejudice against him, but I cook him every way, and then I no like him.' "

FISH.

THE fish-markets of the city of New York and other cities, have become generally known as the depots for receiving all the known varieties of the rarest and choicest fish available for the table. We refer both to the salt and fresh water fish of our coast and inland waters—of fish living altogether in salt water, and those living in fresh, as well as those living in both ; and others still, which at different seasons of the year, exist both in salt and fresh water, such as the salmon, shad, smelt, etc.

The flesh of these fish is eatable, but some species are of a coarse, dry, ill-flavored and indigestible character, although they are not considered poisonous unless they have become so from feeding on poisonous or deleterious substances.

The fresh-water fish appear to be more generally edible; the salt-water fish, however, is more nourishing and palatable. Neither should be eaten when out of season, as they are considered best a short time before spawning, and unfit to be eaten immediately after.

Under the Levitical laws, we find it ordained, that fish with scales present the evidence that they are clean, and are fit to be eaten, while those fish deficient of scales, are placed by the same laws as being unclean, and therefore unfit for food. (No lobsters, crabs, oysters, clams, or other shell-fish are used by them.) This law, with the strict Jews, is observed to this day.

There are some few people who, like the Jews, discard numbers of fish, as well as animals, from the catalogue of edibles, who in time, no doubt, will consider these objectionable fish, etc., to be absolutely necessary to an increased and better informed population.

In the several histories of fish, the authors do not agree in many instances, especially in the varieties, as some appear to have a desire to create new genera, or of multiplying species, which causes much confusion in arranging them under their proper names. No doubt this cause for increasing many of the varieties of the same species, arises from sex, age, the different sea-shores, rivers, lakes, streams, and changes produced especially by what they feed upon.

Large numbers of salt-water fish are brought to our markets from a great distance, principally by steamboats and fishing-vessels; many of the latter are called smacks, which are provided with "fish-wells," placed in the centre of the vessel, by which the sea-water can flow in and out through a latticed bottom, and thus preserve the fish alive and fresh.

These fishing-smacks originated in New York more than a century ago, as will appear from an article taken from an old newspaper, which says: "The plan of bringing live fish to the New York markets, originated with a society of gentlemen, who clubbed together to fit the smack "Amherst" for that purpose."

Then we find in the *Gazette*, July 25, 1763: "Saturday last (23d) was launched the Amherst, fishing-smack, fully rigged and fit for sea. There was a great concourse of people to see her off. She sails for the 'Banks' this day."

The same paper, in the following year (January 30), introduces the following lines in relation to this first fishing-smack here:

"Since on our banks the porgey's found,
A *smack* they've built to try the ground;
But when they have them on the dish,
Deduction finds sauce for the fish;
Plumb-pudding and roast-beef also,
Come from our purses tho' they're low;
And Princess Bay oft brought us up,
By which in plenty now they sup:
But now the case is altered quite.
We bid you, gentlemen, good-night."

The example of these gentlemen induced many others to engage and fit out other vessels for this purpose, which caused the supplies to become so plentiful as to cause the Amherst company to discontinue, and sell their vessel.

The Legislature, also, to encourage the "fishery" on our coast, passed an act in 1773, and introduced it to the public through the following source:

"CHAMBER OF COMMERCE,
New York, 6th of April, 1773.

"*Whereas*, The Legislature of the Province of New York have, by an act passed the 8th of March last, directed that the overplus of the duty of excise, collected in the said city and county, be annually paid for the first year next after the passing of the said act, to the treasurer of the Corporation of the Chamber of Commerce, to be, by the said corporation, disposed of in such manner as they shall think most proper, for encouraging a fishery on the sea-coast, for the better supplying the markets in the city of New York.

"In order, therefore, that the intention of the Legislature may be fully answered, and the inhabitants of this city receive the benefit of so laudable a donation, it is resolved and agreed that the following premiums, hereafter mentioned, be paid by the treasurer of the Chamber of Commerce, to such persons who, upon application and due proof, made to the satisfaction of the Chamber, shall be entitled to the same, viz.:

	£	s.	d.
To the owners and crew of any one boat or vessel who shall supply this market with the greatest quantity of fish taken on the coast with trawl nets (ray and skate excepted), from the 1st of May, 1773, to the 1st of May, 1774, the sum of	£40	0s.	0d.
To the same—with the same exceptions—the next greater quantity	30	0	0
To the same—greatest quantity of live codfish, from the 1st of November. 1773, to the 1st of May, 1774	30	0	0
To the same—and the same time—next greatest quantity of live codfish	20	0	0
The greatest quantity of live sheeps-head, from the 1st of May, 1773, to the 1st of May, 1774	20	0	0
The next greatest quantity of live sheeps-head	15	0	0
The greatest quantity of fresh mackerel, etc.	10	0	0"

In 1783, a curious article on fish originated on the many varieties found in the New York markets at that period, which appears in *Gaines' Mercury*, May 26th, and reads as follows: "One day last week our market afforded us no less than twenty-three different sorts of fresh fish." This brought out in the *Royal Gazette*, two days after, the following: "Mr. Rivington having seen in yesterday's paper that there were twenty-three kinds of fresh fish in the market, I want to know if it will be below the dignity of your royal typographic pen to announce to us their *christened names.* And while you, a very *droll fish*, are *swimmingly* enjoying your post, meridian tide, Goody Burton, or Barley Falernian, you may also tell us which of them will make the best prelude to the noted *Après le poisson toujours*, for much good it has often done to many of the old friends of——*De Grege Epicuri, Porcus.*"

In the next edition of the *Gazette* (31st inst.) appears the following answer: "The *Royal Gazette* of the 27th inst., having ushered into the public to request to you the first—As Mr. Gaine has not favored us with the names of the several sorts of fish which appeared in the market at the same time, we can only judge from conjecture what they were. From often walking through the market, I will venture to offer them conjecture with respect to some of them at least.

"But your correspondent must not expect that I am to announce the Christian names of all of them, as for instance the *jew-fish;* this, we are to suppose, has never had any such: and indeed, although the whole tribe of *pisces* have water dashed in their faces every instant of their lives, yet it will be hard to determine which of them have Christian names. With respect to some of them suspicions may arise, as the *tom-cod*, which being but a diminutive fish, is usually called the *tommy cod;* and there is another called the *jack*, and a third named the *skip-jack*, but the latter I suspect to be the same fish as the *sturgeon*, for as in the improvement of the English language (which probably will not prevail much longer on this continent, and has been much adulterated) it is not impossible that the name of this fish may have been *stir john;* or, indeed, another idea arises, that it originally might have been *sir john*, for why should a loin of beef be knighted in preference to a sprightly fish?

"There are other sorts brought occasionally to the markets, such as *pikes*, *pipers*, *sword* and *drum fish*, but these are found in greater quantities on the area before the bridewell at six or seven o'clock in the evening; and with respect to the *gudgeon* and *sheeps-head*, they are to be met with at every corner of a street, and *black-fish* are not uncommon.

"But among the noted number twenty three, that appeared in market at the same time, we must not omit the probability, at least, of the printer of the *Royal Gazette*, who is allowed by the writer of the queries to be a *droll* fish, and this writer himself, who appears to be a *queer* fish, being of the number, for as Porcus, according to the Linnean system, is a generical term for all sorts of hogs, that part of his signature may be supposed a *sea-hog.*

"With respect to the latter query, which will make the best prelude to the noted *après le poisson toujours*, I shall only answer, *Chacun à son goût. In copia cantus.*"

Twenty years after the above articles appeared, a prepared list of some fifty-six different varieties of fish, then commonly known in the New York markets, are found noticed, some of which appear to possess names not common at the present day. They are found below, alphabetically arranged, with their original orthography preserved.

*Alewives.
Bass or rock-fish.
Black-fish.
*Bregals.
Cat-fish.
Chub.
Clams.
Cod.
Crabs.
*Dog-fish.
Drum-fish.
Eels.
*Fiddlers, plenty.
Flounders.
Gar-fish.
Green turtle.
Haddock.
Hollebut.
Herring.
*Killey-fish.
King-fish.
Lamper-eels.
Lobsters.
Logger-heads (turtle) plenty.
Mackerel.
Mullet.
Muscles.
Oysters.
Pike.
*Pissers (clams).
*Pollock.
Porgeys.
*Prawns.
*Ray.
Salmon.
*Scollops.
*Sculping.
*Sea-bass.
Shad.
Sheeps-head.
Shrimps.
Skate.
Smelts.
Snails or conk.
Snapping-turtle.
*Soles.
Spanish mackerel.
Sturgeon.
*Suckers.
Sun-fish.
Tarrapins.
*Tom cod.
Trout.
Weak-fish.
White perch.
Yellow perch.

—*Daily Advertiser*, Jan'y 9, 1804.

An anxious Philadelphian, who wished to exhibit a greater variety than is noticed above, writes to the editors of the *Philadelphia True American*, and says: "Seeing a list of fish that is brought to the New York markets, I wish to lay before the public a list brought to the Philadelphia market;" and then names over all the above except those marked with a star, but in their places adds the following (which numbers seventy varieties—fourteen more than those found in New York).

Bass (not rock-bass).	Horse mackerel.	Sea trout.
Black backs.	Manhaden.	Sea eels.
Black perch.	Minees.	Sharks.
Brown-back turtle.	Mud shad.	Stink-pots (turtle).
Carpp.	Mud wallepers.	Suckers.
Dolphin.	Ohio cat (fish).	Susquehanna turtle.
Gudgeons.	Oldwives (perch).	Swallow-tailed cat-fish.
Hawks-bill (turtle).	Roach.	Water-turtle, red belly.
Hickory shad.	Salmon trout.	White-bellied cat-fish.—
Horn-fish.	Sea cat.	*Chronicle Express*, Jan'y 17, 1804.

In the above lists, but very few of the fine fresh-water fish are found, and those only of the small or poor kinds; and it is only a few years since a regular business has been established by which the many excellent varieties from the large Western lakes, rivers, etc., have—in their proper season—been found on the tables of the citizens of either New York, Boston, Philadelphia, or Brooklyn. It was thought that when the Great Canal was finished, we should be well supplied, or so it is noticed in a letter dated in 1820: "The fish-markets of the cities on the Hudson will be greatly improved by the canal. New species will be brought down in ice, in a perfect state of preservation, and the epicure of the South will be treated with new and untried dishes of the highest flavor."

The canal, however, did not do as much business in the fresh-fish line as it did in bringing thousands of barrels of salted fish, which were then known as lake trout or salmon, pickerel, white fish, and sisquette, which produced very high prices. There were, however, an occasional lot of fresh fish, and perhaps the first brought for our markets was thus noticed by the press, September 14, 1826: "About five hundred weight of fresh salmon (*lake salmon*) from Lake Ontario, was exhibited for sale in Fulton Market this morning. They were conveyed to this city *via* the Erie Canal, packed in ice and in fine order. Should they command a price that would warrant the expense of transportation, and yield a profit, they can be brought to our market every week during the season. They were sold for thirty-one cents a pound to the first purchaser."

In this manner small lots were received—only, however, occasionally; but when the railroads were established, a more regular supply of the fine fresh fish took place, especially in the cold season, when fish were sold at high prices, and they could be carried in a frozen state; since which, additional facilities for reaching the upper lakes by steamboats has increased the varieties and numbers as well as lessened the prices of the choice kinds in our (N. Y.) city.

The number of fish will be much increased by persons engaging in growing fish in the numerous estuaries, ponds, creeks, etc., for market purposes, as is now done for the European markets.

The culture of fish originated with an humble but intelligent fisherman named John Remy, of Vosges, France, who, although uneducated, by dint of penetration, observation, and perseverance, succeeded in raising fish from the seed or eggs, under various circumstances. Mr. Milne Edwards declares in a Report to the Academy of Sciences, that Remy, with his colaborer Gehin, has the merit of having "created a new industry in France;" and Mr. Geoffrey St. Hilaire, the great naturalist, pronounced Remy one of the "benefactors of his country."

To protect several of the choice species of the fresh-water fish, which sportsmen call game-fish, a law was passed in New York on the 6th of April, 1860, which prohibited any person "to have in possession on exposure for sale—any speckled brook-trout, or spotted trout, or lake trout, between the first day of September and the first day of March, or any salmon trout, or any muscalonge, between the first day of December and the first day of April, in each and every year, under a fine of five dollars for each fish so taken or had in possession.

"No person or persons shall take any salmon trout, save

in the waters of Lake Erie and Lake Ontario; or any speckled brook-trout, or speckled river-trout or lake-trout, or muscalonge, in any of the waters of this State at any time, save with hook and line, under a fine of two dollars for each fish so taken."

The demand for fish in the season of Lent is much greater than at any other time of the year. Then we usually find the numerous stands in our fish-markets loaded down with many varieties, which are sold at prices within the reach of all.

In choosing perfectly fresh fish the following general features will show themselves. The fish should be quite firm and stiff, eyes stand out full and clear, gills quite red, and the fins firm, not hanging, or moving about as the fish is moved.

Fish are seldom subjected to diseases, but sometimes they are found in an unfit or unwholesome state, whether occasioned by some peculiar food or water, or from other causes. A singular phenomenon occurred in the month of November, 1844, when the whole coast was strewed along with dead fish of many kinds. An old fisherman, in the New London *News*, says, the smack in which he was had been unsuccessful, but very few fish having been taken, and on many of the old fishing-grounds not one could be found. In returning along the south shore of Long Island, their attention was attracted to the beach, which was literally strewed with the bodies of dead fish just washed up by the sea.

Blackfish, Cunner's (bergalls), lobsters, and crabs, and many other species which inhabit our shores at this season, lay promiscuously on the sand. On examining the well of the smack, it was discovered that the fish which they had taken were also dead. As far as the shore was examined eastward, towards Montauk Point, it was found to be covered alike with dead fish.

"We are also informed that the smack Caroline, on Friday last, while about fifteen miles from land, passed through a rip (formed by adverse tides) which was filled with dead fish. Soon after this the well of the smack was examined, and every fish in it found to be dead. These remarkable facts require scientific investigation. Similar phenomena have been observed in the Mediterranean after a volcanic eruption on some of the neighboring mountains; and it is quite probable, we think, that the destruction of the finny tribe noticed above was caused by a like eruption at sea, near our coast." A friend of the editor of the *U. S. Gazette*, Philadelphia, "who has just returned from the seashore of New Jersey, informs us that the whole shore, for thirty or forty miles, is covered with dead fish, cast up by the sea. They are of all kinds, from the smallest perch to the largest sturgeon, some rock-fish weighing forty or fifty pounds, and rich sea-bass. Many of the fish are washed up before they are dead. So great is the number, that a gentleman computed that on Leaming's Beach alone there must be ten thousand bushels. What has happened among the fish we cannot tell, as we do not know to what unwholesome influences they are liable in the depths below, but something extraordinary must have been in operation to produce an evil so extensive. Was it a volcanic eruption?"

Several of the different species of fish noticed in the following pages are found with several names to each one—given to them in different places by different persons: such names have been placed with those they represent, that the variety or species may be designated. They are under their several distinct heads, that each may be more easily referred to, beginning under each caption with those which are considered the best, and so in order, as they have appeared to decrease in value for the table.

These captions will appear, 1. *Large and abundant;* 2. *Small and abundant;* 3. *Large and scarce;* 4. *Small and scarce*, concluding with *Shell-fish.* Under the first and second captions are those noticed which are usually found abundant in their seasons. Under the third and fourth headings are those which are occasionally and rarely found in our fish-markets ; while there are many other kinds again noticed, which are not commonly used for the table, but which are edible, or have been eaten under certain circumstances.

I may here add that those under the head of "Large," etc., are usually preferred to boil, bake, or roast, and those under the head of "Small," etc., are better calculated for the frying-pan or gridiron. With these observations, we will proceed with those under the first caption.

LARGE AND ABUNDANT.

Salmon.—This noble fish is generally considered the choicest, most savory, and nutritive of all fish, and usually commands the highest price of any kind sold in our markets, on account of its scarcity, distance brought, and the difficulty of preserving them fresh and in good order.

The best salmon have small heads, and are quite thick through the shoulders. Their usual weight runs from six to twelve pounds each (although I have read of their weighing above sixty pounds). These fish, when on sale, are usually found too large for private families. The retail fishermen, however, cut pieces to suit purchasers. The middle-cut is the choice, though some prefer the head and shoulders, and others again the tail-piece. When cut, the flesh should appear quite red, solid, and flaky.

The Eastern salmon, from the Kennebec River, are considered the best : those from the Penobscot and St. John's Rivers come next. They begin to arrive here sometimes as early as the 1st of March, and continue to the 1st of September. Salmon sold lower in 1860 and 1862 than ever before, or at least within the knowledge of the living : they could be bought for eight and ten dollars per hundred pounds, and it was said some sold at a lower price.

Scotch salmon, brought from Scotland in our steamers, are sometimes found in our markets near all the year round ; but they are not usually in very good condition, and therefore do not rank with our Eastern salmon when in season.

Large quantities of these fish are found in the cured state, either pickled, soused, salted and smoked, etc., sold singly or in packages at much lower prices than in the fresh state, having been cured where taken.

It is very seldom in fact, for many years past, that salmon are taken in the North, or Hudson River, although at an early period they were very plenty. The earliest record of this fact appears in Juet's (Hudson's mate) journal on his passage up the Hudson River in 1609 in the vessel called the "Half-Moon," which says: "Sept. 15. The morning was misty until the sun arose; then it cleared, so we weighed with the wind at south, and ran up into the river twenty leagues, passing by high mountains. We had very good depth, as six, seven, eight, nine, ten, twelve and thirteen fathoms, and great store of salmon in the river."

In 1771 a number of persons in the country of Albany defrayed the expense of procuring salmon from the rivers and lakes where they abound, and placed them in the Hudson River, that they would, by spawning there, soon become numerous. In the same year a law was passed (on the 16th of February) to prevent persons taking and destroying salmon in the Hudson River, under the penalty of ten pounds.

We find, after this period, that they were occasionally taken in this river, and sometimes quite near the city. The Philadelphia *Press*, in 1793, announced the taking of a shad in the month of January, when a New York subscriber says: "A number of your readers are surprised that you would not notice a salmon that was also taken in January." Then follows on—"In January, by a shad, the mighty city was made glad;—A salmon, eke in January, made Manhattans quite as merry.—New York, January 24, 1793."

In answer, the Philadelphia editor says: "On the 21st of January a winter salmon was dined on in Boston by a number of citizens of that capital. The New Yorkers will, therefore, not consider themselves alone in that unusual January regale."

From the New York *Minerva*, June 22, 1796, we find recorded: "A salmon, weighing twelve pounds two ounces, was caught (on Monday 20th) by Captain James Deas, at Little Sligo, four miles up the North River."

This same gentleman is found again successful, and is thus noticed in the *Commercial Advertiser*, June 23, 1808: "A very fine salmon, weighing eight pounds and three-quarters, was caught by Captain James Deas,* at Camperdown, near Weehawk Ferry, on Tuesday morning last. This is the second salmon caught at that place by the same gentleman, within eight years." In the month of June, 1826, "a fine salmon was caught at Red Hook, in a net spread for weakfish. It was brought up to Fulton Market and sold at auction, and bid up to almost ten dollars. It was supposed to weigh about ten pounds." Then in the month of May, 1831, says *Niles' Register*: "A salmon, weighing eighteen pounds, was lately caught in the Hudson River, opposite Catskill—a rarely-known visitor of the waters of that river." Brown, also, in his "Angler's Text-book," says: "A number were taken in nets, in the Bay of New York, in the month of June, 1844." In the London *Times* we find an enormous large salmon "was caught at Chanonry Point, Moray Firth, Fortrose, which weighed sixty-two pounds." Penant, an old writer, also mentions one that weighed seventy-four pounds.

New York City began to be regularly supplied with fresh salmon, from the Kennebeck River, Maine, about the years 1832–3, by some of the coasting schooners, which occasionally brought small lots in ice during one or two of the summer months, or, rather, from about the first of June to the last of July. These were consigned to Mr. John Niles, a produce merchant, No. 212 Washington-street, who immediately announced the arrival thus: "FRESH SALMON.—The

* Captain James Deas died on the 22d of April, 1812, at his residence, New Jersey. He belonged to the St. Andrew's and Marine Societies, of New York.

schooner Pioneer arrived this morning with a fresh cargo of fresh salmon to Mr. J. Niles. The lovers of this delicious fish will have an opportunity, to-morrow morning, to obtain any quantity by calling on Mr. Niles or his representatives, either at the Washington (Messrs. Eldridge and Ashley) or Fulton (N. Rogers) markets."—*Commercial Advertiser*, June 13, 1834.

Spanish mackerel.—This choicest of fish is found very plentiful during some seasons, usually in the months of June, July, August, and September. Their general appearance is similar to the spring mackerel, but a much larger fish, and without the dark lines on the sides; there are, however, three or four rows of pale yellow spots instead.

There is another variety, called the *spotted cybum*, which is known among the fishermen also as the Spanish mackerel. It, however, appears a slimmer fish, more compressed, and with sometimes four and five rows of bright yellow spots, nearer together and running alternately on the sides nearly the whole length. The Spanish mackerel are sold usually at high prices, and their general weight ranges from two to eight pounds.

The *Herald*, August 17, 1862, says: "The largest Spanish mackerel ever captured in the vicinity of New York was caught on Friday, at Long Branch, weighing twenty pounds, and over four feet in length. It was presented to Mr. C. V. Clickner, of the Dey-street House."

Sheep head is a name given to this choice fish from the appearance of the mouth and teeth, which are much like those of the sheep. It is a large, short, deep fish, silvery in appearance, seven or eight dark bands running across it, and with a smutty face. There are many who think it the very best fish for a boil that swims. Weight from four to ten pounds, and in season from May to the first of October. Be careful that you buy them fresh, as they spoil much sooner than many fish, on account of their food, which consists principally of muscles, etc. The editor of the *Commercial Advertiser*—July 3, 1822—gives his experience in the purchase of a stale fish of this species, which he thus describes: "There was a fine-looking stock of sheep head in the market yesterday, killed and dressed, one of which, soon after we had the misfortune to bring it home, forcibly reminded us of the following anecdote: A colored man being once on a time in the market, was detected by the owner smelling a fish. 'What are you about, you black rascal?' said the fishmonger; 'do you smell of my fish?' 'I no smell him, Massa,' said Cuff, 'I talk to him. I ask him what news from sea.' 'Well, sirrah, what does he say?' 'He say he no been dar dis tree week, massa.'"

Several fine live specimens were shown at the Fair of the American Institute, held September, 1860, which were furnished by Messrs. Miller & Co., of Fulton Market, who took several prizes for showing a large and choice collection of "sea-fish." One of these live specimens was taken to Barnum's Museum, where I have seen him several times since, and is yet alive (1864), but grown considerably larger. While at the fair I became much attached to him, for his tameness (in fact, so much so, that he would come up to my hand at the top of the water), that I would not have parted with him but for the great trouble of procuring *fresh* salt water daily for his preservation.

Striped-bass, streaked-bass (known South as) **Rock, Rock-fish**, and **Rock-bass.**—These fish are highly prized by all who have eaten them. Those from a half to one pound weight are best to fry; above that weight to three pounds should be split for broiling, and from four to eight are the choice to boil. The very large fish are sometimes known as "green-heads," and are usually found coarse and rather dry eating, especially when above twenty-five pounds; then the best manner to prepare them is to boil and souse, or pickle the flesh. In color, the back is of a bluish brown, silvery sides, and lighter underneath; the number of stripes running from the head is usually eight, four of which most commonly reach the tail—the rest are shorter. They are never found alive on the stands, and cannot even be kept alive in the "fish-wells," or cars, on account of their wildness, as they soon wear themselves out, or, rather, their fins off, and die. Although they are seldom out of the markets, yet some months they are scarce, viz.: July and August, and again in December, January, and February. They are, however, best in September, October, and November. In the spring months they run quite small and make excellent pan-fish.

Of the immense numbers that have been caught at one time, the following will give the reader some idea. The *New York Packet*, September 1st, 1785, says: "Tuesday evening se'nnight, upwards of one thousand weight of rock-fish were caught at one haul, in the Delaware, near Trenton. Some of these fish weighed near thirty pounds apiece, and generally from eight to twenty."

The *Commercial Advertiser*, August 4, 1812, notices a "Miraculous Draft of Fishes.—On Monday afternoon last, two hundred and twenty-five fine (striped) bass were caught at a single draft, in the Hudson River, below the dam, at the village of Washington. They weighed from five to thirty pounds each, and the whole amount was nearly three thousand weight. What renders this circumstance the more remarkable is, that none of the fisheries on the Hudson have ever been noted for large quantities of bass. The taking of a single one of thirty pounds, in the course of the season, has at all times been considered as very rare and uncommon. Small bass, however, are occasionally caught in considerable quantities, but they are by no means plenty, nor is our market at any time ever tolerably well supplied (except in the spring season) with fish caught in the Hudson."

Then we find in the *Baltimore Gazette*, in May, 1834,—"Yesterday some fishermen, at Carpenter's Point, took, at a single haul, upwards of eight hundred rock-fish, of the largest size we ever saw. Some of them weighed upwards of one hundred pounds, and the most of them averaging between fifty and one hundred pounds. They were selling this morning in the market at from fifty cents to one dollar for the largest—say one cent a pound for such fish as this."

An enormous striped bass was caught with a hand-line at Cuttyhonk, near New Bedford, in the year 1860, which weighed one hundred and four pounds.

Within my recollection, there were particular docks and other places around our city where this fine fish was caught in abundance in certain seasons and tides; and the Battery, on the bridge leading to the Castle Garden, was one of them, which some fishermen held as a favorite place. Here, occasionally, instances occurred of very successful angling. "On Saturday afternoon (says the *Press*, October 12, 1816), a young gentleman of this city caught off the Battery, with a hook and line, nearly two hundred striped bass, weighing from a quarter to one pound and a half. Several others caught nearly a similar number." Another paper, October 17, 1832, notices some "FINE SPORT.—Twelve hundred bass were caught from the Castle Garden bridge yesterday."

Then we have some remarkable and curious incidents, the first of which is found in the *Commercial Advertiser*, September 28, 1816, as follows: "On Wednesday, one of our scientific anglers, Mr. Ellis, brought in three fish upon one hook—the largest, a fine bass, weighing about three pounds. The hook had been baited with a small live chub, which was swallowed by a bass of about one-half or three-quarters of a pound weight, and the whole swallowed by the large fish, leaving the tail of the small bass projecting from its mouth. This spectacle establishes a fact in natural history, we believe, not generally known, that the voracity of this fish induces it to devour its own species."—*Albany Argus*.

The *Connecticut Mirror* notices—"A large bass, weighing between fifty and sixty pounds, was caught a few days since at Haddam, about twenty miles below this city. Upon opening it, it was found to contain a *junk bottle of rum*, which it is supposed must have dropped overboard from some vessel or boat, and caught while sinking by this tippler of the deep."—*Commercial Advertiser*, June 19, 1820.

The following incident was—in the year 1818—related by Mr. John Scudder, proprietor of the American Museum, in this city (N. Y.) "In 1801 or '2, an Albany sloop, becalmed, was gently drifting on her passage through the Highlands: an eagle was observed in the river, fluttering its wings in vain efforts to rise. Some hands in the boat rowed off, and, with a line cast round the body of the eagle, drew it alongside and took it safely on board, together with a large bass that weighed thirty-three pounds, into which it had struck its talons, which became so inserted between the joints of the vertebræ as to prevent extrication. The eagle (of the bald species) was brought alive to this city, and was purchased by Mr. Savage, who at that time kept a museum which Mr. Scudder attended."—*Ibid.*, May 9, 1818.

The same paper, March 21, 1832, also says: "While some men were rowing up Newtown Creek, day before yesterday, they discovered a sea-dog stealing bass from a fuik of a bass-net. They succeeded in taking him, and he was brought to this city, and, of course, was instantly bought by Dr. Scudder for the American Museum, where he is now exhibiting."

Six years after, the same paper (June 16, 1838,) gives the following: "Amusing incident which occurred on board the steamboat Swan, during her passage up Princes Bay. It appeared that quite a group of ladies were assembled before the looking-glass preparing for dinner, while one, more indolent than the rest, was taking her siesta on a sofa, reclining at her ease, in the full enjoyment of all the pleasant visions that a blooming beauty of eighteen summers is supposed to possess, when an enormous rock-fish, or striped bass, suddenly jumped through the port-hole and fell in her lap. Whether the lady or the poor fish was the most frightened, we do not pretend to say; the lady, however, possessing that inestimable gift of nature, the power of making her troubles known, shrieked in such a manner as to drive the others in the greatest consternation among the gentlemen, *sans* hats, *sans* curls, *sans* ceremony! Meanwhile, Commodore Schultz made his appearance in the cabin, and found, to his dismay, a lady apparently lifeless, and a large fish bouncing about the cabin, among his furniture. The Commodore, however, in a few minutes, succeeded, with the aid of a few whose better feelings overcame their fears, in restoring life to the inanimate fair one, and destroying that of the rude intruder."

One hundred years ago, a law (noticed in the *Gazette*, November 14, 1758) was passed, to prohibit the selling or bringing certain fish, called bass or twalft (see Big Drum), to the city, in the months of December, January, and February, in consequence of the "great decrease of that kind of fish," and also of their being unsound and unwholesome in those months. The penalty for such offence "was forty shillings lawful money of New York," and the forfeit of such fish. "And if it be a negro, mulatto, or Indian slave, shall receive such corporal punishment at the public whipping-post, as the mayor, recorder, or aldermen shall think fit, unless the master or mistress shall pay the above fine."

Sea-bass.—This well-known fish is a general favorite for the table. The color is of a bluish black, and the fins of a lighter blue. They are usually found, or caught, from one-half pound up to eight pounds weight, and in season from 1st of May to the 1st of October. The small fish are an excellent pan-fish, and those of a large size, which have a beautiful indigo-blue head, and weighing from three to six pounds, are best for boiling.

A nautical correspondent (in the *New York Journal*, August 4, 1785,) informs masters of vessels bound to the northward of Cape Hatteras, and especially those that fall in about the cape, and are anywise short of provisions, that in latitude 35° 46′ and about the longitude of the cape, there is a large muscle-bank, intermixed with cockles and small pebbles, lying in fifty fathoms water, and abounds with sundry fish, such as sea-bass, sea-trout, flounders, skate, tusk (cusk), and dog-fish. The sea-bass here are very remarkable with respect to their largeness, generally weighing from four to six pounds each, and upon an average twenty to the hundred weight. A vessel has filled two barrels upon this bank in the space of two hours, with only three lines and three hooks, and there is no doubt if two hooks had been applied to each line, they might have got double the quantity. The water upon this bank differs very little in color from the ocean, and in the very height of winter is very little colder. There are likewise to be caught in the winter season, fish, by towing over this bank, if a person has suitable bait, such as the *ballaho*, which they have generally in the West Indies; but particular care must be taken with regard to the quality of the tackling, as the fish are remarkably strong and smart, and generally weigh from twenty to thirty pounds each. Four or five lines have been lost in an hour, and at last been obliged to bend the dipping-line to the inner end of the tow-line, and by the means of having length of line, and keeping the vessel in the wind, the fish have been taken. No common towing will hold them except using the foregoing method: they are supposed to be overgrown blue-fish.

The *Commercial Advertiser*, July 17, 1815, has the following account of some great fishing. "G. Davis, Esq., and a party of gentlemen from Division-street (New York city), went to the fishing banks properly equipped, and in one hour and a quarter caught one thousand seven hundred sea-bass, all of which, except about two hundred, they brought to town in their car. A party from Staten Island, a few days since, had similar luck. It is a fact, that sea-bass were never before known to be so abundant as at present."

The following incident is noticed in the New York *Patriot*, July 17, 1824: "Captain Josiah Ingersoll, standing in Washington Market on Tuesday morning last (1st July, 1824), a person employed by one of the hucksters made a severe blow at a boy with a sea-bass. The boy dodged the blow, and it fell on Captain Ingersoll's thigh, and many of the back fin-bones were left in the flesh, some of which were immediately taken out. Shortly after it became very painful. As soon as he arrived home medical aid was called (Doctors Mott and Coulter), and it was found necessary to lay open the thigh, which was done, and many more bones were found, it is hoped all, but it is feared not. We are sorry to state great fears are entertained for his recovery."

Shad.—This well-known fish is a general favorite among all classes of persons, as its flesh is considered among the best, sweetest, the most delicate, as well as being the most plentiful when in season. Nothing but its numerous bones can be said against it. The color and general appearance are so well known, that description is needless. It is seldom or never found alive on the fish-stands, as they die in a few minutes after being taken from the nets. When fresh, their gills are of quite a crimson red, body firm, and scales very bright; but when their gills begin to turn a whitish blue, eyes sunken, and the fish handles soft, it is then unfit to eat. Weight from three and a half to five pounds. An eight-pound fish is very scarce, although I find in Niles' *Weekly Register*, June 17, 1815, "A shad was lately caught in the Schuylkill which weighed eleven pounds and a quarter; extreme length thirty and a half inches, and round the belly eighteen and a half inches." The editors of the Newark *Advertiser* also say they were presented with a shad which weighed fourteen pounds, a few years ago; but I could not get sufficient testimony to prove the latter weight correct, although I wrote to the editors.

In the spring of 1841 two large shad were taken in the North River, and presented to the Hon. Robert H. Morris, Mayor of the City of New York, by Mr. Alfred G. Thompson, fisherman, of Washington Market. "The female shad measured two feet and three inches in length, and eighteen inches round the waist, weighing six and a half pounds. The other, a male shad, measured two feet and two inches in length, and fifteen inches round the waist, weighing seven pounds." Mr. Peter Vincellette, of Jefferson Market, in 1857, had a very fat shad, which weighed eight and a half pounds, and, what is most singular, it was found without either the roes or melt.

Shad begin to appear in our markets, in small numbers, from the South (Charleston), sometimes as early as the 1st of February, and by the 20th are quite plenty; then from Ochrank (North Carolina) about the 1st of March; Delaware River, the 20th of the same month; North River, on or about the 1st of April; although I read in the *Commercial Advertiser*, January 17, 1807, "A shad weighing five pounds was caught this morning at the Narrows, and sold in our market for one dollar and twelve cents!" Then we have them from Connecticut River about the 15th of April; and so they continue North along the coast to the Bay of Fundy, where they are found to be very fat, fine, and large.

The Southern fish received here are never very large, nor so fat as those taken in the North River. The best, however, are those from the Connecticut River, which are known by their superior size, length, square-shaped back, and a fatter fish. It would almost seem, if we should judge by their uniformity and size, that each river received back again its own productions or births, year after year; which cause, no doubt, produces so many different forms or varieties. This fact appears confirmed by the following testimony. William Ward, of Pennsylvania, who dates "Lower Merion, 10th March, 1814," says: "About thirty years ago (1784), John Roberts, Cooper, and myself, in the fall season, marked a considerable number of young shad, then from four to five inches long, by cutting off a part of the upper fin or fork of their tails, in order, if possible, to ascertain whether they returned to the Schuylkill in the following year. I was informed by Philip Shubert and Jacob and John Colp, that they had caught, the ensuing spring, many full-grown fish marked as aforesaid."

Those which are called *back shad* are sometimes improperly caught, after having spawned and are returning to the sea, when they are always poor, exhausted, and unfit to be eaten ; in fact, no orthodox sportsman will permit a shad upon his table after the 1st of June, as they are usually nothing but head, fins, and bones.

The roes of the female shad are considered a delicacy, and by some superior to the fish itself. The male shad has also roes, or rather a melt ; but they are much smaller and not so seedy-looking or red, but which many prefer, as they think it more delicate eating.

Shad are found salted and also smoked, the year through, and those cured and brought from Connecticut are considered the best.

At a very early period shad were taken so plentiful, that large quantities were used to manure the ground. Of this fact we have the evidence of Edward Winslow (the former proprietor of a part of Daniel Webster's farm at Marshfield), who writes to one George Morton, as early as December 11, 1621, the year after the Pilgrims landed, and says : "We set (planted) the last spring some twenty acres of Indian corn, and sowed some six acres of barley and peas ; and, according to the manner of the Indians, we manured our ground with herrings, or rather shads, which we have in great abundance, and take with great ease at our doors." Morton, also, says, in his *New England Canaan*, "There is a fish by some called shads, by some allizes, that, at the spring of the year, pass up the rivers to spawn in the ponds ; and are taken in such multitudes in every river that hath a pond at the end, that the inhabitants dung their grounds with them," since which period large numbers of shad have been caught all along the coast from Florida to the Bay of Fundy ; but perhaps no place was more prominent as a fishery than at our Narrows, prior to the year 1800. We find in the New York *Journal*, April 26, 1770, the following : "Last week a remarkable quantity of shad fish was taken at the Narrows, on Long Island. One of the seines, as it was drawn towards the shore, was so filled with fish, that the weight pressed it to the ground, whereby great numbers escaped. A second seine was then thrown out around the fish, a third around the second, and a fourth around the third, and all filled in like manner.

"The number of shad that were taken by the first net was three thousand; by the second, three thousand; by the third, four thousand; and by the fourth, fifteen hundred; in all, eleven thousand five hundred!" Another account is given in the same paper, April 16, 1791: "We hear that a draught of shad was taken near the Narrows on Thursday last, which consisted of fourteen thousand fish!—to secure which the fishermen were obliged to add several seines, one upon the other. It is said that this single draught of shad is worth upwards of £200."

The following is an account of the number of shad taken in the fuik net at New Utrecht, King's County, during the following years, by the Cortelyou family, at their fishery in the Narrows, as kept by Peter Cortelyou, Esq., formerly Sheriff of King's County, Long Island: In the years—

1789—15,833—the greatest number taken	on any one	day of	that year—	4,700
1790—24,086	"	"	"	5,266
1791—23,077	"	"	"	4,558
1792—11,460	"	"	"	1,900
1793— 8,145	"	"	"	1,468
1794—16,945	"	"	"	3,575
1795—15,917	"	"	"	1,960
(From 1795 to 1816 the memorandum was lost.)				
1816—10,283—the greatest number taken	on any one	day of	that year—	908
1817— 9,683	"	"	"	1,876
1818— 9,453	"	"	"	459
1819— 8,653	"	"	"	397
1820— 8,233	"	"	"	436
1821— 6,259	"	"	"	1,214
1822— 4,115	"	"	"	391
1823— 3,434	"	"	"	420
1824— 3,115	"	"	"	482

This shad-fishery has been gradually decreasing since the year 1824, so that now it is scarcely worth attending to. The fish now taken (1838) for the whole season, does not exceed the number taken in a single day, as stated, in 1817. All the fisheries in New York harbor are nearly destroyed, and the fish which now supply the markets of that city are brought from the distance of sixty, eighty, and even a hundred miles.*

Mascalonge or **Muskellonge.**—This large fresh-water fish belongs to the pickerel family, and is by many considered the "king fish of the lakes." The color, when fresh, is a very dark green on the back, quite gray on the sides, and sometimes covered with dark or light marks, or white, irregular spots. Their weight varies from five to fifteen pounds, although they have been taken above seventy pounds. They begin to appear in our markets in the latter part of October, last until April, and generally sell at high prices.

A very fine, thick fish of this species—a most beautiful specimen—was sent to me in the month of July, 1858, which weighed above ten pounds. It was what an epicure would call "delicious eating," and I am much indebted to my friends, the Messrs. Miller & Co., of Fulton Market, for this and many other rare species of fish.

An extraordinary large mascalonge, weighing forty-six pounds, was sold by another fisherman (Wm. M. Rogers & Co.) of Fulton Market to the proprietor of the Astor House, in April, 1857, to be served up at the opening of their "restaurant." When this fish was opened, two large silver, or lake suckers were found inside, one weighing above three pounds and the other two pounds.

An interesting sketch of the taking of a large mascalonge near Clayton, on the St. Lawrence, is related by "Rambler," in the *New York Times*, August 10, 1860, who says: "It is not uncommon to see little boys and girls in skiffs, rowing about the river, trolling. One day last week a small boy was thus engaged in the bay, near the vessels lying at the wharf, when he 'fastened' (a local term) to a muskallonge. Being alone in the boat, with no implements to secure him or kill him, and the fish being about as heavy as the boy, it

* Furman's Notes.

was a fair, and for a long time seemed to be a very doubtful resulting fight. The lad, however, had the advantage; for while the fish was being weakened by the struggle, the boy held his own. The boat swayed round and round as the maskallonge struck out right and left, till at last the lad succeeded in getting Mr. Maskallonge's head over the gunwale, and, by one sudden convulsion of the fish, in he came into the boat. And now the reader may suppose the fight was ended. Not so, for it had but just begun; for the boats sit low upon the water, and these fish, averaging about five feet in length, will go overboard, if not prevented, quicker than they came in. The little fellow let go the line and seized Mr. Muskallonge around the body, and a rough-and-tumble ensued upon the bottom of the boat, the fish being first uppermost and then the boy; but he held on and halloed stoutly for help, when one of the guides, seeing his condition, shot out with his boat from the shore and towed in the contending parties. But the little fellow never relinquished his hold till the club was applied to the muskallonge's head, when it was ascertained the fish weighed forty-eight and one-half pounds. Mr. Johnson, the proprietor of the Walton House, sent the fish to the proprietor of the Everett House, in New York." Forty years ago is found in the *Commercial Advertiser* (December 10, 1824) the following: "*Maskeenonjai.*—Among the wonders of our waters will be found the huge and delicious maskeenonjai. This fish is often taken in the nets with the white-fish, on which it feeds with great voracity. It is taken of dimensions from ten to fifty pounds, and we have heard of some that weighed seventy; but the largest that has been caught this season was taken a few evenings since, by Mr. Joseph Loranger, at a fishing-ground a short distance below this city (Detroit); it measured four feet four inches in length, was twenty-seven inches in circumference, and weighed forty-seven pounds. On opening it three white-fish were found in its belly, the largest of which was twenty-two inches in length. A few days ago a fine maskeenonjai was presented to Colonel Smyth, of this city, by Colonel Bunce, of St. Clair: it weighed forty-three pounds. Its skin and head, together with a fine white-fish that was taken from its belly, has been prepared by a young gentleman of this place, and will probably be sent to the New York Museum, as that institution is destitute of this ichthyological specimen."

Black-fish, known as **tautog** in the Eastern States.—This is, by some, considered one of the best fish for boiling: with others, again, it is not a favorite. They are generally found alive on the "stands," as they live a great while out of water, being a bottom fish, and of a very slimy nature.* The name "Black-fish," no doubt, is derived from the color of its back and sides, being of a bluish black, and spotted underneath with very thick, fleshy lips. I have seen them, however, of many colors, where they have lain together in large numbers, with patches or spots of reddish brown, and sometimes white, etc. In season from June to December, weight from three-quarters to five pounds, although I am told the firm of Rogers & Co., Fulton Market, had one which weighed twenty-three pounds, taken in 1845. The *Herald*, of September 29, 1855, notices: "A fine large black-fish, weighing nearly twenty-eight pounds, was caught at McComb's Dam, on Thursday last," etc.

Blue-fish or **snapping mackerel.**—Several years ago this species of mackerel enjoyed the name of *horse-mackerel* and *blue-mackerel*, and is now known in Virginia as *green-fish*, in Carolina as *skip-jack*, and in the Philadelphia markets as *tailors*. The first name denotes its color, although lighter on the sides and underneath. The common size runs from two to six pounds, although sometimes found above ten pounds weight. When fresh from the water this fish is excellent, but grows strong and rancid

* A most remarkable feature in the black-fish is the heart, which shows muscular life sometimes hours after having been taken out of a living fish. I saw one, or, rather, part of one, which showed signs of life four and one-half hours after it was brought to me. The movement was curious, as the point of the heart would raise when the muscular contraction of the sides took place, which it would do at short intervals.

after being out of the water any length of time. In season from 1st of June to end of October. A few fine large fish are found in November.

A blue-fish of twelve pounds' weight was caught by a gentleman of New York, on the 10th of September, 1864, while he, with some six others, was fishing off West Island, near Newport. This fish, when opened, had nine large fish-hooks clustered together in its maw, all of which were identified by the fishermen on the island as having belonged to different parties who had been fishing there during the preceding three days. They were all in a good state of preservation, one of which appeared like a hook that a little while before had been taken off the line of one of the party by some large fish.

Another incident, somewhat of an amusing character, happened during this excursion, which in substance appeared as follows: After this party of seven left West Island, they proceeded to another called "Cuttyhunk," where they arrived in the evening, and directed their steps to one of the two residences or small houses which this island contains, and inquired of the matron if they could be accommodated with meals and lodging for the night. "Wall," she drawled out, after counting over the party; "we can eat you all, but we can't sleep but two—t'other house could sleep the rest on you."

After the evening meal was finished, five of the party made their way to t'other house, while the other two repaired to their sleeping-room above, which they found pretty well filled with all sorts of hunting and fishing traps, besides a pretty good bed. So they sat down for a talk; but to make themselves more comfortable, one drew forth his segar-case, while the other prepared the delicate-looking snells and large hooks for the big ones which they expected to take next day. So they chatted, smoked, and worked on until the tackle was perfectly satisfactory. In the mean time, our smoker had quietly taken possession of a part of one end of the bed, where a reclining position seemed more acceptable to an unusually tired body; and soon after the other thought that he might as well, at least, enjoy the same amount of repose, so he as quietly slipped into the bed, where Morpheus soon after claimed him as his own.

Several times through the course of the evening, the matron's son had mounted the stairway and looked anxiously towards the smoker, who kept the white curling smoke ascending, so that at least every corner and crevice of the room would become somewhat disagreeable quarters for any hungry mosquito that was waiting for a feast. The boy at last excitedly jerked out something about "peowder being dangerous about there," then quickly returned. But our smoking friend supposed that he either wanted him to go to bed and save light, or else fearing that he would set the bed on fire, concluded that as he had not yet completed his usual number of Havanas, he would not heed the boy. However, the unusual noise made by the boy's return again awakened our sleeper, who found the smoker yet enjoying his segar; and then followed the boy's voice, which rang out in his nasal twang—"I say, mister, you'd better be car'ful of that segar, as there is *an open keg of peowder right under the bed, which you mought set fire to!*" It was now clearly understood by both, and enough to immediately extinguish not only the segar, but also a good deal of sound sleep which they expected to enjoy that night. They talked and thought over the matter, but came to the conclusion that the family, by having this keg of "villainous saltpetre" so dangerously exposed, were preparing to give a *warm* reception to the Southern pirates, who had been so lately sneaking around the neighborhood under false colors, and destroying the water-craft belonging to the poor fishermen, but which powder had been so near giving a warming to their Northern visitors and tired friends.

Yellow pike perch, glass-eyed pike, big-eyed pike, pike of the lakes, or Ohio salmon.—This fine and truly American fish is sometimes known as "wall-eyed pike," in consequence of their large eyes becoming white or clouded after death. It is a much larger, rounder, and longer fish than the common yellow perch. The fins are of a golden or yellow color, back and head a purplish brown, the sides yellow, and the belly white. Generally found here in the winter and early spring months, weighing from two to six pounds, and are very succulent and delicate eating, particularly when boiled, as the flesh is firm, flakey, and white. They are caught in immense numbers in principally all the great lakes, some upwards of forty pounds weight, large numbers of which are salted and barrelled for the winter's use, and sent to the large cities.

Gray pike perch appears to be another variety of the above. Those that I saw, on several occasions, were quite different in color, a little slimmer, and a more delicately-formed fish; but perhaps they were poor, and the color changed from different waters or food. I, however, have never seen them so large and fine as the former.

Oblong flounder, fluke, or **spotted flounder.**—These, one of the varieties of flat-fish, are usually found large and plentiful in their season, and are commonly known among fishermen by the name of "fluke." They are quite oblong in shape, the color of a dark olive-green, mottled with dark and light spots, and white underneath. The mouth is large and oblique, and opens on the left side, while the eyes are on the right side—that is, if you stand at the tail and look towards the head, when the back is up. In season in the months from August to November, and average about two and a half pounds.

On the 13th of October, 1864, I found four varieties of the flat-fish in Jefferson Market, viz.: oblong flounder, long-toothed flounder, spotted turbot, and New York flat-fish, all nearly of one size. They were all nicely fried, and my preference was with the oblong flounder, as being the best table-fish, the flesh being close, firm, and well flavored; it, however, was a young specimen.

A remarkable incident occurred in the taking of one of these fish, at the foot of Twelfth-street, North River, Sep-

14

tember 28, 1864. The fluke was caught by a young butcher, who perceived something like an eel partially hanging from his mouth, when he came to take the hook out. A friend of mine happened near by, who took the fish and cut out a small garter-snake, about eighteen inches in length, part of which was decayed. It is supposed that the snake had been crossing the water, near the Jersey shore, and was snapped up by this fish, or had been first killed and thrown into the water.

Toothed flat-fish, or **summer flounder.**—This fish is generally known by the common name of flounder, although some call all the varieties of flat-fish "flounders." De Kay, however, to designate them, the varieties with the eyes on the right side he terms flounders, and those with them on the left he calls flat-fish.

The color of this fish is of a reddish brown, with numerous small rusty-colored spots on the body, and white underneath. The flesh is well-flavored, and they are always found plentiful in the summer months, weighing from one pound to ten. The large fish, however, are not so plentiful as the preceding; the small ones are good pan-fish. The fishermen occasionally skin and bone these (and other) fish, when they are known as "fillets of flounders," and are much more delicate in this manner.

Pickerel (known in Philadelphia as "pike," and in Virginia as "jack").—This fresh-water fish, when in good condition, is very firm-fleshed, sweet, and well flavored, best in the winter and spring months, from September until March, and generally found quite plenty in our markets. They are quite a lengthy and a square-backed fish, with one fin on the back near the tail. Their upper jaw has somewhat the appearance of a duck's bill, and the eyes are quite small and crafty-looking. The color on the back is of a bluish-gray, and sometimes of a greenish cast. The sides are also of a muddy yellow, and quite full of dark irregular marks.

Another variety of this fish, known by the New York fishermen as "pike," is described as a short, thick-bodied fish, rather more spotted than the preceding one, and of a lighter bluish-gray, usually found on their stands, above ten pounds weight. I have heard of pickerel being taken above sixty pounds. It is also asserted that they will eat any thing they can master; and three have been taken on one hook, in their greediness to devour each other. The finest of the variety, called pike, are taken from the Saugerties Creek, which leads into the waters of the Hudson. They, however, are quite scarce, and, when found here, they sell at an extra price.

The third variety of this fish is called the "brook pickerel," which are smaller; they also have a shorter head, and the marks on the side run across the body in a regular manner, but quite clouded. The lower (or ventral) fins are usually quite red; the flesh is also not so delicate as the other varieties, being quite soft, and sometimes it has a groundy taste. Many fine pickerel are brought from Long Island; but they are found in all the fresh-water streams, lakes, creeks, ponds, etc., through the States.

A curious incident of the pickerel is found in the *Post Boy*, March 14, 1765, in the London news, which reads—"A large pike was caught in the River Ouse, which weighed upwards of twenty-eight pounds, and was sold to a gentleman in the neighborhood for a guinea. As the cookmaid was gutting the fish, she found, to her great astonishment, a watch, with a black ribbon and two steel seals annext, in the body of the pike. The gentleman's butler, upon opening the watch, found the maker's name, Thomas Greenfield, Burnham, Norfolk. Upon strict inquiry, it appears that the said watch was sold to a gentleman's servant, who was unfortunately drowned about six weeks ago, in his way to Cambridge, between this place and South Ferry. The watch is still in possession of Mr. John Roberts, at the "Cross-keys," in Littleport, for inspection of the public."

The *Trenton Federalist* has the following curious incident under the head of "*Singular.*—A person in the neighborhood of Crosswicks, Burlington County, having set a gill-net for fish in Crosswicks Creek, on going to examine it, found a large hawk seated on the water over the net. Coming near the place, he also found a pike (pickerel) caught in the net, which had seized one foot of the hawk in his mouth, holding him to the spot. Thus secured, both hawk and pike were taken by the fisherman. On examining the pike, which was entangled near the cork-line, it was perceived that the hawk had struck it with one of his talons in the back, upon which it appeared that the pike had seized him by the other and held him fast. The pike was of a small size, the hawk quite large, measuring three feet nine inches from tip to tip of each wing."

Kirby's "Bridgewater Treatise," speaking of the longevity of fishes, says: "A pike was taken in 1754, at Kaiser's lantern, which had a ring fastened to the gill-covers, from which it appeared to have been put in the pond of that castle by order of Frederick II., in 1437, a period of two hundred and sixty-seven years. It is described as being nineteen feet long, and weighed three hundred and fifty pounds.

White-fish, or **lake-shad.**—This excellent fish is taken in great abundance from the large lakes and rivers. Their general appearance is somewhat like the shad, with a very small head and thick body, color of a bluish-gray on the back, lighter on the sides, and white underneath. When taken fresh out of the water, they have a beautiful, bright, pearly lustre, and show several of the colors of the rainbow. Those caught in the clear, cold waters, and perfectly fresh, are considered the best flavored; and it is said that persons can live longer on white-fish than on any other fresh-water fish. They are found in large quantities in the salted or cured state here, but fresh only in the winter and spring months, weighing usually from two to four pounds, although some have been taken above sixteen pounds.

Seines of an enormous size are used at Wellington Beach, on Lake Ontario. I read of one being two hundred and twenty-two rods long, and about twenty-nine feet deep, covering an area of four acres. In the month of July, 1857, at one haul, forty-five thousand seven hundred white-fish were brought to the beach; and, for nine consecutive days, the smallest haul was eighteen thousand. They are usually packed at the average of one hundred and thirty to the barrel. "About the year 1816 or '17," says Furman, in his notes, "the white-fish from the lakes was held in very low estimation in Ohio and New York. A merchant in Detroit, in 1818, sent about one hundred barrels of them to Cincinnati, as an experiment; but no purchasers could be found, and he lost the whole of them. At that time white-fish were worth about three dollars per barrel; and boat-loads of them were frequently sold at three or four dollars per hundred, and six or seven dollars per barrel; and there were orders in Detroit from Ohio and the western towns of New York for thousands of barrels of white-fish. In 1842, they sold for eight dollars per barrel at Albany and New York."

The *Commercial Advertiser*, December 10, 1824, has the following account: "White-fish, as we have been told by an old inhabitant, were first taken with nets in the Detroit river about fifty years ago. It is said that a British lieutenant, who was stationed at that time at this post, first discovered the movements of the white-fish, and suggested the idea of taking them with nets. He was one night on a visit to the sentinels, and was told by one who was stationed near the shore that he had heard at times a rushing noise in the water. The lieutenant waited a few minutes, and had the pleasure of hearing the rushing, which, as he was somewhat acquainted with fishing, he knew to be caused by an immense number of fish rising to the surface of the water. A small net was immediately got in readiness, and such was the number caught, that, from four dollars, the price soon fell to four shillings a hundred."

Weak-fish, or **salt-water trout.**—This fish is also called "squeteague," and "chequet," in the Eastern States. When fresh caught it is excellent, delicate, and well-tasted; but it is not a firm-fleshed fish, and, when kept some time, its flesh becomes very soft and loses its flavor. It is best broiled. It is said it derives its name from a tender or weak mouth, as it frequently escapes by the tearing out of the hook. Color of a bluish-gray, with speckled back and sides, belly white, fins yellow, and the under jaw or chin quite red. Weight from a half-pound to eight pounds. I saw one of just fourteen and a half pounds weight in Jefferson Market, and have heard of their weighing twenty-two pounds. Their average weight, however, is about one pound. In season from May to October, but best in September and October.

Codfish.—This fish is quite extensively known, and always to be found in our markets. When fresh, its flesh is white, firm, flakey, and very good. When salted and dried, it affords a substantial, wholesome, and cheap article of diet, for which a substitute could not readily be procured. Codfish which have been caught in February, or in early spring months, in the deep water, are split and slightly salted, after which they are laid in piles in a cool, dark place, and covered with salt hay, eel-grass, or sedge, then put under a heavy weight, for two or three months; then again, to finish the process of dunning, they should be repiled and repacked, and stand as long again, which, in the end, will change them all to a clear dun color, and also their name to "dun-fish."

On the fish-stand there often appears codfish of various colors or markings; some will be full of streaks, light and dark, many of the usual gray color, others of a greenish-gray, and others again of a reddish-brown; the fishermen say this is caused by their being taken in different waters, and apply the names of rock-cod, shoal-cod, etc.

They are generally found alive from October to May, after this time they come in boxes, packed in ice, generally from the "Banks," Nantucket, etc., with the heads off and drawn. General weight from two to ten pounds, and often exceeds sixty. Instances are noticed where they have been caught weighing above one hundred pounds. Storer speaks of a "Mr. Anthony Holbrook, a fishmonger in the Quincy Market, informs me he saw taken in the spring of the year 1807, at Newledge, sixty miles southeast of Portland, Maine, a codfish that weighed one hundred and seven pounds, and, to use his own words, upon its head were barnacles the size of the thumb." There are several others of great weight which appear worthy of notice here. In the *New York Journal*, etc., April 3d, 1793: "A codfish was lately sold in the Newburyport Market which weighed ninety-eight pounds. The length of this fish was five feet and a half; its girth, at the thickest part, three feet four inches." In the month of February, 1823, the Marblehead fishermen sent a codfish, weighing eighty-four pounds, as a present to John Q. Adams, the Secretary of State. The fish was frozen with great care, in order to preserve it, incased in a box of ice, and transmitted with a letter from the donors. Then from the *Daily Advertiser*, June 14, 1827, we read: "An extraordinary large codfish was caught off Portsmouth, N. H., in the month of June last (1827), weighing ninety-seven pounds." The Lynn *News*, of January, 1857, also says: "The largest cod we ever heard of was taken last week by Captain Nathan Blanchard, of Swampscott; it weighed ninety-four pounds undressed, seventy-eight dressed, and was sold in Faneuil Hall Market, Boston."

Several parts of the codfish are also used when properly prepared: the tongue is separated from the head when the fish is first caught; this, with the air-bladder, or sack, are called *sounds and tongues*, which are cured and found on sale. They are highly nutritious, being almost entirely pure gelatine. The liver is principally reserved by the fishermen, for the sake of the large quantity of cod-liver oil which is extracted from them by heat and pressure.

Codfish, no doubt, is one of the best fish known to make the excellent fisherman's dish called "chowder," and for the following preparation—which I think is the best one I ever ate—I am indebted to the late Michael Burnham, Esq., by whom it was sent to me:

Fish-chowder.—Take a codfish about six or seven pounds, cut in slices about one inch thick ; take six or seven medium-sized potatoes and cut in slices ; take one pound salt pork, cut in slices, and fried brown ; when sufficiently done, take out the pork from the pot with one half the fat. Now put in a layer of fish, then some of the potatoes and pork, with some pilot-bread ; and so on, alternately, until all is in the pot. Pour over the whole a quart of water and one pint of milk ; add salt and pepper to your taste, and boil twenty minutes. A few onions improve it for those who are fond of them.

P. S.—To the above I add one hundred clams or oysters, in layers with the rest, and a half tumbler of port or a tumbler of claret wine two or three minutes before taking off the fire, stirring it up well.

In 1792, the following was published as a "Curious fact. —At the first discovery of the northern continent of America, few or no codfish were found to the southward of the Banks of Newfoundland and Sable Island. About twenty-five or thirty years ago (1760) they were first discovered off Sandy Hook, in the vicinity of New York. It has been observed that ever since that time they have gradually become more and more plenty on the fishing grounds off the Neversink, in six, seven, and eight fathoms of water, and perhaps equally so many miles further eastward. The present season has afforded an abundance hitherto unknown in that port. Within these few years they begin to be found off and about the capes of Delaware Bay, though in comparatively small quantities, and, it is said, two or three have been caught last year about Chinagoteague Shoals, in latitude thirty-eight, on the coast of Maryland. From these facts it would seem that the codfish is gradually progressing southward, and may, perhaps, in time, be caught along the whole extent of coast belonging to the United States. It is observed by coasting vessels that mackerel are, in the same manner, advancing more to the southward than formerly. We may conclude, from hence, that the Banks of Newfoundland are the original habitation of the codfish, from whence, on account of their prodigious increase, they are annually pushing out colonies in every direction where sustenance can possibly be found."

Haddock.—This fish has something of the appearance of codfish, as to size and color, with a black line running along each side from the gills to the tail. The bones in the head are more prominent and the under jaw shorter. It appears in season with the cod, and is found very good in the months of November and December; then again in June and July, when the flesh is more compact and the flavor excellent, but I think not equal to the codfish.

"*Something curious.*" Captain Stetson informs us that on Wednesday last, while on a fishing party, off Cohasset Rocks, he caught a haddock, and upon opening it for the purpose of cooking, he found in the stomach three hundred and forty dollars in old continental money, new emission! The paper was formed into a roll and was but little injured. —Boston papers, also *Commercial Advertiser*, July 28, 1804.

Halibut.—This is one of the best large cut fish that we have for the table, and is seldom found out of our markets. When placed on the fish-stands for sale, it is always cut as it is wanted. Its flesh is pearly white and very nutritious; and that taken from a fish weighing from fifty to seventy-five pounds is considered the best. The flesh from the large coarse-grained fish is dry and tasteless; and that of a yellowish cast, without the pearly brightness, is apt to be strong and unwholesome. The nape or thin flank part is an excellent piece, being usually fat and juicy, for boiling. Halibut is brought principally from Boston, and is received here alive in the months of March, April (when it is considered best), and May; after this time and through the warm weather it comes packed in ice, until the cold weather commences, after which, if not found through the winter, it is in consequence of severe cold weather or storms, which renders it hazardous to fish for them at sea. In a cured state, pickled, salted, and smoked, they are also found in our markets. A very large halibut was taken by a Gloucester fisherman in 1860, which weighed two hundred and forty-five pounds. Another, still larger, is found noticed in the *American Weekly Mercury*, June 22d, 1732, in the following language: "Our fishermen say they have lately chatch'd an holybote weighing three hundred weight." In the attempt to take a very large halibut, the Portland *Argus* (August, 1847) thus notices a "NARROW ESCAPE.—The two 'fishing women,' somewhat celebrated on this coast, reside on this island (Mt. Deseret, Maine). One of them came near being carried to the bottom by a halibut a short time since. As is their custom, one sat in the bow and the other in the stern, with the little skiff nearly filled with fish. The woman in the bow of the boat hooked a very large halibut, and called her associate to help; but she dared not leave her seat for fear of sinking their loaded boat. The fish was allowed to run to the bottom two or three times to get worried, and then drawn alongside to be killed and drawn in. It seems he did not like to be mastered by a lone woman, and resisted. In the affray, a large codhook attached to the line was drawn into her hand, and then came the danger. The unsubdued monster, being in his native element, now set out for the bottom again; but the heroine, not wishing to accompany him, clung to the boat. She was drawn nearly overboard, but before losing her hold of the boat the line providentially parted, and he thus became disengaged. To this fact alone she owes the preservation of her life. The fish was probably from six to nine feet in length. The 'fishing women' follow their business closely, and are very successful; nothing will induce them to change their employment. They are mother and daughter, the mother being over sixty years of age."

Black (fresh-water) **bass, black perch.**—This is a fine fresh-water fish, when taken from the cold, clear waters of the lakes, and is well known to our fresh-water fishing sportsmen. They are taken from all of the Western lakes, and rivers that lead to them. In size and shape they somewhat resemble the salt-water black-fish, but shorter, a rounder back, and the underjaw longer. The color is of a dusky bluish-black, and the under parts of a bluish-white. I have taken many in Cayuga Lake, from one to two and a half pounds weight; average about two pounds, and are found in our markets scattering from October to April.

The *Commercial Advertiser*, September 8, 1820, states, that "a fish was caught with a hook, in the outlet of Seneca Lake, on Tuesday last, by Horace Teall, called a black-bass, in which was found a copper, or half-penny token, bearing date, 1815, and the size of a cent."

Sea lamprey, commonly called **lamprey-eels**.—These fish are usually taken in large numbers, in the months of March, April, May, and June, but are seldom found plentiful in the public markets, in consequence of their not being much sought after, as their flesh is not generally admired, except by a few country people and foreigners. Large quantities, however, are salted and packed in barrels, then sent abroad. It is said that stewed lampreys were a dish once held in high estimation in England, and that "King Henry the First" died of a surfeit, eating too heartily of this then favorite dainty. My experience, however, in the eating of this fish was rather unfavorable, as I found its flesh insipid and dry eating, dark-colored, and without a hard bone.

The color of this fish is of a brown olive, marbled mixture, fins red and yellow, a bluish tail, and with seven breathing holes along both sides of the neck, and possesses very little tenacity of life—much less than the common eel.

In the months of May and June the lampreys are considered the best, when large quantities are taken up the Hudson River, and especially in the Croton and other rivers. Doctor M. Beardsley says he has taken them in large numbers in the Housatonic, at New Milford, near the falls, with a long pole, having a sharp, crooked hook. When they are seen in the water, sucking fast of the rocks and stones, then, by running the pole down so as to bring the hook just under their bodies, when a jerk up hooks them fast, and they are hauled out. In this manner thousands are taken, and salted down for a part of the family provisions.

The *Canadian Courant* (1831) thus notices a "CURIOUS OCCURRENCE.—On Wednesday last a large sturgeon was observed to leap from the water into a canoe lying at the island in the port, opposite the foot of St. Joseph-street. Immediately means were taken to secure the fish, which, when taken, was found to have two lampreys, about seven inches in length, sticking to its body—one on the top of the head and the other on the insertion of the large fin next the gills. There cannot be a doubt but the fish, in its agonies and efforts to get rid of the lampreys, sprang out of the water with such violence as to precipitate it into the canoe in its descent. The peculiar construction of the mouths of the lampreys show how powerfully they can attach themselves to any substance, and seem expressly constructed to give them a powerful suction ; nor is the rapacity of these fishes less than their power of laying hold of their prey, for when kept some time out of the water, and again placed near the sturgeon, they seized it a second time with much eagerness. The sturgeon measured three feet eight inches ; his little tormentors not a sixth part of his length, nor a sixteenth of his weight."

The **sword-fish** is a very large, round-bodied fish, and, like the halibut, is seen for sale, cut in pieces, on the fish-stands. Its flesh is fine-grained, tender, and well-tasted, and looks much the color of veal. Considered very wholesome, either in the fresh or salted state. It is usually sold at a less price per pound than the halibut. In season in the months of June, July, and August. Its color is of the deepest bluish-black upon the back, gradually growing lighter underneath, the belly being of ashy white, or tarnished silvery shade. They vary in size and weight—from eight to twelve feet in length, of which the sword constitutes about one-third, and from one hundred and fifty to four hundred and fifty pounds weight.

The *New York Sun*, July 7, 1855, says: "A sword-fish, fourteen feet nine inches in length, and weighing five hundred and thirty-seven and a half pounds, was caught off Block Island, by the crew of a pilot-boat, and carried into New Bedford."

The *Commercial Advertiser*, of June 25, 1817, also says: "A sword-fish was caught off the Hook, on the 17th inst., brought to our market, and sold in pieces, at two shillings the pound. The sword, tail, and fins were purchased by Enoch Johnson, Esq., and by him presented to the *Lyceum*."

"This fish" (Dr. Samuel L. Mitchell says) "appeared to have been twelve feet long, and five feet round. I agree with you, that the flesh is excellent eating. The broiled relish prepared for me at Mr. Fairchild s, was in reality very fine.

"My friend, John Ranny, Esq., informs me that another of the same species was taken by one of the pilots near Sandy Hook (as this one of yours was), in the year 1791, and exhibited to the people of this city. That sword-fish is reported to have been sixteen feet in length."

The *Royal Gazette*, July 27, 1782, contains a notice, "To the Curious.—A most surprising fish of an enormous size, called a sea-warrior, armed with a weapon or broadsword, upwards of four feet long, projecting from his head, and so sharp, that in a few minutes it will kill the largest whale; it is by far the greatest curiosity ever seen in this part of the world. To be shown this day and to-morrow at Mr. Jeroleman's Punch House, at the tea-water pump (New York). Grown persons, one shilling; and children sixpence."

The *Pennsylvania Gazette*, October 3, 1751, contains the following attack of a sword-fish (in an extract from a letter dated Boston, September 19). "In our passage from the Main to St. Eustatia, on the 26th of June, in the latitude of 15 and longitude 61, about eleven o'clock at night, was struck by a sword-fish on our starboard bow, which run his sword through our outside plank, and a timber of ten inches thick, and ceiling, and into the hold ten inches, and broke his horn off, and left it into the hold ten inches, which caused our vessel to have four feet and two inches of water in the hold; but by our two pumps cleared her. We reckon that the horn (sword) went through fourteen inches and a half of solid oak."

"The schooner Sarah Millner, of Kingston, in Jamaica, was, on her voyage from thence to this port, struck by a sword-fish, about twelve o'clock in the night, being out three days. The sword penetrated through solid timber thirteen inches thick, and protruding within the vessel upwards of seven inches, passed into a tierce of coffee. He stuck until seven o'clock the next morning, when he broke away, being severely wounded by strokes of the harpoon. The schooner being hove down yesterday, the sword was found and extracted."—*Commercial Advertiser*, November 10, 1809.

An interesting description of the catching of sword-fish, is given by a correspondent at Edgartown, Martha's Vineyard, to the *New York Tribune*, in July, 1855. He says, "one of his companions, whom he was fishing with, discovered a fish to the leeward of the boat; headed for him at once, while his companions commenced to 'clear away' for a fight. Dan's object seemed to be to sail 'head-on' to him, assigning to me as a reason that the fish could not see ahead. After various manœuvres he had succeeded in bringing the boat in range, when he resigned the tiller to his companion and went forward to the bow, taking with him a harpoon. The sword-fish was coming along at a rapid rate upon the top of the water, and I was beginning to fear the consequences of a collision. However, I kept still, and when the fish was within a rod of the boat, Dan made a demonstration which caused the fish to 'wear around,' at which moment Dan hurled the harpoon at him with surprising precision and force, taking him through the neck. Of course there was a line fast to the harpoon, which ran over the side with great rapidity, for the fish, as soon as wounded, dived down perpendicularly. The line was made fast to an empty keg, headed up, which was now thrown overboard, and we started off, to avoid a too close acquaintance with the wounded and excited creature for the present. I should think it was full ten minutes before he again appeared upon the surface, and when he did he went through the water with astonishing velocity (Dan said at the rate of twenty five knots), dragging with him the keg, which was most of the time under water. This rate of speed soon exhausted him, however, and he finally lay still upon the surface. On this we steered for the keg and took it on board, and then cautiously approached the fish. When near enough, Dan dealt him two well-directed blows with a lance (or spade as he termed it) upon his back-bone, which caused him to struggle convulsively for a few moments, when he was taken alongside and rolled on board. In this way we succeeded in capturing four of these monsters, the smallest of which weighed about one hundred pounds, and the largest about three hundred and fifty pounds."

Sturgeon.—The flesh of this large peculiar-looking fish, when found in our markets for sale, is always with the skin off, and cut up as the halibut. The young fat fish are considered the best, when its flesh has a light red or "beefy" appearance and the fat of a pale yellow color. Its flesh is considered wholesome, and, when properly prepared, it is really good eating. Some soak the flesh in scalding water long enough to take away the fatty substance, which is strong if the fish is large; then cut it in steaks and fry it, when it tastes much like veal cutlets. It is much better to roast or bake, than to boil; in fact, sturgeon-eaters seldom boil it. Many also prefer it salted and smoked, when to be had in that state. In season all through the summer months, when it is taken in the North River. They commence to take them about the middle of April and continue until the 1st of September, and are principally of that variety called the sharp-nosed sturgeon, ranging in length from four to nine feet, and in weight from one hundred to above three hundred and fifty pounds.

There appears an account of a sturgeon caught in 1855,

a short distance below Stockton, California, which weighed three hundred and fifty-four pounds, and measured nine feet eight inches in length.

A brisk trade is done in sturgeon meat up the Hudson River, and more particularly at Albany, where no doubt, from its great plentifulness, cheapness, and peculiar color of the flesh, it became known with the name of "Albany Beef." At Philadelphia, also, I saw a great number of colored men engaged in the trade of catching, skinning, and disposing—always in bulk—by the fish or piece (never by weight), great numbers of this fish.

The *Commercial Advertiser*, of 1822, notices an "EXTRAORDINARY HAUL.—Some men who were engaged in fishing for shad in the river Delaware, opposite Tinicum Island, drew up *one hundred and eleven sturgeon* at one haul."

In the north of Europe the flesh of the sturgeon furnishes acceptable food to a great many persons, while its air-bladder is converted into isinglass, and its roe into *caviare.* Dr. Smith in his work on Fish says: "During the long Lent of the Greek Church, and the weeks and fast-days, exceeding in the aggregate four months, sturgeon is the principal food of all European Russia. It was calculated in 1794, that 1,760,405 sturgeon yielded 4,366,800 pounds of *caviare.*" This *caviare* is the roe of the sturgeon or other large fish, prepared by salting and pressing, and was considered a great delicacy when used with roast meats. There is also a very good oil extracted from the offal parts, which is used for the purposes of light."

Pickled Sturgeon, appears to have been introduced in this country at an early day, perhaps before 1750, although I find no account of it until some four years after, when the *New York Weekly Post-Boy* (September 23, 1754) says: "Edward Broadfield is arrived in this city from Trenton, and brought a quantity of pickled sturgeon, and warranted to keep the year round. There is at the house of *Scotch Johnny* [for many years "Scotch Johnny" or John Thompson, kept the "Crown and Thistle," near the White

Hall stairs, N. Y.], a keg opened, where all gentlemen may have an opportunity of seeing and tasting said fish." Some ten years after, the *Gazette*, April 22, 1765, says: "The North American sturgeon is growing in repute every day, so that it is likely to be in great demand in a short time." I should, however, be inclined to believe that it never became much in demand in New York, either pickled or otherwise, as but few advertisements notice it until after the revolution, when one is found which presents many claims for its general adoption. This is found in the *Packet*, October 25, 1784: "Sturgeon put up in spices, equal if not superior in quality to what is done in Europe, no pains or expense being neglected in curing them. This fish, in the way it is put up, is reckoned a genteel dish through many parts of Europe; and as it is ready fit for eating without any addition, renders it very convenient to masters of vessels, who by long voyages, storms, etc., are deprived of an opportunity of cooking victuals. Orders are received at Mr. Bradford's coffee-house, where samples, as they are put up, are left."

This jumping fish is also often seen, by almost every passenger in the summer season, when going up the North River, leaping clear out of the water some eight or ten feet; and occasionally they not only make their last leap, but create some excitement.

The *New York Evening Post*, in August, 1836, notices "An Incident.—A party of ten persons, of both sexes, was crossing the Hudson from Saugerties to Tivoli in a little boat rowed by two of the party. As they reached the middle of the river, a large sturgeon sprang from the water in front of them and threw his huge length into the bottom of the boat, passing directly between the feet of the two gentlemen who sat foremost, and laying himself exactly in the middle under the seats. Great was the surprise and confusion; but one of the gentlemen immediately caught the floundering fish by the tail, and tied it fast with the boat's painter. The creature in the mean time uttered the most plaintive sound, moaning with a noise much like that of a cow. It was taken to Tivoli, where it was found to measure eight feet and a half in length, and to weigh one hundred and fifty pounds. It was cut up and given to the workmen of a foundry on the eastern bank of the river, who made an excellent supper on this "Albany Beef."

A similar circumstance is shown in the *Daily Times*, 25th of July, 1854, which happened in Gardener's Bay, L. I. "Three persons sat fishing in a boat, one of whom, seated in the bow, was knocked overboard by being struck with a sturgeon jumping out of the water near where he sat. He was injured in the shoulder, and cut in the face, and came near being drowned."

Another more singular circumstance is noticed in the *New York Sun*, September 3, 1856: "Captain Simon, of the sloop Science, found a sturgeon floundering about his cabin, which he supposed must have jumped through the stern window, when near Caldwell's Landing, nearly opposite Peekskill, North River."

Then, in the *Commercial Advertiser*, of July 26, 1838, we find noticed a singular death, which occurred in that month in the following manner: "A sloop was sailing up the North River, when a large sturgeon leaped out of the water and alighted upon the deck. All hands immediately busied themselves about securing the stranger; and one of the men being near the side of the vessel, and to the leeward, was knocked or fell overboard with the fish, and was drowned."

Fall herring, or **shad herring** (also called "wee-sick" in Connecticut).—This fish has some of the appearance of a shad, but of a darker color; on the back it is of a bluish-green, with dark-colored spots on the sides, and also with an appearance of spotted stripes running along the back and sides. They are usually taken, with the striped bass, in the months from July to December. Their average weight is about a pound and a half. A fine specimen was sent to me on November 22, 1864, which weighed, plump, three and a quarter pounds, measuring in length twenty and a quarter inches, and six inches in depth. It was very fat, the flesh not so white as the shad, nor was it so sweet, having a little of the herring flavor, and also very troublesome to eat in consequence of the many wiry bones. As it lay on my stall, many pronounced it a shad.

The different varieties of the herring, like the shad, mackerel, etc., when taken from the water, die immediately. Most all kinds of herring, when taken in large quantities, are cured and smoked, and in that way they are often found for sale. When variously prepared they have been esteemed as an article of food from the most remote antiquity. One Guillaume Beuchel, a native of Brabant, in the fourteenth century, discovered a mode of pickling them, which was considered so remarkable, and of so much importance, that the Emperor Charles the Fifth, one hundred and fifty years afterwards, honored his grave with his royal person, and ate pickled herring on the green grass that waved above his bones. "By the corporation charter of the city of Norwich, England, the mayor has to present to the king, annually, a herring-pie. This custom is necessarily practised up to the present day. The pie has a standing crust, modelled in exact representation of Norwich Castle, and filled with herring."

The **Burlington herring** have also had quite a reputation for the table. Large quantities were caught at Dunk's Ferry, says the *Burlington Gazette* (of 1845), many of which were cured by a Mr. Mitchell, at his establishment in Burlington. His method for curing was as follows: "The fish are brought to Mr. Mitchell directly from the nets—all Delaware River fish, and therefore perfectly fresh. They are then cleaned of scales and thrown into pickle, where they remain some hours, whence they are taken and strung on sticks containing a dozen, allowed to dry, and then suspended in the smoke-house, where a choking fog is raised by means of burning sawdust; and, after a week of such fumigation, they are taken down, packed in boxes, and are ready for market. There is a peculiar flavor imparted to the Burlington herring by the pickle in which they are soaked previous to smoking."

Clear-nosed ray.—This variety of the ray is usually found quite abundant, but always cut up, on some of the fish-stands, when it is often sold under the name of skate. The parts sold are only the fleshy side-fins, some of which appear of different forms and colors, showing that they were taken off from the different varieties of the ray and skate. This variety is of a brownish-gray on the back, covered with numerous irregular-shaped dark spots; head almost round, with a small, thin, semi-transparent nose, which feels like a tough jelly; with small eyes, and a double, and sometimes a treble, row of prickles along the middle of the back, down the sides of the tail. The tail is long, tapering, flat beneath, and round above. The flesh is not generally admired, although some foreigners prefer it to either the sword-fish or sturgeon. It, however, improves by keeping, as it becomes more tender and less insipid. A small one, of some ten pounds, was sent to me, of which I prepared the parts to eat; and, although I had it cooked from a French receipt, yet I found it insiped and glutinous. Perhaps the condiments were not so plentifully used as they should have been; but I think I should prefer some other kind of fish.

One of our fishermen, in Washington Market, deals very extensively in this, as well as many other varieties of fish, some of which are not much thought of by other fishermen. The fleshy fins of this ray usually weigh from two to five pounds, and are generally found in season from October to April. There is another variety, called

Spotted ray, of which I saw a small specimen at the Catherine Market, in July, 1864, weighing, perhaps, about four pounds. The head or nose was quite pointed, and the body covered with dark spots. The price of fish was very high that morning. Eels sold at twenty-five cents per pound; fresh blue-fish, fifteen cents; codfish and porgees, ten cents.

This fish, however, was offered, as he lay, for the whole of fifteen cents, and no buyers at that while I was there. Another variety, called

Whip-sting ray, are often taken around the harbor of New York. One was taken in the North River, at the Woodlawn Dock, in 1852, which I supposed would weigh fifty pounds, with a common bass-pole and line; however, it was in the hands of a skilful fisherman, who safely landed it on the shore, with the assistance of another person, in spite of its lashing tail and sharp spines. The color of the body was quite a dark olive-brown, with a short nose, and a long slim tail like a whip. And still another, called

Cow-nosed ray, I saw at the Jefferson Market, some few years after, taken near the same place, by Messrs. Thomas Lawrence, George Starr, William S. Smith, and others. This specimen, however, was a much smaller one than the preceding, weighing twenty-one and a half pounds. It had a double nose, on the side of which were the eyes, instead of on the back like the preceding; the color also about the same. The wings or fleshy fins were more pointed and wider in proportion, and the tail longer and thinner. The flesh of this variety is generally considered the best, as well as it is the most uncommon in our markets. Another, bearing the name of

Smooth skate, is not quite so common as the last-named, having a smooth back, a thick, stout tail, with three rows of short stiff spines, one on each side, and the other on the top of the caudal appendage. Dr. Mitchell notices one that was taken beside a wharf in the East River, November 5, 1815, the length of which was four feet and one inch, and the breadth two feet and four inches, being a large fish.

Broad-sting ray.—This species is rarely found in our markets, but are sometimes caught East. One of my acquaintances took one that weighed one hundred and sixty pounds, which had a great deal more width than length. A part of the fleshy fins was prepared by one of the party and eaten, but was not generally liked.

Porpoises.—These large fish are sometimes caught, especially by sailors who have been long without fresh provisions. They harpoon them, and cut out the choice fleshy parts, enough for a day or two's use, and throw the balance overboard. The flesh is nearly the color of venison, and from a small fish is quite tender, with the flavor resembling beef, but fishy, and, when fried or made into fish-balls, is considered good eating, and much enjoyed by them.

John Josselyn, gent., while on his passage to this country, in the month of May, 1638, writes—"In the afternoon, the mariners struck a porpoisce, called also a *marsovius*, or sea-hogg, with an harping-iron, and hoisted her aboard. They cut some of it into thin pieces, and fryed. It tastes like rusty bacon, or hung beef—if not worse; but the liver boiled, and soused sometime in vinegar, is more grateful to the pallat." (The liver is much like a hog's, both in appearance and flavor.) Soon after "we took a sharke, a great one, and hoisted him on board. The seamen divided the sharke into quarters, and made more quarters about it than the purser, when he makes five quarters of an oxe; and, after they had cooked him, he proved very rough-grained, not worthy of wholesome preferment; but, in the afternoon, we took store of bonitoes, or Spanish dolphins—a fish about the size of a large mackerel, beautiful with admirable varieties of glittering colours in the water, and was excellent food." (No doubt, the *Spanish mackerel.*)

In another part of his account he says: "We took a young sharke, about three foot long, which being drest and dished by a young merchant, a passenger, happened to be very good fish, having very white flesh, in flakes like codd, but delicately cur'd."

Some curious accounts of the taking of porpoises are worthy of notice, the first of which is found in the *Post-Boy*, November 12, 1744, and dated Dublin, June 5: "Yesterday being a great spring tide, a vast army of porpusses came up Lough Foyle in pursuit of salmon. As they rolled by Londonderry, the sailors pursued them in their boats, and killed them all the way, drove them six miles farther up the lough, to the flats about Mount Gavelling. There a new chase began by our fishermen and country people, who stretched a net across the lough, and drove them up to the narrow passages of the Great Island, which lies a mile below this town; there they fell on them with guns, swords, hatchets, and all kinds of weapons, and made a terrible slaughter. There were killed here above one hundred and sixty, besides as many mortally wounded and carried off by the flood. Including those the men of Londonderry killed, there have at least fallen in this battle five hundred porpoises, generally weighing from 1,000 to 1,500 weight, and very good oil. Some of them were full of young ones as big as calves; and some had from six to ten salmon in their stomachs. But we hope that since these grand devourers are destroyed, our fishing will hereafter flourish, and we are pretty well repaid by this oil for the damage they have done."

Another more interesting and laughable scene is found in the same paper dated January 13, 1752. In the news from Annapolis, Md., December 4, 1751: "One Solomon Sharp, seeing a porpoise in a shallow creek, got some of his neighbors to go with him to assist in catching it, who shot at it, but without killing it. At length the porpoise, being pretty much fatigued, did not regard the canoe they were in, but frequently came very near it. Sharp watching his opportunity, leaped upon the back of the fish, and was carried by it for a considerable time, sometimes up to his neck in water, till at length the porpoise running himself on shore, was there killed by the spectators."

Dog-fish.—These fish are occasionally, and sometimes plentifully taken in our harbor, but seldom found for sale in our markets, although they are eatable. Large numbers are taken on the eastern coast, principally for the oil they furnish; and in Truro and Provincetown, Mass., the fish are dried for food for cattle. In Scotland, the flesh of this fish is eaten by the lower classes; there are also many people who eat them here when properly prepared,—that is, they skin them first before cooking, or scald them so that the outside skin is removed easily. I had a piece of a small one (some fifteen inches in length) nicely fried, sent to me, and found it very much the taste of halibut; rather dry, but good. These fish have much of the appearance of young shark (and I am inclined to think they are the young of the same fish), having a small mouth underneath their long upper jaw. The color of the back is of a dark lead-color, lighter on the sides and quite white underneath, and without scales, although the skin is quite rough when stroked backwards, and is considerably used for polishing certain articles.

In the History of Maine, it is stated that "one of Goswold's men (in 1602) had been cured by sassafras, in twelve hours, of a surfeit occasioned by excessive eating of dog-fish, then considered a delicious fish."

In the year 1758, during the French war with England, we find the skins of dog-fish and shark were in some demand in New York. The *Weekly Post-Boy*, July 17, of that year, says: "As there is great plenty of dog-fish and sharks to be caught on this coast, any person that will catch them may hear of a purchaser for the skins, by inquiring of the printer hereof. The said skins must be stretched and dried in the shade, for which an encouraging price will be given."

Shark.—A small young shark, not over two feet in length, is a very good fish to eat, being sweet, with much the flavor of the halibut. The hammer-head variety I also had cooked (with skin on), and several thought its flesh was much like a young halibut, not quite so dry as the common shark or dog-fish; it however was from a fish weighing less than two pounds, which appeared very fat. Shark or dog-fish are seldom offered for sale in our markets, or not within my recollection, although I have known persons who have eaten the young of all the varieties, when they could get them. Sailors enjoy their flesh at sea, as it is "fresh meat." Many years ago, when shark were taken at our wharves, and especially near the Catherine or Old Fly Markets, it was a treat for some of the old negroes, who were not long in cutting out the choice pieces, if the "shirk" was small, for their own particular use. There are many species of this fish, some of which have been taken of an enormous size; and among the earliest account of these captures is one to be found in the *New York Mercury*, July 30, 1764, of one taken at Newport "by a number of whalemen, up the river, who went off from Mr. Bowers' shipyard. It is said to be forty-five feet in length, and that the liver of it will make ten barrels of oil."

Then, *Niles' Register*, 1822, notices "a basking shark, that was caught near Middletown, N. J., on the 4th of June of that year. Its circumference was eighteen feet, length thirty-two feet ten inches." The *Gazette* (15th inst.) says of this *sea-serpent*: "The wonderful *sea-serpent* lately caught at Brown's Point, near Middletown, N. J., is now exhibiting at 253 Broadway, opposite the City Hall. It has two perfect legs, with two joints in each, and a nail projecting out of the palm of each foot. This serpent has no bones, no heart, no tongue, no brains; but a very large liver, which produced four barrels of oil."

Under the head of news from Brighton, November 10, 1812, we find the following in relation to this variety: "The enormous fish, on having been brought on shore at this place, was yesterday sold by the proprietors in the usual way of their disposing of other fish (commonly known by the name of Dutch auction). It was put up at £150, and kept reducing £5 at a time, till it came to £70, when it was purchased by Mr. Weller, who exhibited it during the day, and which produced to him many pounds. The emoluments which this animal has produced to the fishermen have been very large; we are assured by the party that they have received between £200 and £300. The fish, we are now perfectly satisfied, is the *squalis maximus*, or basking shark. Upon opening this fish, the company present were much surprised at the enormous size of the liver, which consists of two lobes, measuring in length upwards of eleven feet, each being sixteen inches thick, and is supposed to weigh considerably above two tons."—*Commercial Advertiser*, January 7, 1813.

Niles again, in 1826 (October 7), says: "A shark of enormous length of thirty feet, whose liver filled ten barrels, has been caught near Eastport. When first seen, it was thought to be a *sea serpent*, and pursued and killed."

Then again in the same paper, June 6, 1835, we find: "Recently at Princetown, a large 'bone shark' was discovered nearly exhausted among a number of herring-seines, several of which he had torn away. A boat put off with a harpoon and lance, when he was immediately dispatched and brought to shore. He measures twenty seven feet in length, girth about fifteen feet, and his liver is expected to yield eight barrels of oil. This is said to be the largest shark ever taken in that quarter."

Then, at an early date, is found a singular and dreadful attack of a shark, noticed in the *New York Gazette and Weekly Post-Boy*, August 12, 1751, in the Boston news, August 5, as follows: "Three men were in a canoe near Well; a large shark came alongside of them, and, by putting his head over the side of the canoe, endeavored to overset it. That he attempted once or twice in vain, but at last effected it, and got one of the unhappy men, who was doubtless devoured by the ravenous monster, as he was never seen after. The other two men, having righted the canoe, got into it and escaped."

A miraculous escape, although a dreadful "fight with a shark," is found noticed in the Greenport, L. I., *Watchman* (September, 1865), which says: "At about nine A. M., of Sunday last, the schooner Catherine Willcox, of Lubec, Me., was proceeding down the Sound, and while becalmed abreast of that port, about eight miles off shore, the captain and a young man, seventeen years of age, named Peter Johnson, belonging at Robinston, Me., formerly a soldier, and who was now working his passage home, stripped off their clothing and jumped overboard for a swim. Johnson swam a few rods from the vessel to pick up a small piece of wood, and, while returning, a huge shark, judged to have been fourteen or fifteen feet long, darted towards him, and seized him about the middle, and instantly disappeared with him, dragging him down, as he says, about thirty feet deep. He struggled and fought with the ravenous monster, fearfully lacerating his right arm in the effort. He finally succeeded in grasping the shark by the head, and by gouging one of his eyes, at the same time dealing him powerful blows about the head, he succeeded in wresting himself free. He then swam to the schooner, pursued by the monster; but, being a man of remarkable physical strength and pluck, he finally succeeded in driving him off, and got on board of the schooner, pulling himself up by the fore-topsail clue-line, which hung overboard, but not until the terrible teeth had left their mark in many a ghastly wound on his abdomen, groins, thigh, and leg, so that he was one mass of gore. The mate and one of the crew took him in the yawl-boat and rowed to the shore, landing at Bokum, whence he was conveyed in a wagon to the residence of Dr. Skinner, who, with Doctors Bryant and Kendall, sewed up and dressed his wounds, the operation lasting nearly an hour, during which time he was kept under the influence of chloroform. There were some thirty-four distinct wounds on his person. The abdomen and groin of the right side were fearfully mangled, the flesh being torn off and left hanging by the skin only, nothing but the thin lining membrane of the abdomen preventing the entrails from gushing out; the femoral vessels were laid bare and the nerves completely exposed. On the left side of the abdomen was another wound, similar in character but less extensive. The right thigh was very badly torn and gashed. Nothing but his indomitable courage and physical vigor enabled him to escape alive. The case attracts attention because of the fact that the shark must have been of the species known as 'man-eater,' which are common in low latitudes, but are rarely seen in shoal water. The common shovel-nose shark of our waters seldom, if ever, attack mankind. Johnson is still living, and, although in a very precarious situation, there is yet some hope of his ultimate recovery."

FISH—SMALL AND ABUNDANT.

Brook trout, or **speckled trout.**—This beautiful and excellent fish (as it is generally considered) is usually found quite small in our markets. The best are taken from the clear, running streams,—the head and back being mottled with a brownish-green and yellow; the sides of a bluish-gray, covered with large yellow and crimson spots; and the belly of a silvery white. The mouth has a black appearance inside. They are sometimes found differently marked, being much darker, with more red and gold colors, etc.; but, as I have before mentioned, the cause is in the different sexes, ages, waters, and food. Their flesh is somewhat the color of salmon, but lighter, and nearly of an orange-color; and as for its table qualifications, although I have placed this fish at the head of this list, yet I cannot agree with a great many epicures as to the superiority of its flesh: for the pot, pan, or gridiron, and plainly cooked, there are many small fish which I prefer before this usually dry-fleshed fish; but when rashers of fat pork, etc., are cooked with it,

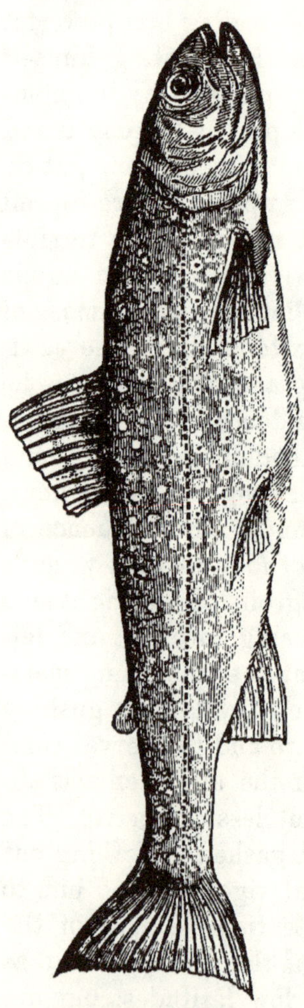

BROOK TROUT.

then the flesh will bear the weight of their testimony in favor of it. The correct way, however, of testing the qualities of a fish, is simply to plain boil it, without sauces or any thing else to make it better or worse.

Brook-trout are found in our markets from half a pound to four pounds weight, in their season, which appears to be from March (rather better in April) until August. A law was passed early in the year 1817, against the sale of this fish from the first day of October to the fifteenth day of March, in any year; nor at any time, weighing less than half a pound.

Among the largest specimens of this fine fish, the *Easton Sentinel*, of 18—, notices:

"MAMMOTH TROUT.—General Cadwallader and lady, of Philadelphia, being on a visit to Bethel, Pa., Mr. G. H. Goundie presented to Mr. Zeigler, of the Eagle Hotel, one of the largest brook-trout perhaps ever known in this country, which was served up in his best style at a dinner last Monday to the general and lady, and a party of ladies and gentlemen of Bethlehem, Pa. The trout measured twenty-two inches in length, nineteen inches in circumference, and weighed seven and one-eighth pounds. It was raised by Mr. Jacob Schnieder, of the Leigh-water Gap, who had kept it for the last six years in a trough in the second story of his house."

Then the *Daily Times*, May 17, 1855, says: "Among the attractions of Messrs. Tiffany, Ellis & Co., at their store in Broadway, yesterday, were three enormous brook-trout, of surpassing beauty. The largest weighed five pounds; they were taken by Mr. J. B. Young, in Killingly, Conn."

The same paper, October 17, 1863, shows "a big thing on ice." "The most superb specimens of brook-trout that we have ever seen have been brought to this city by Mr. G. S. Page, of the firm of George S. Page & Brother, Maiden Lane. They were caught by Mr. Page, in the early part of this week, somewhere north of New York City, about one hundred and fifty miles off. The heaviest of the fish, a huge, fat, plump, glorious fellow, of firm flesh and unequalled complexion, weighed eight and three-quarters pounds; the next largest weighed eight and one-quarter pounds; the next, seven and a quarter pounds; and several of them were five and six pounds a piece. Altogether, fifty-one large trout, weighing two hundred and seventy-three pounds, were taken from a small brook, in eight days' fishing, by two gentlemen—Mr. Page and Mr. Henry O. Stanley." A still larger fish is noticed in the *Tribune*, February 29, 1856, which stated that "Genin, the hatter, had in his possession a speckled (*lake*) trout, twenty-six inches in length, and weighing twelve pounds, that was caught in Lake O'Claire, a hundred miles northeast of Montreal, by Mr. W. Parker." The same paper again, July 14, 1864, says: "Mr. West, president of the Fishermen's Club and proprietor of the Franklin House, Tarrytown, was in the city yesterday. He brought with him the six-pound brook-trout, caught by Mr. E. R. Wunder, of No. 167 Bleecker-street. The fish has been kept in a spring, at Mr. West's house, for some time, and is in as healthy condition as any admirer of Isaac Walton could wish. The trout was formally presented to Mr. Wunder by James Drumgold, secretary of the club."

A curious incident is found in the *Commercial Advertiser*, July 12, 1816, taken from the Boston *News*, July 5th, and headed "FISHING EXTRAORDINARY.—As a gentleman was angling last Thursday, in the mill-dam, Westchester, he accidentally threw his line across a strong white duck, which suddenly turned round, twisted the gut about her own neck, and fixed the hook of the dropper fly in her own breast. Thus entangled and hooked, she soon broke off the gut above the dropper, and sailed down the stream with the end fly trailing behind her. She had not proceeded far before a trout, apparently about one and one-half pound weight, took the fly effectually. Then commenced a struggle the most extraordinary that ever was witnessed—a duck at the dropper and a large trout at the end of the fly! Whenever the trout exerted itself the terrors of the duck were very conspicuous—it fluttered its wings and dragged the fish. In case of no violent struggle on the part of the trout, the duck evidently gave way, and suffered herself at last to be drawn under some bushes, where the shortness of the gut did not allow the trout to shelter himself in his retreat, and the duck to remain on the surface at the same time. The duck's head was repeatedly drawn under water. By chance, however, the gut got across a branch, which hung downwards in the water, and the duck, taking advantage of the purchase which this gave her, dragged her opponent from his hole and compelled him to show his head above water. Then it became a contest of life or death—the trout was in the last agonies, and the duck evidently in a very weak state—when the gut gave way and suffered them to part, each his own way."

King-fish (called **barb** along the Jersey shore, and **whiting** on the coast of Florida, Carolina, etc.) This very fine, small, solid-fleshed, and highly-esteemed fish is especially adapted for the frying-pan. In former years they were quite abundant, but of late they sometimes pass many seasons before showing themselves, not being considered a regular or yearly visitor. The color on the back and sides is of a dark bluish-gray, with silvery reflexions and clouds of a darker hue running obliquely across or forward from the back, and a white, silvery belly. Their usual weight is about three-quarters of a pound, and seldom above two pounds. The largest fish of this species I ever saw weighed two and three-quarter pounds, in the month of May, 1865. In season from May to September.

Smelt.—This pretty, little, and almost transparent fish, is considered one of the very best "pan-fish," if the small size was not against it, which causes it to be somewhat troublesome to prepare. The back is of a pale olive-green, with silvery sides, and a satin-like band extending its whole length. Weight from two to four ounces, and in season from October to April. When fresh (or *green*, as the fishermen term all fish which are not frozen or stale) they have a smell much like that of cucumbers; and when stale they lose this pleasant odor, and also their usual flavor.

Sea-perch or **ruddy-bass.**—This fish is the common sea or river perch, which is found so plentiful when in season. The color, however, is sometimes found quite different when taken from different waters, but all are excellent eating. Its usual color is of an olive-brown tinge, and a golden hue when fresh out of water; the sides are of a yellowish white and with reddish fins. The largest and best are brought from "Old Town Bay," where they are taken above four pounds weight. In season from November to May, and scattering along until July. Usual weight about half a pound.

Frost-fish or **tom-cod.**—This is a scaleless but a delicate and savory pan-fish of the cod species, and of a small size. Its color varies much in the different seasons, from a rich orange to a light green yellow, shaded by a dark brown on the back. Common weight from a quarter to half a pound. In season from September to April.

Silver eel.—This is considered the finest of the eel species, and the color, even "skinned," has something the appearance of silver. Old fishermen say they do not stay in the harbor and bury themselves in the mud as the common eels do, but in the month of November they appear in thousands leaving for the "deep sea," and what is most singular, those of a size leave together, when they are often taken in nets, all of a size. They also say that in spearing for eels through the ice, seldom or never are silver eels taken. In season from April to November. In the fall of 1861, the Messrs. Miller, of Fulton Market, had two skinned of nearly seven pounds' weight. The skins were tanned and made into two pocket-books (by Geo. Evans & Son, No. 1 Jacob-street) of a very flexible and durable character.

Common eel.—They are a very sweet and savory fish, and always in our markets in plenty. Those taken from the seashore are preferred, as they are generally in the best condition. An old fisherman told me that he one day caught several eels at the foot of Fifteenth-street, North River, which he took home and had cooked, but in consequence of a disagreeable taste he could not eat them. He supposed the gas-works or refuse from that place cast into the river had affected them, as he found the taste much as the gas-tar smelled. A curious-looking eel was sent to me, and on laying it alongside of a common eel of the same weight (two pounds three ounces), I found it three and one-half inches longer, a slimmer and a more pointed head, the color on the back of a dark bluish-black, underneath of a grayish brown, and the whole body was covered with short, black, distinct bars, about one-eighth of an inch long, but shorter near the head. These bars were irregularly laid, with three or four in line, or side by side, then across the ends, and so continued throughout.

The serpentine appearance of the eel is not in its favor, and no doubt somewhat injures their sale; but they are as good eating as they are ill-looking, and what is most in their favor is that they are always found "skinned" when for sale on the stands. Usual weight from a half to two pounds, although at times they run much larger. A few years ago Rogers & Co., of Fulton Market, had a box of large eels which weighed from eight to twelve pounds each, and skinned at that. The following notices are of larger ones. The *American Register*, Philadelphia, 1807, says: "On Saturday last an eel of the following surprising dimensions was caught by Captain Howland, between the bridges on the Schuylkill, viz.: length five feet two inches, girth thirteen inches, width twelve inches, and weighing twelve and one-half pounds." Dr. Smith, in his work on "Fish," says: "The largest eel on record was caught in a bay of Long Island, and weighed sixteen and a half pounds." If the doctor had looked in the *New York Gazette*, January 15th, 1727–8, he would have found the following *heavy* eel story: "They write from Shire-Drain, in Lincolnshire, that on the 16th of last month an eel was caught there by one Wm. Townshend, which was seven feet four inches in length, two feet six inches thick; the fat taken out of it weighed sixteen pounds and a half; the ears were eight inches long; the water taken out of its bladder was three quarts and a pint; the weight of the creature was sixty-five pounds."

Eel-skins are found dried for sale in some of our markets, but usually at the Fulton. They are used for various purposes.

Carp.—This beautiful and excellent fish has for several years past been found in our markets. It is not a native of these waters, but having been introduced here, it has made its way into the North River, where many have been taken for several years past and brought to our markets. Their general color on the back is a golden olive-brown, head darker, belly yellowish white, fins dark brown, and a small mouth. They look somewhat like the sucker, with a scale like the mullet. Their growth is slow. They usually weigh from one-half to three pounds, and occasionally above twelve pounds, but average about one pound. In season from October to April.

Lafayette fish, sea-chub, spot, goody, or **river porgee.**—These are a sweet and good little pan-fish, rather a rare visitor, but some years they appear quite abundant. The year that Lafayette visited America (1824) this fish was very numerous; and, at that time, by general consent, it received this new name, as it was thought by many to be a new fish. Color of a grayish-white, with many dark-colored bars running obliquely forward, and pale yellow fins; in season from July to October, when it visits our harbors. Its usual weight is from a quarter to half a pound.

Big porgee, or **porgy, scup, scapang.**—This is a well-flavored fish, although a little dry, and would be more valued if it was less plentiful. They are pretty well known without description, as they are taken in great numbers on the "banks," in the many excursions throughout the summer months, by many of our citizens. Thousands are also taken on the Eastern coast, which are generally poorer, smaller, and darker colored. In the month of April a few of a very large size are occasionally taken, which are found very fine. Their general season begins in May and lasts until December—usually found best in the fall months. Weight from a half-pound to two pounds—the average less than one pound.

In relation to the large numbers of this and other fish taken sometimes, I extract the following from a letter of T. V. Tuthill, dated 1849. He says: "My farm lies on the east end of Long Island, in the town of Southold, Suffolk County. It is bounded on the south by a small bay, where there is an abundance of seaweed, fish, eels, clams, etc. There were taken in this bay, in a few days, last season, nearly *one hundred thousand porgies*, which were sent to New York, and brought over one thousand dollars. There have been taken in our harbor, in the months of May and June, over *eight millions of white-fish* (which we use mostly for manure), in shoals of one hundred to forty thousand at a draught. Our lines are from one hundred and fifty to two hundred and fifty rods long. They are drawn by horses around a capstan."

Spring mackerel, or **common mackerel**.—This is one of the most beautiful of all fish, being of a round, tapering form, back marked with blue and green, and white under. Its appearance, however, is pretty well known, as well as its quality, to all housekeepers, fresh, salted, or smoked. It is never found alive on the stands, and seldom found a fat fish fresh; or rather, there are seldom any found among those brought fresh to our markets that would rank No. 1 salted. They appear smaller, and seldom weigh above one pound. Many fishermen say that it is the same fish that is taken to the "Eastward," and salted in such vast numbers; and, no doubt, when they arrive here on our coast, after having a long and wearisome passage, as they are sometimes met at sea in immense shoals, extending along the sea as far as the eye can reach, followed, worried, and destroyed by hundreds of dolphins, and other large fish, is the cause of their being in such poor condition when found on the fish-stands; but they soon regain their fatness in our waters, and before the large numbers are taken on the coast of Massachusetts, etc., for barrelling, they are in a better condition. They are not, however, the No. 1 fish of forty years ago, when we often found them large and fat enough to weigh from one and a quarter to two pounds, and salted at that. The present No. 1 fish would then rank about No. 3, which were then seldom wanted. The fine large fish have been either driven away, and sought new feeding-grounds, or they have ceased to be plentiful as in former years—perhaps in consequence of the great numbers annually taken, which has gradually diminished the old large fish, and left the small young fish behind. Those mackerel which are brought to our markets fresh, are principally taken off the "Hook," and brought alive in fish-wells, but soon die after having been taken out. In season about the first of May, and found scattering along nearly the whole summer.

A very large catch of mackerel, and other fish, is noticed in the *New York Mercury*, July 15, 1754: "Last Wednesday fortnight, there was taken, off Cape Henry, the largest draught of fish ever known in this part of the world. After several pilot-boats, etc., were loaded with them, there remained on the beach not less than *twenty wagon-loads*, among which were vast quantities of very fine large mackerel."

Thimble-eyed mackerel, chub-mackerel, or **fall mackerel.**—These fish are found smaller than the preceding, and with very large eyes. There is not much doubt but they are the young of the "spring mackerel." My parents told me that, in the fall of 1813, provisions were scarce and high, but, providentially, large schools of these small mackerel came into our harbors, and filled all the small rivers, creeks, inlets, when cart-loads were taken and sold very cheap, which tended to relieve the wants of many of the poor inhabitants, in that season of scarcity and want. When found in our markets they are usually strung together, but are not much thought of for the table. In season from September to November.

Bergall, blue perch, conner, choqset.—There are two varieties of this little fish (blue, or common, and spotted), both much the appearance of the black-fish, but lighter colored, one of quite a bluish cast, the other quite spotted. A very fair pan-fish, but, by taking the skin off (Boston fashion), the flesh appears very white, and is delicate eating. Average weight not over six ounces; in season from June to November.

Winter flounder, or **New York flat-fish.**—This small species of the flat-fish is usually known as the "winter-flounder. The color is of a pale, dirty green, with darkish clouded spots, and white beneath. The mouth is quite small, with the eyes on the left side, and the gill opening on the right. In season from October to July; weight from six to ten ounces, and an excellent pan-fish.

Sand flounder, or **pigmy flat-fish,** is another species, smaller, and not so good for the pan. The color is of an olive-brown on back, and underneath of a bluish-white; weight from a quarter to half a pound.

Yellow perch, yellow barred perch.—This little fresh-water perch is occasionally found quite plentiful on the fish-stands; in fact, it is taken from almost all the lakes and fresh-water rivers in the United States. It differs from the common perch in having a rounder body, head smaller, and tapering towards the snout; eyes, large; color of the back, olive, with yellow sides, and lighter underneath. Four or more bands also run across from the back to the belly. I had a very large perch, weighing above two pounds, boiled (which was taken in one of the lakes on Long Island, with several others quite as large), and found the flesh firm, but quite dry and almost tasteless; no doubt, it would have been much better fried or broiled. Found in the greatest plenty along in the winter months, but in season from September to April.

Sand-porgee.—A smaller fish than the common porgee, but something of the same appearance, except that it has five or six dusky bars across the back. A very fair pan-fish of about six ounces weight. In season in the months of August and September.

Mullet.—There are several varieties of these fish, among which the striped mullet is the most plentiful. They are usually a very fat fish, but for the table they are not much admired, having an unpleasant flavor; the white mullet, however, are considered the best. The striped variety have large scales, color and stripes somewhat like the striped bass, being also a rounder and thicker fish, with a small blue spot on the base of the pectoral fin. They also have a short flat head, and a mouth which raises higher in the centre than on the sides when open. Usual weight is about a half a pound, and in season from September to May. I saw one in November, 1858, which weighed three and a quarter pounds. Mr. R. D. Brower, fishmonger, of Jefferson Market, informed me that in the year 1841, while living on the coast of New Jersey, between Squan and Barnegat, a very heavy storm and high wind drove the sea over the banks, and with it large numbers of mullet, so as to fill all the low-lands and small ponds with water several feet deep. For two or three days thousands were taken with a common scap-net, before the water ran off, and with it carried off the fish. He says they were in excellent condition, and no doubt driven or forced in by the heavy sea.

Sea-robin, banded gurnard, grunter, or **pig-fish.**—This fish is known by the above names, but usually as the sea-robin, among our fishermen. It is at times caught plentifully in nets, in the months of May, June, and July, with the porgee, but it is seldom used as food, as it is an ugly fish to handle as well as to clean, on account of the long bony spines about the head and gills, and also being without scales and quite slippery. The flesh, however, is good; if the head be taken off and dished up as the king-fish, in eating it I could hardly tell the difference. Its usual weight is from six to twelve ounces, but I have heard of their weighing twenty ounces.

Another fish, somewhat like this fish, called

Common bull-head, or **common sculpin**, but usually not so large nor quite so plentiful, is occasionally found among other fish. The body and fins are usually found marked like a toad; head rough and spiny, with large side or pectoral fins, and small ventral, but quite long. The flesh is good eating, but its form and color render it rather objectionable for the table.

Harvest-fish—broad shiner.—This fish is also commonly known by many of our fishermen as *butter-fish.* The name harvest-fish is given it, no doubt, from the fact that they are usually caught in large numbers about that season. They are short, deep, and quite thin above and below, of a silvery color, with blue and green tints, and the sides marked with short creases. They also have large eyes and the nose quite short and blunt; weight about six ounces, and in season from July to October. A very fair pan-fish, but rather unpleasant to clean: in consequence of their food, and from this cause, some give them the name of stinkards; the fishermen of New York, however, have called this fish butter-fish so many years, that it will be troublesome to get rid of it. There is a little fish known as the

American butter-fish, or **spotted gunnel**, about six inches in length, round in form, with a small head and eyes. The top or dorsal fin runs the whole length of the body and is quite short, marked with fourteen black marks; the under or anal fin runs about half way to the tail, which is also short and rounding; the sides are also covered with several dark oval marks, and the whole fish seldom weighs above three ounces. They are seldom found in our markets although often taken in our harbor, or among oyster-beds. A fine specimen of five and a half inches long, taken out of a large oyster by G. Braisted, of Jefferson Market, and presented to me, appeared to have been caught or fastened up in the oyster, perhaps the day before the oyster was taken.

Shiner, or **bay shiner.**—This is a beautiful little silvery-looking fish, being of a little darker hue above than below, and the fins of a yellowish tint. They are very delicate eating, but small and troublesome to prepare for that operation. I have often caught them around the harbor of New York, with other kinds at the same time. I have also taken another kind, called

New York shiner, or **fresh-water shiner,** from some of the fresh-water streams, much like the preceding, but not so delicate eating. They are, however, seldom found in our markets, in consequence of not being salable.

Common sucker.—This is a square, thick-backed, and round-bodied fish of a dusky greenish cast, whitish belly, and a small puckered mouth under, as if it lived altogether by suction. It is found in running (fresh water) streams, lying on or near the bottom quite still, where I have often taken them with a noose-snare made of long horse-hair on the end of a long pole. It is quite a fair pan-fish, but of a groundy taste. In season from October through the winter months. Average weight less than a pound. I saw one at the Fulton Market, October, 1855, which weighed three and a half pounds, and have read of them weighing five.

Cat-fish, or **common cat-fish, horned pout, minister.**—This is a common fresh-water fish, found in our markets in the months from February to May, then again in October and November; usually of a dusky brown color above, mottled sides, and a dirty white beneath; without scales and quite slimy, and with several barbels or fleshy whiskers about the mouth, which gives it somewhat the appearance of a cat's nose. Their color, however, varies much when taken from different waters; as well as, some have larger heads in proportion, being broader, longer, and quite thorny, which some persons give the names of bull-heads, bull-pouts, brown cat-fish, and when found of a very dark or black color, they call them black cat-fish. They are all unfit for the table without being skinned, which adds much to their qualities as a good pan-fish. Perhaps the fish-women of Baltimore understand taking off their *jackets* (skins) better than any others in the trade in the various large cities, with a woollen glove on the left hand, and a knife followed with a pair of nippers in the right; the fish are seized in the left hand, and quickly the skins fly one way while the flesh goes another, and the fish is ready for the pan or pot before the deed could be recorded. Large numbers are also sold in Philadelphia, where they tie them up by the tail in bunches of four or six, and sell them for a fip or a levee according to the size; the smallest fish are, however, the best.

An old black fellow, fishing in the Delaware, near Point-no-Point, several years ago, was seen to haul up several fine rock (streaked bass) fish, which he had no sooner disengaged from his hook than he threw into the water again. When asked the reason of this strange proceeding, he drew himself up, and with a countenance in which it was impossible to say whether haughtiness or indignation predominated, replied: "Ven I fishes for catty (meaning cat-fish) I'll ketch catty, and have nothing to do wid dese ere feller till I want him."

Common herring.—This is the smallest of the herring species, and known by many as the herring of commerce, as the greatest numbers caught are cured as salted herring, or smoked herring, and thus sent abroad; but I think they are not now so plentiful as they were some thirty years ago. They are usually brought here in the frozen or fresh state during the months of February, March, and April. Their color on the back and head is quite a dark blue, tinged with yellow, and lighter underneath. Usual weight about half a pound. Another variety is called the

Spring-herring or **American alewive.**—These fish are usually found much larger than the preceding, and have much of the form of a small shad; in fact, some fishermen call them *hickory shad.* Color of the back of a bluish green, with silvery sides that show a striped appearance, and large scales. They are often caught with the shad in the spring of the year, and sometimes found plentiful, cheap, and not much thought of.

In the news from Havre-de-Grace, Maryland, April 30, 1818, is noticed: "Great Haul of Fishes.—On the 29th inst., it is computed that the almost incredible number of nearly *two millions of herrings*, besides a great number of shad, were taken in the vicinity of this town. We saw two different hauls, each of which, we are informed by those acquainted with fishing, contained three hundred thousand fine herrings and a considerable number of mammoth shad." —*Commercial Advertiser*, May 4, 1818.

Sun-fish, pond-fish, or **pumpkin-seed.**—These little, plentiful, fresh-water fish are generally caught more for amusement than the table; they are, however, found in large numbers, usually from October to April, especially when other fish are scarce. Their colors are beautiful, being of a greenish olive, with red and yellow irregular spots, and also two large dark spots, one on each side or edge of the gill-covers, back of the eye. They are a short, deep fish, of about three or four ounces in weight; I have, however, had them to weigh over half a pound. Their flesh is sweet, but dry and crumbling. Another variety of this fish is called

Black-eared pond-fish, but is not so plentiful. A specimen presented to me November 4, 1864, weighed thirteen ounces, length nine inches, depth four inches, and was a thicker and a little longer fish, according to the width, than the preceding. The scales were less variegated, but with light blue irregular stripes starting from the lower jaw and running back on the gill-cover, and on which was a black ear on a line with the eye. The yellow color was not so brilliant as the above. As a table-fish I found its flesh much like the former. (Since, I have seen several much larger than the above.)

Mossbonker, menhagen, panhagen, white-fish, bony-fish, and **hard-head.**—This fish enjoys more names than any other known. It is a species of the herring that is caught more plentiful than, perhaps, any other kind of fish. The flesh is sweet, but so full of bones as to be almost rejected as food, and of course seldom found in our markets, except the "Catherine," in New York, on a Sunday morning. The color of the head and back is a greenish bronze, with a dark spot on the shoulder just behind the top of the gill-openings, and usually about twelve inches in length. The head is short and blunt, with a sharp chin and belly, and with also a smaller scale than the herring, which firmly adheres to the fish. Now and then we find them brought in by some of the "market-women," ready salted and smoked, selling them under the name of herring. Great numbers of large fish are caught with nets off shore by the fishermen, and salted for their own use, in the fall of the year, when they are fat and fine; in fact, some think they are equal to the shad when salted, and they keep quite as well. Benjamin Tallman writes from Portsmouth to the Newport *News*, which we find copied in the *Evening Express*, November 30, 1859, and says: "Last Friday I caught and saved twelve hundred and fifty barrels of menhaden fish at one set. It was the largest school of fish ever caught and saved at one time with a purse seine." Immense quantities are caught at the fisheries on Long Island, where they are a great deal used; about fifteen thousand on an acre of land being sufficient for any crop, and the price ranging from fifty to seventy-five cents a thousand.

Toad-fish, bladder-fish, or **puffer.** Although this is an unsightly fish, yet its flesh (what there is of it) is good and well-flavored; but it should be skinned, like an eel, when its flesh appears white and much like that fish in taste. Thousands are caught and thrown away on account of their uninviting appearance, and of course it is never found on sale.

LARGE AND SCARCE.

Salmon-trout or **sea-trout.**—This excellent fish much resembles the salmon in appearance and edible qualities; but when placed side by side with the salmon, its back is of a darker green color, with silvery sides, lighter in the color of its fins, and inferior in weight and size. The head and mouth are also smaller. The salmon-trout is never black inside the mouth, like the common brook-trout, although many say (and no doubt it is so) the same fish changed somewhat in color, both externally and internally, and in being of a superior size and flavor, by remaining nearly the whole time in the salt water. The female is considered best for the table, and may be known by a small head and deep body. This is a very scarce fish in our markets, and when found they command a high price. Their usual weight ranges from three to ten pounds, although instances are noticed of their being taken larger. The *Gazette* of the 29th of June, 1821, says: "A very large salmon-trout, weighing thirteen pounds eight ounces, and three feet in length, and seventeen inches round, was caught by Mr. Samuel Carman, Jr., in his pond at Fire-Place, Long Island, on the 24th inst. The *Evening Post* confirms the above "by three of our most respectable citizens."

Another large specimen is noticed in the *Daily Times*, April 12, 1860, "taken on the north side of Long Island, last week, by Mr. J. Crumby, of this city. The trout was twenty and one-half inches long, thirteen and one-quarter inches girth, and weighed four and a half pounds. The nearest approach to the size and weight of this fish was a trout of the same species, taken at Islip, L. I., in March, 1848 (by Mr. F. Dodd, of this city), when he was regularly christened as the 'Henry Clay Trout.' His dimensions were a trifle less than the above, and his weight (after having bled freely) three pounds and fourteen ounces." "Both of the trout as above were of the kind known to some sportsmen as 'creek-fish,' and it is unnecessary to say more than this to the initiated. They have constant access to fresh and salt water, without which the trout can never reach the highest state of perfection. They are the true 'game' trout in shape, muscle, and flavor, and cannot be equalled by any other kind. This is conceded by all experienced judges."

Pompino.—These excellent Southern fish are occasionally caught on our coast, especially on the south side of Long Island and in the Shrewsbury Inlet. There were some eight or ten in our (New York) markets in 1864, and this year (1865) the brothers Miller, and several other fishermen of Fulton Market, had several specimens in the month of July, which were principally eaten by the fishermen, who pronounced them among the choicest fish, and Mr. Samuel Miller thinks they are equal if not superior to the Spanish mackerel. The Southerners also place them above all other fish for the table. In form and general appearance they are somewhat like the harvest-fish, but longer-bodied and a rounder nose. The under side is also of a yellowish shade or color, as well also as the edge of the ventral and caudal fins. In size they appear various; some have been taken as light as half a pound, and others, again, above ten pounds. I purchased one on the 18th of July, 1865, which weighed one pound ten ounces, from which I made a drawing, then afterwards had it fried, and I found it equal to its reputation given above.

Common shad salmon, herring salmon, or **white-fish of the lakes**, is a scarce fish in the markets here (New York), but, no doubt, in a few years the facilities will be so easy for conveying these and other rare species of fish from the great lakes, that they will become as well known to us as the lake salmon, muskellonge, etc. It is said the usual size and form of this fish are about those of the shad, but with a sharper head, having a bluish back, and white beneath. There is also another variety spoken of called the **Otsego shad salmon—Otsego bass**—which De Witt Clinton says "is nearly equal to any fish that swims, for exquisite and delicious food. It is among fishes what the grouse or canvas-back duck is among birds. The flesh is fine, white, and delicate. It is rarely taken with the hook, but has been taken by the seine to the number of five thousand at a draught, in the Otsego Lake, and is daily increasing." The color on the back is of a dusky gray, striped like the striped-bass, and weighing usually about five or six pounds.

Red-bass, branded corvina, or **spud.**—This is said to be an excellent Southern saltwater fish, and is occasionally found in our markets, having been brought by the coasting vessels. Its form is like the king-fish, but much deeper, and the color on the back resembles the weak-fish; the sides have a peculiar streaked look, that is, the bluish streaks are straight until about half-way, when they turn up a little, and then continue on straight to the tail. There is also a reddish tinge (although the two specimens presented to me (February 9, 1865) were more of a silverish, metallic hue, but they had been under others, and were, perhaps, two weeks old) and silvery white underneath. One of mine had a dark, branded spot each side of the tail, and the other had two, besides four others, small and large, on each side between the centre and tail. They were not in the best condition for the table, although good; but I perceived a groundy taste which was not very pleasant. What I saw (some fourteen) would average one and one-quarter pounds each.

Lake trout, or **lake salmon.**—These fresh-water fish are among the best when taken from the fine clear-water lakes. I have seen them that were taken in the Cayuga Lake, weighing above ten pounds. The color and appearance of this fish (as near as I can now recollect) was that of a very large, fat "weak-fish," with the back covered with small spots, and a mouth full of sharp teeth. The flesh was of a yellowish-red color, very much like the salmon; and, no doubt, from that fact, the name of salmon trout is sometimes given it. It is a good table-fish.

In some waters the outside color of this fish is darker on the back and head, being of a bluish-black, with lightish spots, belly white and silvery. They are occasionally found in our markets in the months from October to March. Weight from four to seven pounds.

Mackinaw trout, mackinaw salmon, or **namaycush.**—This species of the trout is the largest known, and often equals, or rather exceeds, in size the true salmon. It is principally taken in the Great Northern Lakes, and is seldom found in our markets except in the salted state. Its flesh is said to be superior to the common lake-trout; but I do not think so, or, at least, with the specimens found in our New York markets, which appeared coarse and not so delicate. The average weight of those taken is said to be from twelve to sixteen pounds; but those which I saw were above twenty pounds, and one over thirty pounds, and I have read of their being taken above one hundred pounds. These very large fish have the appearance of great age, if we should judge from their head, mouth, and teeth. They are also of a lighter color on the back (being quite of a silverish-gray) than the common lake-trout. They are usually found in our markets during the winter months.

Spotted turbot, New York plaice, watery flounder.—This variety of the flat-fish is usually found quite scarce, small in size, quite thin in flesh, or with very little on its bones, and quite round in appearance. It is known among the Jersey fishermen as the "sea-flounder" and "sand-flounder," and seldom sought after by them, as they seem to think that there is but little good eating on them without they are large. Their eyes are full and large, as also the mouth, which opens on the left side, and is found filled with small sharp teeth. Color on the back is dark olive-brown, with darker spots dotted over, which grow larger towards the tail, and rather a bluish-white underneath. Its flesh is white, delicate, and well-tasted. Weight from one to ten pounds, and in season from May to September.

I am told by an old fisherman that he has often taken them with a barbed spear while going along silently with his boat near the shore or inlets on the Jersey coast. He could see them settle themselves down on the bottom, and, by a few motions of their fins, almost cover themselves, with sand, from sight; but the practiced eye discovers their position by a dark spot, when he plunges the spear through them. "Then," says he, "if I strike a big one, his enormous strength would either break my pole or pull me overboard; so I let them run with the pole, which shows itself on the surface after a little time, when the fish is exhausted or dead, and I can take it in without risk; and I have taken them of twelve pounds weight in this manner."

Many persons assert that we have no **turbot,** or **English turbot,** on our coast. Captain Mackinnon of the British Navy (whom, the editors of the *Courier and Enquirer* say, everybody liked, and was known to more Americans than most foreigners are who visit us), says, in a lecture before the Literary Institute, at Lymington, England, "when he first landed here he went to the fish-markets, and found that there were no turbot, sole, or flat-fish. He took a trawl-net to Newport, Rhode Island, and, in three days, caught seventeen varieties of fish, and amongst them several turbot. They had as fine turbot there as we had, but did not catch them, because they only used the hook."

The color on the back differs a little from the preceding, being more of a reddish-brown, and sprinkled with small white specks. It has also six small tubercles near the left eye, with a light ring around them. It, no doubt, is a finer fish for the table, the average being also much larger. I read in *Rivington's Gazetteer*, August, 1773, of "a turbot, weighing only eight pounds, was sold at Billingsgate (London), on Saturday last, for *eight guineas.*" (Had the fish, says the editor, been produced for sale at the Fly Market, in New York, a single piastre would have secured it.)

The *Salem Register* (1817) notices: "A very fine turbot, of about forty pounds weight, was caught in our harbor, and brought to town, on Wednesday night, and sold off at the low rate of four cents a pound. This, we are told, is the second that is remembered to have been brought in here. Another, nearly as large, was also caught near the same place, a few years previous."

French turbot, or **Bay of Fundy flounder.**—There is another variety of the flat-fish brought to our markets in the late winter months, to which the fishermen have given the name of turbot, or French turbot, and an excellent fish it is. In form and color it is somewhat like the pigmy flat-fish, but much larger, longer, and thicker, according to the size. It also has a pointed head, filled full of sharp teeth, with the eyes on the left side. Their usual weight ranged from four to ten pounds. I ate of them several times, and found them choice fish.

Black triple-tail, triple-tail perch, or **black grunts.**—A fine specimen of this scarce fish I purchased in the month of August, 1864, at Catherine Market, which weighed just three pounds, and measured in length sixteen and a half inches; width of body (alone), seven and a quarter inches. It was taken in a net on the Long Island coast, near Flatlands. (Another fine specimen of the same weight was sent to me since.) The color was of a dark greenish-black and bronze, somewhat clouded on the sides and underneath. The dorsal and anal fins extended so far behind as to give it an appearance, with the caudal fin, of three tails. There were twelve stiff dorsal spines, commencing from above the gill-openings, running back, three in front of the anal fins, and one in the ventral fins. I had the fish boiled, and found it excellent eating, being very much like the sheephead. I believe they are only found here in the summer months, often heavier than the above.

Banded ephippus, three-tailed sheephead.—This short, deep, sharp back and bellied fish is occasionally found in our markets, having been taken in the coast-nets, although its home is in the more southern waters. I purchased a fine specimen on the 27th July, 1864, which weighed just three pounds, for sixty-three cents, of a fisherman. Its length, from tip of nose to end of tail, was just fifteen inches; and its greatest width across, from beginning of the dorsal to the same part of the anal fins, was eight inches; the color of a leaden-gray, with six partially indistinct bands running irregulary around the body, commencing across the eye, and ending at the root of the caudal or tail fin. I had it boiled, and found its flesh quite equal to the sheephead; but the bones were more prominent than that fish, or rather less flesh according to the bone.

Siskawitz, or **Northern lake trout.**—This large variety of the trout is usually a very fat fish. It is not introduced here as a fine table-fish, when fresh, because it is too fat and oily; but, as a salted fish, it is found here to be one of the best, and usually sold at a high price. The color on the back appears like a mixture of blue, brown, and green, lighter under, with clouds or spots over the whole body. They usually weigh from four to eight pounds.

Cusk.—This salt-water fish is occasionally found in our New York markets, but more plentiful in those of Boston. Its color and general appearance resemble the codfish, with thicker shoulders and a broader head. The dorsal fin runs the length of the back, and the ventral fins from the vent to the tail, nearly of the same size, with a lancet-shaped tail; and these three fins—the dorsal, ventral, and caudal—are all fringed with a white edge. I have eaten twice of this fish, from six to eight pounds, both fried and boiled, which I found not quite the equal of the codfish, the flesh being a little dry, but firm, and not quite so flaky nor sweet; it had also a shade of a yellowish color through it. This fish, in the warm months, is of a grayish color, mottled with brown spots, and darker in winter; usual weight from three to eight pounds—average about five pounds; in season in July and August, and scattering along through the winter. It is a much better salted than a fresh fish.

Bonita, or **striped bonita.**—This is a rather stout, round, and smooth fish, somewhat of the appearance of a mackerel, but larger and thicker, and the head pointed, with a wide mouth. Several stripes run along the sides from the gill-openings, quartering towards the tail over the back. It has been sometimes taken or sold for the Spanish mackerel, but is altogether differently shaped and marked (see *Span-*

nish mackerel). The flesh is firm and white, but not well-tasted. In fact, I think they are the poorest eating of the mackerel species. The larger fish may be better, boiled, than the small are, fried, as it was from the latter that I formed this opinion. Their season runs from June to October, and some years are quite plentifully brought into our markets. Usual weight from four to eight pounds, although I have heard of their weighing above fifty pounds. Several specimens sent to me weighed less than one pound. I have heard sailors call this fish "skip-jack."

American codling, or **codling.**—This fish is also, by some, called "hake." It appears to be a species of the codfish, but I think not quite its equal for the table. They are, however, quite scarce in the fish-markets of New York. The color of the back and sides is of a reddish brown, and under, or rather along, the edge of the sides, it is full of small black specks from mouth to tail; and the belly, forward of the vent, is of a bluish-white color, while, back of the vent, of a dingy yellowish-white. Inside of the mouth is of a pearly white, but in the throat and roots of the tongue it is quite black. It has large, full, blue eyes, and under the gill-openings hang two long hairy fins, split at the ends, and another long dark one on the first dorsal fins; the second part of the same fins runs about one length down to the tail, and the ventral fin from the vent to the tail. These fish weigh from one to twenty pounds, although those which were sent to me weighed from fourteen to twenty-eight ounces. I found the flesh much like the frost-fish, but with a peculiar smell when alive. In season from September to December.

Hake, American hake (it is also called "Stock-fish" and "Poor John's" in Massachusetts).—These fish are occasionally taken, as also the preceding, with the cod and haddock, and appear of their species, but are longer, and with a tapering, cylindrical body. They have large bony heads, with a thin skin drawn over, which gives them a hard-featured look; to these are added a large mouth filled with sharp teeth, and the lower jaw a little longer than the upper one. The color on the back is of a reddish brown, and below the lateral line a dirty white. In season from June to September, but they are rarely found on the New York fish-stands.

A young specimen of about four ounces weight and ten inches in length, was sent to me November 13th, 1860. Afterwards I saw some twenty about the same size, some of which I had cooked, and found their flesh sweet and tender, but a little dry. This fish, with many other rare species, I made drawings of.

White lake bass, or **white bass.**—This fresh-water fish is also known in New York city as "lake striped bass," no doubt from the fact that their color, and being also striped, has given them this name. They are quite a common fish at Buffalo and many other places near the fresh-water lakes. They have some of the appearance of white perch as to shape, having a small, pointed head, with the under jaw the longest; and some four or five distinct stripes running the length of the body, and others quite indistinct. I saw some at the Fulton Market in the month of October, when they were fat, and I found their flesh quite sweet, except having a little groundy taste. Usual weight from one-half to two pounds. Those which I ate of weighed one-half and one and a half pounds. The larger ones are found here sometimes in a salted state.

Thick-lipped eel-pout, blenny.—The common name applied to this fish by the New York fishermen is "Conger eel." The color of the several specimens which were in my possession was a light brown, with dusky spots on their sides. The fins were also spotted. The head and mouth were large, and the lips thick and fleshy; while the body had the appearance of an eel's tail. Under the jaw, near the base of the round pectoral fins, were two stiff spinous feelers, one and a quarter inches long, which, no doubt, are used to creep along the bottom when in search of shell-fish. I found them good eating, but a little dry; weight from four to six pounds. They are generally caught in company with the codfish, and found in our markets in February, March, and April.

Conger eel, or **American conger**, is altogether a different fish from the preceding, and also a scarce one in our New York markets. Their color is of a dark olive-green on the head and back, underneath of a dirty white, and from three to four feet in length, with the tail ending in a sharp point. The lips are thick and fleshy, with seven small holes on a line back of the eye. Their flesh is not pleasant-flavored. Weight from two to six pounds, and in season from November to April.

"A conger eel was taken in the river Medway, near Romney Marsh, which measured in length seven feet six inches and a half, in circumference two feet nine inches and three-quarters, and its weight was thirty-six pounds and a half." —*Gaz. and Post-Boy*, Feb. 5, 1761.

Groper, or **red groper**.—This is an inhabitant of the Southern waters, and a scarce fish in our markets, but sometimes brought to us in the months of April and May by the fishing-vessels. The shape and size is much that of the sea-bass—not quite equal for the table—of a light pinkish-red, with large eyes. I saw several specimens in the Washington Market on the 7th February, 1857, which, it was said, were taken on our coast. Their appearance showed that they had been taken in very deep water, the eyes having a swelled appearance, almost to bursting, caused by having been suddenly drawn from the pressure of "the deep, deep sea." Since writing the above, I was presented with a specimen of a very light pinkish color, weighing just one and three-quarter pounds (January 2, 1865). A French gentleman saw it on my stand, and said it was a common fish in France, known by the name of "rouget." For the table, I found it no better than described above. Another fish from the Northern waters, much like this fish, called

Northern sebastes, **red sea-perch**, **rose-fish**, and **snapper**, is found here. Many years ago I saw some six of these fish in the Washington Market, which one of the fishermen called "rose-fish," about the size of a two-pound perch. Their color was of a carmine red over the whole fish—perhaps a little lighter beneath—and a dark spot on each side of the head. They were said to be equal to the sea-bass.

Ling.—This fish is taken in company with the cod, and is considered inferior to that fish for the table. I find from experience that the flesh is darker, not solid, and of an insipid, sweet taste. No doubt if it could be bled (as it appears full of blood) in the tail, and hung up until, if possible, frozen stiff, it would be better flavored. Color of an olive-brown, with dark spots on the back and fins. The back fins extend from the head almost to the tail; on the under side the fin extends from the tail three parts of the way towards the head. Weight about six pounds, and in season from November to March, but not plenty, or only occasionally so.

The London *News*, April 4, 1754, notices—"A lusty Fingallon in Pill Lane eat, for a wager of four guineas, twelve pounds of lyng, six pounds of bread, three pottles of potatoes, and afterwards drank very comfortable two pottles of ale."

Pollack, or **New York pollack.**—This fish is another of the cod family, but considered inferior as a table-fish. There appear occasionally in our markets two varieties. Thus, one is of a dark olive-green color on the back, and lighter beneath, while the other is generally known as the "black pollack" or "coal-fish," having a blackish-green back with a silvery lateral line through its length. The fins of both varieties are much in form and place as those of the haddock; the head, however, is smooth and more pointed. The average weight is about five to seven pounds. I saw one of about five and a half pounds' weight in the month of July, 1864, at Catherine Market. On dressing it, the flesh was softer and much darker than the cod; but the fisherman said that many preferred them to that fish, and that he sold them at higher prices when he could obtain them. I, however, should decide in favor of the cod. They are seldom very plentiful, but when found, it is generally in the fall and winter months. In the month of November they were very plentiful in New York, and sold at low prices.

A very small fish, similar to the New York pollack both as to color and location of fins, was sent to me, which was found in a lot of smelts. Its length eight and three-quarter inches, depth two and a quarter inches, and weighed six ounces. The spines in the fins were very indistinct, being both delicate and fleshy. I counted in the first dorsal twelve; second, twenty; third, seventeen; the first anal twenty-five, second nineteen spines, some of which were so small, that perhaps they were not all counted in. I think it was the young of the New York pollack. I made a sketch for future reference. It proved delicate eating.

Drum.—There appears to be not less than two varieties of this fish occasionally found in our markets, one of which is known as the "red drum," and the other the "black" or "brown drum." They are a short, deep fish, with a high round back, covered with large, stiff scales. Their usual weight is from five to twenty pounds, and in season from July to October. They are not prized as food, the flesh being coarse and not well flavored, although a young drum, especially the red drum, is pretty good. Two slices of a large (lightish) red drum, which weighed twenty-three pounds, I had fried, and found it rather dry and insipid; much like poor (large) halibut. These were cut off an excellent specimen, May 9, 1864, brought from the South.

There was a tradition that there were but ten species of fish known to the Dutch when they discovered America, and that when they caught the shad they named it elft (eleventh), the bass twalft (twelfth), and the drum dertienen (thirteenth).

Very large fish, and great numbers too, are sometimes taken of this fish at one haul. The *American Telegraphe*, August 8, 1795, notices one at Providence, Rhode Island, thus: "On Monday last, John Earle and sons caught with a seine, at one draught, in Bristol Ferry, seven hundred and nineteen drum-fish, weighing upwards of fifty pounds each." *Niles' Weekly Register*, July 1833, also says: "Some days ago, a haul was made in Great Egg Harbor Bay, near Bearsley's Point, Cape May, at which two hundred and eighteen drum-fish were caught, their entire weight being from eight thousand to nine thousand pounds. This is said to be the largest haul of that description of fish ever made in that bay." Another still larger, noticed as "A Great Haul of Drum-Fish.—On Wednesday, June 5, 1804," says the postmaster of Oyster Ponds, Long Island, "one seine drew on shore at this place, at a single haul, twelve thousand two hundred and fifty fish, the average weight of which was found to be thirty-three pounds, making in the aggregate two hundred and two tons two hundred and fifty pounds. This is undoubtedly the greatest haul of the kind ever known in this country. A hundred witnesses are ready to attest the truth of the above statement. They are used for manure."

A curious circumstance is noticed in the *Easton* (Md.) *Star*, in the month of October, 1815: "Three men from Kent Island were lately fishing for drum, off Love Point, in about twenty-five feet water, and having been there a considerable time without success, a tlength (Haycock) one of the party felt something move his line, and upon drawing it in, found he had brought up a large earthen jug, and his hook with the bait within it, which, being unable to extricate, he broke the jug in pieces, when, to his utter surprise and astonishment, he discovered a large catfish, fourteen inches in length, which had been enveloped in the jug, and swallowed his hook with the bait. It is supposed the jug was lost from some vessel, and having settled at the bottom in a perpendicular situation, the fish entered it, and not being able to find its way out, continued there till grown too large to get out at the mouth, and the bait having accidentally fallen into it, was seized with avidity by the fish. The jug must have been a long time at the bottom, as there was very long grass and several large oysters adhering to it. Easton, Md., June 20. Attested to by Thomas Goodhand, High Legg, and Solomon Haycock."

Banded drum or **grunts.**—This fish (when found here) has much of the appearance of the preceding, but usually smaller in size. The color of the back is of a dusky brown, sides and underneath lighter, with four dark or black bands around the body. It is sometimes taken with the weak-fish in nets, and makes more noise than that fish when taken from the water, which no doubt is the cause of its being known by the name of grunts. It is said the small fish are equal to the porgee for the table, but the flesh is somewhat coarser. In season from June to October, and weight from two to ten pounds, although one was sent to me less than a half pound.

Fresh-water cusk.—One of these fish was presented to me on Christmas morning, 1860, which weighed just one and one-half pounds, measured seventeen and one-half inches in length, and seven and one-half inches around the shoulders. The color of a brownish green on the sides and back, and underneath of a yellowish white, covered over with black blotches, irregularly. It also had a black spot on each side of the tail where it joins the fin, with a yellowish circle around it.

The fish was covered over with a thick mucus, more so than the black-fish. The mouth full of small, sharp teeth, on the upper jaw they extended back on the roof of the mouth; the lips were fleshy, and the upper jaw, from about half way running to the corners of the mouth, appeared a loose or jointed part, which could drop over the corners of the mouth. The tongue was large and round.

This fish being fresh I prepared its flesh to eat, but found it difficult to clean, from the great quantity of mucus. I then skinned it, with some difficulty, fried it, when I found the flesh very short and tender, but sweet and well-tasted, somewhat like the roes or melt of a he-shad.

Malasheganay or **black sheep-head.**—This is one of the lake, or fresh-water fish, shaped somewhat like the porgee. The color of a dark greenish gray on back, crossed with darkish bands, silvery sides, and yellowish underneath. It is said to be quite a savory fish for the table. Weight usually about three pounds. Another more common fish of the lakes, called

Lake sheep-head, is found much larger and quite plentiful at Buffalo, where it is considered a poor, dry, tasteless fish, and seldom used for the table.

Salt-water cat-fish.—These fish I have taken many years ago, but were quite small specimens. They have but two whiskers on the upper jaw, near the corner of their mouth, and also two very small ones under their chin. Color of a bluish black, with shades of green, lighter sides, and white underneath. Dr. Mitchell notices "a splendid fish of this species, twenty inches long, four inches deep, and three and one-half inches wide. Taken June 30, 1814." When skinned they are a very good pan-fish.

Lake cat-fish.—These are of a much larger variety, and very much poorer for the table than any of the other kinds, without some trouble is taken in their preparation. They are of a muddy-brown color, with an ugly, large, round head, and are caught in all the Western lakes and rivers. I have read of some weighing above one hundred pounds, but they are too coarse to be eatable food; those under ten pounds are, however, thought by some excellent eating, and many of the Western people say they are the "Pride of the Western waters," when properly prepared. They are generally very fat, and of course of an oily nature, which oil is usually strong. The fish should be parboiled to extract the oil, then stuffed and roasted. Then, I am told, they are excellent.

The *Western Spy*, in 1817, notices: "A catfish was taken by a trout line opposite Cincinnati, Ohio, on Monday last, the dimensions of which, by actual measurement, were five feet and a half in length, four feet girth, twelve inches between the eyes, and nineteen across the breast. Weight one hundred and seventeen pounds! Such was the power of this fish, that the man who took him was obliged to shoot him in order to get him ashore." Then again: "A catfish was caught in Peoria Lake, on Friday (May, 1840) morning last, by Mr. George Oakley, which weighed one hundred and forty-one pounds. It was five feet long, three and a half feet round, and twelve inches between the eyes. This is believed to be the largest fish ever caught here, that caught by Mr. Kellar, a year or two since, weighing one hundred and thirty-two pounds only, though it is several pounds less than one caught near Pekin, ten miles below here, about a year ago. Mr. Oakley having presented us with a sample of this, we are able to pronounce the quality excellent, and in no respect inferior to those of smaller size." —*Hazard's U. S. Register*, vol. ii., page 304.

The *Chronicle Express* (January 17, 1804) notices an Ohio catfish "was brought from the Ohio for the purpose of being presented to the largest and heaviest landlord in the city (Philadelphia). Mr. George Brown, sign of the "Falstaff," being the fortunate landlord—he weighed one hundred and eighty and one-half pounds more than any that could be found—he received the fish and regaled forty guests with the same. Weight of the fish thirty-nine and one-half pounds gutted; length three feet six inches; across the head ten inches; between the eyes eight and one-half inches; mouth seven and three-quarter inches. *Pro Bono—Philadelphia.*"

A Cincinnati paper (June, 1844) notices: a monster "Catfish was caught a few days since in the mouth of the Licking, opposite Cincinnati (Ohio), which measured nine feet five inches in length, nine inches between the eyes, and weighing four hundred and forty-seven pounds!"

Golden mullet, mullet sucker, red horse, or **bram.**—This beautiful variety of the *sucking* species is also known by Richardson as the *Gilt Sucking Carp.* A very fine specimen of this beautiful fresh-water fish, weighing just two pounds, was sent to me in 1861. The color was beautifully variegated with yellow, green, red, etc., and the fins quite red. Its shape differs from the common sucker, the body being much deeper, with a smaller head in proportion, and the scales much larger. The flesh was sweet, but a little dry and quite full of small bones. It is not much admired as a table-fish. The season is in the winter and spring months. They are sometimes quite plentiful.

Sea eel.—This large eel, I am told by the fishermen, is occasionally found in the market, but as they are not much esteemed for the table, are seldom found on their stands. Their color is quite brown on the back, and underneath a smutty white.

In the London *News*, January 27, 1764, is found the following: "A salt-water eel, seven feet long, twenty-three inches round, and weighing thirty-six pounds, which had been taken in the shallows near Sheerness, was brought to Billingsgate, and thought to be the largest of the kind which has appeared at that market for some years. It was bought by a fishmonger in Westminster."—N. Y. *Gazette*, April 16.

Tunny, horse-mackerel.—This extraordinary large fish is one of the mackerel species, and has much the form of the common mackerel. The color of the back is of a grayish-black, sides bright and silvery, and underneath nearly white. Inside of the mouth is quite black. Like all the very large fish, such as the halibut, sword-fish, sturgeon, etc., when found in the markets it is cut in pieces. The flesh is considered good, and some say superior to the sword-fish. Dr. Timothy Dwight, in his "Travels," says of this fish: "The horse-mackerel formerly frequented this coast in immense numbers, and, in the season, were constantly to be found in the markets (Newport). But about the close of the Revolutionary War they forsook our waters, and have not made their appearance since. They were estimated a great delicacy, and are the largest of the mackerel species."

Storer also notices one taken near Cape Ann, fifteen feet in length, and weighing about one thousand pounds. "After preparing two barrels of the fish for Boston and New York, the remainder was sold in our markets (Boston), and many of our citizens were enabled to feast themselves on its most delicate meat, resembling much in appearance lean pork, and the best of mackerel in taste."

The *Gazette of the U. S.*, May 24, 1798, says: "A horse-mackerel was lately caught at Provincetown, Cape Cod, which weighed from eight to nine hundred weight. He got entangled in the eel-grass, where the tide left him, and was drawn out with a boat-hook. A large number of the inhabitants were fed from it for several days, sending their children to cut pieces as it lay on the beach. From the caul and remnants of the carcass twenty-eight gallons of oil were obtained." In 1805 a tunny, or a fish of this kind, was stranded at Cat Cove. Its measurement was nine feet and five inches long, weighing nine hundred and twenty-five pounds."

This fish, or many of them, were, no doubt, the cause of a great excitement about the years 1815 to 1818, on the eastern coast, and some quite near the Boston harbor. Every month or two during that period, reports and affidavits were presented to the public of having seen, been chased, or hairbreadth escapes from a—or several—sea-serpents, which were represented as being one hundred or more feet in length, with a body as large as a barrel and a head larger than a horse's. In fact, all sorts of descriptions were given of it, or them. The excitement about it induced a Captain Rich to fit out a vessel with all sorts of instruments for its capture; and this he accomplished, as appears from a letter found in the Boston *News*, dated September 4, 1818. (See *Commercial Advertiser*, September 7, 1818.)

"Last night a messenger arrived in town with news that the sea-serpent had been captured. The town, as you may well suppose, was all in a bustle. This morning a schooner arrived with a fish on board, said to be the monster. Expectation was still on tip-toe—people flocking to the wharves—and every mouth filled with the cry of the sea-serpent is taken. About twelve o'clock he was publicly exhibited at twenty-five cents per sight—and lo! he was nothing more nor less than an albicore, or what is more commonly called a horse-mackerel, measuring nine feet in length, and four or five feet in circumference. It is the opinion of Captain Rich, who sailed in quest of the sea-monster, and who took this fish, that he is the identical one that has long terrified the credulous Bostonians."

"The fish caught," says another account, "is of the mackerel species, and is the thurry, or horse-mackerel." Another account says: "The fish now exhibiting has been well known from the earliest ages. It is the tunny fish, of the mackerel genus. It is sometimes entitled the great mackerel, and by seamen generally called the albicore."

In 1846 one of these fish was found stranded on the flats near the Beverly Bridge, so says the Salem *Gazette*, where it is known as the horse-mackerel, or albicore. "Its entire length was nine feet six inches; girth near the pectorals, seven feet; form elongated; color, back nearly black, sides silvery, beneath whitish; scales on the back very large; dorsal fins, two, the first of which is somewhat peculiar, consisting of twelve very strong rays, connected by a dark-colored membrane, and shutting entirely into a groove, so that, when unexpanded, the fin is perfectly invisible. The second fin resembles that of a shark, and between this and the tail are ten finlets; presenting the appearance of the teeth of a large saw; a similar succession of finlets exists between the tail and the anal fin; tail is lunated, measuring across its extremity three feet and two inches.

"The flesh, which somewhat resembles that of fresh meat, is used as an article of food in those places where the fish abounds."

In the New York *Daily Times*, July 17, 1856, there appears a notice of "an immense horse-mackerel captured on Saturday afternoon at Nahant, which measured nine feet in length, and weighed nearly one thousand pounds."

Dolphin.—This beautiful-colored fish is sometimes brought to our markets, and when found it is not much thought of for the table. They are only handsome in their various and beautiful rainbow colorings while living; in death, however, they lose these changeable colors. Their proportions and appearance are quite ordinary, having a sharp, deep head and a flat-sided body, which tapers down to the tail. A large dorsal fin also extends from the head, and runs tapering down to the strongly-forked tail. The flesh of a young dolphin, of some six pounds weight, I found flakey and white, with a taste much like the common crab, but rather dry eating. The large fish are strong, and not pleasant tasted, but perhaps passable to a hungry man. Professor Kalm, in his "Travels," in the year 1748, says of the dolphin: "They are eaten with thick butter when boiled, and sometimes fried, and afford a palatable food, but rather sometimes dry." Another species, called **bottle-headed dolphin**, I had the pleasure of seeing in Washington Market (August 24, 1855), of about eight pounds weight. Color on the back and sides was a metallic blue, and a dirty silvery appearance under, covered over with small speckled dark spots. It had a large round head, the body tapering gradually to the tail, which was largely forked. The top or dorsal fin running from opposite the gill-openings to the tail, where it ends very small; the under or anal fin running from the tail, and increasing in size, almost half way up the fish; eyes large, and near the mouth. It was called by one of the fishermen of Washington Market a "truter." In the journal of Franklin, who writes 1726, October 6: "We hooked a dolphin this morning that made us a good breakfast." Again he says: "Since eleven o'clock we have struck three fine dolphins, which are a great refreshment to us." The death of Major Job Sumner of the Massachusetts line of the American army in 1789 (September 16), was occasioned from the effects of eating dolphin taken off

Cape Hatteras, which was supposed to have been poisoned. He died in New York city, and was buried from the "City Tavern" (afterwards known as the "City Hotel") in St. Paul's Churchyard. (See *Daily Advertiser*, September 17, 1789.)

Saw-fish.—This large fish is considered a novelty in these waters, as it is seldom taken so far north. However, I have heard of their having been brought to our city, and that they are eatable. The *New York Gazette*, etc., July 29, 1800, notices:—"On the 6th instant, a large saw-fish was caught at Cape May, in shoal water, which is thirteen feet long, girt five feet five, and beak (or saw) three feet in length. It is preserved in Peale's Museum, in Philadelphia." The *Commercial Advertiser*, July 14, 1814, contains news from Charleston, July 6, as follows: "Two saw-fish were caught on Saturday and Monday last, in Mr. W. S. Barnet's mill-pond, on James Island. The one measured fourteen feet long, and four and a half feet across the fins; the other, fifteen feet long, and five feet across the fins. We understand these fish have been presented to the Philosophical Society of this city." We also find in the *New World*, July 24, 1843, notice of an enormous specimen having been taken near Cape May Light-house, in January, 1843, measuring about eighteen feet long, the saw of which was between four and five feet in length." The *New York Sun*, August, 1856, also notices the taking of a monster saw-fish, in a seine, near Mobile. The correspondent states: "They tied a rope to the saw and brought it into shallow water. Two mules, with ten to fourteen persons, with all their strength, could move it only a few feet at a time. After much exertion, they got it in water a foot deep, when began the measuring. From the end of the saw to the end of the tail measured nineteen feet nine inches; from fin to fin, across the back, eight feet; depth, from back to stomach, three feet. Dr. Moore thinks its weight three thousand pounds. The liver alone weighed four hundred pounds, from which a barrel of oil was obtained. A thousand eggs, from the size of a marble to twelve inches in circumference, were taken from it. It presented the appearance of a boat turned bottom upwards."

Bayonet-fish, giant, or **broad-scaled herring.** —This very large, scarce fish, especially in the New York markets, has appeared there, to my knowledge, but four times, and these, I believe, were taken off the Jersey coast. The two specimens I saw in Washington Market, July 12, 1865, were called by some fishermen, "Torpon;" another gave them the name of "carp;" but, as the fish appears not generally known, and had one prominent feature, in the form of a stiff, bony spine (which is much like a bayonet), connected with the lower end of the dorsal fin, I have given it the name of bayonet-fish. The largest of the two fish measured just five feet seven inches in length, and not above fifteen inches wide, which width continued almost down to the tail. I supposed it would weigh about one hundred pounds. It had somewhat the form and color of a slim herring, and with a mouth which opened on the top of the head; or, rather the under jaw was so long that, when its mouth was shut, it presented its chin on a line with the top of its head. The mouth opened *down* very large, the jaws being without teeth, but having very hard, rough surfaces, and of a dark greenish color inside. I purchased the head and shoulders of one (which assisted me to make a drawing of the fish), and boiled the best part of it. The flesh I found full of strong bones, with little flavor and dry eating. One of the fishermen (Moschett) said he had often met with it in the Mediterranean, where it was called *serac;* but, as he had, several years before (1857), given the same name to a very large fish which, from description, resembled the *broad-finned sword-fish,* I concluded he did not know much more than I did about the fish. This latter fish was sold by Messrs. Samuel B. Miller & Brother, Fulton Market, in the month of August, 1857, who called it a **broad-finned needle-fish.** The body was much the shape of a Spanish mackerel, about six feet in length, including its long bill—

the upper one longest—and weighed about one hundred pounds. The color of the back was dark blue, lighter underneath, and with scales about an inch long, pointed, horny, and quite stiff. The back fin was fan-like, and, when closed down, lay hid (to a side view) in a crevice of the back. I heard it was pronounced good eating.

Ribbon-fish, or **silvery hair-tail.**—One of these scarce fish was presented to me by Messrs. Miller & Co., Fulton Market, October 21, 1859. It was a lengthy, flat-bodied fish, with the top or dorsal fin extending the whole length of the body, and ending in a small, thin, hairy tail, and a small fin near the gill-openings on the side. Color silverish, and somewhat the appearance of the Spanish mackerel. This specimen—no doubt, a full-grown one—was just forty-two inches long, and the width, at the widest part (near the head), three and a half inches; about the middle, three and a half inches, and gradually running smaller to a hairy point or tail. It weighed just two and a half pounds. The under jaw was longest, and the mouth contained, in front, four long barbed teeth, and smaller ones along the jaw. Its flesh was white and sweet, but dry and sinewy. Since the above was written, a larger specimen was sent to me by the same parties, on the 30th of June, 1860, which weighed exactly one pound more; and, no doubt, it was an old one, as the under jaw had the long teeth, which appeared to have been, some time before, broken off. This one measured over four feet in length.

Rabbit-fish, or **lineated puffer**.—A fine specimen of this rare fish was also presented to me by the same firm as above, July 8, 1858. The mouth somewhat resembled that of the rabbit, which, no doubt, gave it the name. The four teeth in front close together like the parrot's bill. Color of a dark olive-brown, without scales, and somewhat the appearance of a Spanish mackerel. It had small gill-openings at the fin on the sides, and a soft, white, pouched belly (full of small sharp spines), which it has the power to extend or puff out like a bladder. It weighed just five and a half pounds. This fish, and the following, were too long out of the water to be eaten.

Spotted lampugus.—One of this species of fish was also presented, by the same firm, August 6, 1859. It was quite a flat fish, but beautifully speckled with light blue on the silvery sides, and darker on the back, where were also some fifteen perceptible black spots running along the length of the body on each side. The lower (or ventral) fins, lay in an indenture under the belly. It measured sixteen and a half inches in length, three and a half inches across the widest part of the body, and weighed just one pound.

Sea-wolf, sea-cat, or **tiger-fish.**—To the same firm as above I am again much indebted for a fine specimen of this ill-looking fish, presented April 29, 1858, which was taken off the coast. The length was three feet, color of a bluish-gray, with twelve dark stripes running across the body, and with a flabby dorsal fin running nearly the entire length of the back; pectoral or side fins large and broad, with a mouth full of teeth—those in front being long and sharp, and also irregular, while those in the upper jaw, or roof of the mouth, were flat and very hard, as, no doubt, its principal food is the oyster, clam, and other shell-fish. They are regarded by the fishermen as unfit to be eaten; but De Kay says "his flesh is by no means unsavory; when smoked, it is said to have somewhat the flavor of salmon." I have also since been informed they were delicate eating either fried or boiled.

American angler, fishing-frog, sea-devil, monk-fish, goose-fish.—This big-headed, ugly-looking fish is not an uncommon one in our waters, as they have been taken in our harbor occasionally. A specimen was caught by George Bowman, in Gowanus Bay, on the shore, stranded, in the month of November, 1855. Mr. Bowman was going to dig soft clams, when he discovered it on the shore alive. He put his spade out towards its mouth, when the fish seized it, and held fast until taken to a house, where it lived some six hours after. It measured three feet two inches long, and would weigh above sixty pounds; much the form of a toad-fish, with a very large mouth and throat. The color of the upper surface of the body was brown, the lower part white. It had a pair of strong fins under the jaw, some the appearance of a hand, with which it is said to stir up the mud and sand when it wishes to conceal itself from its prey. The flesh had much the appearance of that from a large codfish. I have no knowledge of its flesh having been eaten, yet I believe it to be good from its looks. In the month of November, 1858, one of these ill-looking monsters was captured at the foot of Christopher-street, North River. "It was," says the *Tribune*, "about four feet in length, and weighed twenty-five pounds. The head was similar in shape to the rim of a man's hat, the body resembling the body of a codfish. On the top of the head, about six inches from the snout, were two eyes as large as a cent, while just beyond were two small horns, surrounded at the base by long hair. The mouth was set around with sharp teeth, and of sufficient capacity to take in the head of a child six or eight years old, and its great tongue seemed to be covered with little prickles. It had no gills, and the only breathing apertures were two holes in the snout. On each side were two great fins, while, protruding from the belly, were two hands with five fingers, and almost as perfect as a human hand." A curious account of this fish, and a wild sea-duck called "old wife," is found in the Philadelphia Repository and Register, as follows:

"Near Salem, in the month of October, 1803, some lads were fishing near Baking Island, when they discovered a fish struggling on the surface of the water; on a nearer approach one of the lads took the gaff and pulled it into the boat. It proved to be a monk-fish in a swollen state. The lads, in want of bait, cut the fish open, when, to their utter astonishment, out hopped a live bird, commonly called an *old wife*. It was too feeble to escape, and the lads secured it and brought it on shore. It is still living, and may be seen at Mr. Whittemore's tavern at Beverly."

The following anecdote is thus told: "Decatur, when at Tunis, in 1805, frequently amused himself in pulling about the harbor in his barge with his gun. On one of these occasions he saw on the water a very remarkable fish, more like a *devil-fish* than any thing else he had seen. His fondness for natural history, which subsequently led to his making a very valuable and rare collection of marine animals, made him very desirous of possessing this novel specimen. He pulled near, fired, and struck the animal, which sunk in shoal water, where it could be seen on the bottom. Decatur, eager to secure his prize, asked Reuben James, who was his coxswain, to dive down and bring it up. Reuben hesitated, and replying, 'I don't like to trouble that chap; he looks as if he would make an ugly customer,' declined the unprofitable exploit. Decatur immediately went over himself, and soon brought the strange monster to the surface. It should be remembered that though Decatur was a captain of a frigate, he was yet a young man, with a young man's love of enterprise and adventure."

Lump-fish or **jelly-fish.**—One of these singular-looking fish was presented to me on the 17th of June, 1858. The color of the head and upper part of the body was of a grayish-blue; on the under side, a very light pale-blue, and the whole fish has a semi-transparent look of a soft, tremulous mass of flesh. The back also raises up, somewhat like the comb of an old fowl, with a short, square head and a small, round mouth, when open. Just behind the lower jaw, on the under side, is a round fringed suction, which it no doubt uses to attach itself to the hard bottom or rocks under the water, as its whole appearance denotes it a sluggish swimmer. Three rows of horny tubercles run its entire length—one commences above the eye and runs to the tail, the next, at the gill-openings, runs below the tail, and the third at the bottom, on each side of the belly, which runs its length. It had no scales, but a rough, thick skin, and weighed about five pounds. One fine specimen of ten pounds weight was sent to me, which I had boiled, and so soft was the thick, blue skin, that I could cut it and peel it off the flesh very much like common jelly. The flesh, however, yet adhered to its soft bones, but a little more boiling and it came off easily. The skin was soft and well-tasted, while the flesh was harder but sweet: the bones were soft and porous and easily cut with a table-knife. "Richardson informs us that the Greenlanders eat its flesh either cooked or dried, and its skin raw, throwing away the tubercles." They belong to the Northern Seas, but are occasionally taken in our waters, from three to four pounds, although they are sometimes found to weigh above ten pounds.

Western mud-fish, or **lake lawyer.**—On the 18th of November, 1858, I received a fine specimen of this scarce fish (here), from the Messrs. Miller's, of Fulton Market, brought, among other species of fresh-water fish, from Lake Ontario. Its weight was just three pounds, and in excellent condition, full of seed (or eggs), which appeared much like flax-seed, and, like the black (and other bottom) fish, covered with slime. Its color was mottled, of a greenish-brown on the back, and lighter underneath, covered with large, thin, oblong scales. The dorsal, or back-fin, which was about one and a half inches long, commenced half way on the back, and ran along almost down to the tail. The tail, of a lancet form. It had two fleshy points, half an inch long, on each side of the nose; small sunken eyes, and a small oblong horny plate, back of the under-jaw or throat. I had a small photograph taken of it, and afterwards prepared it for the table. I found the flesh short and tender, but with a disagreeable, rank smell and taste. It no doubt would have been much sweeter if skinned, but I consider it unfit for human food.

Fresh-water gar, buffalo bony pike, or **lake bill-fish.**—This appears a species of the gar, but rather a formidable one, if we should judge from its appearance.

It is usually taken in the large lakes, where it is found very large. Its flesh has but few admirers. The body is almost round, armed with a hard coat of mail, and a bill or mouth about one-fifth of its whole length. Common weight from two to ten pounds, although the following will show that they are taken occasionally above one hundred pounds. Niles, in his *Register* of November, 1823, notices one which is called a pike, as having been "killed with a rifle in the Forked Deer River, near the town of Jackson, in the Chickasaw country. Its length was six feet, girth three feet, and weight one hundred and fifty pounds. Mr. Webb saw him in the water the day before he was killed, and shot him in the side with his rifle; but the bullet seemed to make no impression. The next day he got into a tree, sloping over the water, and at his approach shot him at the juncture near the gills, between the head and body, and killed him. Three or four other bony-scaled pike have been seen near the same place, and fired at repeatedly by Mr. Haroldson and Dr. Collier, but without effect. All of them have a practice of rising every few minutes to the surface and of spouting up water, frequently to the height of ten feet, and the blowing could be heard from one to two hundred yards."

Another of our city press of 1859, has a notice of a "Mr. L. W. Scales, now in this (Keokuk Gate) city, has a fish called alligator gar, which beats any thing we ever saw before that came out of the Mississippi. It is over eight feet long, three feet in circumference, and weighed rising three hundred pounds when taken out of the river. It was killed in the Arkansas River, a few miles above its junction with the Mississippi. It is his intention to exhibit it."

The following, however, is either a pretty tough or a curious fish-story, which is found in the *New York Sun*, June, 1856. Mr. E. W. Fuller, writes to the *Franklin* (St. Mary's) *Journal*, and says: "Yesterday my workmen hauled up into my saw-mill a hollow log, in which we found a large fish of the genus filibuster, judging from his equipments. It resembled both the alligator gar and shark, apparently being a cross between them, with the tushes of the gar and a triple row of worked teeth. It was about seven feet long, in girth measuring thirty-one inches, with a coat of mail similar to the gar. In his stomach were found three dollars and seventeen cents in small silver and copper coins —there being twenty-nine pieces—together with a good-sized bowie-knife and scabbard, and a revolving pistol with five barrels, all loaded and capped ready for instant service. He appeared as ferocious as a tiger, and would snap and bite at every thing in his reach. The power of his jaws was immense. He bit the end off from a piece of plank two inches thick by four wide. Altogether he was an ugly customer, which I would not fancy to meet in his own element."

Great sun-fish or **head-fish.**—This singular-looking fish is occasionally taken in our bays near the coast. The name—head-fish—given it, is caused no doubt from its appearance of a fish's head, and of sun-fish from its roundish form, with the latter half of its body fringed with fins or flippers, which gives it an appearance of the sun's rays. The color on the back is of a dark gray, and shades down to quite white underneath. Only the very young are considered fit to eat. (Storer calls this peculiar-looking fish *the short sun-fish*.

The *Essex Register*, September, 1835, notices a "Rare Fish.—On Tuesday last a pleasure party, in a boat from Beverly, discovered a large sun-fish between Baker's Island and Halfway Rock; they succeeded in taking him, and carried him into Beverly. He weighed six hundred and forty pounds, and it is said to have been the first ever brought into Beverly or Salem. His skin has been taken off and stuffed, and will probably be exhibited as a curiosity. We understand that one was carried into Marblehead about twenty years ago." *Hazard's U. S. Register*, vol. iii., 1840, notices: "A monster fish, called sun-fish, was taken near Mr. Veazie's bathing-house, end of Warren Bridge (says the *Bunker Hill Aurora*). It was alive and swimming in the creek. It was attacked with boat-hooks, and exhibited a good deal of fight and ferocity, for which it was knocked on the head, and having also swam with great violence against the stone wharf, it was easily captured. It measured about four feet in length, two and a half in width, and a foot thick, and weighed two hundred and twenty-seven and a half pounds. We are told that above a gallon of oil was obtained from the liver alone."

Then we find in the *New York Tribune*, August 4, 1857, another notice of "An enormous sun-fish was captured at Hempstead Bay, Long Island, on Saturday last (August 1st), by a party of gentlemen on a pleasure-excursion. The supposition was that it had come in the bay at high-water, and the receding tide prevented its return. Its dimensions were some nine feet six inches in length, by about four in breadth, and its weight was nearly or quite one thousand pounds. This one is supposed to be the largest of the kind of which we have any record."

The same paper, one year afterwards (on the 6th of August, 1858), says: "Two of these clumsy inhabitants of the briny deep were captured at Sianconset, Nantucket, last week, one weighing over *five hundred pounds!*"

Dr. Samuel L. Mitchell notices another specimen, captured in the lower bay within Sandy Hook, weighing about two hundred pounds.

White porpoise.—An enormous fish, called by some white (whale or) porpoise, was caught in the Saginaw River, by three Canadians, and was exhibited here (in New York) in the month of January, 1860, under the name of *white whale.* Its weight was said to have been two thousand three hundred and sixty pounds, and about twenty feet in length. It was considered a rare specimen of the porpoise.

O'Callhan notices "A certain fish of considerable size, snow-white in color, round in its body, and blowing water out of its head," made its appearance in the North River, in the month of March, 1647, at the time of a great flood. He says "all the inhabitants were lost in wonder, for, at the same instant that this fish appeared to us, we had the first thunder and lightning this year." Barnum has shown several live specimens in his American Museum, among his collections of rare fish, and at the time (July 13, 1865) of the burning of his Museum, he lost two fine specimens which cost him some seven thousand dollars.

Torpedo-fish, cramp-fish, or **numb-fish.**—This fish is one of the ray species, with a body and head almost circular, and the tail tapering down to a point. Its color is of a dull yellow, marked with spots, eyes very small. The flesh is considered equal to the common ray, and the usual weight is from five to fifteen pounds. We, however, notice one in *Niles' Register*, November, 1823, that is represented as weighing above one hundred pounds. This extraordinary fish was "taken off Martha's Vineyard, by one of the persons who were angling for cod. The animal was computed to weigh from one hundred and fifty to two hundred pounds. It was anteriorly of a roundish or circular figure, ending backward in a tail, making the whole resembling, in some sort, an old-fashioned periwig, with a tie behind. When displayed on the deck, it, on being touched by the fishermen, struck them with a cramp through the hands, arms, and shoulders. It had been hooked through one of its fins, just fairly enough to hold it securely and have it on board. The flesh was very tenacious of life, and during its twitching and velications made the murderers (who were flaying it) feel its narcotic and sedative effects. The skin was finally taken off, and with its ichthyological character is now in New York." Length five feet, breadth three feet two inches, and the color of the back a pale chestnut brown, with a white belly. The *Commercial Advertiser*, August 12, 1822, also contains an account of a "torpedo which was found in shoal water, near one of the islands in the harbor of Portland (Maine). It was kept in a tub of water for ten or twelve hours, after which it languished and died."

Vampyre of the ocean, or **devil-fish.**—One of these monsters of the ray species was taken and brought into New York in the month of September, 1823. It is particularly described in the press by Dr. Mitchell, who says the fishing-smack "Una" had returned from a cruise off Delaware Bay. "She sailed about three weeks before (9th September) from New York, for the express purpose of catching an enormous fish, which had been reported to frequent the ocean a few leagues beyond Cape May and Cape Henlopen. The adventurers in this bold enterprise have been successful" in taking this vampyre of the ocean. "Its strength was such that, after the body had been penetrated by two strong and well-formed gigs of the best tempered iron, the shank of one of them was broken off and the other singularly bent. The boat contained three intrepid men, John Patchen, Theophilus Beebe, and William Potter, was connected with the wounded inhabitant of the deep by a warp of the line. The celerity with which the fish swam could only be compared with that of a harpooned whale. The weight of this fish after death was such, three pairs of oxen, one horse, and twenty-two men, all pulling together, with the surge of the Atlantic wave to help, would not convey it on the dry beach. It was estimated from this to equal four tons and a half, or perhaps five tons.

"The size was enormous. From one wing or pectoral fin to another, expanded like the wing of an eagle, measured eighteen feet, the distance from the snout to the end of the tail fourteen feet, and length of the tail four feet. Width of the mouth two feet nine inches."

This monster, or the stuffed skin, was exhibited as a show, in the month of December following, in a wooden building. "A little boy, attempting to gratify his curiosity by looking through an aperture of the building, was struck in the eye by the blade of a penknife from the interior, and it was thought he would lose it. The people thereupon took the law into their own hands, destroyed the building, and tore the vampyre to pieces, and secured the person of the offender."

In the month of August, Niles, in his *Register*, notices "a very large individual of the species, the devil-fish, was taken in Delaware Bay, near the lighthouse on Cape May, Saturday afternoon last. It was harpooned near the shore, but broke loose, however; having returned to shallow water, it was a second time harpooned and secured. It was about nineteen feet in breadth, and about twelve feet in length from head to tail; weight appeared to exceed a ton."

Whale.—There are several species of this enormous fish, among which those commonly known are the great Greenland whale, the spermaceti, the humpback, razor-back, finback, right whale, and the grampus; some of which are occasionally taken in or near our New York harbor, when they are usually cut up to extract the oil. The flesh is edible, and, although very coarse, is eaten by many nations and by some whalemen. I was informed by Judge Meigs that while he was in Bermuda in 1794, he ate of the whale's flesh, and thought it much like coarse, tough beef. He also says the negroes there are very fond of it, and the old wenches beg of the whalemen for pieces after the blubber has been cut off.

Charles Francis Hall, in his "Arctic Researches, and Life among the Esquimaux," informs us that "the skin of Greenland whale is a great treat to the Esquimaux, who eat it raw. The black skin is three-fourths of an inch thick, and looks like India-rubber. It is good eating in its raw state, even for a white man, as I know from experience; but when boiled and soused in vinegar, it is most excellent.

"I afterwards saw the natives cutting up the krang (meat) of the whale into such huge slices as their wives could carry; and as they worked, so did they keep eating. When I saw the natives actually feasting on the raw flesh of the whale, I thought to myself, 'Why cannot I do the same?' and the response to my question came rushing through my brain, independent of prejudice, 'Because of my education —because of the customs of my people from time immemorial.

"As I stood upon the rocky shore observing the busy

natives at work carving the monster before me, my eyes caught a group around one of the vertebræ, from which they were slicing and eating thin pieces of ligament that looked white and delicious as the breast of a Thanksgiving turkey! At once I made up my mind to join in partaking of the inviting (?) viands actually smoking in my sight. Taking from the hands of Ugaring his seal-knife, I peeled off a delicate slice of this spinal ligament, closed my eyes, and cried out, 'Turkey!' But it would not go down so easy. Not because the stomach had posted up its sentinel to say, 'No whale can come down here!' but because it was tougher than any bull-beef of Christendom! For half an hour I tried to masticate it, and then found it was even tougher than when I began. At length I discovered I had been making a mistake in the way to eat it. The Esquimaux custom is to get as vast a piece into their distended mouths as they can cram, and then boa-constrictor-like, first lubricate it over, and so swallow it quite whole.

"One old woman kindly came to me and offered a generous slice of the 'whale gum' she was feasting on. Reaching out my hand, with one stroke of her 'ood-loo' (a woman's knife—an instrument like a mincing-knife), she severed the white, fibrous strip quick as thought. It cut as old cheese. Its taste was like unripe chestnuts, and its appearance like cocoa-nut meat. But I cannot say this experiment left me a very great admirer of whale's gum, though, if the struggle was for life, and its preservation depended on the act, I would undoubtedly eat whale's gum until I got something better to my liking."

The great Greenland whale is the kind mostly sought after by the fishermen. It is said to be a large, heavy animal, and the head alone makes a third of its bulk. It is usually found from sixty to seventy feet long. There is, however, one noticed in the Liverpool *Mercury* much larger. "On the 3d of November, 1827, an immense species of the Greenland whale was found on the coast of Belgium, dead, about twelve miles distant from Ostend, by a crew of fishermen. Their boat being of too small tonnage to move so enormous a mass, they hailed two other boats to their assistance, and the three together towed the whale towards Ostend harbor, on entering which the warps by which it was towed snapped, and it was cast on the sands east of the harbor, where it was dissected, and afterwards exhibited in Paris and London, I believe. Cuvier and the professors of the *Jardin des Plantes*, estimated its age from nine hundred to one thousand years; and one proof of its great age is in the cartilages of the fingers of the hands or side fins, which are completely ossified, or converted into bone. Its total length, ninety-five feet; breadth, eighteen feet; width of tail, twenty-two and a half feet; weight when found, two hundred and forty-nine tons, or four hundred and eighty thousand pounds. Quantity of oil extracted, four thousand gallons."

Another species, called the razor-back whale, was found near Willett's Point, on the north shore of Long Island, fast between two rocks which the receding tide had left dry, on the morning of the 10th of August, 1859. It proved to be a young one, and probably strayed in the Sound in search of food, where it got bewildered or frightened, and ran ashore. It was nearly twenty-five feet long, and the tail measured six feet across.

Niles, in his *Register* of 1846, says: "On the 3d (April) instant, about thirty-six young whales were discovered in York River, Virginia, driven ashore by the late heavy gale, about a mile or two from Yorktown, of Revolutionary memory. Boats were fitted out rapidly, and proceeded to capture the prizes." Another account of "something like a whale:"—"A whale of an enormous size, measuring upwards of seventy feet in length and fifty in breadth, was on Wednesday towed alongside of a South Sea whaler lying at the mother bank, where it was decimated in the usual manner for obtaining the largest quantity of oil. This fish was observed on Friday, following a shoal of small fish through the Needles' passage, which, though sufficient for a seventy-four to pass, was inadequate to that of this unwieldy monster, as it soon found itself on a shingle bank, with the tide ebbing: consequently, notwithstanding the most violent exertions to get off, which were seen for many miles by the prodigious quantity of water thrown fifty or sixty feet high, he remained an easy prize to several fishermen, who went off and cut his throat, from which, and other wounds inflicted on itself, the sea was dyed for several miles. The supposed value is £500. A similar occurrence never happened before within the Isle of Wight."—Found in the *Commercial Advertiser*, November 13, 1813. The same paper, of the 11th of July, 1815, gives another account of whales. "A gentleman from Long Branch informs us that, on Wednesday last, three large Greenland whales were discovered off that place. One of them, supposed to be eighty feet long, ran ashore on the bar at nearly low-water, where he remained about three hours, roaring loud enough to be heard at the distance of two or three miles, and dashing the sand in every direction with his tail. While he was lying in this situation, his associates were plunging about as near to him as they could approach with safety, constantly spouting and throwing around the water, and manifesting the liveliest sympathy for their afflicted companion. When the tide rose, he worked himself from the bar, wheeled about several times in the water, joined his companions, and, spouting in triumph, steered his course to the northeast.

"By his weight and his struggles to extricate himself, he had formed a deep gutter in the sand.

"On the 4th of July a large whale was caught near Cheesequake, on the Jersey shore. It was discovered asleep near the beach by a man who was mowing in a salt meadow. The laborer, supposing the whale was dead, took an oar and waded out to it; while attempting with the oar to open its mouth, it awoke, and rolled itself, like a log, seventy or eighty yards upon the beach. The laborer, who had escaped with difficulty, collected the people in the neighborhood, and with scythes and other instruments soon killed it."

FISH—SMALL AND SCARCE.

Black perch, black bass.—These excellent perch are taken in large numbers in the months of May, June, and July, on the coast of Massachusetts, and sent to our markets, where they are found in limited numbers. The color is usually of a dark-brown or black, above (the head is more of a bronze green), and lighter beneath, covered with large scales. Uusual weight from one and a half to three pounds.

Another variety, called *small black-bass* or *black-perch*, are occasionally found here, but are generally very small; when found, however, of a large size, are then quite as good as any of their species. They are taken in the fresh-water lakes, and many are brought from Long Island; usually of quite a dark-brown color, sometimes almost black (especially after spawning), with an indistinct appearance of stripes on the sides. In season in the fall and winter months, but are caught through the spring and summer months.

Dory, monkey-fish, pig-fish, or **John Dory.**—These names are all given to this, no doubt, rare fish here, of which a peculiar specimen was presented to me September 30, 1862. It was a short, deep fish, with a face or head that looked more like a pig's than a monkey's, having but two long, slim, hairy fins, one of which, the dorsal, commenced just behind the centre of the fish, and ran out, inclining towards the tail, about five inches long, to a point, then from the base it continued down to the tail, of about half an inch long; underneath, the ventral began about the centre, and continued the same as the dorsal, both ending at the root of the tail, which was strongly forked. The lateral line raised with the line of the back, and ran distinctly to the tail. The color was bright and silvery, and quite white underneath. It weighed just twelve ounces, and I found it excellent eating. I preserved a small drawing of this one, as it appeared different from any that I have yet seen or noticed in the drawings before. Another variety, called

Hair-finned dory, or **hair-finned argyreoise,** has some of the appearance of the preceding, but the head is more compressed, body shorter and smaller. It is also furnished with two dorsal hairy fins. The colors are also darker. I have no doubt but it is also excellent eating. There is also another, called

Rostrated dory, or **rostrated argyreoise**, so much like the preceding as to be almost taken for their young. They are occasionally caught in nets on the coast of New Jersey, where they are known as the *dollar-fish,* being about the size of a silver dollar, and much the color of a new specimen. They are seldom used as food, being too small. Another *dory,* under the name of

Blunt-nosed shiner, or **bristly dory**, is a much larger fish than the preceding, and with a head, form, and color more like the first (monkey-fish), except that it has no long hairy fins, but instead it has several short, sharp spines, hidden in a groove in the back. A specimen of this thin, sharp back and belly fish, was sent to me September 29th, 1864, with the name of *moon-fish,* by some New York fishermen. It measured nine and a half inches in length, in width (the widest part) four and a quarter inches, and through the thickest part three-quarters of an inch, and the weight just seven ounces. The flesh was delicate and sweet, but the quantity was small compared with the large amount of bones.

Hair-finned blepharis, or **hair-finned dory.**— A fine specimen of this scarce fish was sent to me August 4, 1865, which had been caught on the coast of Long Island. The length from nose to end of tail was just six inches, and four inches deep. Color, palish-blue on the back, and silvery-white beneath, having fine lightish brown bands across the body, those near the head quite indistinct. The hair-fins, of which there were seven dorsal and six in the anal, measured (four of the longest) twelve inches in length, the others suddenly shorter. The ventral-fins were long-shaped, somewhat like a sword, and quite black. Its small quantity of flesh was delicate eating, and much the flavor of the dory varieties. A drawing was made of this, as it differed from the others I had seen.

Long-finned harvest-fish.—This fish is also known South as the *rudder-fish,* where it is found more plentiful, but occasionally it is found here. It is a short, deep, long-finned fish, with large eyes, small mouth and teeth, and a short nose. The color is of a blue and green tint on the sides, darker on the head. The body has some of the appearance of the short-head fish in shape, but very much smaller, seldom over one and a half pounds. They are a very fair pan-fish, the flesh being white and delicate.

Speckled red-mouth, speckled grunts.—This scarce fish, one of which was sent to me October 31, 1862, has some of the shape and position of its fins like the porgee; the color is somewhat different, being of a bluish-gray or slate-colored, covered with brownish-yellow spots on the back, running diagonally across to the top, from the lateral line; underneath of the same color, but lighter. This was a fine fat fish, the flesh tender and sweet, but in cooking it had quite a strong fish smell. Its weight was just one and a quarter pounds. Another species, somewhat like the preceding in shape, called the

Yellow-finned red-mouth, is rather a rare visitor in our markets. The mouth is large and red, and the lips fleshy. Color of body is much like the porgee, with indistinct stripes across it, and it is said to be quite as good for the table as that fish. Occasionally found here in the months of July, August, and September.

Carp, or **common carp.**—Although these fine fish are not natives of this country, yet for their introduction here, some thirty years ago (1832), we are indebted to Henry Robinson, Esq., of Newburgh, Orange County, who introduced them into the North River, by which they have become plentiful, and are taken every season by the fishermen in their nets. They properly belong to the fresh-water, and no doubt do not visit the sea, or even venture into water that is too highly tinctured with salt, which accounts of their always being taken near where they were first introduced. Their color is of a golden olive brown, on back and sides, and yellowish white underneath. Those usually found in the markets are from a half a pound up to three pounds. They have much the appearance of large gold-fish, but are a much better table-fish.

White perch, gray perch, little white-bass, or **silver perch**, is one of the varieties of the sea-perch, and much the form and appearance of the common perch, except in color; the back of which is of a light-blue shade, sides silvery, and white beneath. The scales on the sides appear like spots; fins pale-yellow, and tail slightly forked. They are usually quite small, seldom weigh above a quarter of a pound, although they have been taken in the North River above a pound weight. Their size is somewhat against them as a table-fish, as they are delicate eating when properly fried. In season in the winter and spring months. In the fisheries on the Potomac River, at a place called Warburton's Landing, says the *Commercial Advertiser*, April, 1802, "there was the greatest haul of large white perch perhaps ever known in America; above ten thousand were taken from the seine, after letting numbers get away by lifting the seine." I found these fish plentiful in Philadelphia.

Dusky balistes, or **iron skin**.—A fine specimen of this rare species, weighing one and a half pounds, was sent to me on the 2d of August, 1866, which I made a drawing of, as the one I had did not represent some of its prominent features. In dressing it for the "pot," I found its skin so tough that it fairly turned the edge of my knife; I, however, succeeded in getting the head off, and drawn, but before I got through I concluded that it ought to enjoy another name, and the most suitable one appeared to be "*iron-skin.*" Under the throat ran a round stiff spine, which showed some half inch near the ventral, directly under the pectoral fins, which ran under the skin down to the jaw. The front dorsal spine (of which there were three) was very stout and long, and when laid down, were hid in a crevice in the back. The fishermen called it a *rabbit fish*, but I think they mistook it for the *lineated puffer*. De Kay, however, notices it as the dusky balistes. The flesh was firm, flaky, and well-tasted, but perhaps a little dry.

Northern barracuta.—One of these rare or scarce fish was presented to me on the 2d September, 1862, which measured fourteen inches in length, and weighed one and a quarter pounds. The color on the back of a dark green, with a yellowish lateral line, and underneath a silvery white. Two dorsal and two ventral fins were placed almost directly opposite each other, with small pectorals, and a strongly forked tail. The body was almost round, with large eyes and mouth, and the under jaw considerably longer than the upper one, in which one long tooth appeared in front, which closed between two in the upper jaw; behind these were several large and small teeth, all raking backward, and a very rough tongue. This specimen was taken at the east end of Long Island, and for the table it was very good.

Spotted codling.—A fine specimen of this small, scarce fish was presented to me, September 27, 1864. The general appearance was somewhat like a large frost-fish, with a small head and large eyes, scales thin and easily removed, and the lateral line black, but disconnected, or only in stripes a quarter of an inch long.

The first dorsal has a black spot near the top edge, the tip of which is white, and underneath it has two long barbels, or hair-fins, which seem split near the end just under the gill-opening, and forms four ends, the main being the longest. It is an excellent pan-fish, much like the frost-fish. Its weight was just half a pound, and length eleven inches. I have had several specimens since, some of them much larger.

Long-toothed flounder, or **spotted flounder.**—This variety of the flat-fish appears rather scarce, or at least they are not often noticed by the fishermen ; and if so, they are only a spotted variety of the fluke, or oblong flounder, although their bodies are longer in proportion. The specimen sent to me (October, 1864) measured in length sixteen inches ; width, including fins, six inches, and weighed one and three-quarter pounds. It had four large, round, distinct spots, somewhat like eyes, that were bordered with white, two near and on each side of the base of the tail, and two about the centre of the fish, near the base of the caudal and ventral fins. The flesh was well-flavored, but not so fine as the oblong flounder, nor so plump or fleshy ; but perhaps this fish was not in the best condition.

Southern caranx.—A beautiful small fish of this species, weight seven ounces, was sent to me September 27, 1862 (since that period I have had several specimens). The color of the back blue, on the sides yellowish, and a small dark spot on each side of the opercle, or gill-opening, in range of the eye. I found the flesh a little dry, but sweet and good. Another variety much like it, called

Yellow caranx, or **yellow mackerel**, was also sent to me August 29, 1864, which weighed four ounces. It had a more yellow or golden appearance than the preceding, and a longer bodied fish. The flesh was not quite so delicate, being a little dry and insipid eating.

Rock bass, rock perch, stone perch, or **golden-eyed perch.**—This greenish fresh-water bass is almost equal for the table to the black-bass, its near companion, as I have taken them both at the same time and place. They are, however, a smaller, deeper fish, weighing usually from one-half to one pound weight. The color is of a very dark green above, sides of a golden-copper, with several rows of dark spots, and the fins of a bluish-green. The nose is also inclined to turn up. In season with the black-bass, but are not usually so plentiful, I suppose on account of its size.

Calico bass, speckled bass, or **partridge-tailed**

bass.—This fish is also known among our fishermen as the "strawberry bass." Their form is somewhat like the sun-fish, but not so deep, with a hollow, compressed head, and a mouth which inclines to open upwards, the lower jaw being much the longest. Color of quite a dark green on the back, lighter on the sides, and covered with dark, irregular spots, more distinct near the tail. The fins are also placed like those of the sun-fish, excepting that there are eight stiff sharp spines in the dorsal, four in the anal, and one in the ventral fins.

I have eaten of them several times (the largest specimen seen weighed one pound ten ounces, measuring in length fifteen inches, depth six inches), and found their flesh quite sweet, but a little dry. Found here in the winter months.

Sole (or **soal**), or **New York sole.**—This is another species of the flat-fish, but usually quite small, and unlike, especially about the mouth, any of the other species. Several were sent alive to the Fair of the American Institute in 1860, measuring from five to six inches in length (which department was under my charge as a manager). On the dark side of these fish appeared several brown spots and bars, which ran across the fish, and the inner side reddish-white, with a rough skin. I found their flesh delicate eating, much better than I expected from their looks, but a very small quantity of it, and somewhat troublesome to pick from its many bones.

The N. Y. *Gazette and Post-Boy*, September 18, 1760, in the London news notices a "Mr. William Davis, of Caermarthen, South Wales, who was fishing in a boat a little distance from the above place, caught a small *soal*, and just biting the head, as the custom there is, in order to kill it, the fish slipped so far down his throat as to choke him immediately." Another instance of the same kind is found in the Columbia *Sentinel*, November 19, 1806: "In Swansea (Eng.), Mr. David George was in the act of disengaging a sole fish from a net, when the fish made a spring down his throat, and choked him to death."

Gar, sea-pike, bill-fish, banded gar-fish.—This is a long-billed and a lengthy fish, the under jaw being longer than the upper one, and the mouth crowded full of sharp teeth. The color on the back is of a dark-green, lighter on the side, and silver-white under, or below the two raised bands on each side; there is also a band running along the back. I have eaten them several times, and found the flesh sweet, something the taste of an eel, but not so juicy. The backbone is of quite a light-green color. In season from July to October, and usually weighs from one to six pounds. P. Vincellette had three in Jefferson Market, in 1862, which weighed sixteen and a quarter pounds—largest over six pounds.

Northern bill-fish, or **Northern gar,** is another of the same species, with the jaws not quite so long as the preceding. The color is also much like that fish, being of a darker green. It has also a silvery band along the body, and silvery-white under. They are taken in large numbers off Cape Cod, and found to be very nutritious and sweet fish. In season in the fall months.

Needle-fish.—This name is given by some New York fishermen to a very rare fish which was sent to me June 14, 1865, in a fresh condition. The name, no doubt, was given to it in consequence of its long, peculiar bill, altogether unlike any fish I ever saw or read of. The whole length of the fish was just fifteen inches, while the bill, from the opening of the mouth to the point, was two and a half inches long, and, unlike the sword-fish, the mouth opened on the top, or upper side of this bill, which, when pressed downwards, opened the mouth, and upwards, the mouth closed. The bill appears a continuation of the lower jaw, and is of a horny substance, covered with a soft, dark skin. The mouth was quite small, the upper jaw being only about an inch in length, having many small, minute teeth on both lower and upper jaws, as far as the mouth closed on the bill. The body of the fish was squarely formed, having quite a flat back and belly, the deepest part measuring one and a half inches, round the body four and a quarter inches, and weighed just six ounces. Color on the back of a dark-blue, which abruptly met a broad silver streak and merged into a white silvery color underneath; and I may say it was a beautiful-colored fish. The fins lay in nearly the same position as the pickerel's. The tail, however, was strongly forked, the upper fork being shorter and smaller than the lower one. It was covered with large scales, which easily came off. Its flesh tasted much like the gar. I preserved a drawing of this rare fish (at least, in New York).

Brilliant chubsucker, or **chub of New York.**—This is a perch-shaped fresh-water fish, having a dark slate-colored head and sucker mouth; the back of a dark dusky green; sides silvery and yellow, interspersed with darkish-clouded marks, being covered with large scales and a considerable quantity of mucus. They usually weigh from a half to a pound and a half. A specimen sent to me weighed the latter weight; measured, in length, thirteen inches; depth, four inches; and I found it a good, sweet, juicy fish. In season in the fall and winter months—the latter the best. Another kind I received at the same time, called

Large-scaled sucker, or **blue sucker,** which weighed eleven ounces, measuring in length ten inches, and in depth three inches. Color of a dark pale blue on the back, and lighter beneath. It was not so good a table-fish as the above; season the same.

Horned sucker, horned dace, or **barbel.**—This species is also from the fresh water; in form and color somewhat like the brilliant chubsucker. The distinctness, however, is in the little points or horns between the eyes and nose. For the table it is about the same quality, and is in season at the same time. There is another species, called

Red dace, red-fin, or **rough-head**, usually found a smaller fish, also from the fresh water, which has much of the head and jaws covered with small pointed tubercles. The fins also are marked with a crimson red color, and altogether it is a beautiful little fish, but usually too small for the table. Another variety, called the

Shining dace, white dace, or **shiner**, principally found in the great lakes, is a much larger and better fish for the table. The color on the back is of light olive-brown, head darker, and the sides silvery. Another, still larger, called the

Black-headed dace, lake dace, or **lake chub,** with a brownish-black head, dark olive-green back, lighter beneath, and of a glossy white underneath, and of about the same quality for the table.

Variegated bream, dace, or **yellow-bellied perch.**—This perch-shaped fish is about the size of the white perch, but, as its name denotes, the variegated colors on the body show the green, blue, and yellow, with a silvery mixture throughout. It is occasionally found in the winter months; but, in consequence of its small size, it is not much esteemed, although a sweet fish.

Spotted thread herring, thread fish.—This is rather a scarce fish, althcugh occasionally seen here. The peculiarity of this herring is found in the latter end of the dorsal or back fin, and is a long, thread-like ray, nearly three inches in length. It has also a round black spot back of the head, in range of the eye, and is shaped much like a shad. It seldom weighs above one pound, and is in season in September and October. Another scarce variety, called

Slender herring, is long, round, and a smaller fish. Color of a silvery-blue on the back, lighter beneath, and the dorsal and caudal fins tinged with yellow. It is a summer fish when found here. Another more plentiful variety, called

American alewive, or **spring herring**, is taken with the shad, and is much the form but smaller than that fish. The color, however, is darker on the back, with several indistinct spotted stripes running lengthwise on the sides, and silvery underneath. They are a better table-fish than the common herring.

Spotted shadine, New York shadine, is another shad-looking fish, but smaller, and a scarce variety. It has a distinct dark spot behind the gill-opening, on a range with the eye—in fact, nearly all the shad and herring species have this spot, sometimes, however, quite indistinct. These fish, when found, are seen here in the fall months. This is the poorest fish of the species for the table.

Saury, round herring.—A fine specimen of this sea-fish was presented to me, October 10, 1862, which weighed one and a quarter pounds. It had a long, round body, greenish shade on the back, and silvery sides, with the tail strongly forked. It is correctly described by De Kay, but is a much longer fish, according to its size, than appears in that work. As an edible fish, I found the flesh sweet, but quite full of small wiry bones.

Sisco, sisquette, or **lake herring.**—These fresh-water fish are usually found in our markets in the autumn and winter months, and generally very fat. They have some of the appearance of the common herring, but with a sharp-pointed head, and a round form. Several specimens were sent to me, the heaviest of which weighed one and a quarter pounds. I found their flesh very sweet, but a little dry, and not so full of bones as I expected. I am inclined to believe they are the young of the common shad-salmon or herring-salmon. I was informed by the historian of Jefferson County (F. B. Hough, Esq.) that the name "sisco," given to this fish, originated from the name of Dr. James D. Seisco, who had an excellent fishery on Chaumont Bay, about the year 1805, where he took these and other fish by thousands every year.

River moon-eye, or **river herring.**—One of this species of fresh-water fish was presented to me in the month of November, 1859. It had some of the appearance of the common herring, but shorter, and with very large eyes quite near the mouth; it also had large scales and silvery sides. The tongue was covered with small teeth. Weight, three quarters of a pound, and about the same as the above for the table. Another of the same species, called

Lake moon-eye, which has much of the same appearance as the preceding, but not so deep or so flat-sided a fish. They, however, are seldom seen here.

Pilot-fish.—Several fish of this name were sent to me in the summer of 1862, which so much resembled the *banded seriole* that I was inclined to think them the same fish. The only difference I discovered was, that they were without the first dorsal fin; the pectorals and ventral were also smaller, and the tips of the tail and all the other fins were fringed with white. I found them indifferent pan-fish. The banded seriole are also known by some of the fishermen as "rudder-fish." Another variety of this species I named

Brown pilot-fish, as I could not find any thing like it. Its general appearance and form was much like the preceding, but a larger fish. In length it measured twelve inches; depth, three and a half inches; weight, fourteen ounces. It was sent to me in the month of August, from which I preserved a sketch. The first dorsal fin is composed of seven short and stiff spines; the second, of thirty-three soft spinous rays, running to near the tail. The ventral has one short stiff spine, and some twenty soft rays, commencing one half inch from the vent, and running back the same as the dorsal, and tinged with white. Color of a reddish brown on the back; quite dark, and a lightish brown streak on each side. The pectoral fins were short, roundish, and quite delicate. The ventral fins counted nine stiff rays: eyes blue, and the flesh about the same quality as the preceding.

Remora, or **shark-sucker.**—One of these curious fish was presented to me, October 3, 1862, by Mr. R. D. Brower, fisherman, of Jefferson Market, which measured just twenty inches in length, and weighed one and three quarter pounds. This specimen is called by De Kay "white-tailed remora," and correctly described on p. 307 of the "New York Fauna," excepting that the "broad black band," running lengthwise, was not found on this fish, but merely a light narrow line. For the table I found it quite indifferent eating, although without the skin it was more palatable. Fishermen generally call it the "shark-sucker," as it is often found fastened to the shark; and so closely is the back of the head (or suction part) imbedded or fastened to the under part of the shark's body, near the head, that it has no trouble to feed upon whatever escapes the shark's terrible jaws.

Flying-fish, or **New York flying-fish**.—These winged fish are occasionally found in our markets, having been brought here by the fishing-smacks, or other fishermen, more as curiosities; but I am told by sailors that they are much enjoyed by them, when found on the decks of their vessels when trying to escape from their water enemies. Their side or pectoral fins are their wings, which cause their flight; but it is only for a short distance, when they fall either in the sea or a passing vessel. Their color is of a darkish green, and white beneath, and from ten to twelve inches in length.

There are also many varieties of small fish found in the markets which are usually too small to be profitable as human food, such as gold-fish, killi-fish, small dace, minnows, sticklebacks, etc., which are kept purposely for fish-bait; but, when of any size, most all are found to be delicate eating. I have eaten of killi-fish, among which were several called striped killi-fish, weighing above six ounces each, and I found the flesh very sweet, but a little dry.

A friend, on Long Island, has a stock of gold-fish which multiply so fast that he occasionally takes them, from a half to one pound weight, for the use of his table. Several curious specimens were also taken, some of which had three tails; others, again, were quite round or flat, mottled with black, silver, and gold, and had different heads and forms of fins, which would lead many to think that they were of different varieties; but he informs me that all were bred from the common gold-fish. They are generally found to be more ornamental than useful, and are sought after for their beautiful colors and domestic habits or tameness.

SHELL-FISH, &c.

UNDER the above head I have placed the crustaceous and the molluscous species of shell-fish, commencing with those generally placed under the first named.

Lobsters.—These shell-fish are too well known to need description, as they are usually found in great plenty in our markets in all months of the year, except December, January, and February. They are, however, better in some of the months than others; that is, the female or hen lobster is generally preferred through the summer months—especially June and July—and the male, or "ram" lobster in the winter months, when found. The latter is distinguished from the hen not only for its want of eggs under the flap, or tail, but by the longer and narrower back, running quite to the tail and including the fan or fins. When the eggs, or berries, of the female are large and quite brown, the lobster will be found exhausted, watery, and quite poor. The largest are not always the best, but those ranging from four to six pounds in weight, when fat, are the choice and most delicate.

A very fine variety called *blue-backs*, with quite thin shells, brought from the coast about Cape Cod, in the months of May and June, are sought after by the lobster epicure. The average weight is usually from two to four pounds, although I have heard of their weighing above twenty. I am told that one was sold in Fulton Market, several years ago, of twenty-eight pounds!! The female seldom weighs above eight pounds. When fresh they are always lively, and the tail will spring strongly back under them when lifted from the stands. Many are found cooked in some of the markets, more particularly the Fulton, of New York, and Faneuil Hall, of Boston, who send them all over the country. The whole lobster is good to eat, except the shell and craw, or stomach, which lies between the eyes.

Professor Kalm, in his travels here in 1748, speaks of lobsters as being "plentifully caught hereabouts," and further says: "I was told of a very remarkable circumstance about these lobsters, and I have afterwards frequently heard it mentioned. The coast of New York had already European inhabitants, for a considerable time, yet no lobsters being in this part of the sea, they were therefore continually brought in great well-boats from New England, where they are plentiful; but it happened that one of these well-boats broke in pieces near Hell-gate, about ten English miles from New York, and all the lobsters in it got off. Since that time they have so multiplied in this part of the sea that they are now caught in the greatest abundance." The *Gazette*, etc., September 11th, 1766, says: "A live lobster, which weighed thirteen pounds and a quarter, was sold (in the previous month of July) at Billingsgate Market Garden (London) for twenty-four shillings (at New York, in 1765, one of eighteen pounds sold for two shillings and sixpence)." Some considerable difference in the weight and price.

Some time before the Revolution, "A Wm. Richards, of Philadelphia, famous there for pickling sturgeon, came to New York and planted lobsters near Hell-gate, East River; they grew and became plenty, and he had a vote of thanks from the 'Assembly.'" At the commencement of the Revolution, the harbor of New York, it is said, abounded in fish and lobsters of the largest size; but immediately after the cannonading by the vessels of war in the Battle of Long Island, and the taking possession of New York by the British army, they all at once disappeared, and but few were taken until within the last fifty or sixty years; since when they appear to have been gradually "creeping down," so that they have been often taken opposite the city.

An amusing, but no doubt a painful incident, called "The lobster's revenge," found among the trials before the Paris Tribunal of Correctional Police, in 1852, was that against a dealer in fish, who was summoned by a Madame Grebuchet, who claimed thirty francs damages for the injury caused to her nose by one of the defendant's lobsters. The plaintiff, wishing to regale her husband with a delicacy for his dinner, went to the market and was bargaining for a lobster, which she took up in her hand, but threw it down again, saying it was not fresh. The fishwife protested that it was alive, but Madame Grebuchet asserted the contrary, and that it even stunk. To satisfy herself that such was the case, she a second time applied her nose to it, when the lobster, as if in defence of its owner's veracity, seized hold of Madame Grebuchet's nose with its claw, and held it fast. She screamed for assistance, but, instead of immediately rendering it, the dealer and her companions around burst out into a laugh, and it was some little time before the nose of the lady could be released. The fishwoman, in her defence, maintained that she was not to blame, and that the mischief was solely caused by the imprudence of Madame Grebuchet in applying her prominent feature so closely to the lobster's claw, when she had been told that it was alive; and the Tribunal, taking the same view of the case, dismissed the complaint, and the plaintiff ordered to pay costs."

Crabs.—The crab is not so generally used as the lobster, but it certainly is of a better flavor, if more troublesome to prepare. The middling size, when heavy, lively, and with large claws, are considered the best and sweetest. If light, they are poor and watery: when stale, the eyes look dead and the claws hang down. The female is usually thought inferior to the male, and she may be known by the claws being smaller, and the flap, or apron, larger, which appears on the white or under side.

In taking them up with the hand, catch them by the fla fin or leg, behind, next to the body; they then cannot reach you with their large claws. They are in season from June to January, and considered the most wholesome in the winter or cold months. In the year 1817 an ordinance was drafted prohibiting the sale of crabs in the public markets, "from the 15th of December to the 1st of March in each year," but afterwards rescinded.

The process of casting off its old shell occurs annually (between June and October), and when taken just before that time they are called shedders, or

Shedder crabs, when they are readily known by those who deal in them. The flap or apron has a red and blue appearance, and by breaking a point of the old shell the new or soft one is discovered under it. In this condition they are principally used for bait in "fishing." When they are taken with the old shell off, and the new, yet soft, shell on, they are in a helpless state, and are generally found near the shore ; they are then called

Soft crabs or **soft-shelled crabs.**—These are considered a great luxury, when fried, and also by the fishermen for bait, when high prices are paid for them. They are found in this state in the months of June, July, August, September, and part of October. The female crab, when full of eggs or spawn—that is, under the apron will be seen large numbers of these little brownish-green eggs, which, as they grow in size, presses this apron out until it stands at a right angle ; in this state they are known as the **cow-crab,** and are then usually found in the channels or deep water, where they go to deposit their eggs or young, and are then unfit to be eaten ; but as the cold weather advances they soon after become fat again. The severe cold weather, however, drives them into the mud, where they are raked up and brought to our markets through the winter in a fat condition.

From the *Sun*, July 7th, 1855 : "*Crab Extraordinary.*—We were yesterday shown a crab of the most extraordinary dimensions, taken by Mr. John Carlyle, of Brooklyn, in Gowanus Bay. It is of unusual size and weight, and the fishermen in the neighborhood had never seen any thing equal to it. It measures three feet in length from tip to tip of the claws, and weighed when taken full eight and a half pounds."

Horse-foot or **king crab.**—Great numbers of this species of crab are taken in the spring of the year ; but they are seldom sold in our markets, although, it is said, when the flesh is carefully separated from the other parts and boiled it becomes a delicious, savory food. Their form is that of a horse-foot, with a long, stiff, horny, triangular, sharp-pointed tail, which appears their weapon of defence. They come to the shore to deposit their eggs in the sand on the coast. So numerous are they on this occasion that the beach is covered with them for miles. Many thousands are shovelled up with their eggs in wagon-loads, of which the eggs are used to feed poultry, and the crabs to feed hogs, or in making a rich manure. Several other species are sometimes found in our markets, but more for curiosity than food, among which are the **spotted crab** or **sand crab,** the **lady crab,** the **oyster crab.** This latter crab is considered a delicacy when found in the oyster, while the two former are inferior or seldom or never eaten. There is also another little shell-fish, about the size of the first joint of the finger, called **fiddler** or **soldier crab,** that has only one large claw, which it carries before when it runs, and at the same time it is ready for defence or attack, the claw being about the same proportion as the big fiddle is to the violoncello player in an orchestra. They are found in the soft banks along the salt-water ditches, where their numerous holes denote their presence. Their flesh is eatable and quite sweet—when you can find it.

Shrimp.—This lively little animal, somewhat the form of a lobster, is not much used for the table, but large quantities are taken and sold for "fish-bait." When of good size, however, they are found to be sweet and well-flavored. Many are used in making sauces, stewing, etc.

Prawns, **American prawns**, or **big shrimp.**—These are usually found larger and quite differently formed from the preceding, having a larger head and eyes, with a saw-like beak or crest, which bends upwards: also a sharp back (especially near the tail), flat-sided, and the claws, especially the large biting ones, quite small; in fact, it is unlike either the lobster or shrimp. The two hair-fins are also three times the length of the shrimp. Many years ago they were taken on the shores of Long Island, but now they are brought from the South, especially from Charleston, already cooked, usually sold by measure. They are excellent eating. In season from April to November.

Oyster.—Of this famous shell-fish, but two principal varieties appear here: these are the Northern and Southern, although the oystermen have many names to distinguish the particular place where from, such as East Rivers, York bays, Saddle-rocks, Mill-ponds, Shrewsburys, City Islanders, Cow Bays, Blue-points, Chingaroras, Virginias, Delawares, &c.

The Northern oyster has a broad, thin, tough shell, with a pleasant smell, savoring of the odor of marine plants, while the Southern oyster has a thick, spongy, soft shell, and of less flavor. There is no doubt the oysters taken on our coast, in our bays, inlets, and especially the East River, attain their most luscious flavor. They are in season almost the year through, except when spawning; then they are milky, watery, poor, and considered unfit and unwholesome food. The months of their spawning appears in May, June, and July. It is said that planted oysters—that is, those that have been transplanted from their native beds and placed and fattened on others prepared for them—are never milky, and, no doubt, by their being thus removed or disturbed before they have commenced to spawn, has caused them to stop this process, while in their natural beds they were always subject to this objection.

An unusual excitement, or, rather, an "oyster panic," occurred in New York City, in October, 1855, which prevailed against the use of oysters as an article of food for several weeks. Several highly-esteemed citizens died very suddenly by cholera, which it was thought was occasioned by eating diseased oysters. Various causes were assigned for their poisonous quality: some attributed it to drouth; others, that the oysters had been taken up during their spawning time, and thus become diseased. The same complaint and fatal instances existed at Baltimore, Alexandria, Georgetown, and other places.

Dr. James R. Chilton, a noted chemist, after making a chemical examination of them, says: "It is not an unusual circumstance that oysters and other shell-fish, when eaten after having been kept long during the warm season, will produce serious illness resembling cholera; but no such ill effects would be likely to arise when they are received fresh from our waters."

Several years ago oysters were seldom seen for sale in their general spawning season; it was not only against the laws (as it is now), but the people would not buy or have them in their possession. An ordinance was passed in 1839 which reads as follows: "No person shall bring into the City of New York, or have in his or her possession, in the said city, any oysters, between the first day of May and the first day of September, in any year, under the penalty of five dollars for any quantity not exceeding one hundred, and the further penalty of two dollars for every additional hundred."

No shell-fish should ever be used as food when their shells remain open, as they are then dead, unfit, and one such will spoil the whole dish.

Wholesale dealers usually have four qualities or sizes on sale. The best are known as extras, then follow the box, cullings, and bushels. Other dealers sell at retail, and also open them, which they sell by the hundred, gallon, or quart to private families; and others again make a large business in pickling them for home and foreign consumption, which are sent throughout the "States," and for shipping.

I have always found the best and finest flavored oysters were those of a middling or even a smaller size to eat out of the shell, either raw or roasted. The clusters are seldom found as good as single oysters, and especially those of unnatural length, are usually found poor and watery. I have known twelve large long slim oysters standing endwise and upright, like the quills upon a porcupine's back, all growing upon one stem.

In the month of September, 1859, a discovery of a great

oyster-bed was made at Eaton's Neck, on the Long Island shore, by five fishermen from Darien, Conn. It is stated that "they found themselves drifting too far out; and dropping overboard an oyster-dredge to bring their boat to anchor," when ready to draw it in again on board, they found it very heavy, and after raising it to the surface, they had it filled with fine large oysters, when they soon loaded their boat, and entered into a mutual compact of secrecy: but it was broken; the information was sold, and the valuable discovery was soon made public. Thousands of bushels were taken and replanted, and those which were planted in deep water, produced some extra fine large oysters, which found a ready sale in our markets.

Perhaps the largest oyster ever taken on the coast of the United States, or which we have any record of, is noticed in the Mobile *Advertiser* in the month of April, 1840. This says: "The large oyster taken by Xavier François, while oystering on Monday last, was brought up from the wharf on a dray last evening. An oyster measuring three feet one inch in length, and twenty-three and a half inches across the widest part of it, is a curiosity. Mr. Ayres, the purchaser, will exhibit it at the Alhambra this day at eleven o'clock, when it will be opened and served up in his usual good style."

An oyster of pretty good size, out of a lot of *East Rivers*, was opened by Braisted, of Jefferson Market, January 27, 1865, which contained a small fish known as the *spotted gunnel*, or *butter-fish*, measuring six inches in length, and a half an inch in depth, flat or compressed sides, and a dorsal fin extending from back of the head to the tail, filled with sharp spinous rays; the anal fin from about the centre or vent, also to the tail, with two small pectoral fins, and a roundish tail. It was quite dead.

Hard clams, hard-shelled clams, round clams, and (the Indian name) **quahaug**.—This bivalve is the most in use in and about New York, and is much prized by many of our citizens as an article of food, especially from some localities, when it is so savory as to be almost equally valued with the oyster. They are a ered very nutritious and healthy, and used by pe every condition in life. The best qualities are those from Fire Island, Cow Bay, Little Neck Bay, Flushing B. Oyster Bay, City Island, Egg Harbor, Rockaway, Shrewsbury, Shinecock, New Inlet, etc. A very large amount of these clams are sent or distributed all over the States, and also in our steamers, in a fresh and pickled state. I have known two or three incidents of this shell-fish catching rats, which occurred in the following manner. When lying on the stands quiet some time, they open their shells, no doubt in search of water or food, and while in this state, one night, a large rat took a fancy to extract all that was most valuable to his clamship's existence, by inserting one of his fore-paws into the partially open door of the bivalve's household. This sudden and unwelcome introduction was so unexpected and sensitive to the shell-mailed inhabitant, as to cause the quick closing of his doors, by which the intruder was tightly fastened and secured. A considerable squealing and dragging around was the result, but there was no let up, until the rat as well as the clam paid the death penalty. Another curiosity is found noticed of the

Giant clam, which is the largest of all the testaceous animals. "Only one shell in Mr. Turell's cabinet weighs four hundred pounds. Upon a moderate calculation, the animal which it contained would afford a meal for a hundred men. It is a native of the shores of the Indian Ocean, where, it is said, at low-water the tiger comes down to seek for food: he puts his paw into the shell to get at the animal, when the shell closes and holds him so fast that he either loses his paw or is drowned by the rising tide."—Boston *Weekly Mag.*, 1803.

Soft clams, soft-shelled clams, long clams, and **piss-clams.**—This fine clam enjoys several names, as appears above, but the most common one is soft clam, from the fact that it has a thin, brittle, or soft shell. It differs in shape from the hard-shell, being some longer, and the taste

..ı and luscious; they are also considered very nu- They are found in great abundance along the ..nd the numerous creeks, at low-water, in groups or ..lies, about nine to twelve inches under the sand. .Vherever you find the shore full of round holes, about the size of a small finger, there you may be sure to find soft clams. It is through these small holes they feed at high-water. They are usually found opened in our markets; and the best are here in the winter months, or from September to May, after which they are not so good. When the tides are very low, or the water has been driven off the shore by high winds, then large, fine clams are dug up, and found on sale as soon as they can be brought to the markets.

Beach clam, dipper clam.—This is one of the largest clams known; of an olive-brown color, shaped much like the hard clam, but the flesh is tough and not so sweet as the latter clams, although some persons enjoy them; they are, however, principally used for fishing-bait. Many are taken on the shores of Long Island, but are only occasionally found on sale in our markets.

Razor-shell clam.—This is a singular-looking shell-fish—long, curved somewhat the shape of a razor-blade, and by some the flesh is esteemed as a good article of food. It is not usually much larger than a jack-knife. Seldom found in our markets.

Clams ashore. The Hempstead, L. I., *Enquirer* (February, 1839) says: "During the recent gale large quantities of clams of all descriptions were thrown upon the beach for an extent of nearly eight miles, and so great is the quantity now lying high and dry, that it is supposed it would require all the horses and wagons in the town of Hempstead, for months, to carry them away."

Scollops, or **scallops.**—These are found in plenty in our markets, when in season; are best from September to March. Only the muscular part, or, as some call it, the heart, is used as food. They are good boiled and pickled, but much better fried; many, however, do not like their peculiar sweetness, which is somewhat like the flavor of a rich soft clam's, but much more cloying and satisfying.

Muscles.—These shell-fish are generally found best—in fact, only fit to eat—in the fall and winter months, and seldom in great quantities, as they are not generally esteemed very high as food. They are best boiled and pickled, but, on account of their solid texture, etc., they do not readily digest, and therefore do not agree with many stomachs. Summer *Sunday mornings* they are plentifully found at the Catherine Market.

Fresh-water muscle.—This muscle, or clam, is taken from fresh-water streams, but seldom used as food, being very tough, and considered unwholesome. Pearls of value, however, are sometimes found in them. I saw some in 1856 that were sold to jewellers at from one to five dollars apiece. Since that time many have been found worth as many hundreds apiece.

Winkles, or **periwinkles.**—There are several species of this shell-fish sometimes found in our markets, usually at the Catherine Market, on a Sunday morning. They are caught and brought from the Long Island shore, and sold here as an article of food; but they are not generally relished, being somewhat strong-flavored. They are mostly used by the poor who live near the coast. Found in the summer and fall months. In England they are called "wilks."

Cockles.—These shell-fish are often picked up with the round clam, in the mouths of rivers and bays near the ocean. Their form is shaped like the clam, but wrinkled and rough. They are not much thought of as food, are quite scarce, and seldom seen in our markets.

Snails.—From the French journals, we learn that snails have become a fashionable article of diet in France. "That there are fifty restaurants, and more than twelve hundred private tables, in Paris, where snails are accepted as a delicacy by from eight to ten thousand consumers. The market price of the great vineyard snails is from 2f. 50c. to 3f. 50c. (forty-seven to sixty-six cents) per hundred, while those of the hedges, woods and forest bring only from 2f. to 2f. 25c. (thirty-eight to forty-three cents.)" Snails are, and have been for several years, imported from Europe, but are principally used by foreigners. They are generally stewed after having been scalded out of their shell.

Green turtle.—This fine turtle is well known to the epicure for its delicious steaks and the savory soup which it affords. The flesh appears to be of three colors, and it is said to combine the taste of fish, flesh, and fowl, although one of the members of the "Turtle Club" (Denman), who appears well informed on the subject, says: "The dark red flesh is called beef, a lighter part veal, and the other part lamb." The fat is of a green color. The veal part is generally used for steaks, which are taken from the fore-quarter. Those under fifty pounds weight are called "chicken turtle," and from fifty to eighty pounds weight are considered the best.

In preparing them, after having hung them up by the hind-fins, and taken off the head, some five or six hours after, they should be taken down, and the shells, both under and top, nicely cut off, then drawn or emptied, and cut up as desired. They are found in our large markets, sometimes as early as May, and continue to cold weather; occasionally to be had in the winter months. They are kept alive in large cars, and fed with cabbage-leaves, beet-tops, etc., of which they appear to be fond. The dealers have them to weigh from ten to upwards of four hundred pounds.

Green turtle are occasionally seen and taken in our waters, although they belong in the warmer latitudes, West Indies, Florida, etc. The *Columbian*, August 23, 1819, says: "On Thursday last, a smack, coming from Whitestone through Hell-gate, chased a large green turtle some distance, but the game escaped by sinking under the small-boat at the moment of seizure." Better luck had Mr. Van Ranst, of the Williamsburgh ferry, who, next day, off Bushwick Creek, with a hook and line, caught one which weighed forty-eight pounds, and refused five dollars for it at the dock.

Some few years ago one of our dailies told an amusing

story of a distinguished politician from the rural districts, who came to New York, and resolved to give a splendid dinner to some of his party friends. In order to make sure that every thing should be of the best quality, he went to market himself, and bought first a turtle. After taking great pains to select one of the finest specimens in the lot, and ordering it to be sent home, he said to the fisherman, by way of making it quite right—"This is a right-down genuine turtle, ain't it?" "Certainly," was the reply; "one of the very best." "Because," he added, "although I ain't been in the city long, I ain't to be humbugged; it won't do for you to try to put off any of your confounded *mock* turtles on to me." The turtle-dealer stood astounded at his customer's sharpness.

The *New York Daily Times*, September 29, 1864, has "*A Curiosity.*—Mr. Brittan, of the Mansion House, corner of Bleecker and Crosby streets, several weeks since, imported a lot of green turtle. They were killed shortly after their arrival, and nothing more thought of the affair, until yesterday, when about thirty young ones were found crawling about the premises. On examination it was found that several eggs had been laid near a wall heated by a range, and in that manner incubation had taken place. The little ones are quite a curiosity, being probably the first native-born green turtle ever seen in this city."

Salt-water terrapin.—This is the well-known terrapin of the epicure, and the best of the turtle tribe. They are usually cooked with the shell on for the various dishes, and considered best and fattest in the months of November, December, and January. Almost any old New Yorker recollects Alexander, or rather "Sandy Welsh," who kept the "Terrapin Lunch," under the Museum. He could prepare a dish of stewed terrapin that would make an old-fashioned alderman shake his full round front and sides with laughter, and, in the end, burst the buttons off his waistcoat, while enjoying this luxurious feast. Sandy was the great purchaser for all the terrapin at the Washington Market in his day. The largest portion come from the South, and occasionally we have a few from Long Island.

A remarkable specimen is noticed by the editor of the *New York Commercial Advertiser*, in the month of October, 1826. He says: "We have this morning examined a young terrapin, caught yesterday at Staten Island, by Louis S. Korkie, and by him presented to Mr. (Reuben) Peale, for the Pantheon Museum (at this period stood No. 252 Broadway), which is a very great curiosity. It has two heads, and but four legs as usual. The heads and eyes are perfectly formed. But what appears more singular, is the fact that they are endowed with different instincts or intelligences—that is, there is no concert of action between them. One head often pulls one way, and the other another; and it is often a matter of some struggle in which direction the animal shall move. Sometimes one is the master, and sometimes the other, during which time the progress is slow. Now and then, however, when they *put their heads together*, and have apparently the same object in view, they walk off with the ordinary speed of common terrapins. It is really a curiosity which will afford much gratification to naturalists."

Soft-shelled turtle.—The color of this turtle's shell is of a dark slate, with numerous spots over it. The head has a white stripe on each side; the neck, feet, and tail, are covered with white and black. The flesh is much esteemed as wholesome and nutritious food.

Logger-head turtle.—This turtle is sometimes brought to our markets for sale, but are not much sought after, and, of course, do not sell well, especially the large ones. A small fat one makes tolerable soup for a hungry man. They have quite a smooth shell on their back, a large thick head, and appear quite helpless on land.

Hawks-bill turtle.—This is a scarce turtle in our markets, but is sometimes found here. It has a small mouth resembling the bill of a hawk. The shell is the "tortoise-shell" used in combs, etc., but the flesh is considered poorer eating than the logger-head.

Leather-turtle.—These turtle are sometimes taken on the coast or Sound, usually of very large dimensions. Their mouth is different from either of the above; the upper jaw is somewhat like a parrot's, pointed down, which, when shut together with the lower jaw, fits like a tooth of a steel-trap. The shell on the back has five long raised ridges running lengthwise.

An enormous specimen is now (1860) exhibited in Barnum's Museum, which was taken on the 27th of September, 1811, by Samuel Coon, and other pilots, off the coast, when it was said to have weighed eight hundred pounds. The *Columbian*, September 28, 1811, says of this "mammoth turtle:" "Yesterday the pilots on board of the boat Young Pilot, at sea, fell in with a sea-turtle, harpooned it, got it on board, and brought it up to the city, when it was weighed in the hay-scales at Whitehall, and found to weigh eight hundred pounds, being by far the largest we have any account of in this country. We understand Messrs. Coon, White, and Torrey, the pilots who took it, have disposed of it to Mr. Scudder, of the American Museum (then kept at 21 Chatham-street), where it may be seen." This turtle may yet be seen in Barnum's famous museum, and thousands of curiosities besides, for the small sum of twenty-five cents.

Another, no doubt of the same species, I find noticed in an old paper, September 7, 1773, as having been taken on the coast or Sound near New Rochelle, N. Y. "A turtle of an enormous size, and singular form and marks, was taken with a harpoon by Mr. Bleeker, and some others, near New Rochelle; his length is eight feet from fin to fin, and seven feet three inches from stem to stern. He is spotted under the fore-fins like a leopard, and discovered amazing swiftness after having been struck with a harpoon. He had been seen among the rocks for three or four years, in the neighborhood of New Rochelle, but was not known, before the capture, to be a turtle. He is found to be upwards of eight hundred pounds weight."

Snappers, or **snapping turtle.**—This is an ugly,

savage-looking specimen of the turtle species, with a large head, feet and claws. Sometimes known to weigh above forty pounds. The flesh of the young—from two to five pounds—are the best, being very nutritious and savory food, but the large and old are sometimes quite strong, and of a musky flavor. The eggs are esteemed by the epicure. When found in our markets, the head is curbed or fastened, as their jaws are like a vice when it takes a hold. It will allow its head to be severed from its body before it will yield, and I have heard of there being life in it seven days after.

In the month of July, 1820, the *Commercial Advertiser* notices how a snapper was caught on Long Island: "A lad of this Island, by the name of Robert Shella, recently adopted the singular mode of catching snapping-turtles with a rat-trap, and actually succeeded in catching one by the nose, weighing twelve pounds nine ounces, by baiting the trap with pork, sinking it to the bottom of a mill-pond, where those turtles are plenty, and making it fast to a stake. The one above-mentioned was taken by the trap, and from the trap by Bob, in less than one hour after setting it."

In the year 1848, while on a hunting excursion, in crossing a meadow in Westchester county, N. Y., we came across a large snapper, about the size of a peck measure, which afterwards proved to weigh above twenty-five pounds. A few days previous, I was told by my hunting companion, that his daughter, then some twelve years of age, went to a spring (some distance from the house) for water, and in stepping on the stones near it, a large snapper, being under one, suddenly snapped and caught the toe of her shoe, which so frightened her that she had no power to call for help for several moments; she was, however, heard, and before the ill-looking animal could be taken off, a sharp axe was brought into action, which soon separated the body from its vice-like jaws.

The Shenandoah *Herald*, 1824, relates the following curious incident, which happened within two miles of Woodstock: "On observing a large hen-hawk fluttering near the ground, it was discovered that he was held by a snapping-turtle, who retained so firm a hold of one of its feet, that it was with difficulty extricated after the hawk was killed." It was supposed that the hawk intended to capture the turtle, but got captured instead.

Another more remarkable incident occurred with one of these animals, which was caught by an acquaintance, who informed me that he put the snapper in hot water after taking off his head, and a minute had not elapsed before quite a large snake came out of the body and ran over the floor, when it was killed. It was a hard story to believe, but if a snake could be swallowed by the animal without injury, then I must believe it, and therefore give it as I heard it.

Red-bellied terrapin, or **red-legs.**—This variety of the terrapin is much the largest, but not equal to the salt-water kind for the table. Many are found in the Philadelphia markets, and occasionally seen in the markets of New York, usually brought from New Jersey, where I have taken them in the streams and mill-ponds, and also on the land. Some persons consider them, in the winter season (when fat), almost or quite the equal of any of the terrapin species.

Fresh-water terrapin, or **wood terrapin.**—This variety, I believe, is not the common fresh-water terrapin, but much like them. They wear a brown-colored shell with a reddish tinge, with also a reddish neck and feet, speckled with black. Their flesh is considered equal to the preceding, especially by those who take them, as they generally use them in their families, seldom sending them to market.

Smooth terrapin.—This species is sometimes found in the markets, with a smoother shell than the salt-water terrapin, and considered almost its equal for the table. The legs are shorter, and the head without the black spots.

Painted tortoise.—This is the handsomest of our fresh-water species, and but seldom seen for sale. Not much esteemed as an article of food.

Spotted turtle, or **speckled turtle.**—This is the common "skillepot" which inhabits almost every muddy pond or sluggish stream. It is not generally eaten, its flesh being of a muddy, insipid, and strong taste.

Frogs.—The edible frogs are known as the "Gibbou's green frog," although I believe most all of the varieties are eaten, or rather the hind-quarters. They are sold in our markets by some of the fishermen, ready skinned, at so much per piece or dozen, according to the size. They are very delicate, and quite sweet eating; those who try them once, seldom refuse to eat again of them. Foreigners, however, use them most, and think they are more delicate than the thigh of the woodcock, and praise the exquisite dishes of which it forms the component part. They are usually stewed, fried, fricasseed, etc.

Preparing fish for cooking.—The great thing to be attended to in the preparation of fish, is to cleanse away every particle that is offensive, and yet to do this in such a manner that the fish may retain its stiffness, which is frequently destroyed by the knocking about and handling it while the process is going on. By this means the firmness and fine flavor, if not wholly destroyed, is in a great degree impaired. Another thing to be kept in mind is, that many different kinds of fish require to be opened in a different manner. Some require great pains to be taken in the scalding of them, or cleansing them from their slime; others may be dressed without undergoing this process at all, or even gutted; and some there are, as fresh-water eels, cat-fish, etc., for example, that require to be stripped of their external skins altogether. Fish which are taken from ponds, or stagnant waters, often have a muddy taste, which exists only in the skin, and in the process of cooking this flavor is communicated to the body. To remedy this, they ought to be skinned, as they do with cat-fish, bull-heads, eels, etc., or by soaking them in salt and water before cleaning them for half an hour, then rinsing them with cold water. But never leave a good fish one moment in the water after it is thoroughly washed—by this means the flavor is often materially injured.

Preserving fish fresh.—Draw the fish and remove the gills, then insert pieces of charcoal in their mouths and bellies. If they are to be conveyed any distance, wrap each fish up separately in linen cloth, and place them in a box with cabbage-leaves above and below them.

THE FISHERMAN'S FISHY F. FORT.

The *Comic Times* gives the following finished f-fort on the fisherman's daughter, Fenella, which fun, fancy, and fame will finish and fill up the catalogue of fish.

"A famous fish-factor found himself father of five flirting females—Fanny, Florence, Fernanda, Francesca and Fenella. The first four were flat-featured, ill-favored, forbidding-faced, freckled frumps, fretful, flippant, foolish, and flounting. Fenella was fine-featured, fresh, fleet-footed fairy, frank, free, and full of fun. The fisher failed, and was forced by fickle fortune to forego his footman, forfeit his forefathers' fine field, and find a forlorn farm-house in a forsaken forest. The four fretful females, fond of figuring at feasts in feathers and fashionable finery, fumed at their fugitive father. Forsaken by fulsome, flattering fortune-hunters, who followed them when fish flourished, Fenella fondled her father, flavored their food, forgot her flattering followers, and frolicked in frieze without flounces. The father, finding himself forced to forage in foreign parts for a fortune, found he could afford a faring to his five fondlings. The first four were fain to foster their frivolity with fine frills and fans fit to finish their father's finances. Fenella, fearful of flooring him, formed a fancy for a full flush flower. Fate favored the fish factor for a few days, when he fell in with a fog. His faithful filleys faltered and food failed. He found himself in front of a fortified fortress. Finding it forsaken, and feeling himself feeble and forlorn with fasting, he fed on the fish, flesh, and fowl he found, fricasseed and fried, and, when full, fell flat on the floor. Fresh in the forenoon, he forthwith flew to the fruitful fields, and, not forgetting Fenella, he filched a fair flower, when a foul, frightful, fiendish figure flashed forth. 'Felonious fellow, fingering my flowers? I'll finish you! Go, say farewell to your fine, felicitous family, and face me in a fortnight!' The faint-hearted fisher fumed and faltered, and was far in his flight. His five daughters flew to fall at his feet, and fervently felicitate him. Frantically and fluently he unfolded his fate. Fenella forthwith, fortified by filial fondness, followed her father's footsteps, and flung her faultless form at the foot of the frightful figure, who forgave her father, and fell flat on his face, for he had fervently fallen in a fiery fit of love for the fair Fenella. He feasted her till, fascinated by his faithfulness, she forgot the ferocity of his face, form, and features, and frankly and fondly fixed Friday, fifth of February, for the affair to come off. There was festivity, fragrance, finery, fireworks, fricasseed frogs, fritters, fish, flesh, fowl, and fermentry, frontignac flip, and fare fit for the fastidious, fruit, fuss, flambeaux, four fat fiddlers and fifers; and the frightful form of the fortunate and frumpish fiend fell from him, and he fell at Fenella's feet, a fair-favored, fine, frank freeman of the forest. Behold the fruits of filial affection."

VEGETABLE PLANTS.

We have shown the abundance of meats—fish, flesh, and fowl—with which our markets teem. If thus bounteously supplied from the animal kingdom, we have ample reason to rejoice at the plenty afforded to us by the yieldings from the vegetable kingdom. By the progress of the science brought to bear upon that branch we now term "kitchen-gardening," markets are supplied with the asparagenous plants, spinaceous plants, edible marine plants, allicaceous plants, acetaceous plants, edible fungi, leguminous vegetables, esculent roots, the cabbage tribe, sweet herbs, plants used for tarts, salads, and pickles, and the native and several of the foreign species.

"Vegetables, as food for mankind, are used in larger proportions than any other nutritive substances," some of which are eaten while young and tender, but when more advanced in growth become unfit for use. The leaves and stalks of some, and the roots and seeds of others, are used for food.

It is not many years ago when the suburbs—or say twenty miles around the City of New York—from Long Island, Westchester, and New York counties, and New Jersey, furnished the city with a plentiful and cheap supply of vegetables. Long Island always bore away the palm for producing the earliest and finest vegetables: with the increase of the population of our city a larger and wider area of land for the supply of these articles became requisite, which increased the distances from the general marts, whilst greater facilities to bring these products of the earth to market became paramount: from these causes the prices of vegetable-marketing necessarily became greater.

Upon Connecticut, Massachusetts, Western New York, New Jersey, and Pennsylvania, requisitions were made, and now the Southern States, Bermuda Islands, etc., send their early supplies to our markets—not only vegetables, but fruits, fish, nuts, etc.—for months anticipating our native supply. From Charleston, Norfolk, Savannah, and the Bermudas, tomatoes, potatoes, peas, cabbage, onions, strawberries, cherries, are brought at least twice a week during their seasons. Some of these articles are brought by hundreds of barrels at a time.

Early in the spring from the South, and still later from the North, many rare vegetables and other edibles are brought to market by the facilities afforded by the railcars and steamboats, thus inducing, as it were, in these latitudes, artificial seasons. But when in their proper seasons, which differs but a few days or weeks between the different cities, from various directions they are daily gathered in vast quantities; then dispatched by the numerous railroads, steamboats, sloops, and vehicles of all sorts to their destinations, and we find them in the various public markets the next morning fresh and good. So great is the competition of market-gardeners, and so immense the demand for vegetables of all kinds, that all are sure to meet with a ready sale at remunerating prices.

In noticing the following vegetable plants they will be found placed in alphabetical order, and under two separate heads, as follows: *vegetables*, and together include *pot-herbs*, and *medicinal plants.*

VEGETABLES.

Artichoke.—There appears to be two distinct plants of this name used as food—the top or head of one kind, and the root or tuber of the other. The best variety of the first kind, or that preferred here, is called the *globe artichoke*, although the *conical*, *oval*, *large flat*, etc., have many friends, both here and in Europe. The part eaten is the fleshy portion of the leaf of the flower or head, before it blooms, which forms on the top of the stem. The plant itself much resembles the thistle. (The whole heads are, however, sometimes pickled.) The fleshy leaves are prepared as a salad, or are best when stewed or boiled, and are found in season from July to November. The French and Italians bend down the leaves and stalks, bind them together, then cover them with earth to blanch like celery, when it is known as *artichoke-chards.* These are eaten raw in winter, with salt, or vinegar, oil, etc., as a salad or substitute for radishes.

The other species, of which the tuber only is used, is called *Jerusalem artichoke.* The roots, or tubers, of this plant are much like small, ill-shaped potatoes, which grow in clusters of various sizes, forms, and colors, some of which are white, yellow, red, and purple skinned; but I believe that all the varieties usually boil watery; some, however, stew them afterwards with butter and wine, w... be found as pleasant-tasted as the real artichoke.

They are also very good cut up raw into thin slices, with vinegar, etc. They should be taken out of the ground in September or October, and preserved in sand for winter consumption.

Asparagus.—This is one of the best and choicest luxuries of the vegetable kind, being a wholesome, digestible, and a light food. Among the best varieties the green giant asparagus is generally preferred, as its young shoots grow thick and very tender. I have known it to grow so large and fine that the cuttings from sixteen stalks weighed four pounds, and many of them, singly, eight inches of tender eating. Some prefer the white, others the purple top, but neither kind is so sweet or tender as the green giant, grown in the light sandy soil near the sea-shore. In boiling the shoots, all should be tied up in one bunch, put into the pot standing up, so that the water is up about half way; then boiled some ten to fifteen minutes; then laid on its side, so the water covers all, and thus finished, when principally all the parts may be eaten.

The season of asparagus commences, with quite small shoots and short bunches from the South, in the month of April; from New Jersey and Long Island in May and June, and seldom fit for the table after the close of the latter month. On the 17th of May I saw a bunch of green asparagus, of twenty-four stalks, weigh exactly four pounds, raised by Mr. Underhill, of Oyster Bay, and presented to Hedden & Sons, Jefferson Market. A month later, Mr. J. B. Mingay, of the same market, showed a white bunch of nineteen stalks weighing the same weight.

Beans.—The varieties of the bean are very numerous, although they appear to be divided into but two sorts—the garden, runner, or pole bean, and the field, bush, or dwarf bean. These are used for the table in two ways: those eaten with the shell or pod are called string or snap beans, while the seeds of the others, called shell-beans, are alone

...a, cranberry, kidney, dutch-caseknife, etc., ...of those I have known to be used in and out ...r pod, when young and tender. Then, again, some of these varieties are subdivided into various kinds: for instance, the lima is of two varieties, the white and green, but are known as the potato lima, Carolina lima, common lima, small lima, and so the names go through the whole varieties. Among all the shell-beans the lima is considered the queen, as the Neapolitan is thought of the string or snap beans; but all the varieties of the latter should break or snap crisply, else they are not in their proper state. The potato lima yields, when shelled, almost one-half more than the common lima; it has a short, thick shell, and the seed also is much thicker, usually producing three seeds or beans in a pod. The season commences with the string-beans from the South—about the 1st of April—and continues, with a succession of new crops, until the middle of November. These are followed by the shelled-beans, or those to shell, generally about the 1st of May, and continue throughout the year, although in the last few months they are in a dry, or sometimes found in a soaked state in the markets.

Beets.—There are also many varieties of this plant; and among the best for the table are the turnip-rooted, long-blood, long-smooth, early bassano-turnip, etc. There are also larger varieties, but these are generally used for feeding cattle, such as the yellow turnip-rooted, mangel-wurtzel, sugar beets, etc. The table beets are numerously used as a pickle, in stews, soups, pies, etc., and, when new, their season commences about the 1st of June (being brought from the South) and continues throughout the year.

Beet greens, or **young beets.**—The whole of the very young plant (top and bottoms) of the early turnip-rooted are usually boiled as greens, and are best in the months of May and June, when they are very tender and excellent. The young tops are also good alone.

Borecole, or **green curled kale.**—This fine table-vegetable, of which there are several varieties, should be well frost-bitten before it is fit for use; after which the frost should be drawn out by placing it in a cool cellar, or in cold water. The parts used are the tender tops or crown of the plant, with the side sprouts, which should be well boiled, so as to be tender before being dressed and eaten. In season as soon as the frost takes hold of them, and continues good nearly all winter.

Broccoli.—This excellent plant is a variety of the cauliflower, but considered not quite so delicate in flavor, the head or flower of which being somewhat of a purple cast, while that of the cauliflower is of a creamy white. However, the qualities and varieties of both broccoli and cauliflower have become, by cultivation, so nearly alike—especially of the white varieties—that it requires the botanist to distinguish between them. Broccoli are in season from September to November, and may be kept longer if hung up by the roots in a cool place.

Brussel-sprouts.—This plant is one of the species of the cabbage kind, producing in the axils small heads resembling those of the cabbage on a large stalk. They are very tender, and much esteemed by those who use them, which is generally in the winter-time, cooked as greens. They stand the frost well, are in season from September to January, but are not much cultivated here.

Cabbage.—There are several varieties of this excellent plant. The "early York" is a great favorite, and widely cultivated, on account of the excellence of its flavor, and its early maturity. There is also the "early dutch," "flat dutch," which the Dutch commonly slice and call it kohl-slaw, or salat, meaning simply cabbage salad; but the progress here has corrupted it to cole or cold slaw. There are also other kinds, more particularly used for *saur-kraut*, or *sour-krout*, called the drumhead, Bergen, etc. Another, called the "savoy," a curled-leaf cabbage, is by some considered the finest of all varieties, it being very tender, of a fine flavor, rather a small head, but solid, and generally sold for higher prices than those that are much larger. The red cabbage is another variety, and is generally used for pickling. Young cabbage is found in our markets in May and June, when it arrives from the South; but the season about here commences in July, and continues until cold weather; then, if they are put in a good cellar, or properly buried, they can be kept almost the whole year. The *London Chronicle*, of 1765, gives the following account of a large cabbage: "A gentleman of honor and veracity has furnished us with the following surprising instance of the fertility of the soil and mildness of the climate of the South American provinces, viz.: He saw, a few days ago, in a gentleman's garden, near Savannah, in Georgia, a cabbage-plant, which, having stood the winter three years, and seeded annually, rises from one root and spreads over a circular form of thirty feet, measuring ten feet every way." In the year 1813, in the month of October, a cabbage was sold in the New York Market, which weighed forty-three pounds.

Capsicum, or **peppers.**—*See Peppers.*

Cardoons.—This plant is a species of the artichoke, but much larger and taller; the stalk part of the leaf and midrib, when properly blanched, will be crisp and tender. They are used for soups, stews, salads, etc. The *Gardener's Chronicle* says: "When a cardoon is to be cooked, the solid stalks of the leaves are to be cut in pieces, about six inches long, and boiled like any other vegetable, in pure water (not salt and water), till they are tender. They are then to be carefully deprived of the slime and strings that will be found to cover them; and, having been thus thoroughly cleansed, are to be plunged in cold water, where they must remain until they are wanted for the table. They are then taken out, and heated with white sauce or marrow. The process just described is for the purpose of rendering them white, and of depriving them of the bitterness which is peculiar to them. If this is neglected the cardoons will be black, not white, as well as disagreeable." In season from September until March.

Carrots.—There are several varieties of this vegetable, of different forms and colors—white, yellow, scarlet, etc.—used for the table. They are a very useful root, either in soup, stews, haricot, puddings, pies, etc., and are to be found nearly or quite throughout the year in our markets. The young carrots, which commence the season, are from the South, which arrive about the 1st of May; then from Long Island, about the 1st of June, and continue on, with new crops, until November, when those intended for the table are put in earth or sand for winter and spring use, in fact, until the young carrots are again found on sale.

Cauliflower.—This fine vegetable, of which there are several varieties, is one of the luxurious plants which generally command a high price. The large, solid, creamy, white heads are considered the best. When the leaves are much wilted, and the head has dark soft spots through it, they are stale and not good. The early kinds appear about the 1st of May, and so continue on, in succession of crops, until the frost destroys them. Besides plain boiling, they are much used for pickling, soups, etc.

Cavish, scavish, or **scabious.**—This is a common field-plant, which, in the early spring months, makes excellent greens. The young leaves grow in tufts of a longish shape, pointed at both ends, of a light green color, but of a pleasant taste. The young stalk is also good, both of which are soft and mucilaginous. The stalk produces a small yellow flower when in bloom. They will bear considerable boiling to be good.

Celeriac, or **turnip-rooted celery.**—This tuberous-looking root has a sweeter taste and stronger odor than the common celery, and, when properly cooked, is very tender and marrow-like. The tops look much like celery, but are quite short and green, and are much used in soups, etc. The root, however, is large, stout, and quite rough, and when sliced and stewed German-fashion, it is excellent. It is also boiled, then prepared as a salad. It is found for sale in the fall and winter months.

Celery.—There are several varieties of this excellent plant, of which the white solid, red solid, and the white dwarf are now generally preferred. The latter, I think, is the sweetest and tenderest in February and March. In buying, select the solid, close, clean and white stalks, with a large, close heart, as they are apt to be the most crisp and sweet; however, early in the season all celery is a little bitter. The season commences about the middle of August, and as soon as the frost is found, celery becomes sweeter and better. It is found constantly in our markets afterwards, until about the 1st of April.

Chard, or **Swiss chard.**—This plant is one of the best of the beet tribe, but, unlike that vegetable, the root is not usually eaten, but the large succulent leaves, which have a very solid rib running along the middle. The leafy part, being stripped off and boiled, is used as greens; while the midrif, or stalk, are dressed like asparagus; and when they have been properly blanched, by art, they have a pleasant, sweet taste, and are considered very wholesome. They are not much cultivated here, however.

Chicory, or **wild endive.**—The part of this plant used is the long root, which looks somewhat like salsify, and the leaves, when young, can be used as a salad. The root has a smell like liquorice, and is principally used in the making or mixing with coffee, when the root is properly prepared; that is, by cutting it up in half-inch pieces, then dried in the air, after which it is browned in an oven or kiln, then ground with either coffee, rye, beans, corn, potatoes, carrots, parsnips, acorns, or other cheap substances, when these mixtures are attractively placed before the public, and sold at high prices—often for pure coffee. Chickory mixed with either roasted rye or coffee, is considered wholesome; but as it is a cheap article, and when mixed with half coffee, should reduce the price to at least one-half—with rye, about one-quarter. Either article, however, should be purchased separately, then prepared to suit the taste, when the purchaser would know what he was using.

In an examination by commissioners in London, who found out of forty-two specimens of coffee, thirty-one to be adulterated with chickory only, while twelve had roasted corn in addition to chickory; one had beans, and one had potato-flour. The total result was, that one-third of the whole weight consisted of adulterants, and in some cases chickory was present to the extent of more than one-half. "It was found that some of the grocers use a 'coffee colorer,' of a rich brown color: it consists chiefly of burnt sugar, and appears to be used to deepen the color of poor coffee, or of coffee which has been chicoried. The sellers of cups of coffee at a cheap price are said to be very familiar with this 'improver.' The commissioners adduce some curious examples of the discrepancy between the quality and the high-sounding names of particular samples; thus, a packet of 'celebrated Jamaica' was found to be nearly all chicory; 'finest Java coffee' consisted of half coffee, much roasted corn, and a little chicory; 'superb coffee' was principally chickory and roasted corn, with very little coffee; 'fine plantation Ceylon' was nearly all chickory; 'fine Java' contained much chickory and potato; 'delicious drinking coffee' contained a large quantity of chickory and roasted corn."

The commissioners also examined thirty-four samples of chickory itself, purchased indiscriminately at different places, "and amongst them found carrot, parsnip, mangel-wurzel, beans, acorns, roasted corn, biscuit-powder, and burnt sugar. It had been stated in other quarters that such strange substances as burnt rags, red earth, and rope-yarn have been found in chickory; but this belongs to the transcendental regions of rascality."

Cives, chives, or **shives.**—This plant is a species of the leek, with small, awl-shaped leaves, growing in tufts; and these are only fit for use so long as they remain green and fresh. They possess a flavor peculiar to the onion family, and are principally used for flavoring soups, salads, omelets, etc. The Germans also make use of it in their smear-kase, etc. It is in season from April to June, and usually found tied in small bunches. Foreigners are its principal consumers.

Colewort, or **collards**.—This is a kind of small cabbage, cut young and eaten as greens, but it is not much used in this country. It is, however, used in England throughout the winter, and is in season from August until March.

Corn.—*See Indian Corn.*

Corn salad, **lamb's lettuce**, or **fetticus**.—This plant is principally cultivated as a winter and spring salad, and is of a mild, agreeable taste and flavor. The leaves should be eaten while young. They are sometimes boiled as spinach, etc.

Cress.—There are several species of this warm and pleasant-tasted plant, the shoots of which are much used as an early salad. The most common is the water-cress, which appears in abundance from March until May, and then again from September until November. Another kind is called the

Garden-cress, or **pepper-grass**, which is also eaten when young as a salad. It has a pleasant, refreshing, pungent taste, and may be had during the spring. Another species, called

Winter-cress, or **early hedge-cress**, which is a much larger plant, and is considered a species of the mustard, is very pungent and biting. The young leaves are most of the year used as a salad. There is also another species of this plant, called by some

Indian-cress, or **nasturtium**.—*See Nasturtium.* I might add another small variety, called

Small water-cress, with much the taste of the family of cresses.

Cucumbers.—This vegetable is called a fruit in botany, and a cold one it is, although pleasant to the taste of most people, yet they are not easily digested, nor is there much nourishment in them; but when pickled, or made into pickles, they are then considered less unwholesome. There are several varieties found in our markets, among which are the early, short and long, prickly, green, white Turkey, etc. The quite young or small ones, of various sizes, are used to make pickles—in fact, many persons call them pickles when asking for them. The very small ones are used for gherkins; the large, or those nearly full-grown, are hard, and commonly used as a salad; and when they begin to soften and turn yellow, or rather ripe, the Germans and others prepare them in such a manner as to make some very good dishes, among which frying is one of them. Cucumbers begin to show themselves from the South in April, from Long Island, etc., about the 20th of June, and so continue in our markets until November, after which they are found in a cured state, or pickled. Several other species of the cucumber have been tried, but with little success, for the table.

Dock, yellow dock, or **patience dock.**—The curly and narrow-leafed dock is much used in the spring months as greens. The broad, smooth leaf-dock, known as "horse-dock," is considered not fit for use, and some say it is poisonous. The former is often found in our markets when young, is tender and sweet, and makes a very fair dish of greens. The root is much used as a purifier of the blood.

Dandelion.—This well known wild plant, by some called "piss-a-bed," is now much cultivated, and is found a very wholesome vegetable. Early in the spring—March and April—the young leaves are used for salads and greens, when it is found slightly bitter, but rather agreeable; and as it increases in size, it becomes full of bitter milk. However, by proper cultivation and blanching, it is found to be both pleasant and wholesome. The roots are also used, and much valued for their medicinal properties. In 1856, Messrs. Hills & Stringer, of New York City, introduced "dandelion coffee," made of the roots of this plant, which I found a very pleasant drink. It was then prepared for the visitors to the Fair of the American Institute, then held in the "Crystal Palace."

Egg-plant.—This plant is called "guinea-squash" at the South. There are several varieties of this excellent vegetable, of which the large, purple, oval-shaped kind is the best for the table. When cut into thin slices and fried, they have the taste of an oyster; but they should be firm and hard, or rather, not ripe. They are much used in other dishes, in soups, plain boiled, stews, etc. The white variety is much smaller, being about the size and shape of a goose-egg, and but seldom used—grown rather for ornament than use. The egg-plant is in season from June until October.

Endive, or **succory.**—There are several varieties of this plant, of which the curled are found the most numerous. The green curled is very crisp and tender; but the white curled is more so, but less hardy, and usually found quite scarce. The broad-leaved Batavian—called, by the French, *scaroll*—is much cultivated, but principally used by the French and Germans. The leaves (only) are generally used in soups, stews, ragouts, roasts, etc., but, when blanched, they make a good salad. In season from September until March. The roots of endive are also much used in Europe; the Germans prepare them like *salsify*, and they are also dried and ground into powder as a substitute for coffee.

Garlic.—This plant is a species of the onion, with an acrimonious taste, and a most disagreeable smell. The root grows in the shape of bulbs which are enclosed. It is much used by the French in a great many dishes for seasoning, soups, stews, and other dishes, and has also many medicinal qualities. It is in season throughout the year, and usually found strung as onions, in ropes or bunches.

Gherkins, or **Jamaica cucumber.**—This small, oval, light-green, prickly fruit appears to be a species of the cucumber, but more thickly covered with prominent fleshy spines or prickles, and usually about the size of a common egg-plumb. It is also very full of small seeds, and a round stem, three or four inches long, which is firmly attached to

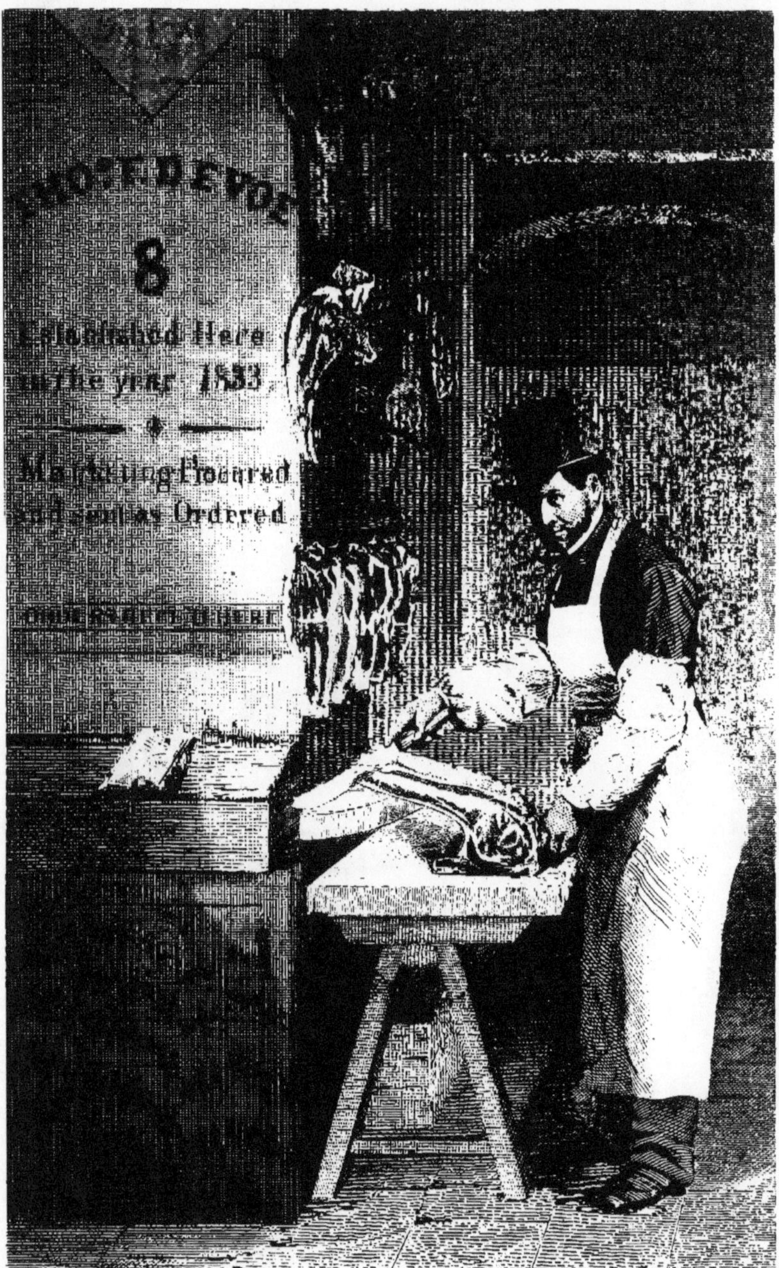
8
Here
1833
Ordered

the fruit. When cut its smell is like that of a cucumber, and its uses are generally for pickling; but it should be pickled before the skin grows tough. It is not much cultivated here, but, when found, it is usually in the months of August and September.

Gourd, or **calabash.**—This creeping plant, perhaps, ought not to be placed among the table-vegetables; but, as its fruit, when young and tender, can be—and is, sometimes —used for pickling like cucumbers; and also, as this fruit grows old, its shell becomes hard, light, and strong, which can also be made useful either for water-dippers, substitutes for buckets, etc., I concluded it was worthy of space somewhere in this volume.

Horse-radish.—This is a common kitchen-plant, the roots of which are used ground, or cut into very small pieces for salads, sauces, etc. It is, however, boiled by some. The tops are also used when young as greens. It is always in season. When freshly ground, it has an agreeable pungent taste, but soon loses it when left open or exposed.

Indian corn, or **maize.**—The useful qualities of this important plant are very numerous, and easily prepared into a variety of forms fit for human food. Before it becomes hard and ripe the ears are fit for roasting or boiling; cut from the cob, and cooked with beans, makes the dish called "succotash;" or it can be dried and kept a long time for future uses. When ripe and hard, it is prepared by coarse or fine grinding for hominy, samp, mush, johnny cake, bread, etc. There are many varieties, of which the *sweet-corn* is considered the best for boiling; and of this quality there are several kinds, caused from peculiar culture, soil, and climate. It begins to arrive from the South (Charleston), about the 1st of June; then from Philadelphia, say from the 10th to the 15th of July; from New York, about the 1st of August; and continues, by a succession of crops, to be soft and good until the 15th of October—although I have eaten it in a good condition on the 1st of December (1855). It was raised on Long Island, near Fort Hamilton, by Mr. Richard Bennett, and sold in the Jefferson and other markets. But a few years ago, it was the custom for colored women to sit around at the various corners of the market, with their pails and tubs of hot-corn, which had been previously boiled; and others, again, perambulating the streets half of the night, with the cry of "Hot corn! hot corn! hot! just come out of the boiling-pot."

"The full-eared corn, at every well-known spot,
Prompts now the vender's cry, 'All hot! all hot!'"

It is recorded in the *Onondaga Standard* (September, 1846), that the Onondagas and other Indians have a grand feast annually, which they call *suckatash*, or *succotash*. It states that "the great *suckatash* was served up in the big kettle, composed of all sorts of vegetables, mixed with corn and beans, and seasoned with pork and a great variety of meats. It is a luxury highly prized by the Indians as the consummation of their harvest."

Kale, green-curled.—See *Borecole.*

Kohl rabi, turnip cabbage, or **Dutch turnip.** —This vegetable was formerly known as "Egyptian kale;" is considered sweeter, more nutritious and solid than either the cabbage or white turnip. On a stem, just above the ground, it grows or swells out in a round, fleshy bulb, about the size and form of a large turnip, on the top of which it sends forth its leaves. Among the varieties, are the white, green, and purple stemmed—the latter usually preferred for winter use, as it can be kept sound and good until late in the spring. They are usually found in the market about the middle of June, and are best

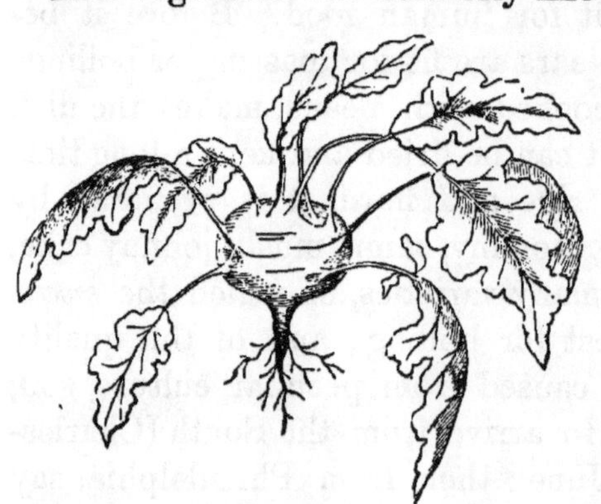

KOHL-RABI.

for the table when quite young, being then more tender and delicate. They may be cooked like the cabbage or turnip, and eaten with the same condiments; or they may be cut in half-inch slices to boil; then change the water once or twice, and then serve it up with butter or cream poured over it. They should be preserved like a cabbage for winter use.

Lamb's quarter.—This common plant or weed, when young, makes early greens, which are much used by country people. The leaf is somewhat the form of a lamb's quarter, which, no doubt, has given it the name. The root, stalk, and leaves have a pinkish color, and, when boiled, are quite pleasant tasted. Best in the month of May.

Leek, or **flag onion.**—This common plant of the onion tribe shows large flag-leaves running up from small, fine roots. They are generally found tied in bunches, or one or two with a small bunch of parsley, tied up, being a quantity sufficient for a soup or stew, etc., for a small family. The leeks, when properly blanched, are boiled, and served with toasted bread and white sauce, and eaten as asparagus. The young leeks are found in August, and continue throughout the winter.

Lentils.—These seeds or beans are not much used or grown in this country, but are a favorite food with the French and Germans, who consider them nutritious and better tasted than the common bean, which they much resemble. They are found in a preserved state in some of our best grocery stores.

Lettuce.—This fine tender plant is by many called salad, for which it is almost wholly used, and for which it is unrivalled. It is sought after early in the spring, even at high prices, which cause many to grow it under glass. There are many kinds, each of which is excellent—the early cabbage, butter, drumhead, silesia, cos, etc. The hard lettuce raised in the open air is generally found in the month of May, but most abundant in June and July, and continues throughout the year, except at short intervals through the winter.

Mangel wurtzel is a variety of the beet, but much coarser and larger, although a wholesome vegetable either for men or cattle. The leaves, when young, are quite as good as the common white or red beet, as well also as the thick, fleshy stalks, stripped of the leafy part, peeled or scraped, then boiled.

The *Commercial Advertiser*, July 25, 1814, through the Norfolk *Chronicle*, quotes the following: "The culture of the Mangel Wurzel, or Root of Scarcity, which reaches the size of from twelve to twenty pounds, is increasing rapidly in this country. This esculent has proved its value and use to many, particularly in the late severe weather, in affording food for sheep, while the turnips were so long buried in the snow. Fifty tons per acre have been obtained of this valuable root, upon good sandy loam, and applied to the purpose of fattening oxen, sheep, and pigs, and feeding milch cows, for which purpose it equals any food whatever."

Martynia.—This coarse, annual plant shows large flowers, which grow into a curved pod, somewhat like a cow's horn; these, when green, and so tender as to allow the skin to be easily cut with the thumb-nail, are then fit for pickling. When ripe they are so hard and woody as to be useless. They are not much grown here yet, but, no doubt, they will become quite plentiful, as they make an excellent pickle.

Milk-weed or **milk-vetch.**—The young shoots, or stalks, when sprouting out of the ground, say some four to six inches high, make excellent, tender greens, even after the young leaves become detached from the stalk they are good. These and the young poke-weed, when sold in the markets, are usually tied up like asparagus, in bunches, but are shorter and of a lighter color. They are usually found best in the month of May, and when grown in the shade are more tender and sweet.

Morel, morill, or **mascul plant.**—This vegetable is closely related, or is a species of the mushroom, from which it is distinguished by the cap, which is hollow within, and adheres to the stem by its base, and latticed on the surface with irregular sinuations. It grows in moist places to the height of about four inches, and should be gathered when the plant is perfectly dry. They are found to be rich and succulent, when used the same as mushrooms or truffles. They are better to dry than the mushrooms, as they do not lose their flavor. They are found growing from May to September.

Mushrooms.—The edible mushroom is considered by some as one of the most delicious, as well as one of the most dangerous, delicacies of our table; it, therefore, requires some knowledge to select the right or edible kind. The young button, as it is sometimes called, has the top or cap quite white, the gills or under part are loose, of a light red or flesh color, and as it increases in size and age, the top changes to a chocolate brown color, and looks scurvy, when the gills also change to a darker red. The stem is also white and round, and changes dark with age. The button is sometimes found almost of a globular form, and when smooth and white it is the best and most savory. Every eatable mushroom has a decidedly pleasant odor, and is never slimy, while those which are dangerous are of a bad odor, or are devoid of or have very little smell.

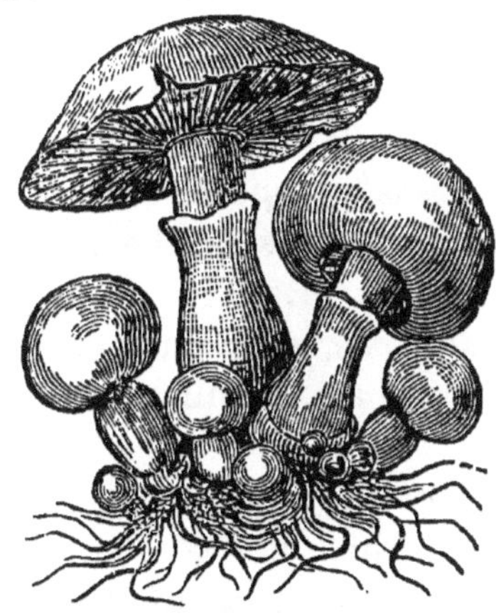

MUSHROOMS.

The following test, in some occasions, may be found useful: "Sprinkle salt on the spongy part or gill of the mushroom to be tried. If they turn yellow they are poisonous; but if they turn black they are good. Allow the salt to act a little time before you decide the color." They are extensively used for making catsup, stewing, pickles, etc. They are in season during September and October, but by artificial culture may be had throughout the whole year.

I found in one of the London papers, of 1817, of the rapid and large growth of a mushroom. It was found growing in the middle of a blacksmith's fire-place, and measured "ten inches long in the stalk, and five and one-half inches in diameter; it was proved by the root of the plant that it had grown there since eight o'clock the preceding evening, at which time" the blacksmith left off work.

Mustard.—The leaves of the young, white, broad-leaved kind is best for a mixed salad, or to boil with meat as greens. It may be had at any time in a few days, by being sown in a box and kept in a warm place. The excellent sauce is generally made from the foreign ground seed, which invariably appears on the table for a well-prepared dinner. The seed is used for pickles and medicinal purposes. Black mustard is also extensively used here, and is of the same flavor as the former; but I think it stronger. The country people prepare this kind for their table use, when but a small quantity is required to make the tears come, unwillingly and unbidden sometimes.

Nasturtium or **Indian cress.**—This plant by many is called *stirtion*, the young leaves of which are excellent in salads. The flowers serve as a garnish for dishes of cooked meats, while the buds scarcely formed, and the green seed (pods or fruit), are preserved in vinegar, which make an excellent small pickle (used as the caper) for summer use, and should be gathered in the month of August.

Okra or **gumbo.**—The green seed pods of this West India plant, while young, are very highly esteemed, especially at the South, where it is much used, and also considered a very wholesome vegetable, as it produces a great deal of mucilaginous and nutritious matter. The pods should be young and tender. Of the three varieties—the long-green, white-ribbed, and the short-green (which has smooth, round pods)—the first is considered the best, either green or dried. By slicing the pods into narrow rings, and drying them on strings, they can be preserved for winter use. It is much used in stews, soups, pickles, etc. The ripe seed, when of sufficient age and carefully parched, can be hardly distinguished, it is said, from genuine coffee. The new okra is in season from August until the end of November.

Onions.—This well-known vegetable is used, in many various ways, especially in seasoning soups, boiling, and, in fact, it is an indispensable vegetable in cookery. Among the principal and best varieties are the white, or silver-skinned, yellow, and red, and they have also various names according to their size, shape, season, and flavor. The very small of the white kind are much used for pickling; the larger and other kinds are applied to other and various uses.

The first new onions are received from the South about the 1st of May, usually from the Bermudas, packed in palm leaf hampers, holding from a-half to one bushel, which onions are large, flat, and red colored, but sweet and excellent: then they follow from New Orleans, 1st of June, and from New Jersey, Connecticut, Rhode Island, etc., from the 15th to the 20th of July. About thirty-five years ago the common red onions were principally sold, fastened on a wisp of straw about the size of a man's thumb, which were called a "string" or "rope of onions," and I have heard them called "bunch of onions." These were principally brought from the Eastern States. They were tied three or four dozen on this rope of straw with twine, by placing the foot on one end, which end they commenced to tie on the onions closely, round and round, until they reached the height of the knee. However, when loosely tied, or the string broken, many onions were lost to the purchaser, and sometimes also the strings would be quite short, both in number and length; this, however, was soon accounted for by the seller, as having been tied up by a "short girl." In the olden time a certain weight was demanded by law, which appears in 1761 that a bunch, or "rope of onions," "shall weigh at least four pounds net weight, under penalty of forty shillings." A large onion was sent to the editor of the *American Agricul-*

turist, raised from Mexican seed, grown in Denver, Colorado, which weighed two pounds.

Orach, or **orache**.—This plant is not much cultivated here for the table, but in some parts of Europe the leaves, with the tender stalks, are cooked and eaten, in the same manner as spinach or young beets, to which it is generally preferred; they have a pleasant, acid taste. The stalk, however, must be used while young, or they will be stringy and worthless.

Oyster-plant.—*See Salsify.*

Parsley.—I know of but two kinds of this valuable condiment—the double-leaved, or curled, and the plain, or single-leaved. The leaves are used largely in cooking or garnishing. It is always in season, except at intervals through the winter months. The roots are edible boiled as carrots, etc., but not much used here.

Parsnips.—This wholesome and nourishing root is very desirable during the winter and spring months, when other vegetation is scarce. Among the best varieties are the "large cup" and "long-smooth;" but those free from side roots, being large, heavy, smooth, tender, and sugary, are the choice. They are one of the vegetables which the frost improves; good to boil, for soup, making bread, and it is said they make a good wine, resembling Madeira.

Parsnip chervil, or **turnip-rooted chervil.**—This tuberous-rooted plant is yet but little known here. In the south of Europe, however, it is spoken of as a valuable esculent root. In form and size it is much like the early horn carrot; skin of a grayish black, and the flesh white, with a taste or flavor between the chestnut and potato, or so I am informed, not having yet tasted or even seen the plant. In season in August and September.

Peas.—This fine vegetable is familiar in the domestic cookery of every country, and is here most extensively cultivated and used when in season. In their proper season, over three hundred wagons-load have been counted at one of our public markets (Washington), laden with this pleasant and nourishing food. Among the best varieties are the early emperor, Warwick, may, dwarf, Prince Albert, cedo-nulli, marrowfat, Japan, sugar, etc., the latter being usually cooked in the pods, like string beans, and are truly excellent; but the marrowfats are undoubtedly the best for summer use. Peas should be always purchased in the pods, and those should feel cool and dry. If closely packed they have a mashed or wet appearance and a warm feeling, which much injures their natural flavor; and when the shells or pods begin to turn to a lighter shade, or look rusty, the pea has usually a black spot upon them, and is then found too old to be good. But to have them in the greatest perfection—if it is possible—they should be cooked immediately after being picked. The first new peas received here are generally in small quantities and at high prices. They come from the Bermudas about the 1st of April, from Charleston about the middle of May, from southern New Jersey about the 1st of June, from Long Island, etc., generally from the 10th to the 15th of June, and so continue until September. Large quantities of dry, soaked, and split peas are sold throughout the winter season. The Japan pea is one of the best varieties; they, however, should be boiled with salt meat to give them a delicious flavor.

Peppers, or **capsicum.**—The several varieties mostly cultivated here of this hot plant, are the common red and green, of the long and round kinds. The pepper pods, when ripe, are red. The long red is dried and ground for cayenne pepper. The green round pod makes a hot pickle mixed with cucumber, as also does the stuffed pickle, or mangoes, etc. The small kind, called the bird or cherry pepper, is the most acrid of all the varieties. The bell pepper is the least pungent. This plant comes plentiful in market about the 1st of September.

Pie plant.—*See Rhubarb.*

Pig-weed.—This common plant is much used by some country people for early greens, and when gathered in a young state—generally in the months of May and June—

it is quite good, but somewhat troublesome to prepare. I have not seen it on sale in our markets.

Poke, or **poke-weed**.—This common plant, when young and the shoots are just appearing above the ground in the spring (from four to eight inches high), makes a dish when boiled, almost equal to asparagus, which it somewhat resembles. It is usually found tied in bunches when for sale. I have found it more plentiful in the Philadelphia market than in any other, a great deal of which is brought by the colored people and herb-gatherers.

Potatoes.—This most excellent edible root is, without doubt, the most useful, wholesome, and nutritive of all the roots now in use. Scarcely a dinner is prepared without having this vegetable on the table. "They furnish flour without a mill, and bread without an oven."

There are many ways of cooking this vegetable, but when boiled or roasted, they are the best. They are also used in bread-making, starch, and many other ways. They should never be used when frozen and thawed, by the action of the weather, as they are considered unwholesome and unfit for use; but when in a frozen state, they should be placed in cold water, which slowly draws out the frost and renders them edible.

The sooner potatoes are placed in a dark cool place after being taken out of the ground, the better they will be both for keeping and eating; but if exposed to light and drying wind it will detract from the flavor and otherwise injure them.

Among the best varieties are the Carters, kidneys (black and white), mercers, buckeyes, peach-blows, Prince Alberts, Western reds, Dikemans, yellow pink-eyes, Jackson-whites, rockwhites, northern-whites, Junes, Dovers, etc., etc., etc.

The Carters (at this period) are considered best for the table, and are usually sold at the highest prices. The kidneys or white pink-eyes are not far behind them (once thought the best); both, of late years, appear not successful growers, and the Carters especially are subject to the rot, as are also the mercers, which have been very successful above twenty years; but, for the last four or five years, the peach-blow is taking the lead.

The first new potatoes received in the New York markets in the spring are the highly prized Bermudas, in the month of April. They are said to be the common Western reds grown in the Bermuda soil. Then from the Southern States, about the 1st of June, we receive the Charlestons; about the 20th, the Norfolks; and from New Jersey and Long Island, early in July, the early varieties appear, viz., the yellow pink-eyes, rock-whites, northern whites, Dovers, etc., which are only cultivated for their early growth, as they are usually watery and not well-flavored. The old potatoes are, at this time, found to be scarce, poor, and not much sought after. A great quantity of Nova Scotias are received here throughout the winter months, especially when the prices are high.

I find an enormous Bermuda potato noticed, above one hundred years ago, in the *Weekly Gazette*, dated October 3, 1748, as follows: "This day a potato, of the sort called Bermuda potatoes, was brought to this city, being the produce of Plumb Island, in this province, which weighed seven pounds and a half, is entirely sound and good, and was made a present to the printer hereof by one of his customers."

"Doctor Fuller, of the 'Connecticut Retreat,'" says the *Hartford Courant*, of 1839, "has gathered from one true Rohan potato, presented him last spring, and which weighed only four ounces, *ninety-six pounds five ounces.* One of the potatoes weighed two pounds ten ounces, and the yield being four hundred to one."

Sir Robert Banks says: "The potato was first introduced into England from America, by the colonists sent out by Sir Walter Raleigh, in 1586. In the year 1619, the common market price was *one shilling* (English) per pound." Bowen, in his picture of Boston, under date January 1, 1636, says: "The ship Rebecca arrived from Bermuda with thirty thousand pounds of *potatoes,* which are sold at two pence a pound." For a long time the potato was treated as a fruit, baked in pies with spices and wine, or eaten with sugar; and it was many years after, before it was cultivated as a field-crop. The date of the introduction of potatoes into New England is generally stated as about 1720. In the Charleston, S. C., news, *New York Journal*, etc., July 21, 1768, it is stated that "Irish potatoes are now produced here in so great plenty that we have begun to export them to other parts." More interesting history of this vegetable is found in the same paper, June 22, 1791, which reads: "Potatoes were first known and discovered in America in the reign of Queen Elizabeth. John Hawkins first imported them into Europe from St. Fee, in Spanish America. For the first time, they were planted in Ireland by the brave Sir Walter Raleigh, he having, at that time, an estate in that kingdom; but their history was so imperfectly understood, that Sir Walter Raleigh was resolved to renounce the expectation of bringing that exotic to any degree of perfection: for, in some time after he had planted them, the stalk shot forth, and, perceiving balls upon them, he concluded that they were the delicious fruit; but, upon boiling; he found them not to be productive of either a pleasing or salubrious beverage, whereupon concluded he had lost his labor; but, upon digging up the ground for other purposes, he discovered, to his great surprise, that the fruit he was in quest of lay concealed beneath the earth, which he found to be most pleasingly grateful to the taste. Upon experiment, it was found that treble the quantity of potatoes could be raised from the same parcel of ground than of any other exotic. They immediately became the principal food of the Irish peasantry, and so remain to this day, being in as high esteem among their first European propagators as *punkins* are in New England. From Ireland they were spread into England, where they likewise met a most favorable reception, and from whence it has been erroneously asserted that *potatoes* were natives of Ireland, although it is not above two hundred and twenty-six years since they were first imported into that kingdom."

Sweet potatoes.—There are many varieties, differing in size, shape, color, and taste, of this vegetable; but it is seldom that there are more than two kinds found in our markets—the red or purple rooted, and the white or yellow rooted. The former is mostly cultivated in the Southern States, and are much esteemed for their large size, sweet flavor, and nutritious qualities. Our climate produces the white or yellow rooted in more perfection; and of this kind great quantities are grown in New Jersey, from whence they are brought to our markets in their season. They are a much lighter food than the common *potato.* Thirty-five years ago *sweet potatoes* were considered a luxury, and seldom found on the general table; then they were also known as *Carolina potatoes.* When eaten raw these *potatoes* taste much like *chestnuts,* when freshly taken out of the ball or bur. The young leaves, and also the tender shoots, are sometimes boiled as pot-herbs, and esteemed as a wholesome food. They are in season from August until December, after which they begin to lose their flavor, and, towards spring, get quite spongy and poor, without they are carefully preserved in dry, cool cellars.

In California the sweet potato grows to an immense size. The editor of the *Sacramento Union* says he was presented with one that measured two feet three inches in length, and weighed five pounds. Another, of the *Nashville Gazette,* received one which weighed nine pounds.

Pumpkins.—There are several varieties of this vegetable much esteemed, and among the best is the cheese, West India, sugar, striped, etc., which are excellent for the famous "pumpkin pies," pumpkin bread, etc. Their season commences in September and lasts until January, when they generally disappear, although, if kept dry and from the frost, they will keep until spring. By cutting them in rings or pieces, and plain drying them, they will also keep well. Another process of drying them is noticed in the *Ohio*

Farmer, who tells us to "cut them up and stew until they are soft and dry; pound and strain through a cullender; then grease pie-pans, and spread it on about a quarter of an inch thick, and dry it; roll it up, and put it away, in a tight box or bag, from the insects. Each one of these rolls will make a pie." I have tried what was called "pumpkin meal" or flour, but it did not give satisfaction.

In the year 1839, the *New Jersey Journal* notices "a pumpkin raised in a garden in Elizabethtown, which weighed, when taken from the vine, one hundred and eighty-seven and a half pounds, and measured seven feet in circumference. There were also raised, in the same patch, six other pumpkins, the average weight of all of which exceeded one hundred and five pounds." Another, much larger, is also noticed as having been raised by S. G. Allen, Esq., of Jersey shore, Lycoming County, Pennsylvania, which weighed two hundred and thirteen pounds.

In the *Commercial Advertiser*, October 19, 1813, Grant C. Thorburn advertises "a *pumpkin* weighing two hundred and twenty-six pounds, and measuring seven feet five inches in circumference. It is one of eight *pumpkins* produced from two seeds, whose weights, added together, amount to one thousand and seventeen pounds. It was raised on the place of D. Gelston, Esq., in the neighborhood of this (New York) city. Eight days after, is found, from the *Boston Gazette*—"*Extravagances of Nature.*—Under this head, the *Centinel*, of the 23d instant, asserted, rather hastily, that 'the *Yankee* land is *beat* all hollow,' because a *pumpkin* had been raised in New York State, weighing two hundred and twenty-six pounds, and a *squash* weighing one hundred and eighty pounds. These productions of nature are no doubt remarkable; but the fact is, the *Yankee* land is *not* beat, and, instead of knocking under, claims the victory! In proof, I beg leave to inform you that there has been raised, in Scarborough, a *pumpkin* weighing three hundred and five pounds, and nine feet in girth. This *beats* the New York one by eighty-one pounds, at least. Further: in Windham, *turnips* have been raised weighing twenty-five pounds, thirty inches in girth, and six inches deep. Further: in Stroudwater, a *carrot* has been raised, twelve inches in girth at the head, and three feet four and a half inches in length. *Further still:* in Gorham, an ear of *corn*, eighteen inches in length, containing sixteen rows, and one thousand one hundred and twenty kernels of large, sound *corn*."

Extraordinary product from two pumpkin-seeds is thus noticed in the *Commercial Advertiser*, October 20, 1818, which were planted in May of that year, and "gathered last week on the ground of the late Rev. Dr. Blair, Germantown (Penn.), when it appeared that the exact weight of the whole was *fifteen hundred and twenty-eight pounds*, one of which measured six feet four inches in circumference, and weighed one hundred and thirty-one pounds. There were several others nearly as large. We have heard of no increase in any part of the United States which has exceeded this, at any time or in any season." In this opinion we also concur, and think it has never yet been equalled.

A curious custom prevails in Paris of annually proclaiming the King of the Pumpkins, "and of making a solemn procession in honor of the largest vegetables of the species which can be discovered. The 'king' of the present year (1855) was grown at St. Maude, and weighed three hundred and forty-eight pounds, being a little less than seven feet in circumference."

Purslain or **parslane.**—This very common plant has fleshy, succulent, tender, round leaves, which, when cultivated, become much better and larger. The whole plant is used, or rather it is best to cut the young growth off when some five or six inches long. It is good boiled and eaten as *Spinach* (when it is quite slimy), and considered wholesome; it is also used in *salad*, pickled, etc.

Radishes.—The cry of "Red-chis" is generally a welcome sound, as a harbinger of summer, being one of the first vegetables that grow in the open air and make their appearance here in the spring. It is not very nourishing, but rather pleasant, chiefly on account of its spicy, aromatic flavor. Among the best kinds are the *long-scarlet*, *long-white*, *white*, *red*, and *yellow turnip*, *black Spanish*, etc., etc. The young leaves are sometimes used in salads. Their season commences in the month of April, and continues with a succession of crops until the appearance of cold weather, when the black Spanish and the winter varieties can be buried in dry sand for the winter's use, and in fact can be kept until the new *Radishes* are again in the markets.

Rampion.—This European plant has not yet become much known here, although its character ought to recommend its common cultivation. The root is long and white, resembling the *Radish* in form; has a pleasant, nut-like flavor, and can be eaten raw like the Radish. In the fall and winter months it is considered best, when the leaves as well as the roots can be cut together for a salad. The whole plant is found filled with a milky juice. There is another species called

German rampion or **evening primrose,** which is a common plant in this country, growing on the roadsides and pastures; but with cultivation the roots (only part used) grow to the length of ten or twelve inches, in form like a long *carrot*, but with a whitish skin on the outside, which should be taken off, when its white flesh is fit to be eaten in its raw state; or, if for a salad, it is best quite young. If, however, it is full grown it can be cooked as the *parsnip* or *skirret*, etc.

Rape.—This plant of the cabbage species, with its fleshy stem and leaves, is sometimes used in the same manner as *spinach*, in salads, etc., and much better when touched with the frost. It is rather scarce in our markets, at present, but it may not continue so.

Rhubarb or **pie-plant.**—The stalk of this early and highly-esteemed plant is the part used when the leaf has grown a sufficient size. This fruit stalk makes wholesome, cooling, and delicious tarts, pies, puddings, jellies, preserves, wines, etc., resembling those made from apples and gooseberries.

Among the many varieties, the Giant and Victoria are generally preferred, as they produce the largest, finest, and most succulent stalks, or petioles, which are most sought after. In season from April until September. The leaves of this plant, boiled as greens, are considered poisonous, as they are said to contain a considerable quantity of *oxalic acid.* In the month of May, 1844, the entire family of Mr. Havens, of Bedford, New York, was poisoned by means of rhubarb leaves boiled as greens. Four of the children came near dying.

Rhubarb dries very well, and will keep good quite as long as wanted; it will shrink a great deal and resemble soft wood, but before it is used it should be soaked one night.

Mr. Bergen, at the "Farmers' Club," N. Y., June 6, 1859, stated "that he had seen four stalks of this plant weigh twenty-eight pounds!!"

The editor of the *Commercial Advertiser,* May 15, 1830, thus notices the introduction of this fine plant: "We can not forbear mentioning that Mr. William Neale (who kept a garden in Fifth-street, a few doors east of the Bowery) has a large supply of that choice vegetable, the *rhubarb,* now just coming into use in this country, as an esculent of excellent properties."

Salsify, oyster-plant, or **vegetable oyster.**—This fine vegetable has a grassy top and a long, tapering, white root, somewhat the form of a *carrot,* which, when cooked, has a flavor much like the oyster. They are also sometimes thinly sliced, and, with proper condiments, served as a salad.

The tops, when young, are sometimes used as greens; the root, however, furnishes an excellent dish throughout the winter. They are usually found for sale tied up in bunches of about a half a dozen roots together. There are one or two more species, one of which, called

Scolymus or **Spanish oyster-plant**, the roots of

which are nearly white, fleshy, long, and tapering, some of them from twelve to fifteen inches in length, full of juice of a milk-white color. They are cooked in the same manner as the preceding root, when their taste is found to be of a pleasant and delicate flavor, and considered wholesome. Another species of this plant is found, called

Scorzonera or **black oyster-plant.**—The root of this plant is long, tapering, with a grayish-black skin and white fleshed, which is tender, sugary, and well-flavored. They are cooked as the *parsnip*, *salsify*, etc.; but before cooking the rind should be scraped off, and then left in cold water for a few hours, for the purpose of extracting their bitter flavor. In season with the *salsify*, etc.

Sea-kale. This plant is one of the hardiest of the *cabbage* tribe, and grows about four feet high. In the fall the plant is covered with earth; in the spring the blanched white shoots and stalks, which begin to force themselves through this earth, are cut off, from three to six inches. These, when properly prepared, cooked, and served, are very delicate, sweet, and tender vegetables. The ribs of the leaves, when skinned or peeled, are also prepared and eaten as asparagus. In season in the spring months.

Shallot or **eschallot.** This plant is another of the *onion* tribe, which is sometimes preferred, on account of its peculiar flavor. The largest bulbs are best for seasoning of soups, stews, salads, in vinegar, etc. In the green state it is not used, but in the dry state it may be kept throughout the year, About midsummer the new bulbs are found in the markets.

Shepherd sprouts. This ragged-leaved plant is among the first that sprouts in the spring, when it makes good early greens. It grows somewhat like the *dandelion*, in a tuft or cluster of long leaves, and remains fit for use until the flower stalk begins to grow, when the leaves become tough and bitter. It is one of the plants which lose but little of their bulk when boiled.

Skirret.—This hardy vegetable is cultivated for its excellent root, of which is sweet and white-fleshed, having somewhat the taste of parsnip, and is generally cooked in the same manner. It is not, however, much esteemed here. It is in season in September, and lasts until the approach of frost, when it should be preserved in earth or sand.

Sorrel.—There are several varieties of this plant, known under the names of English, French, broad-leaved, blistered-leaf, round-leaved, heart-shaped or wood-sorrel, etc., and also a species called *Tuberous-rooted Wood Sorrel.* The leaves of the former varieties are much esteemed, especially by the French and Germans, who think it not only excellent but very wholesome, especially with those who use much salt provisions. It is boiled as *spinach*, used in sauces, salads, soups, and many cooked dishes. The other kind, called

Tuberous-rooted wood sorrel or **tuberous-rooted oxalis.**—The tubers as well as the leaves and flowers of this plant are used in various ways. Professor Morren says: " The uses of the *Oxalis* are many. The young leaves are dressed like *Sorrel* in soup, or as a vegetable. They have a fresh and agreeable acid, especially in the spring. The flowers are excellent in salad alone, or mixed with *Corn Salad, Endive,* of both kinds, red *Cabbage, Beet*-root, and even with the petals of the *Dahlia*, which are delicious when thus employed. The roots (or tubers) are gently boiled with salt and water, after having been washed and slightly peeled. They are then eaten like *Asparagus*, in the Flemish fashion, with melted *Butter* and the yolk of *Eggs.* They are also served up, like *Scorzonera* and *Endive,* with white sauce, and form, in whatever way dressed, a tender, succulent dish, easy to digest, agreeing with the most delicate stomach." It is not much cultivated here.

Spinach or **spinage.**—This fine, hardy plant is considered to be always in season, by a succession of crops, the leaves of which are very succulent and wholesome, and usually boiled for greens. The best varieties are the broad-leaved, savoy, or curled-leaved, and the prickly-leaved. On the 24th of October, 1856, Mr. Joseph Cudlip brought to Jefferson Market a head of spinach which weighed two pounds and appeared to be quite tender.

Squash.—The varieties of this vegetable are very numerous and most extensively cultivated. Among the most esteemed are the Boston marrow, Valparaiso, summer and winter crook-necked, yellow butter, acorn, or Turkish cap, apple, custard, early bush, etc. The latter is one of the earliest, or first ready for use, about the middle of June, the yellow butter about the 1st of July, the Boston marrow about the 1st of August, and some of the varieties continue by proper care to be good until the 1st of January. Another new variety has been lately introduced and spoken well of. It is called

Japan squash.—This new species here was introduced by Commodore M. C. Perry, who brought the seed from Japan. It has some the appearance of a large watermelon, but much heavier and quite solid. A specimen raised by Judge Livingston, was by him presented to the Farmers' Club, American Institute, in November, 1858, which weighed seventeen pounds; the seed ordered to be distributed. The judge and others spoke highly of it for the table, cooked as the *egg-plant*. One other larger specimen was burnt up in the Crystal Palace fire, which took place October 5, 1858. There were several very large squashes exhibited at the Horticultural Fair of the American Institute held at their rooms October, 1866, among which were two of the *custard* variety, raised at Clifton, New Jersey, on the farm of James Brown, Esq. These splendid squashes were, perhaps, the finest and largest of this variety ever raised, and well deserved the *special premium* awarded. Mr. Brown also received, at the same time, another *special premium* for some extraordinary large ears of very excellent white corn, which attracted much attention. The *Commercial Advertiser*, October 8, 1813, speaks thus of a *Mammoth Squash.* "There was yesterday brought to market a *squash* which measured six feet eleven inches in circumference, and weighed *one* *hundred and fifty-two pounds.* Fifty dollars was offered for it."

Sweet corn.—*See Indian Corn.*

Sweet potatoes.—*See Potatoes.*

Talta-ruben, or **German turnip.**—These very small species of the *turnip* appear to have been lately introduced in our markets. Those which I saw were about the size of the common white *radish,* but not quite so long, having two rows of fine roots growing on their sides from top to bottom. The Germans and French purchase them principally. They were on sale in the months of October and November.

Tomatoes.—This excellent plant, many years ago (1830), went by the name of *love-apple* altogether, and was grown more for ornament than use; but now it is considered a most valuable article of food, containing important medicinal properties. Dr. Bennett says "that the tomato is one of the most powerful aperients of the liver and other organs; where calomel is indicated, it is probably one of the most effective, and the least harmful remedial agent known to the profession—that a chemical extract may be obtained from it that will supersede the use of calomel in the cure of disease—that he has successfully treated diarrhœa with this article alone—that when used as an article of diet, it is almost sovereign for dyspepsia and indigestion—that it should be constantly used for daily food; either cooked, raw, or in the form of catsup, it is the most healthy article now in use." Among the best varieties are the large red, or common tomato, smooth red, apple and pear-shaped, large and small yellow, fig, cherry, etc. They begin to arrive from the South in the month of April, and weekly grow more plenty; then from lower New Jersey, Pennsylvania, in the month of June, and New York along from the 1st to the 15th of July. Their season ends in November, although they are to be had, in sealed packages, fresh and good until the next year.

Truffles.—This species of *mushroom,* or fungi, is not

grown in this country, I believe, although it is often found on the tables of our epicures and some of the first-class hotels; brought here by the aid of the steamers from Europe.

The external appearance of the *truffle* is not at all inviting, being almost black, and having rather a rough coat, with a warty and ridgy surface, and usually about the size of a small *egg*. The flesh is white and firm, of a close contexture, and the taste, which is quite savory, resembles that of the *walnut* or *almond*, and improves all it touches in cookery.

They appear in great abundance in their native place during the fall and winter months. Those which are sold *dried* are devoid of flavor, and considered of no use. The *Morel* is the only one of the tribe that will bear drying without losing the properties for which it is held in estimation for food. *Truffles* are found for sale either in fruit stores, large hotels, or some of the eating saloons.

"Very little has hitherto been written about the *truffle*," says the *Horticulturist*, "and we look in vain for any account of its habitat or methods of propagation in botanical works. In scientific treatises it is classed in the ranks of the esculent fungi, like the mushroom, and is named the 'Tuber Cibarium.' 'There are few of nature's productions,' says an English authority, 'so extraordinary as this family of the fungi; and in no other country than our own are there so many varieties of the class to be seen, with their curious shapes, their beautiful colors, and their fairy rings springing up like magic after a night's rain or a damp day.' Unlike the mushroom, this strange fungus is propagated *under* the surface of the soil. They are found where the soil is black, loamy, mixed with flint, or is composed of chalk and clay. They grow close to the roots of large trees, and seem to be propagated by the partial decay of their long, fibrous roots, and nourished by the drippings from their branches. They are found in shrubberies, plantations, and woods, and sometimes in banks and ditches, but always where trees abound, beneath them or at a little distance from their stems. They grow in rings of clusters of six or seven round each tree. 'Nor will they flourish beneath every kind of tree, but frequent the oak, the lime and cedar, and appear especially to love the beech, since wherever that tree grows with the richest luxuriance, the truffles are found in great abundance and of the best quality.' The usual season when truffles are found in England is the month of September; but their appearance depends very much upon the state of the weather. In a dry season, the truffle-hunter will not look for them before October or November, and until sufficient rain has fallen for their production. In favorable situations and in damp weather they will grow in a few days. They will increase from a quarter to half a pound in weight, and, in rainy seasons, they will sometimes reach a pound, while they measure from four to six inches in circumference. The truffle resembles, externally, a rugged knot of an old oak, or a piece of decayed wood. This is the large truffle. There is another kind well known to the truffler, though ignored in scientific accounts, called the red truffle on account of its color, and is of the size of a pea, and equal in flavor to the larger kind. This larger truffle, when examined through the microscope, is found grained with fibrous lines, and is of a firm, tough texture, white in color when young, and growing darker until its ripeness is shown by becoming entirely black. As the truffle grows *under ground*, there would be some difficulty in finding it were it not for the fact that, before it is cooked, it possesses a peculiar odor—so powerful and so peculiar that no imposition can be practised in its commerce. The raw truffles, when ripe and fit to eat, possess this pungent and oppressive odor, which will pervade the whole house; and they must be boiled or stewed, when this odor will disappear. This peculiar perfume is nearly imperceptible to the human senses when the fungus is growing beneath the soil; and, for this reason, the truffle-gatherer is assisted in the search for them by a peculiar breed of dogs that are trained for this purpose. 'Clever little dogs they are, and trained from puppyhood to hunt the truffle out by the nose, and then to scratch it up with their long, sharp claws. It is curious and interesting to watch the powers of nose possessed by these small dogs; how directly they perceive the odor of the hidden truffle; they rush to the place, straight as a dart, even at twenty yards' distance.'"

Tuckahoe, or **Indian bread**, somewhat resembles the *truffle*, but is found in New Jersey, Virginia, etc. Its qualifications are not yet much known. The Hon. James M. Garnett says: "It has neither root in the ground nor stem above, but grows a few inches below the surface, apparently as unconnected with the soil as a buried cannon-ball would be. It is oval in shape, and varies in size from that of a goose-egg to that of a man's head. The coat is rough, and of a dark-brown color—the inner substance very white, similar in texture to that of the *yam*, and of an insipid taste; when fresh, however, it is somewhat acrid.

In the *Commercial Advertiser*, August 21, 1816, an article taken from the South Carolina *Telescope* says: "The (name) *tuckahoe* is supposed to be of Indian origin, and has also been applied to the *truffle*, a vegetable that grows entirely under ground, and is a favorite dish at many tables."

Turnips, or **turneps**.—There are several varieties of this common vegetable. Among the best are the early white or greentop, yellowstone, cowshorn, red or purple top, goldenball, Aberdeen, Ruta-baga, or Russian *turnip*, the last of which (there are several varieties) is excellent for winter use. The middle-sized common *turnips* are the best for the table, as the large ones are apt to be spongy. They are useful in broths, soups, etc., and more especially with a boiled *leg of mutton*.

The season of new *turnips* commences about the 1st of June from southern New Jersey, and continues with all the varieties throughout the year.

The editor of the *Commercial Advertiser* (November 20,

1832) says: "We have this morning been shown by Mr. Grant Thorburn one of the most striking natural curiosities that we ever saw. It is a *turnip* raised in Minden, Conn., which resembles a man's hand so closely as to startle the beholder as it is unrolled from the paper in which it is wrapped. The fingers are nearly perfect; as also is the thumb, save that it is withered a little since it was taken from the ground. The fingers are also properly fitted to each other, even to the natural crook of the little finger. Mr. Thorburn gave five dollars for it."

Vegetable marrow.—This vegetable is said to be a species of the gourd, but found useful for culinary purposes in every stage of its growth. When young, it is cut into slices and fried with butter; when more mature it is cut into quarters, stewed in rich gravy, and seasoned to taste. It is said to be both wholesome and nutritious.

Water-cress.—See *Cress.*

Yam.—The common *yam* is an excellent vegetable, grown in the Southern States; but some seasons find it plentiful in the Northern cities, and sold quite cheap. By some it is more highly esteemed than the potato, which it nearly resembles. It is much larger, more irregularly formed, being of a long flat, and quite darkly colored. They usually weigh from one to three pounds each; but I have seen them weigh over twenty pounds. They are in season, and generally found here, in the month of September, and last until January. Another species of the *yam*, called

Japanese yam, or **Chinese potato,** has been introduced into our country through the Patent Office, in the early part of the year 1855. In the fall of the same year, Mr. Boll, a florist, exhibited at the Fair of the American Institute several fine roots, which had some the appearance of long white *sweet potatoes.* When fully matured and plainly cooked—either boiled or roasted—with a little salt, its flavor is much like that of the common *potato,* being quite dry and farinaceous. One drawback, however, to its large cultivation will be from the great depth it grows into the ground.

POT-HERBS, MEDICINAL AND OTHER PLANTS.

The pot-herbs, or certain aromatic plants noticed in the following pages, are those selected which appear to be the most used in seasoning or flavoring other food, whether in salad, sauces, stuffings, dressings, or other articles of cookery; while those deemed medicinal plants are commonly used more or less in every family.

Alexanders, or **allisanders.**—This plant somewhat resembles *celery*, with a smell of *myrrh*, and a pleasant aromatic taste; generally used as a pot-herb, or in salads, etc., after being properly blanched. It is now seldom cultivated, as the *celery* is almost universally preferred.

Angelica, garden—This plant, many years ago, was much used. The stalks were blanched and eaten as celery; but now the stalks and leaves are made into a candied sweetmeat by the confectioners, when cut in May. The seeds are also used in cordials, and sometimes medicinally.

Anise-seed.—The seed of this plant is much used in confectioners' candies, liquors, etc., medicinally, having an aromatic smell and a pleasant warm taste. The green leaves are also used for garnishing salads, and seasoning.

Balm.—This perennial plant has a light aromatic taste, and the smell of lemon. The leaves are employed green and dried, both as a medicinal and culinary herb.

Basil.—There appears to be two or three kinds of this wild. The first is more generally used for making salads, soups, especially mock-turtle. The flavor resembles cloves. The common wild is seldom used in cooking.

Bene plant.—This plant is much used in the South for culinary purposes. "The blacks in Georgia boil some of the seeds with their allowance of Indian Corn. A few leaves, when green, plunged a few times in a tumbler of water, make it a thin jelly, without taste or color, which children afflicted with the summer-complaint will drink freely, and it is said to be the best remedy ever discovered." An excellent oil is made from the seeds, after it has age.

Birch.—There are several varieties of this plant or tree, all of which are found useful, either for cabinet purposes, building canoes, paper, etc. The sweet *birch* juice and buds are used in candies, wine, etc., while the twigs are made into brooms, etc. (See *Birch-brooms*, under head of "*Dairy and Household Products.*")

Bloodroot.—This plant, in the spring, brings forth a beautiful small flower, which rises upon a single stem, and enclosed in a single leaf. When the plant is broken, a red juice oozes out, which has some the appearance of blood, the root of which is used in medicine for coughs, croup, fever, etc., and is considered a valuable wild plant.

Boneset, or **thoroughwort.**—This is a common herb, brought by the herb-gatherers to our markets and sold principally for medical purposes.

Borage.—This annual plant smells somewhat like a cucumber. The young leaves, which have a wrinkled, rough, hairy appearance, are, with the young shoots, boiled as spinach, or prepared as a salad. The seeds are also used. The flowers are also used for garnishing.

Brook-lime.—This plant grows in wet localities, some ten to fifteen inches in height. The stem is quite smooth and tender, with small fibrous roots growing out at the joints. The whole plant can be used as a salad, or the same as the *water-cress*. It is also excellent as a medicinal plant.

Burdock.—The long yellow roots of this weed (as the farmers call them) are found on the herb-stands, where they are principally sold for medical purposes.

Burnet, or **garden burnet.**—The parts used of this plant are the young oval-formed leaves, which have a warm, piquant taste, and, when bruised, they have a smell like *cucumbers*. They are sometimes used as salad, or in soups, etc. The roots are used medicinally.

Calamus, or **sweet flag.**—This plant is found in wet meadows, the roots of which have a pleasant aromatic flavor, and found plentifully for sale, more especially by the colored people, on a Sunday morning, at Catherine Market. It is used for flavoring and medicinally.

Capers.—These little buds are much used here, but they come to us preserved. I find, from the Patent Office Report, of 1854, that Mr. H. M. Bry, of Louisiana, has succeeded in raising two crops of this kind, equal to any he had ever seen in Italy. They are used principally with boiled meats.

Caraway.—This plant is chiefly cultivated for its seed, which is generally used in confectionery, distillation, and medicine. When young and tender, the under leaves are sometimes used in soups. The seed is ripe in the autumn; and the root, when cultivated, is of a sweet, pleasant taste, and was formerly boiled and eaten like the *parsnip*.

Catnip, or **catmint.**—This plant is gathered green while the flowers are out, and often brought in that state by the country wagons as a perquisite for the boys. The flowers, leaves, and small stalks are much used as a medicine for *young* mankind. The cats are also exceedingly fond of it, which no doubt gave it its name.

Chamomile, or **camomile.**—The flowers of this plant are used as a medicine, being very bitter. Extracts are also made for medicinal purposes and bitter beers.

Chervil, or **Cicely the sweet.**—There are several species and varieties of plants under the name of *chervil*. The leaves of all the kinds, however, are generally used either in salads, soups, etc. They have all an aromatic taste, some quite strong of *anise-seed*, others, again, of other flavors. It is much used among the French and Germans. The young leaves can be used as they come up in succession through the season.

Chickory.—The root of this plant has somewhat the

appearance of the *parsnip* and *salsify*, etc. It is considered edible when cooked in the green state, like *salsify*, *endive*, etc., and, when dried, it is used to adulterate coffee, and also in brewing porter. It is rarely found in the green state in our markets, but large quantities are sold in the dried.

Clary.—The leaves of this biennial plant are used in flavoring soups, stews, and also in medicated wines, etc. It is very good for digestion; it has somewhat the appearance of sage. It is found in the dried state, occasionally, in the markets, on the herb-stands.

Coltsfoot.—The leaves of this plant are principally used in colds and pulmonary disorders. They should be cut in July and September, then dried in a shaded place.

Comfrey.—The root of this rough-leaved perennial plant is considered nutritious for man or beast, and the leaves are good for cattle. It is only occasionally found here for sale. It is also good as a medicine.

Coriander.—The seeds of this annual plant have a pleasant flavor, and much used in confections and medicines. Its leaves are also used in soups and salads.

Costmary, or **alecost.**—This perennial plant has also a pleasant taste as well as smell. The tender parts of the plant are used as a pot-herb. The leaves alone are sometimes used as a salad, or to flavor ale or beer. Fit for use in the summer or fall months.

Dill.—The parts of this plant particularly useful are the small, slim, green leaves—which appear somewhat like the *feathery* leaves of the *asparagus* when fully grown—as also the anibels and seeds are much used in pickles, etc. The leaves alone are also used in some kinds of soups and by some foreigners. The best time to gather this plant is the month of July, when it is covered over with the small yellow flowers, and hang it up to dry.

Elecampane.—The root of this perennial is of a bitter aromatic taste, which is principally used in medicine; but not much thought of. Found best when not less than two years' growth.

Fennel.—This plant is not yet much cultivated here, but it is much used in Europe. Among the several varieties most used is the *common* and *sweet fennel;* the first is used in soups, broths, sauces, pickles, etc., and the young leaves make a good salad. The stalks of the *sweet fennel* are the edible part when parboiled or stewed. The odor is usually found disagreeable. Generally found in season through the months from June to January by successive plantings.

Hoarhound.—This perennial plant, or the parts used, are found on the herb-stands ready prepared for sale. It has a bitter aromatic taste, but is made quite pleasant in candies, etc.; is much used for colds. Large quantities are gathered and prepared by the Shakers.

Hops.—The domestic use of the *hop,* or flower of this plant, is pretty well known to almost every country housewife, and the brewer for malt liquors, small beer, ale, porter, yeast, poultices, etc. There are several varieties, among which are the English cluster, grape, and Pompey *hop.* The young shoots are good for the table, when cut in the spring, some five or six inches high. They are eaten as salad, or boiled and served as *asparagus,* which they resemble. The flower, or hop, should be gathered in August.

Hyssop.—This dwarfish perennial has a strong aromatic scent, and the leaves and flowers are of a warm, pungent taste. The young leafy shoots and flower-spikes are usually cut as they are wanted. It somewhat resembles thyme, and is used in salads, etc., and also medicinally. They are also cut and dried, and used as other pot-herbs.

Juniper berries.—These small, dark, purple-colored berries, about the size of a pea, but ovate in form, are found growing on a low, flat-spreading sort of a cedar-bush, and are sometimes brought to our market by the herb-gatherers. Used principally to give an aromatic flavor to gin, and also medicinally. They are also said to be one of the best antidotes for the rot in *sheep*—about a half a gill per day, until all apprehension is removed. There is another variety growing on the common cedar, called

Cedar berries, but much smaller, which are much sought after by robins, cedar, and other birds, when migrating in the fall months. When simmered in neat's foot oil, makes a good ointment for lame backs, etc.

Lavender.—This short, hardy plant, is generally more used medicinally than in cookery, and more in the toilette than either, as lavender-water, or oil of lavender, and also to perfume clothing.

Licorice, or **liquorice.**—This useful perennial plant is not generally cultivated here; but its fleshy roots are much used in colds, and by some porter-brewers. The roots are best when grown several years.

Lovage.—This plant in appearance is somewhat like *celery*, but quite warm and pungent; sometimes used as a pot-herb or a salad. It is, however, medicinally valuable, both seeds and roots; the seeds more especially by the distillers for preparing a liquor called *lovage*, as also by confectioners.

Marsh-mallow.—This is an excellent mucilaginous herb in making syrup or tea for a cough or colds; but it should be procured by *one* or from *one* who is well acquainted with the plant.

Marsh marigold (called *cowslip* in the Eastern States). —This is a common swamp or water-plant, which grows from eight to ten inches high, with quite a thick stem; and when young the leaves can be used as greens as well as a pot-herb. In Europe the flowers are used for flavoring soups, stews, etc.

Marjoram, sweet.—This hardy plant, or rather the tops and leaves, are much used both in a green and dry state, and is a relishing herb in soups, broths, stuffings, etc. The branches are cut in July or August, for drying, before the flowers open, for the winter use.

Mint.—There are several species of this plant, which are used in culinary, medical, and other purposes. Those most in common use are the *spear*, or *greenmint*, *peppermint*, *pennyroyal mint*, etc. (See the following.)

Pennyroyal.—This common aromatic herb is sometimes cultivated for making an essential oil, and is also used medicinally. Its odor is very annoying to some insects, especially ticks; therefore it is useful. It is found for sale in our markets, sometimes in great quantities.

Peppermint.—This is the plant which is mostly used for distillation, in manfacturing the oil of peppermint, of which great quantities are used by confectioners, druggists, liquor dealers, etc. I have also read of its being used as a pot-herb. Another variety, called

Spear mint, green mint, or **common mint,** is more useful in cookery, in soups, green *peas*, or mixed with salads, or sauce for roasted *lamb*, and also in preparing a drink called *mint-julep*. The young leaves and tops, of from one to six inches in length, are the parts used. As a domestic medicine it is also popular, and deservedly so.

Pokeberries, or **pigeon-berries.**—Strings of these dark-purple juicy berries are occasionally found in our markets in their season, which are principally used for dyeing a purple color. I have also heard of pies being made of them.

Rocket, or **roquette.**—This is an annual plant, indigenous to France, the young leaves of which are used in summer in succession as a salad. The flowers have an agreeable odor, like those of an orange. But it is not much used here.

Rosemary.—This pleasant aromatic plant is both useful and some kinds quite ornamental, especially the *gold* and *silver-striped* varieties. The common, or green-leaved, however, is sometimes used for flavoring soups and stewed meats, etc.; also in drinks, as well as in the manufacture of *Cologne water*. Its flowers and stems are also one of the ingredients used in making "Hungary Water," and the stems alone as a garnish.

Rue.—This plant is now but seldom used other than as a medicine. It has a strong, bitter taste, also very pungent and penetrating, so much so, as to inflame the skin when much handled. The ancients used it much in their cookery, both in soups and in vinegar. There are a few yet left who use it for cooking purposes. It is seldom found for sale.

Sage.—There are several varieties of this perennial, of which the *common green* is among the best. It has a strong, fragrant smell, and a bitter, warm taste. Its leaves are much used in stuffings, sauces, and in various other articles of cookery. It is also remarkable for its medicinal properties. Usually found tied in small bunches, green and dried.

Samphire, or **sea fennel.**—This plant is but little grown here, on account of its difficult cultivation; but its leaves have a pleasant, warm, aromatic flavor. The fleshy leaves and young branches are pickled in vinegar, and also used in salads as a seasoning.

Sassafras.—From this small tree is gathered the young shoots, which are sometimes used in the place of *okra*, when that is found scarce. The bark gives an excellent flavor to spruce and other home-made beer; that taken from the root is, however, the best and most aromatic. This latter is much used as a medicine, or in flavoring candies, or giving a pleasant odor to soap, etc. Large quantities are prepared and sold.

Savory.—There are two kinds of this plant which are used for culinary and medicinal purposes—the summer and winter varieties. The aromatic leaves of the latter, as also the tops, both green and dried, are much esteemed, and used in seasoning *peas, beans,* dressings, salads, broths, etc. It is also found for sale in a dried and pulverized state, sealed in packages.

Southernwood.—This hardy plant produces leaves of a bitter, aromatic taste, with rather a pleasant odor. These, with the young branches, are employed in medicinal purposes altogether.

Spruce, black or **double spruce.**—From the young twigs of this tree are made the so much used spruce-beer in summer; it is also used medicinally. A great deal is brought here by the herb-gatherers. It is also brought here in tops and branches as an evergreen ornament. (See *Christmas Green,* under *Dairy* and *Household Products.*)

Sumach, or **smooth sumach**.—This is a common bush that grows on rocky, barren places; the small fruit grows in clusters, and when ripe (in September) is found of a crimson color. They add much to make a pleasant drink, especially for the sick. The leaves are much used in tanning morocco, etc.

Tansey.—Large bunches of this peculiar-flavored plant, or rather its leaves, are found on the herb-stands; which I now find is principally used as a medical tonic. Formerly it was used in many culinary preparations. It is found best in the spring months, when it is young and green.

Tarragon, or **dragon's wort**.—This plant, or rather the leaves and young tops, are frequently used in salads, soups, pickles, etc. They are of a hot and biting character, and when put in vinegar (*tarragon vinegar*), it is highly esteemed as a fish-sauce. They are usually ready for use in the fall months.

Thyme (**common** and **lemon**).—This sweet little shrub has an agreeable smell, with a warm, pungent taste, the leaves and tops of which are much used in stuffings, soups, sauces, etc. Of the two kinds, the *broad-leaved* and *narrow-leaved*, the former is generally preferred. It is gathered green in the fall, then dried, and is so found for sale in our markets tied up in small bunches.

Wormwood, or **common wormwood**.—This plant is one of the bitter perennials, with a strong aromatic odor. Its leaves and tops are sometimes used to flavor cordials, and medicinally.

FRUITS.

"They are gold in the morning, silver at noon, and lead at night."

Fruits, although not absolutely necessary as articles of food, or even nutriment, with but few exceptions, yet, from their very peculiarity and seasons and rarity, comparing them with other productions, they have become a necessity to man, in all climes, whether in the civilized or savage state; they are his luxury, nay, his *dessert*, whether partaken of from the prolific hand of nature, or forced by man's hot-house ingenuity; whether eaten at the rich man's table, or munched by the laborer on the roadside; whether dealt out to the million, or picked from the gutter by the ragged urchin. Fruit is man's luxury under all circumstances—his dessert. Apart from the general taste for fruits, "in their seasons" and "out of their seasons," an inward voice—which we call craving—demands these gifts of a beneficent Providence for certain ends to the physical welfare of man. They are not only nutritious, but they are also medicinal in their properties. They produce certain beneficial changes in the blood (which medical men term "alterative"), which alters the blood from an unhealthy to its healthy condition; consequently, by the use of ripe fruits, many diseases lurking in the system are either neutralized or removed. Many fruits have the peculiar medicinal property of "cooling" the blood as it is termed, or in other words, rendering it less liable to feverish or inflammable excitement. In European countries, where the vast multitudes of populations actually encumber the limited space upon which they exist, fruits, although largely cultivated, rarely fall to the lot of many millions of beings cabined, cribbed and penned in the numerous large cities and towns. Even to the wealthy, fruits are a luxury—a dessert. To the poor they are a *Tantalus*: few live under their own "fig-trees;" and, where fig-trees grow, they are dealt out to those who neither work nor delve. May we not attribute very many diseases affecting the pent-up, impoverished artisans and laborers of all large towns? In the United States, happily, the people have an opportunity to seek and to obtain a portion of God's favors to man; and although fruits are not sufficiently plentiful to supply the wants of all, yet fruit, to a certain extent, may be obtained by the poorest of city populations.

It is worthy of remark that, notwithstanding the lavish liberality of many of our *housekeepers*, with their willingness to pay the largest prices for the best productions of our markets, we find few fruits offered for sale of first-class production. Surely the fifty to one hundred per cent. higher prices paid for the very few superior cultivated and perfected fruits found and sold in the markets, would be an all-sufficient premium to induce the fruit-grower to devote his attention to procure the choicest varieties of different kinds of fruit.

Fruit in perfection should be full sized, sound, ripe, fresh, and of the best varieties; and, when most plentiful, they possess the best and highest flavor. When not intended for culinary purposes, the earlier in the day they are eaten the better, as they will be found the most invigorating stimulus for other food.

With wondrous adaptation to man's convenience and enjoyment, one delicious fruit succeeds another: thus, when strawberries and currants begin to fail, raspberries and cherries are ready, succeeded by blackberries and whortleberries; then comes the sweet, juicy, beautiful peach, the nectarine, and plum, followed by the luscious grape, the mellow pear, and the crisp-snapping apple, in all their various sorts and sizes, which continue on, and we never tire of them.

> "The luscious peach, the blooming nectarine,
> Among the precious fruits of earth are seen.
> Fruitful Pomona supplies the busy mart,
> And suits man's palate, whether sweet or tart."

On the use of unripe fruits, the *Journal of Health* thus sets forth: "It is very pretty to talk of fruits as the gift of nature, which, as meant for man's refreshment, cannot, we are told, be injurious. But people ought to define what they mean by fruit. If it be the matured production of a tree or shrub, in which the saccharine matter is properly evolved and distributed through the pulpy matter, which has itself lost its early tenacity; in other words, if it be ripe fruit they mean, we can see no objections to moderate eating of it. But if they libel the worship of *Pomona* to such a degree as to call early green apples and pears, little shrivelled peaches, water-melons without a particle of saccharine juice in them, plums as hard as bullets, fit offerings at her shrine, and suitable food for either a rustic or a civic population, why then we would condemn the immature dietists to eat what they recommend. As well might we insist on the consumption of darnel because it grows with nutritious grain, or of ergot because it is part of the rye, as talk of such vile trash as half of the fruit which is hawked about being fit food for any animals except swine, and they will give many an extra turn after a meal of it." And then, again—"Be it remembered that the eating of ripe fruit does not imply the necessity of swallowing the skin and stone or seed, as many are in the fashion of doing. Certain it is—to say nothing of the labor to which the poor stomach is put on the occasion—nature never intended those parts of the fruit to be eaten: the one is an external covering for the purpose of protecting the nutritious part proper, the other for perpetuating the plant."

The numerous varieties of fruits cultivated and wild, foreign and domestic, received here and sold in our markets, show the necessity, as well as the importance, of their being perfectly cultivated. The several fruits will be found in their order, alphabetically arranged.

Apples.—This excellent, healthy, and useful fruit is found usually in great abundance in our markets throughout the year. We have the early or summer *apples* from the South sometimes as early as the months of May and June; one month later, we obtain them from our own district; and, still later, they are brought to us from further north; and the same supplies of *apples* apply to the fall and winter varieties.

Apples for summer.—We have the white-juneating early harvest, early strawberry, golden sweeting, yellow bough, summer pippins, pearmains, rose, belle-flower, red astracan, beswick, codlin, etc.

Fall or **autumn.**—From the month of September until December, fall pippins, autumn pearmain, strawberry, St. Lawrence, sweet swaar, porter, seek-no-further, Jersey-sweet, spice-sweet, pound-sweet, maiden-blush, Gravenstein, Hawley, or Dowse, etc.

Winter and **spring.**—From the month of October until March, Rhode Island greenings, Newtown or winter pippins, Spitzenbergs, pearmains, baldwins, vandeveres, swaars, talman-sweets, winter-sweets, golden russets, etc. Sometimes the Newtown pippins, Wagner's northern spy, Roxbury russets, etc., are found on sale through the month of June. The Newtown pippin, no doubt, ranks highest for all general purposes. Riker says it was first cultivated in an orchard near Newtown by one of the *Moore* family.

The Rhode Island greening is a very tender, rich, early apple, but late in the season it loses flavor, and becomes soft and insipid. It is said that it takes its name from the cognomen of the gentleman on whose land it was found. The fruit was first found—says Furman—in Rhode Island, a short distance from Newport, near an inn kept by Mr. Green; hence it was called the Green inn *apple*. A slight change, however, has come over the old appellation, which is now simply "Greening."

The Spitzenberg and Baldwin are fine table-apples; but I might name fifty varieties, and each would have as many admirers as being the best.

The kind of *apples* principally used for preserving or ornament, are the red Siberian crab, large Siberian crab, yellow Siberian crab, large yellow or Hagloe crab, lady apples, etc. These beautiful crabs and lady apples are usually found in the month of September, the latter generally in November, and some of the varieties will keep until May.

When wanted for preserves, they should be used before growing mealy, as in that state they cook like sauce.

The numerous and various uses for apples of various kinds are almost as many as the fruit itself. They are prepared for drying, apple-sauce, apple-butter, cider, pies, tarts, jellies, fritters, dumplings, stewing, baking, the dessert, etc. Large quantities of dried apples, apple-sauce, apple-butter, and cider are prepared and made by the

Shakers and others; which are usually found on sale in the fall and winter months.

Among the largest *apples* I ever saw, one was shown at the American Institute Fair, held in September, 1860, which measured eighteen inches in circumference, and weighed *three and a half pounds.* It was of the kind called Gloria Mundi.

Apricots.—This fine smooth-skin fruit is among our earliest kinds, but never appears very plentiful, in consequence of which it is sold usually at high prices. In flavor it resembles the *peach* more than any other fruit—not quite so juicy, but tender, well-flavored, and highly esteemed. When not fully ripe, they make excellent tarts, preserves, pastries, marmalades, jellies, jam, etc. Among the best varieties are the breda, moorpark, peach, early golden, purple or black *apricot,* etc. They ripen generally before the peach, either in July or August, according to the season.

Bananas.—This delicious, wholesome, and nourishing Southern fruit grows and appears here in bunches. They grow separately on a stout twig or branch, in a spiral form, to the number of from twenty to sixty in a bunch. They appear in our markets in the month of March, both the red and yellow varieties. The former is considered the best, but it is found to be of the shortest season, as it is scarcely ever found for sale after the 20th of July, while the yellow variety continues on until the 1st of October.

Bananas differ some from the *plantain,* being much shorter, rounder, more mellow, and can be eaten raw, sometimes roasted in fritters, preserves or marmalades, and pies; and the fermented juice makes an excellent wine. It resembles fruit in its nature, very much like a luscious pear more than any thing else, and hence my reason for calling it fruit.

Large quantities are brought from the West Indies, principally from Baracoa, on the island of Cuba, and other Southern countries.

Barberries, berberries, or **pepperidge-bush berries.**—This little crimson fruit grows in clusters, and so found on sale ; is seldom eaten fresh on account of tartness, but principally used in pickles, jellies, sweetmeats, soups, garnishing, and cooling drinks, etc. They grow on a prickly or thorny shrub, and ripen in September and October. Sometimes they are quite plentiful in our markets. The leaves of this fruit are eaten for a salad, and taste somewhat like *sorrel*.

Beach plum, or **sand plum**.—These small purple, and sometimes crimson, fruit are found on or near the sea-beach on Long Island, or in sandy fields near the salt water. When ripe, the fruit is somewhat astringent, but rather agreeably so, and is thus found in September.

Bilberries.—These small purplish-red fruit are somewhat the appearance of the *whortleberries*, but generally smaller. They, however, grow upon a good-sized tree, like in form of the apple or *horse-chestnut*, and the leaves pointed like those of the *birch*. *Whortleberries* of the smaller kind are sometimes called *bilberries*, but they differ in taste, the latter being of a much richer tart in flavor. They are found quite plentiful north and east of New York ; usually ripen in the latter part of August or first of September.

Blackberries.—There are several varieties of this fine, wholesome fruit, among which the Lawton, Kittatinny, Wilson's early, Dorchester, etc., are considered the choicest kinds. The Lawton, however, is the largest and finest which cultivation has yet produced. The Wilson's early ripens from five to ten days earlier than either of the other varieties, but the Dorchester soon follows it, being a much sweeter and finer-flavored fruit, somewhat like the orange. Perhaps, however, the first to ripen are the *running blackberries*, or *dewberries*, which in certain localities grow very large and fine, on a creeping ground-vine ; and, especially when exposed to the sun, they become sweet and excellent. The common *low-bush blackberry* is the poorest kind, being small, round, irregular in shape, of a reddish-black, and rather a tartish taste. Another variety, called the *thornless blackberry*, is a fine-looking berry and pleasant-tasted, but very scarce. The name given to this variety is in consequence of the bush being nearly or quite thornless.

Blackberries commence to ripen about the 10th of July, and continue until the 1st of September, although I have seen the *Lawtons* in the market until the 1st of October; but the fruit was rather flat-tasted, or had lost its rich flavor. To have these berries in perfection, they should be ripe enough, that when the bush is shaken those which drop will be found just about as good as you can have them. They also make excellent wine, syrup, puddings, etc. Many are also found dried on sale. The root of the bush makes an excellent decoction for summer complaint. The *white-fruited* variety seems to be grown more for novelty than for use.

Black gumberries, sour gumberries, tupelo, or **pepperidge-berries.**—These small, blue, oval berries, with large pits, are found growing on large trees. Of a sour taste, until the frost has taken hold of them, when they become ripe, and with an agreeable, tartish flavor. Their taste is so pleasant that I should think they could be used in jellies, tarts, etc. They are generally found growing two together on a thin twig, and might be properly called *twin-berries.* When a boy I knew them to be called *Drams* in Westchester County, N. Y.

Buffalo-berry.—See *Shepardia.*

Cherries.—These are some of the first delicious summer fruits, which are always grateful and acceptable, especially at the dessert, and are much improved in their flavor by placing them in ice an hour or two before serving them up. The first of this fruit which we receive are generally from Norfolk, etc., from about the 10th to the 15th May, and so continue till near the month of August. Among the many varieties which appear in our markets are the White-hearts, May-Dukes, Black-hearts, Dikemans, Black-mazzards, Black-tartarian, Black-Eagle, Honey, Oxhearts, Kentish, or common sour cherry, etc., with the small wild cherries. A great many of the sweet varieties are used for the dessert, and in a canned state; for improving the flavor of brandies, used in the dried state, etc. The Kentish, or common sour, is much used in pies, tarts, preserves, puddings, etc.

Citron.—This fruit is of the lemon species, but larger warted and ribbed, or furrowed. Its thick, fragrant rind is generally found here in a preserved state ; this and the pulp, which is subacid, are used in confectionery, sweetmeats, plum-puddings, preserves, etc. The best of this fruit comes from Leghorn, Nice, etc.

Cranberries.—This berry is pretty well known for the fine tarts, pies, and jellies it makes. Of this there are several varieties, but only two that are at present extensively cultivated or found in our markets, which are the *cherry* and the *bell cranberries*, the former being the prettiest and that most sought after, and looks much like that fruit, after which it is named. The *Bell Cranberry* is oval, somewhat like an *Egg*. The cultivated fruit are the largest, most perfect, and of the best flavor. The season for the fresh fruit commences about the 1st of September and continues until April. In Southern New Jersey many are left on the vines all winter, or until the snow and ice admit of their being gathered. These are usually quite ripe, sweet, and of a dark color. In February, 1865, they sold at *wholesale* for forty dollars per barrel.

The *American Cranberry* is found growing in a wild state in the Eastern, Middle, and Western States, and produces large crops without cultivation. It is said that this fine fruit was first noticed by the botanists who accompanied Captain Cook, in 1778, who found it growing spontaneously on the northwest coast of America and about Hudson Bay. It was taken to England, and for many years cultivated in the garden of Sir Joseph Banks as a curiosity. In 1813 he produced, from a bed eighteen feet square, three and a half Winchester bushels of cranberries, being at the rate of four hundred and sixty bushels to the acre.

Captain Henry Hall, of Barnstable, Massachusetts, is noticed as having cultivated this fruit almost fifty years ago,

(1866), with perfect success. The Eastern States have the credit of preparing them for the market in the most cleanly and best manner, so that they arrive in our markets looking fresh, plump, and sound.

Currants.—This useful, wholesome, and cooling fruit is much used in its green and ripe state for many purposes and preparations. The green *currants* are much sought after, just before they begin to color, or grow red, for pies, tarts, stews, to can, etc. They are generally in market about the first of June, and grow ripe in July, when they will hang on the bushes, especially if covered, until September, and are used for jellies, etc. A very pleasant drink is also made from them. Among the best varieties are the *Cherry*, *Red*, and *White-dutch*, *White grape*, *Black Naples*, etc. The *Black currant* is a different species, not having the same flavor as the common *currants*, but a flat and strong taste, and are the best for jam, jelly, etc., when made for the sick.

Dried currants.—These are usually sold in our fine groceries, and when plenty, at the markets. They are prepared in foreign countries, and are best from the Levant and Grecian Islands. The new dried fruit arrives here in the months of December and January. There are a few of the common currants dried in this country, but are not much sought after,

Custard apple.—See *Pawpaw.*

Dates.—This is a fruit of a palm-tree, of an oval drupe form, somewhat like the acorn, and of a yellow color; the pulp is soft, sweet, of a vinous flavor, and encloses a large oblong stone or kernel. They are found here in a preserved state, pressed into a sort of matting called trails, and when sold by retail they are cut or broken in lumps. They are usually sold by the pound. The fresh fruit arrives here in the months of January, February, and March. The first cultivation of the *Date* in North America, says Furman, was made in the summer of 1826, by Dr. Grant, of St. Simon's Island, in Georgia, successfully.

Dewberries.—See *Blackberries.*

Elderberries.—These small, black berries are pleasant-tasted, when ripe, and are brought to our markets to be used for various purposes. They make the *Elder-paste,* for the sick, which is considered excellent, *Elderberry* wine, a wholesome and agreeable beverage, sometimes used for making pies, etc., and when gathered while in flower make the *Elder Flower Tea,* etc. The bark also makes an excellent ointment; in fact, the whole plant is much used in medicine. The berries are in season in the months of August and September.

Figs.—The fresh, ripe *Fig* has an insipid, sweet taste, are considered nutritive and wholesome, and when a person becomes accustomed to eating them they are usually fond of them. In this climate it requires some artificial assistance to bring them into a ripe and perfect state, although I have read of two crops being produced annually. It is usually ripe in August. (I, however, have eaten them ripe in July.) Preserved figs are found here quite plentiful, brought from foreign climes. They are considered best when fresh brought here, in the months of December and January, after which they will bear close examination, especially those which are "hawked around" are apt to be wormy and are often spoiled.

Fox grapes or **wild grapes.**—This fruit is found very plentiful in their season, or when in a green and in the ripe state. The green *grapes* appear about the 15th to the 20th of August, when they are used for pies, preserves, etc., then about the 20th of September they are found ripe and changed to a dark blue color. They are very round and soft, with rather a pleasant tart taste, but a little *foxy,* and last until November. (See under head of *Grapes.*)

Gooseberries.—There appears to be many varieties of this fruit, but I do not deem it necessary to name only the different colors as they are found in our markets. The red, yellow, green, white, and those of a medium size, free from rust, are generally found the best. They first appear from the South in May, and continue until the 1st of August.

They make excellent tarts, pies, sauces, preserves, gooseberry wine, etc.

Granadilla or **May-apple.**—This fine fruit is known at the South as the *Granadilla*, where it grows in the greatest perfection, generally about the size of an *Apple*, and larger, with a sweet, yellow pulp. I have never seen it in our markets, but am told it is found sometimes in the Philadelphia markets, more especially in the Southern cities, where it is used as a dessert.

Grapes.—There are several species of the native, hardy grape, of which the Isabella is the most popular. The Catawba ranks very high, as also the Concord, Diana, Clinton, etc., all of which are favorites. There are also several new varieties, among which are the Rebecca, Delaware, etc., which promise well. *Grapes* commence the season about the 1st of September, and last until November, and when properly kept, a month or two later. They are principally used for the dessert, preserves, jellies, or to can.

It is interesting to know that at least three of the best varieties were cultivated by ladies. The *Isabella Grape*, which thrives best and is most productive in the neighborhood of New York and other places, was introduced by George Gibbs, Esq., of Brooklyn, Long Island, from North Carolina, about the year 1814. His wife, Mrs. Isabella Gibbs, who took a prominent part in its further cultivation, was complimented by having her first name given to this fine, large blue *grape*. The *Diana Grape* also took its name from Mrs. Diana Crehore, Massachusetts, and the *Rebecca* from Mrs. Rebecca Peake, of Hudson, N. Y. The origin of the *Clinton Grape* is also worthy of notice, as found from Professor North's statement (see Journal of the N. Y. S. A. Society, vol. 7, 1864), who says: "The *Clinton Grape* was so named from our village, and originated in the horticultural amusement of a student at Hamilton College. The original *Clinton Grape*-vine is growing over a tall elm on the east side of Dr. Curtis's house, on College Hill. It was planted there in 1821 forty-three years ago, by Hugh White, of Cohoes, then a junior in college. Having a fondness for gardening and tree culture, he planted a quantity of grape-seed two years before in his father's garden, in Whitesboro'. Out of the many hundreds that came up, Mr. White selected one that looked more promising than the others, and planted it east of the house of Dr. Noyes, with whom he then boarded. This seedling vine proved to be a rampant grower and wonderfully productive ; with bunches long, compact, quite uniform, with berries small, a very dark purple when fully ripe, quite palatable early in September, yet improved in flavor by the frost. As a grape for making wines and jellies, the Clinton is quite a favorite in latitudes where the *Catawba* will not ripen."

We have also the luscious foreign grapes in perfection, by the assistance of the hot and cold graperies, from April until December, among which are the Black Prince, Black Hamburgh, White Muscat, White Sweet-water, Tokay, etc. The Syrian (a white species) produces the largest clusters. Those raised by artificial culture are sold sometimes at very high prices, varying from fifty cents to three dollars per pound, and are usually found at the large confectioneries and saloons. The White Malaga, of foreign growth, is found at our large fruit and grocery stores.

Grape-fruit or **forbidden fruit.**—This is a species of the orange, but of a bitter and tart flavor. The inside skin, which surrounds the fleshy cells, is of a disagreeable bitter. They have much the appearance of the shaddock, but smaller. In season usually with the *Orange*, and not much admired.

Ground cherry.—See *Vegetable Cherry*.

Honey bean or **sweet locust-fruit.**—The fruit or pod is flat, crooked, and long, of a reddish brown color, and full of hard seeds, enveloped in a sweet, pulpy substance, much like honey, when it is ripe, but becomes sour after a frost. In my boyhood I have travelled miles to get "honey beans."

June berries, wild service berries, or **May**

cherries.—These are a small, pear-shaped, purplish, red-colored fruit, about the size of large *Bilberries*, of a sweet, pleasant taste, when ripe. They grow on a bush or small tree, usually from six to ten feet high, and ripen in the month of June, when they continue about one month. Birds are very fond of them.

Lemons.—This is one of the most common of the foreign fruits, principally used in cooling summer drinks, and for various culinary as well as medicinal purposes. The rind or peel is also used in flavoring a variety of dishes, and also in preserves. They are almost always to be obtained. Fresh fruit, both of this and the following, arrive in the winter from the West Indies, and in the spring from the Mediterranean islands.

Limes.—This fruit is a small species of the lemon, of a paler color, thinner skin, and the taste of a bitter acid, although quite cooling. The green fruit is much esteemed for its preserving qualities, but is seldom to be found here. It is usually more scarce than the lemon.

Mandrake, **May-apple**, **raccoon-berry**, or **wild lemon**.—This fruit is a stranger in our markets, and only occasionally found among our citizens; and, no doubt, if it was esteemed at all, it would be cultivated and become more plentiful. It is found growing in many parts of our Northern States, more particularly on new-cleared lands. It grows singly, and seldom two are found on a stalk; with much of the appearance of an *egg-plumb*, and with a sickish sweet taste. It ripens in September and lasts until frost. There is another peculiar-looking fruit, which, some forty years ago, became known to me, and, in fact, to many boys of my acquaintance, as the *May-apple*. However, afterwards, I found it generally known as *pinkster-apple*, and *hog-apple*. It was not at all like an *apple* either in form or flavor, being in shape irregular, without pits or seed, of a light green color, sometimes nearly white, and juicy without a pleasant flavor. It grows on a small bush, and ripens in May and June. I have often gathered them on the grounds now occupied by that beautiful place known as the Central Park.

Medlar.—This fruit is quite round, and about as large as a plum, though some varieties are as large as an apple. The pulp is thick, and contains five wrinkled stones; but they are not much esteemed until they have been touched severely with the frost. The large Dutch *medlar* is of the best quality. They are, however, but very seldom seen here.

Melons.—It is said that there are but two species of this fruit—at least, that we cultivate successfully: the rough or embroidered coated is called the *musk-melon,* and those with a smooth thick skin are called *water-melons.* These are divided into many varieties. From the *musk-melon* are the *nutmegs, citron, cantaloup, pineapple,* etc. Of these, the citron is most valued for its sweetness, richness, and high flavor. They appear from the South—usually from Charleston and Savannah—about the 1st of August. The nutmeg is preferred by most people for its high musky flavor and large size, and the skin appears as if covered with a net, ribbed or crossed like the nutmeg spice. They are in season a short time previous to the former, and are found more numerous. The cantaloup is the first ripe *musk-melon,* but it is not so much cultivated as the two former. It, however, enjoys a sweet and pleasant flavor. The *musk-melon* appears not to have been generally cultivated around New York, prior to 1818, as we find, in the *Commercial Advertiser,* August 28th, of that year, the following in relation to this fact:

"*Musk-melons.*—The cultivation of this fragrant fruit has long been a disgrace to the New York market. Although every care has been repeatedly taken to distribute seeds of the best species, such repeated carelessness has always attended every effort to improve the breeds, that we had almost abandoned every hope that our market would rival Philadelphia in the production of this exquisite fruit. We are indebted, however, to Mr. Aaron R. Jones, from that quarter, for having supplied us, most abundantly, this season with *musk-melons* of the first quality, and of the most delicious flavor, and at very reasonable prices. He has, by experiment, convinced our horticulturists that good *melons* are as easily cultivated as bad. *This is the second year* which has amply, we trust, rewarded this enterprising person. Last year he commenced his experiment at Hoboken; but the present season he removed to Guanos, Long Island, a kindlier, earlier soil. The following calculations, founded on inquiry and pretty accurate estimates, will show the reward he is likely to reap from his enterprise.

"Mr. Jones has cultivated *eight acres* of land with *musk-melons* solely. He planted sixteen thousand hills, which will certainly yield for market *three* melons per hill, is forty-eight thousand melons. These forty-eight thousand melons will probably average ten cents per melon, is four thousand eight hundred dollars, which gives a product of six hundred dollars per acre. Allowing one half for the expenses of manure, culture, and bringing to market, will leave a net profit of two thousand four hundred dollars—equal to three hundred dollars per acre.

"This instance of successful enterprise is held up as an incentive to gardeners and farmers in the vicinity of this city to follow this profitable example. Instead of the toil and trouble attending the cultivation and bringing to market boat-loads of unpalatable fruit, how much more productive will it be to cultivate from the choicest seeds, unmingled with any other inferior qualities, and thus secure a certain profit!"

Among the best varieties of the *water-melon* are the Spanish mountain sweet, orange, Carolina, apple-pie, citron water-melon, etc. The Spanish variety is certainly one of the best, being very sweet, rich, and excellent. The skin is of a dark green, and slightly marbled rind, moderately thick, with a red, solid flesh. This variety is extensively cultivated on Long Island, New Jersey, etc.

The orange *water-melon* is of a round shape, and of a smaller size, and, when ripe, must be cut through the skin like an orange, and the rind taken off without breaking the pulp, then divided by cutting between the lobes, when it will be found delicious eating. The Carolina *water-melons* are very good here when fresh, and are found here in the latter part of July. The citron *water-melon* ripens late, and is quite small and round, with a very thick skin or rind, and generally used for preserves.

Apple-pie *water-melon.*—This Japan species of melon is but lately introduced here, and appears, with the aid of a little lemon-juice, to make excellent apple-pie, or one that you cannot hardly tell the difference. It will keep quite well all winter.

To judge *water-melons,* when ripe and fit to eat, they should, when pressing them between the hands and knees, make a sort of cracking noise, and, when knocked on by the knuckles, will emit a sort of hollow sound, but never by their great weight. It, however, requires practice to judge them properly.

The common use of melons, some one hundred and fifty years ago, is referred to in the following extract from Sir John Chardin's Travels in Persia, in 1720: "*Melons,* in the common season, which lasts full four months, are the daily food and sustenance of the poorer sort of people. They live upon nothing but *melons* and *cucumbers,* the last of which they eat without paring them. There are some that will eat five and thirty pounds of *melon* at a meal, without making themselves sick. During these four months they come in such vast quantities to Ispahan, that I can't help believing that they eat more there in a day than they do in France in a month. The streets are full of horses and asses that are loaded with them, from midnight till morning, and all the day till sunset."

Mulberries.—There are several varieties of this excellent and wholesome fruit. The red, black, and white are the only varieties with which I am acquainted. The best of these is the red, being full of seeds and having an agreeable acid, sugary taste. The black is larger, more sugary, or rather more of a sickening sweet after several of them have been eaten, but are best when not too ripe.

The white is smaller than either, with also a taste similar to that of the black. These I have gathered and eaten from the trees along the walks to the Elysian Fields at Hoboken, N. J., about the year 1830. Usually ripe on the 1st of August.

Nectarines.—This fine-flavored fruit very much resembles the peach, except in the smoothness of skin and firmness of flesh. But few of them, however, find their way into our markets, and it requires much trouble and care to produce good crops. Among the choice varieties are the early violet, French white, late yellow, etc. They begin to ripen about the 1st of August, and continue good until October.

Olives.—This foreign fruit is found here in a preserved or pickled state, although they are cultivated at the South, in Louisiana, South Carolina, etc., and said to fully ripen. It is, however, not a very profitable crop. They are used here principally by foreigners. The oil made from this fruit is the common sweet or olive oil, so much valued in salads, cookery, etc.

Oranges.—There are several varieties of this most excellent and refreshing fruit. The largest and best are from St. Augustine, and sell at the highest prices. The Havanas are equal in flavor, but have a thick and rough rind, and the pulp of either is very juicy and delicious. The Maltese have also a very thick and spongy skin, and the pulp is quite red, and sometimes without juice. The Sicilian fruit are smaller, with a thin skin and a sour taste, but usually most abundant and cheap. Ripe oranges are a wholesome hand or table fruit, while the green are used for preserves and confectionery. The rind and pulp are also used in cookery, as well as the flowers for perfumery. The West India oranges are found here from October until April, and those from the Mediterranean, in boxes, from January until May, after which periods they lose flavor and become dry and spongy. Another variety, called the *bitter orange* or *Seville*, is not much used here, the pulp being quite bitter, sour, and sharp, and the rind of a very pungent nature. It is only valued for marmalade, candy, etc.

Partridge-berries, or **nanny-berries**.—These little black berries grow in clusters, on a tree-like bush, on uncultivated grounds or along hedges. When fully ripe, they have an insipid, dry, sweet taste, and a large pit. They are edible, what there is of them, and birds are very fond of them. Found ripe in September, and continue on the bushes until winter sets in. I have never seen them on sale in our markets, but have eaten quarts while hunting.

Paw-paw, or **custard apple**.—This fruit is found plentiful in the Southern and Western States, and appears somewhat, in form and color, like a small *cucumber* when ripe. Its pulp is rather too luscious to be agreeable, although palatable to some, having a flavor like custard, of a saffron color, and quite full of hard seeds, which look like those from the *water-melon,* but larger. It is said to be best when touched by the frost, and many persons like them best when boiled in the green state. They usually ripen about the middle of September. Judge Law, of Evansville, Indiana, says "that having met at the house of a friend where there was some paw-paw brandy, the distiller remarked that the *paw-paw*, which is indigenous to our bottom-lands, yields more spirit to the bushel than any other fruit, and that he has contracted for one thousand bushels to distil the coming season (1859). A bushel of the fruit will yield two gallons of the spirits." They ripen in the month of August.

Peaches.—This is one of the most tempting and luscious fruits in the catalogue, having a great many varieties, although generally known under two principal names—the freestones and clingstones. Among the best variety of the first is the early York, Crawford early, rare-ripes, Morris whites, melocoton, honest John, etc. Of the varieties of clingstones are the lemon cling, orange cling, white heath, Oldmixon late heath, blood cling, etc. Peaches first make their appearance from Bermuda about the 25th of April, in small numbers and at high prices; from the Southern States the latter end of June and first of July, and from lower New Jersey (a few unripe ones) about the 20th of July; but they do not appear in large quantities, or in a ripe state, save from the 10th to the 20th of August, when they commence to be plenty, and continue so until the 20th of September, when they gradually decrease with the large hard winter peaches until November, after which they are found in the dried state. Their principal use is for dessert, many for preserves in various ways, in brandies, etc.

We have previously noticed Mr. Aaron R. Jones, who started a new life in the cultivation of fine *musk-melons* in the year 1818. He afterwards, says the *Commercial Advertiser*, August 26, 1826, "directed his attention to a new field of industry, having purchased a handsome tract of land in Shrewsbury, N. J. About three years since (1822) he set out a peach orchard of twenty acres, it is understood, which this year (1824) has begun to requite his care and attention. *Jones' peaches* are the order of the day—and most excellent they are in size and flavor—and are now selling from two to three cents each, and from fifty to seventy-five cents a half a peck."

Pears.—There are many varieties of this excellent fruit, and but few of the very choice kinds are seldom found plentiful in our markets, and those few command high and paying prices to the producers. Among the choice summer *pears* are the Bartlett, summer Doyenne, Madelaine, sugar pears, Bloodgood, Brandywine, small harvest pear, etc. The autumn pears are the Duchess d'Angoulême, Bartlett, Virgalieu, or white Doyenne, Sheldon, gray Doyenne, Seckel, Buffam, Flemish beauty, Louise Bonne de Jersey, Washington, Bell, etc. Winter pears are the winter Nellis, pound, Columbia, Vicar of Wakefield, Lawrence, Easter Beurre, etc.

The first pears begin to show themselves in June, and sometimes earlier, but seldom ever good. The best are received in August, September, and October for the *dessert*, of which the Duchess d'Angoulême, Bartlett, and Virgalieu stand first; the former has been known to have sold at *one dollar each*, and often from three to six dollars a dozen. Many kinds are used for baking, stewing, preserving, etc., and a drink called Perry is also made of them. Several of the winter varieties will keep well through the winter, and last until April.

The origin of the Seckel pear is thus noticed by "the venerable Bishop White (in the Philadelphia *Gazette*, 1835), whose memory is remarkable for its strength and correctness." He says "that when he was a boy, about seventy years ago, there was a *bleeder* in this city known by the name of Dutch Jacob, who was a great sportsman. At a certain season of the year he was known by his neighbors and others to bring home from his excursions very *delicious pears*, but he would never tell anybody where he procured them.

"About that period the London Land Company, which owned some land below the city, made a sale, and Dutch Jacob purchased the lot upon which his *pear-tree* stood. It afterwards became the property of Mr. Seckel, and now belongs to the estate of the late Mr. Girard. The Seckel pear is now known all over the United States."

Persimmon or **American medlar.**—This fruit seems to be a species of the *Plum*, when ripe, somewhat the color of an *Orange;* others, again, are red, and some quite black. The fruit is not fit to eat until it has felt the frost, which somewhat shrivels the skin and makes it tender, luscious, and quite sweet, but a little puckerish. In the settlement of Virginia, Captain John Smith called this fruit the *Putchamins*, when he says: "We daily feasted with good bread, Virginia pease, pumpions, and *Putchamins*," and "if it be not ripe, it will draw a man's mouth awry with much torment. If ripe, it is as delicious as an *Apricot*." The ripe fruit are about as large and much shaped like a *Date*, and grow on trees, in bunches. Cultivation has much enlarged and otherwise improved the fruit as well as the tree, which is ornamental and worthy to be placed in every lawn, the foliage being rich and beautiful, and the bearing trees, when loaded with ripe fruit, present an admirable appearance.

Persimmons are found in our markets in October, and if very ripe they appear broken and mashed. They make an excellent syrup and good table-beer; whiskey is also manufactured from them.

Pine.apples.—This excellent-flavored fruit is found in our markets quite plentiful in their season, which commences about the 1st of April and lasts until September. They are known here under two general names, or kinds: the birds-eye and the sugar-loaf; the first is considered best for eating out of hand, the latter for preserving in different ways. They certainly have a delicious flavor, but they usually disappoint the palate, by having so much wood and fibrous substance to swallow along with it. They are brought from Havana, Nassau, Matanzas, etc. Their usual weight is from two to five pounds.

Pine ivy.—See *Wintergreen berries.*

Plantains.—This is an invaluable tropical fruit, and is used by many of the West Indians for bread. It grows in smaller bunches or spikes than the bananas, each one being from eight to twelve inches long and about three in diameter, somewhat the form of a *cucumber*, but pointed at both ends. The flesh is firm, solid, and nutritious, and may be prepared for the table, either in a green or ripe state, for tarts, sweetmeats, and confectionery, and it is also good for roasting, frying, broiling, or even when boiled, with salt meat or fish. It is found in season from February to September.

Plums.—Among the varieties of this fine fruit stands the green gage, which ripens about the middle of August and lasts until October. Then there is the Washington, the Jefferson, white and purple Damsons, the white, red, blue, and frost gage, the purple and yellow egg, magnum bonum, apricot, common blue, or horse plum, etc. They are used for the dessert, preserves, etc., and are generally found in our markets from the latter end of July until the middle of October.

Wild plums.—There are several varieties, and different sizes, colors, and tastes of this fruit, some of which are red, yellow, and purple color, with tastes of sweet, tartish, and sour, and again some quite hard and almost uneatable. Several varieties of the best kinds have been introduced into the States of New York, Connecticut, and New Jersey, and successfully grown, producing crops as regular as any other fruit-crop. I have often seen a fine, cherry-looking fruit in our markets, which was called *Illinois Cherry*, about the size of large red or sour *cherries*, without the stem. The skin was quite tough, while the flesh appeared tender, with rather a tart taste and a slight touch of bitterness ; the pit, however, was a regular *plum* pit. I understand they grow wild in some of our neighboring States, but when cultivated they are much improved in size and flavor. They are used and make very good tarts, sweetmeats, etc. In season about the middle of September, and last until November.

Pomegranates.—This fine-looking fruit is brought here from the Southern States, but not in large quantities, as it is not much thought of. It is about as large as a good-sized apple, having some of the appearance of a smooth apple-*quince*, but with a red cheek, full of seeds and divided into sections. When it becomes ripe there is a soft, juicy, agreeable acid pulp around the seeds : the rind and inside partition is hard, tough, and highly astringent. Ripens generally in September and October. It makes an excellent medicinal syrup, either for fever or inflammations.

Prickly pear or **Indian fig.**—This little fruit I have never seen in our markets, but have often gathered and eaten them. The fruit is in the form of a fig, or long little pear, very troublesome to handle, being full of little, yellow, prickly spines, which should be brushed off before handling or gathering, and when ripe they come off readily. Its pulp is subacid and palatable (with the taste of a fig), and of a red and purple color. It is found on thin, dry soil, on the top of rocky surfaces, growing in tufts on a few thick, fleshy leaves.

Prunes.—This is one of the foreign varieties of the plum, dried or preserved; a fine, wholesome fruit when fresh. Those from Turkey are generally the best, but there is a great deal of difference in the quality; if they are heated or sweat on their passage, they become candied, with a whitish appearance, which impairs their quality. The best are put up in glass jars, boxes, and other small packages. Those in baskets or casks are considered not so fine. A free use of them will be found beneficial as a medicine. The fresh arrivals are generally from December to May.

Quince.—This beautiful fruit is never eaten without being cooked in some fashion or another, when it is much esteemed for its fine flavor. For marmalade, preserves, jellies, sauces, stews, syrups, tarts, wine, etc., and also medicinally, it is everywhere valued. Among the several varieties are the apple-*quince*, pear-*quince*, Portugal, etc. The apple, or orange *quince* is the most popular, as it is the most tender and excellent-flavored; the Portugal is quite scarce, but is considered as good as the first, and the pear-*quince* is usually the most perfect, but quite hard and tough, although the flavor is equal if not superior. Select the smooth large ones, as they are the most tender and perfect, and not so full of waste. The small knotty ones are tough, worm-eaten, and wasteful. This fruit is in season in October, and lasts until December.

Mrs. B. Willis, in Orange (N. J.), produced a *Quince* in 1844, which weighed *one pound five ounces*, and measured fourteen inches, being in a plump and perfect state.

Raisins.—This foreign-prepared fruit are grapes dried either in the sun or the oven. The Malaga, or muscatel, is the largest and best for the table. The sultana, without seed, the Smyrna, etc., etc., principally used in pies, puddings, etc. They are found the best in boxes, also in kegs, etc., sold in the best groceries, fruit-stores, and when plenty are in our markets. They are in season throughout the year, but best from December to June, when they are fresh.

Raspberries.—This is an excellent and pleasant-flavored fruit for the dessert, especially the choice qualities, among which are the red and the yellow, or white, Antwerp, Franconia, Fastolff, etc., which ripen from the 5th to the 10th of July—the common red a little earlier. The black cap, or common black *Raspberry*, is the wild fruit found along the hedges and fences, which have a very rich acid flavor. They ripen later and last about six weeks. Favorable seasons *Raspberries* are found in our markets early in June, and often as late as the 10th of August. Many uses are made of this berry—in preserves, jams, ices, tarts, syrups, vinegar, wine, etc.

Shaddock.—This tropical fruit is like a large, coarse orange, with a very little of that fruit's flavor, and a good deal of stringent bitter, especially when any portion of the skin, or parts of the division which separate the fleshy pulp, are eaten. Therefore, for a hand fruit, it is not of much value ; but for preserves, it, no doubt, is good. I am, however, told that when it has fully ripened on the tree, its juices are saccharine and subacid, and those which are heavy and soft are usually found the best.

Sloes.—This is a species of the *wild plum*, but smaller, more solid, and much better when ripe. It is occasionally seen here, and found in abundance in the Western States, where it is used for pies, preserves, etc. In season from September to November.

Shepardia, or **Buffalo berry.**—This fruit is of the size and appearance of a large currant, of a red or scarlet color, and grows in clusters, with a rich taste ; used principally for, and makes excellent preserves.

Strawberries.—There is no kind of fruit more delectable to the sense of taste than the *strawberry ;* and there are few more agreeable to the sight when fully ripe, large, and fresh taken from the stem. There are several varieties of this fruit brought usually in great abundance into our markets; those, however, which first appear are found placed in the smallest baskets that the article of wood can very well be formed into, and these generally bring the highest prices. Among the earliest and best varieties are the Early scarlet, Hovey seedlings, McAvoy's superior, Burr's pines, Scotch runners, Black Prince, Boston pines, etc. From the South they appear in small quantities about the 1st of April, and so continue for about one month, daily increasing, so that by the 1st of June New Jersey lays them on our tables in abundance; and daily after that period the neighboring counties pour them into our (New York) city by thousands and tens of thousands of baskets, boxes, bowls, etc. They, however, begin to fail about the 25th of June, and generally disappear by the 10th of July. The use of this fruit is various, but principally used for the dessert, ices, syrups, preserved in cans, etc.

"About t[illegible]r 1800," says *Furman* in his Notes, "garden *strawbe*[illegible] ere first introduced into the New York markets. Be[illegible] that there was none except a few wild *strawberries* which were brought in by women from Tappan and New Jersey. The person who has the honor of having first gratified the New Yorkers with the taste of this most delicious fruit in its cultivated state, was Robert Debevoise, of Brooklyn, who cultivated a strip of land between Samuel Jackson and H. B. Pierpont, Esq. (lying between Fulton-street, the East River, and immediately north of Pierpont-street). His price was then two shillings for a pint bowl of them. He refused to sell any of his plants, and thus kept the run of the market alone for about three years, and thereby made a great deal of money. After that he gave old John V. Swartcope, also of Brooklyn, some of the plants, and in a short time he also came in for his share of the profits."

There were occasionally a few large *strawberries* produced at an early period, one of which is thus noticed: "A *strawberry* raised this season in the garden of Mr. J. Wooston, of Wilmington, Delaware, measured *three inches and three-quarters* in circumference, and weighed one hundred and sixty-one grains." (*Commercial Advertiser*, June 14, 1816.) Of late years we have much improved in the size, but I think not much in flavor.

Tallow-berries, or **ground-berries.**—These small red berries are found growing on a small, tender vine resting on the ground, in the cleared woods; and when eaten, they have a sort of sweetish, tallowy taste, but rather pleasant. Found ripe in November, but seldom in our markets.

Tamarinds.—This fruit, or rather pod, is found here in a preserved state in our grocery and fruit stores. It is generally used without preparation as an article of food, and occasionally as a medicine. William M. Singleton, Esq., of Winchester (Va.), has succeeded in raising *tamarind-trees* which bore fruit, in 1854, of a quality equal to that imported. The best are cured with sugar, and are known as the sugar *tamarinds.* Another kind is also cured with molasses, and known as the common molasses *tamarinds*, or West India *tamarinds.* This fruit is in season all the year round, but is best in the months of May and June.

Thorn-apples, or **haws.**—These small red fruit are usually found about the size of a *cherry*, but in form and appearance of miniature *apples*, quite filled with seeds, which render them almost worthless. Some varieties, however, have some flesh on them, and they can be used in preserves, etc. Found ripe in August and September.

Vegetable cherry, ground cherry, raspberry tomato, or **strawberry tomato.**—These small fruit grow on a straggling-looking weed or plant, and are found covered with a bladdery husk. When ripe they are usually of a purplish red, and others again quite yellow, but all have an agreeable acid flavor. Dr. James Knight, chairman of the Horticultural Society, writes to me: "There has been some new varieties introduced and cultivated for the fruit, as some people consider them quite palatable, and call them the *raspberry tomato*, as they possess somewhat the flavor. Some again call them the *strawberry tomato.* Among the new varieties a much larger sort has been introduced, called *vegetable gooseberry*, having the taste of a ripe *gooseberry*." This kind, however, I have not yet seen. I have eaten several kinds, and found some quite sweet and others again of a subacid flavor. Ripen in September about the locality of New York. I kept some of them with the husk on over five months, when they were perfectly dried.

Whortleberries, huckleberries, or **blueberries.**—There are several varieties of this prolific fruit known, among which those growing on the high bushes are usually preferred. The best variety is called the *swamp huckleberry*, or *blueberry*, which yields the largest berry, of a purplish black; when ripe is subacid, rich, and juicy. Another variety, called the *common*, or *high-bush berry*, is also a rich, fine berry, of a dark-blue color. The common low-bush blueberry or *huckleberry*, is commonly known among the Jersey pickers or gatherers as the "cracker-berry," as they crack or snap in the mouth on account of their tough skin. They are smooth, quite black, full of seeds, and of a tartish taste. Another better variety of the *low-bush*, known as the "sugar-berry," being quite sweet, of a bluish coat, or like a coat of flour dusted over them, and with very small seeds. When found in our markets they are usually mixed up together, and are in season from about the 15th of July to the 20th of September.

Wild cherries.—These little purplish-black cherries (or drupes) are found on strings like currants, and, when ripe, have rather a pleasant bitterish-sweet taste, which some people are fond of, and are considered wholesome. They are much used for making cordials called *cherry bounce*, cherry brandy. Cultivation has improved them much, both in taste and size. The bark of the tree is much used for medical purposes, and the wood for making furniture, etc. They are found ripe about the 1st of September.

Winter grapes, or **frost grapes.**—These are a small clustering species of the *grape*, of a pleasant acid flavor when ripe, and also when touched with the frost.

They grow in clusters, and are thus found on sale in the month of November.

Wintergreen berries, checker-berries, tea-berries, pine ivy, etc.—These little red edible berries look much like a miniature crab-apple, and are found growing on a shrub, from four to six inches high, on low sandy soils, usually among the *pines*. This berry's taste is much like the bark from off the twigs of *sweet-birch*, with the flavor of *wintergreen*. They are used in syrups, confectionery, and pleasant out of hand, and sometimes put in whiskey or spirits, when it is called "tea-berry rum." The leaves make the essence of wintergreen. These berries are sometimes found in our markets in the winter and spring months, as they remain on the bush throughout the winter and early spring months.

NUTS.

Almonds.—These excellent nuts are not usually found on sale in our public markets, yet in plentiful seasons they can be purchased in some of them. The choice nuts are usually sold in our fine groceries, fruit-stores, and confectioners. The parts eaten are the meat of the dry pit or shell of the sweet almond, some of which are so soft that they are broken by the fingers; these are known as the sultana, but usually called *soft* or *upper-shell*, and *ladies' thin-shell;* the thick-shell are known as the *Jordan* or *hard-shell*. They are now cultivated in the central and Southern States, but our large supplies are brought from the south of Europe. The fresh or new nuts usually arrive in our cities in the first winter months, when they are found very tender, sweet, with much of the "nutty flavor;" while the old nuts are hard, dry, and with but little of this excellent flavor.

Beech-nuts. or **beech-mast**.—These little nuts are occasionally found for sale, but are not sought after, or only when wanted for particular purposes. They are, however, eatable, and even nutritious; of a triangular form, or shaped somewhat like a buckwheat kernel, but much larger. They are sometimes known as *mast*, or *beech-mast*, and serve to fatten hogs, especially in new countries where *corn* is scarce. Squirrels are particularly fond of them. In some parts of Europe they make oil from them.

Black walnuts.—These excellent nuts, when ripe, and with the husk off, are very rough, black, and round; found in the markets during October and November, and will keep for many months. The ripe kernel is large, sweet, and wholesome. The immature fruit, while in the green, tender, outside shell, and before the internal shell becomes hard (which is usually in the months of July and August, according to locations), makes the walnut catsup, or for pickling. The hard wood, which is of a dark purplish color, is much used by the cabinetmakers, and for gun-stocks, etc.

Brazil nuts.—These nuts, as their name denotes, are a native of South America, and are of a dark brown, being rough-shelled and three-cornered, with a large white kernel, having the flavor of the hazel-nut, and very oily. The season of the new nuts arriving here continues from March until May.

Butter-nuts, white walnuts, or **oil-nuts.**—These are a species of the *walnut*, resembling, when young, the *black walnut*, but elongated and smaller. When ripe they are of an oval, oblong form, not quite so large or rough as the black walnut, and are of a different flavor, with an agreeable taste, and rich in oil. When green and soft they are excellent for pickling. They ripen in the month of September. In the Eastern States these nuts are known as oil-nuts, and in Southern Ohio, etc., as the *white walnut*.

Cashew nuts.—This is a native of the Indies, but sometimes found here. The nut or fruit is in size like an apple, some of a white, red, or yellow color, and, like the cherry, tastes sweet and pleasant, but sometimes sharp and astringent. The kidney-shaped seed grows on its summit, and, when roasted, is superior to almonds.

Chestnuts.—I know of but two kinds that are represented here—the common American *chestnut*, and the large Spanish *chestnut*. Great quantities of the latter are sold roasted in a hot state along some of our public places and streets. The common *chestnut* is, however, the best flavored, especially when fresh, and is excellent either raw, roasted, or boiled. Their season commences in September and continues good throughout the winter.

Chinquapin nut, or **dwarf chestnut.**—This is a small variety of the *chestnut*, growing on smaller trees, and considered about the same quality. It is seldom seen here, but quite plenty in the markets of Baltimore and Philadelphia, and is known by some as the *dwarf chestnut*.

Cocoa-nut.—This nut is the best flavored of all the foreign kinds. They come principally from Baracoa, Brazil, and other places. The white kernel, although hard, woody, and tough, in its fresh state, is said to be very nutritious, and, when grated, makes excellent puddings, pies, cakes, in candy, etc. It contains a white liquid called milk, which is sweet and nourishing, and they should never be purchased but when this milk is heard to shake within them. The *cocoa-nut* tree furnishes food, raiment, milk, oil, toddy, cups, bowls, cordage, brushes, mats—in fact, it is difficult to say what it does not furnish the Indian.

"The Indian nut alone
Is clothing, meat and trencher, drink and pan,
Boat, cable, sail, and needle—all in one."

Filberts.—These nuts are said to be an improved variety of the common *hazel-nut*, but a great deal larger. The best kind is called the red *filbert*, known by its crimson skin; another kind, called white *filbert*, with a yellow white skin; and also another, called the large Spanish *filbert*. They are found throughout the year; but the new nuts are received only from November to February.

Ground-nuts, chufa, or **earth almonds.**—This little oval tuber having the name of nut, led me to place it under that head. They are very seldom seen in our markets, no doubt in consequence of its smallness, although they are considered esculent, nutritious, and worthy of culture, when they improve in size, and are ready for use in the fall months. When roasted, their taste is much like a boiled *chestnut*, being white, mealy, and good-flavored, and, when dried, their taste is somewhat like the almond. In some parts of Europe they are used for making an *orgeat*, which, with water, makes a milky drink, much used in Spain, and other hot climates where it is known.

Mr. G. F. Waters, of Waterville, Maine, in a letter noticed in the *Tribune*, of January, 1860, says: "The plant has been growing in a wet corner of my garden for years. I have obtained tubers two inches in diameter. There are two kinds of this plant indigenous hereabouts. The tuber in one kind is quite round, and has a sweet taste, yellowish meat, etc. The other, which is the most common, tapers towards the ends, one being whiter than the other; meat, white, sweetish, and quite gummy. I have been told by one of our oldest inhabitants, that many people lived upon this ground-nut during the winter of 1817 and 1818, the nuts having been collected in the fall for food. The flower of this plant is quite showy and fragrant—the odor strongly resembles that of orris-root."

Hazel-nuts, or **wild filberts.**—These are much the shape, form and color of the filbert, but are smaller, thicker shell, and better flavored. They grow on bushes, alongside the borders of the woods and fences, into a cluster of frizzled husks; and when they begin to open, or show the end of the nut, they are fit to eat. They usually appear in August and September.

Hickory-nuts.—There are several varieties of *hickory-nuts*, which are often found mixed together in our markets; and it requires some knowledge of them to select the best. The choice nuts are generally known under the name of

Shell-barks, or **shag-barks**.—These grow on the shaggy-bodied trees, having a thin shell, a large well-tasted full kernel, of a good size, and ripen in October. They are also flatter made, with eight edges or corners, and easily to be cracked. The next best is called

Mocker-nuts, or **thick-shelled hickories**.—These are usually a larger and rounder nut, but with a very thick shell, while the kernel is small but sweet. There is also a smaller thick-shelled nut, which some call the *white-heart hickories*, but I think it the same grown in a poorer soil. The wood of this tree is the best kind for firewood. Another variety is called the

Pig-nut hickories, which are smaller, fig-shaped nuts, having a kernel with a bitterish taste, although I have eaten them when quite sweet. This tree produces the toughest wood of all the other kinds. Then another variety, called

Bitter-nut, **hog-nut**, or **swamp-hickories**, which are the poorest of all the varieties; in fact, the kernel is so harsh and bitter that even the *squirrels* will not eat them. All the varieties ripen in October.

Horse-chestnuts, or **buckeyes**.—The fruit grows in fleshy, prickly capsules, and ripens in the fall months. These nuts are not edible without some preparation. The *Cultivator* says: "The bitter green oil is removed by first grating them to a pulp, then adding one fiftieth (1-50) by weight of carbonate of soda. The mixture then is thoroughly washed and racked by means of a clear fountain, and a white and agreeable paste subsides, which is manufactured into bread and cakes. In Paris they are manufactured into starch."

Madeira, or **English walnut**.—Great quantities of this foreign fruit are annually imported here, and found in the fine groceries, fruit-stores, and markets. The Grenoble nuts are considered the best, and are in season throughout the year. The nuts begin to arrive here in December, and continue until April, when they are considered best.

Peanuts, earth-nuts, pindar-nuts, or **ground peas.**—This common nut is found for sale in all our principal cities, and in all seasons of the year. They are brought principally from the Southern States, Africa, etc., in large quantities, and may be found chiefly in fruit stores, and after having been roasted, everywhere, in the markets, on the street corners, apple-stands, basket pedlers, etc.

The fresh or new nuts arrive here in November (until June), as the first frost kills the vines and ripens the nuts.

In relation to the culture of this nut, the *North Carolina Advertiser* informs us that "the annual exportation to the Northern States and Canada considerably exceeds one hundred thousand bushels. A single planter in one of our Eastern States obtained from it a yearly income of six thousand dollars. He raised from fifty to seventy-five bushels to the acre, and cultivated five acres to the hand, which at one dollar a bushel, the ordinary price—though one dollar and twenty-five cents was frequently realized—yielded an income of from two hundred and fifty to three hundred dollars to the hand. No such result, under the old system of labor, could be obtained with the staples, on similar soils. Our cotton planters contented themselves with a crop yielding from twelve to fifteen dollars per acre, and it was the summing up on a large surface that gave a living result. The cultivation of no crop is so easy, and only the simplest implements are required—first the plow, to break the land, and then simply the sweep and weeding hoes.

"The average crop, as we have stated, is from fifty to seventy-five bushels to the acre, besides which there will be left in the ground enough to fatten one hundred pounds of pork. The vine, when the pea is removed, makes an excellent forage for cattle—said to be equal to the best Northern hay. From the nut is expressed a most valuable oil. During the war just closed this oil was universally used in our machine-shops, and its lubricatory properties are pronounced, by competent authorities, to be superior to those of whale-oil, for the reason that it does not gum at all. One of the qualities of oil is extensively employed in the composition of medicine; another is used for burning purposes, and possesses the virtue of not smoking; while still a third makes a really excellent salad condiment. Such, and so varied and important are the uses to which this simple product can be devoted; uses which the uninformed, who have perhaps regarded it only in the light of an indigestible bulb, would never suspect to proceed from its cultivation."

Pecan nuts.—These nuts are brought from the South and West, and are taken for a species of the *Hickory Nut*, known by some as the *Illinois Hickory*. It is almost an inch long, as large as the end of a common-sized finger, with a smooth shell, and oblong shape. They are of an agreeable taste and wholesome. Brought here principally from the Southern States and Texas, and in season from December until April.

DAIRY AND HOUSEHOLD PRODUCTS.

Butter.—This most useful article of the dairy is known so well, that it would be almost impossible to give the least information in relation to it. We, however, find that it was unknown to the ancient Greeks, and the Romans employed it only for anointing or as medicine; but as an article of food it originated with people of the middle ages, whose generations have continued on with its use to the present day.

It is always to be found in great abundance in our markets, as well as in the grocery and other stores. It is brought from almost every county in ours, as well as the neighboring States, but the counties of Orange, Chemung, and Cortland (in New York) have the reputation of producing the best qualities and largest quantities; there are, however, many towns in this and other States, especially in Pennsylvania, which are producing the article in all its excellence, especially that which is packed by them for winter's use. I think in this, as well as many of the dairy products, that the farmers who supply the Philadelphia markets, excel in having their *Butter* well made, neatly done up in nice clean packages, and—I won't add that it is better-flavored than some of the New York or Boston *Butter*—but it certainly is more generally good.

Some of the Western butter is not always to be depended on, as it will be occasionally of all colors, kinds, and flavors, and also in all kinds of packages. It is used largely in all the delicate operations of cookery, and an almost indispensable accompaniment with bread. The best is made in the spring months, it then being of the finest flavor and color; the next best is made in the fall months; the next in the summer, and the poorest quality is the white "chimney-corner *butter*," made in the winter, which is usually found with a bitterish taste, quite mealy-looking, and made up into various sized rolls, of from one to three pounds weight.

An enormous pyramid of *Butter* was exhibited in the City of New York, in the year 1838, by Colonel Thomas S. Meacham, of Richmond, Oswego County, New York. This large mass of *Butter*, the press says, "weighed upwards of one thousand two hundred pounds." Another he had forwarded to Washington, weighing over one thousand four hundred pounds, to receive the critical judgment of the representatives of the nation. "We hope that he may get as good a price for it as he did on a previous occasion for a like specimen sent to the capital—fifty cents a pound." One of these large truncated cones of butter, weighing one thousand three hundred and fifty pounds, was on sale at Griffith's, in South-street, one door below Coenties-slip, in New York. The press says that it was afterwards removed to the City Hotel, in Broadway, for exhibition, and afterwards cut up and sold to purchasers. It was tastefully ornamented, and bore the following inscription: "The great Western Pyramid of Fine Table *Butter*—manufactured, erected, and inscribed in honor of the Civil and Judicial Officers, Editors,

Merchants, Mechanics, and enterprising Citizens of the great and flourishing City of New York."

Cheese.—This well-known substance is found in abundance in our markets, provision, and grocery stores, and seen of several varieties, sizes, forms, colors, and flavors. The best is made from what is termed the *creamed or whole milk*, then from the *half-creamed*, and then from the skim-milk, which produces at least three qualities of *Cheese*. Some of the choicest comes from Herkimer and Jefferson counties, in this State, and the much admired "English dairy cheese." Connecticut claims to produce the largest quantity as well as the best quality. In choosing *Cheese*, we must first find that which will please our taste, at the same time it should be compact and of a buttery texture, free from holes within, with a smooth, firm rind, sufficient salt for a pleasant relish and to preserve it untainted. Their usual weight varies from ten up to seventy pounds, although some dairies produce them above one hundred pounds, and some, again, above one thousand pounds. The "*Great Cheese*," presented to President Jefferson (January 1, 1802), by several farmers of Cheshire, Massachusetts, weighed one thousand two hundred and thirty-five pounds. In the year 1835 several very large *Cheeses* were made by Colonel Meacham (previously noticed), who then kept one hundred and fifty-four cows, and made that season three hundred *cheeses*, weighing one hundred and twenty-five pounds each. He also made one for President Jackson, weighing one thousand four hundred pounds; and nine others whose aggregate was eight thousand one hundred and fifty pounds. In relation to the disposition of some of these "*mammoth cheeses*," the *Commercial Advertiser* (December 8, 1835) says: "One of these large *Cheeses* was purchased by the St. Nicholas Society, and served up at their anniversary dinner, at the City Hotel, yesterday. It attracted great attention, and the quality of the article was pronounced excellent.

"Col. Meacham removed the *cheeses* yesterday from Masonic Hall (where they had been on exhibition) to the store of Messrs. S. & W. Hotaling, No. 29, west side of Coenties Slip, where they will remain a few days. It has already been mentioned in the public papers that one of these noble *cheeses* was intended as a present to Daniel Webster. Col. M. this morning called upon Mr. Webster, and requested him to walk over to Coenties Slip and examine these specimens of the product of his dairy—a request, we need not add, which was readily complied with.

"The Eastern senator was highly gratified with the view of these extraordinary articles, the taste with which they have been prepared and preserved, and the apparent excellence of their quality. He seemed to be perfectly at home upon the subject, and entered into the spirit of agricultural pursuits with a familiarity of conversation which proved that he had not forgotten the knowledge he had obtained when himself a youthful farmer, guiding the plough with an arm as vigorous as the intellect which he is now consecrating to the service of his country in the high councils of state.

"In the course of the interview Col. Meacham said to Mr. Webster that his occupation was that of a farmer, in the county of Oswego, and that he had a dairy of one hundred and fifty-four cows; that with a view of giving an impulse to this particular branch of husbandry, he had made these *cheeses* during the last season. His intention was, to present one of them to the President of the United States, another to the Vice-President, and a third to the Governor of the State of New York, and a fourth to some other distinguished citizen. His fellow-citizens of the County of Oswego had manifested a lively interest upon the subject; and it was no less in accordance with their feelings (and, indeed, with their particular desire) than with his own, that this distinguished citizen should be the gentleman whom he had now the honor to address, but whom he had not anticipated the pleasure of meeting in this city. With this view one of the *cheeses* had been inscribed to him (Mr.

Webster) before it came from his own farm, and of this he now begged his acceptance.

"Mr. Webster replied, in substance, that he appreciated the compliment very highly, and accepted it with much gratification. These *cheeses*, he remarked, were the finest specimens of an American dairy that he had ever seen. Not only were they highly creditable to the enterprise and public spirit which had prompted their manufacture, but they bore direct testimony to the character and prosperity of the district of country in which they had been produced. He begged Col. Meacham to accept of his thanks for the very handsome present, and to convey his kind regards to those of his fellow-citizens of Oswego who had united with him, in feeling at least, in the bestowment of this mark of their favor toward so humble an individual as himself."

In the year 1849, at the Fair of the American Institute, a *mammoth cheese* was exhibited which was said to weigh one thousand seven hundred and fifty pounds! without doubt the largest ever made. It came from Austin, Ashtabula County, Ohio.

Pineapple cheese.—These pineapple-shaped *cheese* are formed by being pressed in a net the form found, and the rind is toughened with the assistance of hot water, which assists in keeping them a long time. Their usual weight is from six to twelve pounds.

Cream cheese.—Another article made from milk, and is sometimes found in our markets, but more particularly in those of Philadelphia. It is made from rich sour cream tied up in linen cloth to drain, then laid on a deep dish, still covered around, and turned every day, and sprinkled with salt for ten days or a fortnight, until it is ripe. If wanted to ripen quick, cover it with mint or nettle leaves. This, however, is only one way. There is another article much used called

Smearkase, a German name for *churds.* It is made into pies, cakes, spread on bread, and also eaten with pepper and salt. I ate some in Philadelphia made into a cake, which I found was very good.

Eggs.—With all the nations of the earth *eggs* more particularly have been a favorite and wholesome food. Here they may be considered as being in season the year round, although in the spring months they are more plentiful and cheap ; the winter months, however, they are found usually quite scarce and high, and, of course, but few families can afford to use them, or only in mixed preparations. In certain seasons they come by thousands, in fact I may truly say thousands of barrels, containing almost a thousand in each, from Ohio, Indiana, Michigan, Illinois, etc. They come nicely packed with clean oats, etc., in good flour-barrels, when they arrive here in good condition, with no loss on the oats, as they are a ready sale.

Among the various kinds of *eggs* there appears to be two qualities, viz., the fresh-laid *eggs* and the preserved *eggs.* The latter are preserved by the use of lime-water, salt, scalding, etc., which appears to destroy the vital principle, when they are not considered so valuable in their general uses as the first, or *fresh-laid eggs.* The *fresh,* or *newly-laid eggs* appear semi-transparent when placed between the eye and a strong light. The large end placed against the tongue will also feel warm. If it shakes it is apt to be stale or quite bad ; in fact, a good fresh egg when placed in water sinks quickly, but if stale, they either float or sink slowly.

Some imagine that because eggs are different shades of color, size, and looks, they cannot be all fresh alike. "To every hen belongs an individual peculiarity in the form, color, and size of the egg she lays, and it never changes so long as she remains healthy. Some hens lay smooth, cream-colored eggs, others rough, chalky, granulated ones ; then there is the buff, the snow-white, the spherical, the oval, the pear-shaped, and the emphatically *egg-shaped egg.*"

Duck eggs are of a bluish cast, a little larger than the common fowl's, and the flavor not so delicate; only found in the spring of the year, and then occasionally.

Goose eggs are much larger, whiter, and usually less esteemed. They are scarcely ever seen more than a few lots in the spring.

Guinea hen's eggs.—These are very small, speckled, and considered one of the best flavored; generally found among the *common fowls' eggs.*

Turkeys' and **pea-fowls' eggs** are seldom or ever found in our markets. All of the above are usually mixed with the *common fowls'* when brought to us direct by the neighboring farmers or market-men.

Egg-powder.—The eggs are solidified, or condensed into a dried powder. The white and yolk are reduced by evaporation, then packed in tins, which can be kept any length of time. This *egg-powder* can be used as the fresh eggs for many purposes in cookery.

How to preserve eggs.—Pour a gallon of water upon a pound of quick-lime in a jar. Let it remain about twenty-four hours to cool after its effervescence; procure *eggs* as fresh as you can, and drop them into the jar *gently;* place the jar where you can take out the *eggs without disturbing it,* so the *eggs* will keep good for a twelvemonth. (Trans. Am. Inst., 1855.)

Honey (*in the comb*).—This delicious and nutritive matter is found in our markets, sometimes in great plenty, in the summer and fall months. It is estimated according to the nature of the flower from which it is extracted. The best is found in small boxes (showing one or two sides with glass), the comb well filled with white and handsome honey, which is supposed to be made principally from the white clover; the buckwheat (flower) *honey* is darker, but very sweet. Large hives of *honey* are also found, but it is generally inferior to the above.

Honey (strained), or **Southern honey.**—I believe this kind of *honey* is now seldom found in our markets, or in fact much sought after. Years ago it was very plentiful and cheap, but seldom found as pure as nature made it, which, no doubt, is one cause of its being so little used.

Beeswax.—In the fall months *beeswax* is found quite plenty, in *cakes*, brought in by the dealers in *Southern* and *Western honey*. There is much sold that is impure, not worth half the price of pure.

Maple-sugar.—This product of the forest is found in its season in large quantities for sale in our markets. It begins to make its appearance about the 1st of March, and found quite plenty in April, May, and June. It is often found in small cakes from a quarter to half a pound each, and also in square bars. Some of it is very white, nice-looking, and not very sweet, having been through a bleaching process, which not only takes out the sweetness, but a share of the *maple* flavor; and, again, it is found mixed with common sugar.

Maple syurp and **molasses** is also made in large quantities, but usually sold in large groceries, etc.

A very large production of *Maple Sugar* from one tree is found noticed in the *Commercial Advertiser*, June 13th, 1808, as follows: "Mr. Luke Baker, of Princeton, in the County of Worcester (Massachusetts), during the past season, inserted twenty taps into one maple-tree on his farm, by means of which he drew twenty-three gallons and three quarts of sap in one day, which being boiled into *Sugar* made seven pounds and a quarter; and the whole quantity of *Sugar* made from the same tree this season is thirty-three pounds, which must have required, according to the above proportions, upwards of one hundred and eight gallons of sap. The above facts are given under Mr. Baker's own hand."

Another article in the same paper (January 24, 1814), shows the profit and its advantages in its making at that period. "The high price of foreign sugars will render the manufacture of *Maple Sugar* the ensuing season an object of very great profit to the manufacturer, and of great importance to the country, particularly the interior. With the view of exciting early attention to the subject, we annex some data, derived from a person of experience in the business. He states that his sugar-works, consisting of three hundred and sixty trees, yielded him last season one ton of sugar, and sixty gallons of molasses ; and that the whole labor was performed by one man and a boy, with a yoke of oxen and a sled. Calculating troughs and buckets to last eight years, and to cost twenty-five cents each, the expenditures and receipts would stand nearly thus :

"*Expenses.* Wages of one man six weeks, $30. Do. of one boy the same, $20. Twelve and one-half per cent. of the cost of buckets, $10. Miscellaneous expenses, $25.86. Total expense, $85.86.

"*Receipts.* 2,000 pounds sugar at $20 per cwt., $400. 60 gallons molasses at $1.50 per gallon, $90—makes $490. Deduct expenses—$85.86—leaves clear profit, $404.14."

Sorgum syrup is another *sweet* article lately introduced in our markets, made from a species of cane, somewhat like that of *Broom Corn.* It is very pleasant-tasted, and will readily take the place of the common syrup, or molasses, in the principal uses where the latter is employed. Its sweetening strength is said to be much greater, as a less quantity is required, and with buckwheat and other griddle cakes it is excellent.

Hominy.—There appears but two kinds of this excellent and healthy food prepared for sale, which are usually known as the *small* and *great hominy*, either of which are seldom or ever prepared or cooked ready for sale in the Boston or New York markets ; but in the public markets of Philadelphia, Baltimore, and Washington it is sold in large quantities, not only to the poorer classes, but to all. There the people come as much prepared to purchase it and bring it in their kettles, or dishes, as they do their *Butter.* Many families, no doubt, in either New York, Boston, or elsewhere, who have not the convenience, knowledge, or the time to cook it (and it requires a considerable time to do it properly), would purchase it as quickly as they would *Sausages*, *Head-cheese*, or even *Butter* itself. However, in point of economy for human food, it is said that one *Bushel of Hominy* is equal to *Eight Bushels* of *Potatoes.* The "Plough" says, to prepare it: "Wash slightly in cold water and soak twelve hours in tepid soft water; then boil slowly from three to six hours in the same water, with plenty more added from time to time, with great care to prevent burning. Don't salt while cooking, as that or hard water will harden the corn. When done, add butter and salt; or the better way is to let every one season to suit his taste. It is good hot or cold, and better when warmed over."

Since writing the above, I have found another kind, called **lyed hominy,** which is differently although easily prepared. That is, boil the white field *corn* in *ashes* and water until the husk or skin of the grain is loosened, which takes place in a few minutes; care, however, must be taken that it does not remain too long in the *ashes,* or it will taste of the lye. So soon as the husk is loosened, it must be washed and rubbed through the hands in cold water, until the grain is cleansed from the *ashes* and husk or bran. When wanted to be cooked for the table, it must be scalded and then put to boil in plenty of water, having plenty of hot water to add to it as the first boils down. The grain will burst into a white ball, and become soft when sufficiently done, when it is ready to be eaten, either warm or cold, with milk, cream, etc.

Captain N. Uring informs us how *hominy* was made in Virginia one hundred and forty years ago (1726). He says: "They put such a quantity of corn in steep (*soak*) as they design to boil the next day; and then take a small quantity at a time, and beat it in a wooden mortar, which is made by hollowing a piece of tree, and, with a pestle, beat the corn till it is broken into small pieces, and the husk separated from the grain, which is facilitated by its being soaked in water all night; when they have beaten the quantity they design, they winnow the husk from the grain, and put it into a pot with some few kidney-beans, and a sufficient quantity of water, with a piece of beef or pork, and boil it, and it is excellent, hearty food, very wholesome and well-tasted, and is what most of the poorer sort of people in that country live upon."

Apple-butter is another domestic article which may be properly called a *sauce*, being made of sweet cider, and apples, and is occasionally found in our markets. Large quantities are manufactured in some of the States, more especially in Pennsylvania, where its use is almost universal, being considered one of the necessaries of the table. In its preparation, "the cider is boiled in large kettles, holding from thirty to forty gallons, into which apples, properly pared and quartered, are thrown—say two bushels of prepared apples to twenty-five gallons of cider. After six to eight hours' boiling, during which the liquor is constantly stirred, it begins to thicken, and, when reduced to a tolerable paste, and about the color of chocolate, it is taken from the fire, deposited in earthen jars, and, after standing a few weeks, is of good flavor for use."

Apple-sauce is another similar-made article, except the mashing of the apple. Both of the above are made in large quantities by the Shakers, who put it up in neat and proper packages, when it is readily sold.

Saur-kraut, or **sour-krout**.—This article is found quite plentiful in our markets, usually prepared by the Germans. To make it, take as many hard, firm cabbages as you wish to preserve, tear off the loose leaves, then quarter them, cut out the hearts or stalks, and chop, with a machine or hand, the quarters into small pieces. Then, to every one hundred pounds of cabbage, take three pounds of salt, a quarter of a pound of caraway-seed, and two ounces of juniper-berries; mix them all together. Procure sweet, clean, iron-hooped casks, lay the chopped cabbage three inches deep, then sprinkle each layer, as it is pressed in, with the mixture of salt, caraway-seed, and juniper-berries. After each is full, it must be covered with a linen cloth, and wooden head, then pressed down with heavy weights, and allowed to ferment for a month. The cabbage produces a great deal of water, which must be poured off, and its place supplied with a mixture of warm water, whole black-pepper, and common salt; keeping the cabbage always well covered with brine, and have the casks placed in a cool situation as soon as a sour smell is perceived.

Feathers.—There are two kinds of *feathers* found on birds. The strong and hard kinds found in the wings and tails, especially from *geese* and *swans* are called *quills*, which are used principally for pens; those from other large species are sometimes used in making toys, etc. The soft feathers which cover the bodies of poultry, and most all kinds of birds, as a protection and ornament, are principally used for beds. The best *feathers* are white and downy, and especially those picked from live *geese*, etc. This operation takes place about three times in a season, or when their *feathers* begin to fall, which appears about the 1st of April, then again the middle of June, and again the 1st of September. The *feathers* from birds which were dead when picked are not so much valued, in consequence of the blood being left in the ends, which causes them to smell bad and pack more closely.

Cat-tails, or **meadow-flag.**—The fur or hair of the fruit of this meadow-plant is picked off, when ripe, for several uses, but principally for beds. The broad leaves or flags are much used for chairs and by the coopers, to put between the staves to tighten casks. They are sometimes found here for sale ready prepared for use.

Bulrush, or **rushes.**—I have occasionally seen bunches of these harsh, grating stalks, or rather a sort of green, rough spikes, sheathed into one another, for sale; but for what use here I do not know. In the country they are sometimes used to scrub with. There is, however, a softer kind, which is much used for chair-bottoms, mats, coarse basket-work, etc.

Broom-corn.—This species of the Indian Corn is grown principally for making the common whisk-brooms. There appears but two kinds, and both have friends; these are the *tall* and *dwarf*. The seeds are used more for replanting, but are frequently sold for feed, and, by some, considered nearly as good as oats. Many years ago *whisk-brooms* were made by some farmers, who brought and sold them in the markets. They were rather clumsy-looking, but excellent wearing brooms; the handles, more especially, if not handsomely turned, claimed smoothness and great strength. A "broomstick," then, laid across the shoulders or head by the angry housewife, was generally a *settler*.

It is recorded in the *Washington Sun* (1837), that broom-corn, now cultivated to so profitable an extent in this country, owes its cultivation to Dr. Franklin's acute mind. A lady of Philadelphia held an imported clothes *whisk* in her hand, and, while examining it as a novelty, he found a single grain still attached to the stalk; this he planted, and a large, increasing article of usefulness has been thus perpetuated in the United States.

Christmas greens.—A few days before Christmas, a great many wagons, etc., are brought to the markets loaded with the tops, limbs, and young evergreen trees of spruce, pines, firs, cedars for "Christmas-trees;" also the running ground-vines, or running pines, etc., tied up in bunches, ropes, stars, hoops, figures, etc., ornamented with little red winter-berries, painted paper-flowers, etc., to ornament various public and private houses on Christmas day. The streets about some of our public markets are sometimes piled up along the gutters, or on wagons, from square to square; besides, hundreds of loads are brought in and delivered directly to the purchasers.

Birch brooms.—Large numbers of these coarse *brooms*, made principally of *birch twigs*, or *shoots*, by many of the farm laborers, when there is nothing else to do in the winter months, are sold at, or peddled about, the markets. Many are used by the butchers, street-sweepers, etc.

Baskets.—Many years ago *baskets* of all sorts, sizes, and kinds, among which were the *bushel* (full measure), the round handle, the flat and the square baskets, were sold in our markets, usually in the spring of the year, by our thrifty farmers, being the productions of their winter's labor; and if they were not so handsomely *turned*, they were strongly made, "not for a day," but until you were satisfied that your money was not laid out in *trash*. These remarks will lead me to notice the

Bushel baskets.—Large quantities of apples, pears, peaches, potatoes, etc., are sold by the *basket*, and often represented as a *bushel basket*. *This bushel basket* is a mere figure of speech, which signifies that if filled with peaches, pears, or plums, they will actually measure about *half a bushel*—if apples or potatoes, about *three pecks*, or five baskets out of three. If the fair-dealing producer should ask a reasonable price for an honest *bushel basket* of apples, say one dollar, and another dealer close by, with a *bushel basket of three pecks*, asks eighty-seven and a half cents, the latter will sell his produce much sooner than the other, because the price for his *bushel basket* of *three pecks* is lower, when, in reality, the honest *bushel basket* is the cheapest.

The only reason that I can give for this is, that many who go to market imagine that every basket represented as a *bushel basket* should contain a bushel *measure*, and that no one would *dare* to sell short measure in such a *basket*, and in such a public place; therefore, for the protection of both the purchaser and the honest dealer, a law should be so framed and put in force, as to either compel the restoration of the *full bushel basket*, or else have every *basket* marked according to its true capacity.

There are also a great many *barrels* of articles which come to our markets, like the *bushel baskets*, are frauds on the purchasers, and in defiance of the law which regulates the size of apple, pear, and potato barrels; the uniform size of which is fixed at that of a flour *barrel*, and none smaller than that can be used, on penalty of the loss of whatever the *barrel* may contain, besides a fine as an additional punishment for swindling.

This also calls my attention to a truthful statement

found in that excellent paper, the *American Agriculturist*, headed—

"FARMERS' TRICKS OF TRADE.—The following from a correspondent needs no comment: 'Of two Long Island farmers, one warmly contended that *custom* sanctioned putting the largest and finest potatoes, apples, pears, peaches, etc., on top of the basket or barrel, for if this is not done, they bring lower prices. The other, who was more conscientious, said he could not do it, notwithstanding custom sanctioned it, and he was aware that he got less for his fruit and vegetables than his neighbor did. As a buyer for family use, I listened attentively, and regretted to find that the majority of buyers, or market-men, at least, are thus paid a premium for what I should term deception, if not dishonesty. For a long time I have observed this tendency to make the finest show upon the outside; and when I wish to buy a basket of apples or peaches, I have to ask the dealer to pour them out, to see how the bottom compares with the top. What says the *Agriculturist* to so glaring an evil? Shall we not rather encourage uprightness in all our dealings, than countenance deception in any way? I know of parties who have bought what they supposed to be fine baskets of fruit, judging from the outside appearance, and finding them so very inferior generally, they have resolved never to deal with such sellers again. As it now is, a person is certainly liable to be deceived, unless he overhauls every package of fruit or vegetables coming to market. As far as one purchaser is concerned, I am resolved to purchase of such persons as the conscientious dealer referred to, when I can thus encourage honesty rather than duplicity.'"

What usually makes a bushel:—"Sixty pounds of *wheat*, *Irish potatoes*, *beans*, or *clover-seed*; fifty-six pounds of *shelled corn*, *rye*, or *barley*; forty-five pounds of *timothy*, *flax*, or *hemp seed*; seventy pounds of *corn on the cob*; thirty-six pounds of *oats*; fifty-two pounds of *buckwheat*; fifty-seven pounds of *sweet patatoes*; forty-seven pounds of *onions*;

thirty-three pounds of *dried peaches;* twenty pounds of *bran*, etc.

I will also add here a few remarks on the articles usually sold by weight, that come in kegs, boxes, or other packages, which, to those who don't know, will be information, under the head of

Gross, tare, and **net weights.**—In buying large quantities of butter, lard, honey, etc., in the packages in which they are brought in, either barrels, boxes, firkins, tubs, etc., if the whole package is weighed it is called the gross weight. The *tare* is the weight of the empty barrel, box, etc., which should be weighed before the article is put in, and marked distinctly on the package, directly under the *gross weight.* The *tare* is deducted from the *gross*, which leaves the net weight of the article to be paid for, and the package as agreed upon.

Pot-plants, roots, and **bouquets,** in the spring and early summer months, are found on some of the stands, which are usually located on the outside of the public markets, where light and air are advantageous to the life and growth of the numerous varieties of *plants* and *roots*, commonly wanted at this period of the year. Here are found the delicate hot-house and open-air plants, usually ornamented with many beautiful and varied-colored flowers, while young fruit-trees, bushes, and shrubs are looking their greenest and prettiest close by; then behind these are seen the rusty-looking grape-vines and other roots which partially lie covered and cared for, so that at least there is life enough left to successfully transplant each one to a more generous home. Most of the flowering plants are usually found in bloom, having been forced into that state by the florists, as they are found to be most salable, or rather that they more readily take the fancy of the general purchaser. So numerous are the varieties found, that to give a proper description of each of them would require so many pages—already fully described in other works—that to attempt a description here would perhaps deter those in want from at least a visit to the various stands, where these natural and cultivated beauties of the floral life are sold.

Among these are many rare and choice plants, besides elegant *bouquets*, some of which are quite elaborately prepared for those whose purse corresponds with their tastes, while thousands are found merely formed of a few of the common or wild flowers of the season. Their sale is not confined to the outside stands altogether, but also to many hucksters and others, who have them in various months of the year ; all, however, are usually sold at reasonable rates, by which a large business has grown up in this department of the public markets products.

ECONOMY IN THE USE OF MEATS:

AND

HUNG MEATS.

Economy in cooking should be studied and practised by all, as many a wholesome dish or dinner can be prepared for a very small sum, especially butcher's meat, the principal part of which is sold and used in a fresh state.

There are many parts of an animal which are sold many cents per pound cheaper than some which are called choice cuts or pieces ; at least *three parts* of the animal is of this former class of meat, which will not generally bring the first cost per pound that the whole animal cost, and this is one reason why the other *quarter* part brings the higher charged prices. This large portion of the animal comprises the chuck-ribs, rounds, cross-ribs, tops-of-sirloins, plates, navels, briskets, flanks, neck-pieces, leg-pieces, legs and shins of beef, shoulders of mutton or veal, liver, haslets, hearts, sheep-heads, etc., all good for various dishes, either a roast-in-the-pot (a country cooked dish), stewing, boiling, bouilli, soups, and some are even good for a plain roast or a good steak, etc.

The English make excellent dishes of cow-heels, sheeps-trotters, melts, lights, etc., while the Germans of the entrails of calves make into a dish which I found to be excellent eating; and we find that each nation, as well as family, has its peculiar manner of cooking nearly every joint of meat as of other articles of food.

There are many people of limited means who "do marketing," seem to have no desire or wish to practise economy, but rather to appear extravagant, if it lies in their power, by purchasing every thing at the highest prices, more especially where credit is given; others do this rather to live on the labor of other people than rely on their own. Some there are who have a large family, for instance, want a roast of about twelve pounds weight, of either beef, veal, or mutton, who think nothing else will do but a choice rib or sirloin, or a fillet or loin of veal, or leg or saddle of mutton, will answer, which, at a cost of eighteen and three-quarter cents per pound, amounts to two dollars and thirty-five cents, when a cross-rib, or chuck-rib, or shoulder of veal, or fore quarter of mutton, of the same weight, would cost about one dollar or one dollar and twenty-five cents; then the latter, if prepared by a plain country cook, would make either joint quite as tender, juicy, as well relished, and in reality more eatable than that which costs nearly or quite half as much more, when prepared by *many* of our modern cooks.

Again, there are some who, if they had but twenty-five cents in the whole world to lay out in meat, they would select a "pound of the best porter-house steak," or a "pound of veal cutlets"—not a taste hardly for two persons, but it must do for six—when, if laid out for a three or four pound piece for bouilli, or soup, or a common stew, would be a bountiful supply of food for all. Yes, twenty cents worth of meat and ten cents worth of beans or peas, or some other good, low-priced vegetables, would make a much more wholesome, nutritious, and economical meal than would a four-pound sirloin steak make alone, at a cost of seventy-five cents or a dollar. I have often observed that those who plead against the dearness and extravagant prices of meat, and who I have offered a six or seven pounds beef's heart, which would make them *two good nutritious meals*, refuse to take it at a cost of fifteen cents only ; they would rather pay their last dollar for half as much meat in an expensive *steak* or *chop*. This is one of the chief causes why the few prime parts are so high-priced.

Sometimes, however, we find persons who were brought up in the country among our thrifty farmers, fail not to remember the precepts the good housekeeper, their mother, who had taught them the great domestic *accomplishment* of producing an economical dinner from an ordinary part of any joint of meat. I am also sorry, as I am free to say, that this *one* accomplishment, so necessary to every woman housekeeper, and so useful to the economy of every-day life, is not taught now-a-days ; it is not even hinted at in any of our schools or seminaries.

Hung meats.—Meats should be *hung* long enough to grow tender ; if too long it becomes dry, loses its juices, flavor and weight, and if not hung long enough it is found tough and hard. It should also be hung where the air is clear and cool, but not in a strong current, as then it will dry out its juices. It is said that if you steam a tough piece of meat for a half an hour, then roast it in the ordinary manner, it will be tender. I have no doubt but this process will assist it, but I think at the expense of a loss of much of its sweetness. The loss in cooking meats—when roasted is about *one third*, and in boiling about *one quarter*.

BLEEDING ANIMALS.

The practice of bleeding cattle, calves, sheep, and lambs before slaughtering them, is almost done away with in the city of New York ; there are, however, a few who still continue it.

The public generally begin to understand which is the

best meat—that from the animal which has been *bled* two or three times, until all the *sweet juices* have been extracted, or that from animals which have not been *bled*, having all the natural excellent juices remaining.

I think it must convince every thinking person that by taking (two or three days before the animal is killed) from thirty to fifty quarts of blood from a *steer* or an *ox*, such practice, by drawing the life of the flesh, which is *blood*, will reduce and weaken the animal to such an extent as to render it incapable of eating its usual quantity of food, thereby causing a sick, feverish, and thirsty condition. Water being placed before the animal in its feverish state, it drinks largely to supply the liquid deprived from the flesh by this bleeding, as well as to relieve a feverish thirst. As a consequence the rich, thick, red blood is drawn from the animal and newly replaced by a large quantity of water. This watery mixture is drawn back through the veins and flesh, which has the effect of thinning and whitening, or of producing the desired handsome, light, and clear-colored beef, so stupidly sought after, and which is generally so much admired by those who have more regard for and knowledge of appearances they possess for these negative attributes, which alike demonstrate the unsterling value, not only in man but in the meats of beasts as well.

In *Calves*, this bleeding process is still worse, as it—for the sake of whiteness—exhausts what little juice or sweetness there is in *Veal*, leaving it a dry, insipid, and tasteless flesh.

If, however, the calf should be immediately killed, fresh or direct from the cow, without bleeding, the *veal* will be natrally white, tender, juicy, and wholesome food. On the other hand, the startling facts present themselves that much of the flesh called *Veal*, sold about our cities, really is not fit for human food, in consequence either of its tender age, starvation, bleeding, and the inhuman manner of conveying these (and some other) animals through our streets to their destination, or all combined. I have known instances where young *calves* have been taken from the *cow* in the morning, rode some fifteen or twenty miles through a hot sun to the market-boats or railroad station, then through the night brought on to the city, the next morning purchased up by the butchers (or rather by some of those who conduct the business), who are sometimes cruel enough to pack some fifteen or twenty in a cart, with legs tied and heads hanging over the sides; then carried over the rough pavement to the place of their destination, when they are often found injured and in a half-smothered condition; this, with their continued bleating and starvation, for sometimes from twenty to fifty hours (and I have known them to be in pens afterwards for a week or more without proper food). When killed, the veal of such treated animals will be very red, veiny—the result of this feverish state. Such veal would not sell so well as if it had been whitened, as is usually done, by the bleeding process. This is one of the just causes for complaint against this poor, insipid, tasteless, and unwholesome veal.

Thousands of *calves*, or their flesh, are brought and sold in our cities, of an age altogether too young for human food. Sometimes they are found not above three days old, while the majority of all brought are not ten days old; and this kind of flesh is principally sold throughout our cities, especially in those places called "cheap meat shops" or "private markets," often by men who purchased it ready *dressed*, and who really do not know whether it is the flesh of a dog or *calf*.

This fact is shown in a police court, by the testimony produced before Justice Perry, of Williamsburg, Long Island, which is set forth in the *Daily Tribune*, April 6, 1855. One of the witnesses—George Pessinger—who had been a regular butcher for forty years, states that "he saw nine quarters of plated veal hanging up in a meat-shop in Grand-street, which, if the whole nine quarters were tried out, after taking away the pork-fat, which the kidneys were plated with, enough fat could not be got out to grease a jackknife. Butchers call this *bob-veal*. I consider this meat very unwholesome; it was very young, and had been starved either here, or while it was being brought here."

The defendant wished to procure the Washington Market butcher of whom he purchased the flesh, to prove that it was *good veal*.

"Pessinger asked accused if he knew whether the meat in question was *veal* or *dog-meat*. The accused answered that he '*did not know*, but he supposed it must be *veal*, as he bought it for that.'"

Another instance is worthy of record, in which *justice* was done to a *Justice*, found in the *Herald*, March, 1857, and headed "*Unsound meat venders*—justice to New Jersey.—The case of Justice of the Peace D——n, from Ramapo, N. J., came up for trial. It will be recollected that Justice D——n was arrested for selling *premature veal* in Washington Market a few days since, and in the absence of bail to the amount of five hundred dollars, was locked up in the Tombs. He plead guilty to the charge. Judge Russell was disposed to send him up for the term of thirty days, but upon the representation that Esquire D——n had already suffered great loss in this transaction—1st, the veal, valued by him at sixty dollars; 2d, time, five days in the Tombs; 3d, twenty-five dollars which he paid to certain 'Tombs' skinners or 'shysters,' who pledged to procure him bail, and of course failed to redeem their pledges. His Honor, Judge Russell, after giving him unmistakable assurance that a repetition of the offence would demand the severest penalty of the law, let him off with a fine of twenty-five dollars, which he promptly paid. Justice D——n, after congratulating himself and friends upon his safe deliverance from the Tombs, took the cars for his rural home in Ramapo."

No calf should be permitted to be sold (for *veal*) until it is four weeks old; again, more care should be bestowed on the feeding and conveying them from place to place.

Many country people, however, carry them in a proper

manner; that is, untied in a pen placed on wagon-wheels, which plan should be employed in our cities, either by the large dealers or the cartmen, who would be patronized by those, at least, who had a spark of humanity towards dumb animals.

I have known sheep to have been similarly bled, and even have heard of lambs having also been bled. This, I believe, is now seldom done in this country. In England, however, it appears much practised, and lately I read of a butcher having been arrested at Oxford for "cruelty to animals," and fined five pounds, with one pound costs. The cruelty stated was, the butcher "having possessed himself of the knife, he seized the head of one of the *lambs* and made a deep incision under each of its eyes. The knife was blunt, and the blood not flowing freely at first, defendant again applied the knife, drawing it across the creature's face several times, until the blood spirted out in a stream. The same operation was repeated on the other *lambs*, one of which fainted from the loss of blood," etc. The butcher said in his defence "there was no cruelty at all in the act complained of, in proof of which he had practised it himself for nearly forty years." He added, "that if these animals were not bled in the manner complained of, the flesh would not look so white as some *carcasses* to which he directed the officer's attention."

Ram mutton is generally of a dark color, and I have often seen them bled in this manner to whiten the meat, so that it would appear like wether mutton; this, however, is a cruel way of torturing before killing the animal. As I have before observed, this bleeding practice is almost discontinued. I am happy to say few respectable butchers are now guilty of this cruelty. It is a wrong and barbarous act, which secures nothing but whiteness or presumed handsome-colored meats, at the expense of weight and the fine sweet juices which make the sappy, sweet-flavored, and wholesome meats.

COOKS AND COOKERY.

It was the saying of some ancient Epicurean philosopher "that eating is the chief end of man." If this view be correct, and we will admit that it is correct, so that the subject of cooks and cookery can be here illustrated by another popular axiom, that the Almighty sends us meats and his Satanic majesty sends us cooks. As a rule, our readers will admit this to be a truism. The object, then, of good cookery is paramount to the happiness of man. To this end good cooks become a necessity, and no doubt would be, and are, highly estimated when possessed. We, unlike people of other nations, call cooks *cooks*, and nothing else. We do not recognize them by the name of *artists.* To a certain extent, however, they are artists—artists catering to the *internal*, contra-distinguishing those artists who appeal to the *externals.*

The extent of attributes, invention, practical experience, genius, taste, are all to be found in cooks of the first class. Cookery has become so important an art, that the highest order of cooks are acknowledged as well as admitted as one holding an honorable and important position in society.

An eminent author says: "No person can be a good cook who is not at the same time a chemist, a botanist, a physiologist, a draughtsman, and even something of a geometrician. Independent of these required requisites, he had need be endowed with many natural gifts; for he must have a keen scent, a delicate sense of taste and touch, with a quick ear, else he will ever be liable to be deceived as to the state and maturing of meats, the due seasoning of ragouts, the *doneness* of the boiled and roast, the stewing of the viands, the condition of the various pastes. It is of the last importance, therefore, that a cook should be perfect in his corporeal senses, and ready in his mental ones."

"A master cook! why he's the man of men
For a professor. He designs, he draws,
He paints, he carves, he builds, he fortifies,
Makes citadels of curious *fowl* and *fish*.

"Some he dry-dishes, some motes round with broth,
Mounts *marrow-bones*, cuts fifty-angled custards,
Rears bulwark pies, and for his outer works
He raiseth ramparts of immortal crusts!"—Ben Jonson.

Some families are fortunate in securing good cooks, while hundreds complain daily of having bad ones; and their usual complaints are: "We cannot get them; they are not to be had, even at very high wages. We look through the advertisements in the daily papers, and numbers we find which, from description, are just the thing we want; so we note down in our memoranda some ten or twenty of those who are 'to be seen between the hours of twelve and two—for two days.' When we look over our list they appear so scattered, that we feel almost discouraged; but their advertisements read so well—just such as we want exactly—that we expect the first visited will suit us.

"Our start is made, and we run ourselves up and down a half-dozen 'third-story back rooms,' from one side of the town to the other, in the most filthy places of our city; in fact, so filthy that we would prefer almost anybody to cook for us rather than take up with persons that advertise in such quarters, their boarding and lodging retreats; finally we are worn down, sick, and tired almost to death, without the possibility of being suited. As a last resort, we then apply at the Intelligence office, and find it crowded with some fifty or a hundred servants. Ten or fifteen *good cooks* are presented to us that 'can come well recommended.' We question them as to their knowledge, etc., and find they know something; but they, in turn, like the 'advertisers,' want to know how large the family is, how many afternoons and evenings they can have in the week, what nights they can have a '*little company*,' what perquisites are allowed, etc. The first six girls will also tell you that there is work enough in your family for one or two assistants (besides your other help); others will say they have always been allowed two or more afternoons in a week, etc., etc.; and finally they will dwindle down to *one*, which you in despair conclude to try for *one week*. The first day she has a *steak* to cook. She puts it down to broil over a miserable, poor, *hard-coal* fire, where it is left to dry up (instead of cooking), when, by the time dinner is ready, the steak having previously passed through the process of what they call *broiling*, has been placed in the oven to keep hot until ready to be served. At the table it is brought before the carver, who enters upon his duties; he commences by complaining of his *dull knife*, and by the time he has served all, the 'dull knife' complaint has become general all around the table, until some one discovers that it is the *steak*—a *tough steak*—dry, insipid, tasteless; and all now believe that the fault is alone in the *steak*. Then the *butcher* 'takes it,' not on, but behind, his back, and it may be with truth that he is the guilty individual. But the *good cook* will certainly know whether the *steak* is tough or not before it is laid on a bed of hot coals." If she finds it a really tough *steak*, she will have the rough-faced mallet to work until she is satisfied that there will not be much complaint when it is served up direct from the quick fire and the gridiron. It is not alone the steak, but to all joints of meat, more especially corned beef, that this language applies. Corned beef seldom if ever is properly cooked. I here illustrate an instance where such complaints as here mentioned came from two of our most respectable families. The complaint came from the family of the married daughter, in relation to corned beef. I was repeatedly told that I gave to her father's family better corned beef than to the daughter. I wished to impress her mind such was not the case; that the apparent inferiority of the corned beef supplied to her was caused by inferior cookery! "That," she said, "could not be, as their cook was old, experienced, and a very good one." I replied, "The next piece of corned beef you receive send it to your father's cook, and let her prepare it for you." Previous to this I had (from these causes of complaint) taken two of the same kind of pieces, and from the same animal, and arranged it so that they both had their corned beef near at the same time. The usual report came back, that the father's meat was excellent, and that of the daughter very indifferent. Not long after this, the daughter, making her marketing, frankly confessed to me, "I begin to think that it is not so much the fault with your corned beef, as it is in the cooking of it. I ate of your corned beef, which I sent to my father's yesterday, and there had it cooked; it was perfectly delicious. In fact, I always get good corned beef there." "Yes," I rejoined, "they have a good cook there, especially for preparing corned beef."

I was once informed by an old patron how he and his wife learned to cook corned beef. He said: "Soon after we were married, some 30 years ago, I had a job of carpenter work to do on Staten Island, which required some three or four hands to complete, and as we could not work the regular hours, in consequence of having to conform to the ferry-boats' time of leaving at both ends of the route—that is, to go down with the first boat in the morning and leave with the last in the evening—which made the hours of work between eight, A. M., and four, P. M., so that we had only time enough to make a hasty meal at noon, and then continue until the time for the last boat. Well, as I had to furnish this *hasty* meal, I thought it best to have a piece of corned beef boiled that night, so that we could carry a part with us. A good-sized piece was procured, and it was quite late before it began to boil; my wife, however, not being very well, retired to bed, and as I had been hard to work all day, two hours watching the pot and beef began to tell upon me, and I concluded to lay down and leave a slow fire under the pot, not thinking, however, but I would wake up about the time it was done; or, I concluded if it did cook pretty well it would do no harm; and sure enough, it must have simmered slowly until the fire went out, perhaps some seven or eight hours. We awoke early, and the first thought was of the meat in the pot, with the conclusion that it would be all in pieces, or else soggy and tasteless; it was, however, lifted out whole, and being almost cold, it was cut and tasted; we found it to be tender, sweet, and juicy, and my men thought, as well as all who tasted it that day, that never was eaten such a delicious piece of corned beef. Since that time my corned beef, hams, tongues, or any kind of salted meat intended to boil, is put over early and left to slowly boil or simmer a long time, and after it is done the pot is lifted off the fire, when the meat is allowed to cool in the pot from twenty minutes to half an hour. Following this process we always have good boiled meat, and so say all our friends who sit at my table and partake of them."

Very many of our *good* cooks, if asked "if they know how to cook a potato?" "Why, yes; anybody can cook a potato!" they most indignantly reply; but when their capability is tested (it may not be the first or the second day) the potatoes will be found either underdone, or overdone, spoiled by being too hard, or heavy, or soggy and watery—when this *good* cook will tell you the potatoes have been boiled the usual time.

My experience informs me that a cook knowing how and always cooking potatoes well, that she will generally be found a tolerable *good plain cook*, she having then at least the character of watchfulness and ordinary judgment, two qualifications very essential to the cook.

Cruikshank, in his "Omnibus," gives some humorous remarks, while relating the trouble in obtaining a good cook. He says: "We have just had another new cook; but too sure I am that, like the whole tribe of cooks that enter our family, she will never pass the boundaries of the cognomen of new cook. All our cooks have been new. The oldest one we have ever had, in my remembrance, was a prodigy of a month's service in our kitchen; and although it must be confessed that, even during that period, she was twice threatened or warned by my mother, her long stay was astonishing to us all. Compared with her predecessors she was quite a fixture in the house.

"It would take up too much room to detail one-half of the discrepancies of our cooks. One, as my maiden aunt delicately observes, becomes quite inebriated—off she goes. Another has *followers*—off she goes. Another increases her kitchen stuff, at the expense of the fat of the meat, which she cuts off to a nicety (and my father is particularly fond of fat)—off she goes. Another cannot cook a potato—off she goes. Another forms a clandestine match with the butler after a week's intimacy—off she goes—he, too, falling a victim and losing his place.

"When I say that my mother seldom overlooks the first offence, I explain pretty clearly how it is that every week finds us with a new cook. On the day of their engagement, my sanguine parent invariably tells us she has found a treasure; a cook with such a character—never drinks—no followers—so honest—can cook any thing—such a woman for making made-up (sometimes called French) dishes, etc. In a few days this treasure of a cook turns out to be, without a single exception, the very worst we ever had to endure (for it rather singularly happens that each in succession is the very worst). 'Oh, that dreadful woman!' is the cry. She boils what she should roast, and roasts what she should boil; she is a snuff-taker, and almost every thing she cooks is supposed to savor of *Lundy-foot* or *Prince's mixture*—off she goes, before we find out a fair half of her intolerable propensities.

"The last treasure we had only cooked our dinner on one day! She must have been a practitioner in some wholesale cooking establishment—cook to an ordinary on a grand scale, where dinner for a hundred and forty was daily prepared. We had to dine on cold meat for a week after she left us. You must know, that, on the first day of her instalment in office, the butcher had been directed (we live a few miles from town, and at a distance from any market-place) to send us a supply of animal food sufficient to last for about eight days. There were a leg of mutton, a saddle of mutton, a sirloin of beef, a round of beef, and various other small knick-knacks for side-dishes. Well, my dear, credulous mother received the new cook as usual. She found her to be a most enormous treasure; and she can, at this day, make affidavit, if necessary, that she gave her the proper directions about the dinner. On the day the circumstances I am about to relate took place, we had merely the family at dinner. On entering the dining-room, I observed my mother gently start, as her eye encountered a great number of large dishes round the table. She, however, suppressed her astonishment, took her place at the head of the table (my father never carved), said grace, and was sinking slowly into her chair as the servant raised the first cover. My mother instantly started up, exclaimed in a tone of alarm, and with turned-up eyes, 'Mercy on us! the leg of mutton!' All eyes turned in a moment upon the uncovered mutton, and then on my agitated mother. The servant, after a pause, laid his hand upon the second cover, upon which my mother had bent her looks. Up went the cover, amidst curling wreaths of steam. 'Good gracious! look at the sirloin!' cried my mother. We all looked accordingly at the sirloin, but without discovering in it any thing peculiarly different from other sirloins. The removal of the next cover exhibited the round of beef: another exclamation from my mother. We now all commenced staring, first at the joints, then at my mother, and then at each other. We certainly began to think, when a fourth joint had appeared in view, that *there was* 'something wrong.' A pause ensued; my father broke it. 'In the name of wonder,' said he, 'what's the matter?' 'O that new cook!' answered my mother, with a groan. 'What has she done?' inquired my father. '*The whole week's marketing!*' said my mother, sinking into a chair, for she had been standing all this time."

Many families, hotels, steamboats, etc., leave all their household and other accounts, as well as the choosing tradesmen, in the hands of their stewards, housekeepers, waiters, cooks, or other help. Many of these make it a rule to select such tradesmen only who, by them, are either compelled or voluntarily pay them bribes (or *vails*, as they are called in England), sometimes to very large amounts, to retain them as their customers. For such perquisites to the servants, of course, the employers are overcharged to make up the amounts paid.

Then, again, the *help* is generally complimented in kind or pay, in proportion to the amount of the *bills*—that is, the greater the amount of the bills, the greater the bribe is given. The consequence of all this is, that such kind of *help* will manage to consume or waste, as much as possible, the various articles, in order to receive a bribe in due proportion to their consumption. This bribing custom has been introduced by the *foreign airs* and *foreign* practices of our *foreign help*, who have introduced and taught their art and usage from the large cities of Europe, and who, absurd as it may appear, will not *employ any of our respectable families*, unless they are permitted to act the financial medium between them and their trades-people. These foreign *garçons* must select the grocer, the butcher, the baker, the poulterer, the fishermen, etc., and of course those tradesmen are selected who have the most elastic consciences and purses, and who will faithfully screen the servant's rascalities and merited disgrace.

While showing up the dishonesty of our foreign help, perhaps it may not be deemed impertinent to the point to show the *modus operandi* of those who encourage in this respect the servant's dishonesty. A respectable and conscientious cook, in whom her employers had the utmost confidence, informed me that a butcher close by my stand had offered her a *ten-dollar bill* to induce her employer to trade with him: finding that he could not bribe her to trade with him, he attempted to pass off the proposition as a joke; but as similar attempts had been made by him upon other servants with success, he was treated accordingly.

The worst feature befalling these persons in such cases is, that although these dealers may occasionally be successful in inducing servants to change trades-people by such discreditable means resorted to, yet sooner or later, they are apt to be discovered, and then the trader or family is not only lost to both the new as well as the old dealers, and very often the market also; as many conscience-stricken do not like to be seen changing from one dealer to another, they of course do not wish to acknowledge their mistakes by returning to their old places of dealing. The fact is there are heads of many families who are not aware of the iniquity and injury done by many of these named dealers, with their *foreign aids* and domestic *help.* My evidence, however, is now in relation to the two latter, proceeding with several instances from my experience of the peculiar *help,* which many families have found, to their cost, more plentiful than those of the more faithful.

The family of a prominent merchant, residing in the Fifth Avenue, for several years had dealt satisfactorily, I believe, with the author. This family was *fortunate!* enough in securing the services of foreign help (respectively cook and waiter), in the persons of man and his wife. The wife (cook) was supplied with a pass-book to market with, and thereby not having the opportunity of cheapening, or purchasing articles of inferior qualities, and *pocketing* the difference in her favor, as if she had been supplied with the ready money daily to make the market purchases; but at the end of the month, when the monthly bill was paid by her, she demanded "*percentage,*" as she called it, for herself. "What do you mean by *percentage?*" I demanded. "Why," she says, "I mean five per cent., of course, on all butchers' bills, and other tradesmens' bills, as are allowed in England." "Well, to be sure," I replied, "as yet we have not, in this country, arrived at that state of tradesmen's perfection in trading with servants, when we shall have to rob the employer to bribe the servants with *five per cent.* on their bills when they are paid. If your employer does not pay you wages enough ask him for more; but you cannot introduce those terms here."* She was highly indignant, and flounced away with a threat that she would not patronize me again; *and she did not.* Soon after she was successful in finding a place to trade, where, I suppose, she received her *five per cent.*

In a note to her employer (with whom I was not personally acquainted; he, as many other heads of families, never go to market), I informed him of the circumstances. The note was *not answered,* and I felt as if their absence, under the circumstances, was more profitable and satisfactory to me than their custom, so long as they countenanced the dishonesty of their help.

The following presents another phase. The cook of one of my patrons, who had been dealing with me twelve or fourteen years, who once in a while came to me for her marketing, about Christmas time gave me several hints that something from me was expected for her "Christmas-box." Christmas came, and with it her importunities. "Well, what can I give you?" I asked. She replied "that their trade was large, and it was by her repeated intercession or I would have lost it long ago," and finished up the unblushing demand, that she could not expect less from me than a *ten-dollar gold piece!* "Now," I observed, "do you think that I would be doing right to present you with this amount of money? If so, then I ought not to give less than one hundred others, who have the same right to ask from me the same amount as you have demanded."

This reasoning did not strike her with sufficient force to satisfy her. Before she left she had reduced her demand to a *five-dollar gold piece* as a 'Christmas-box' gift. I am pleased to put it on record, *she did not get it.* As she was leaving, she gave me to understand that it was the last month the *family* would patronize me. I paid no attention to her threat. About two weeks after this incident I had a

* On one occasion an employer, being informed of his servant's act, valuing her services, authorized me to pay the percentage and add the same to his bill.

visit from (the lady) the head of the family, who told me the meats I sent her were not so good as those formerly sent, that her cook complained very much about the quality, etc. I told the lady that I expected to have heard this complaint before, and I also told her about the demand for a "Christmas-box"—and further, that I must decline serving her so long as she kept that cook, as she would *spoil* every joint of meat I should send her, unless she was watched. In a few days the lady sent me word that she had changed her cook.

Another instance of a character different from this occurred a few years ago. A young (and no doubt a happy) couple commenced their career in marketing by dealing with me. As their family (of course) was not large, they often had a small steak or a few chops. The young husband (as he had, jokingly, once or twice before) observed to me, "Why don't you send me some *tenderloin* in our steaks?—we always have it when we *dine out*." "I generally do," I replied, "when you order such." "Well, but we don't get it," he rejoined. "Then there must be some wrong with my help or your cook," I continued. "I will send you a steak to-day, with a good *tenderloin* in it;" which *tenderloin* I marked in his presence, which I requested him to see whether his cook or anybody else cut any of it off, before it was placed on the table. He went home and informed his wife of the intended watch on the *tenderloin*. When the steak was served, lo! the *tenderloin* was missing, and he informed me that the cook shortly after was also *missing*.

The following *squib* offers another feature of similar doings. A gentleman addressed his servant, "James, I have always placed the greatest confidence in you; now tell me, James, how is it that my butcher's bills are so large, and that I always have such bad dinners?" "Really, sir, I don't know, for I am sure we never have *any thing nice in the kitchen, that we don't send some of it up in the parlor*."

INDEX

TO THE VARIOUS JOINTS AND OTHER PARTS USED IN THE DOMESTIC OR TAME ANIMALS.

WILD ANIMALS.

POULTRY.

WILD FOWL.

BIRDS CALLED GAME.

FISH.

VEGETABLES, POT AND MEDICINAL HERBS, POT-PLANTS, ROOTS, Etc.

FRUITS AND NUTS.

DAIRY AND HOUSEHOLD PRODUCTS.

GENERAL INDEX.

THE MARKET-BOOK.

BY THOMAS F. DE VOE,

MEMBER OF THE NEW YORK HISTORICAL SOCIETY.

In Two Volumes, Octavo, (about 650 pages each.)

THE introduction of the First Volume of "THE MARKET-BOOK" has brought forth several commendatory notices from the "press" and from several prominent individuals, of which extracts have been introduced in the following pages. The first edition having been long exhausted, another (revised) will appear, with the Second Volume, which will soon be ready for the press.

"It furnishes a mass of information difficult to be found elsewhere, and gleaned by you from sources few seek, and fewer investigate with the care and patience which you have exhibited. There are many recitals and telling incidents which deepen the interest and give attraction to the work.

"In its perusal, I was reminded of a remark made by Hallam in his 'Middle Ages,' when referring to the 'History of France' by the Fathers of St. Maur, that you might dive at random in it, and could not fail to bring up some curious fact. I write from memory; but such is the purport, if not the words of his observation. So I hold the result to be in regard to your work.

"What a contrast between the 'Old Burgher Butchers,' whom you characteristically describe, and their *fast* descendants! The change in the spelling of the ancestral names are not greater than the altered mode of living and the luxurious habits which mark their generations, in our day. Some have reflected honor on the parent stem, whilst others have endeavored to kick away the ladder on which they rose. The human race but repeats itself, and with innate tendencies would run into excess, but for the file which a growing religious sentiment applies to remove its defects and polish its surface.

"Your well-arranged index is a most valuable aid, and is copious and sententious. The theme of your second volume is fruitful with varied and useful topics of great public utility." — *Frederic De Peyster, Esq.*

"I must take leave to add how very creditable it is to you as an historian and an author.

"Your research is thorough, so that you are an example to others for its fidelity: you are never led away by chimeras that form the romance of history; but show yourself in every page a lover of truth and a diligent and successful searcher after truth.

The style of your work has everywhere that first merit of clearness; and is often more elegant, I assure you, than that of many who are professed scholars. I am glad, too, to respond to the fine patriotic spirit which pervades your work: I agree with you fully that 'we must watch, guard, and battle, if necessary, that the Union may be preserved.'" —*Hon. George Bancroft.*

"It has been so much the habit to make History the mere record of wars, of the quarrels of kings, and the intrigues of politicians, that of the more immediate interests of the daily life of peoples, their customs, their sports, their markets, their household existence, we are left in comparative ignorance.

"It seems quite fitting that in this, our peoples' form of government and society, a new historical path should be struck out, and you have proved yourself a careful and skillful pioneer therein." —*Hon. Charles King.*

"I have read it carefully through, and as the period over which it extends is one to which I have given considerable attention, it affords me great pleasure to say that it contains more original and accurate information in respect to local events and manners in the early history of the city than any work upon the subject that has appeared during my lifetime. It is chiefly commendable for its industry and its accuracy, and will for this reason be more serviceable as a record of past landmarks than other productions in the same line of inquiry of much greater pretensions. You have not only shown great industry, patience, and care in the collection of materials, but have enhanced the value of the book by an index so copious and minute as to enable all co-laborers to get at the large amount of original information you have brought to light with the least possible loss of time. This is a matter which the writers of books, and especially of books of this description, attend to but indifferently; the consequence of which is that their labors are not as available to others as they might be, and are overlooked by subsequent inquirers, who would otherwise refer to them as standard sources of information." —*Hon. Charles P. Daly.*

"The very thorough examination which I have been enabled to make of this, tho first fruit of your historical labors, has enabled me to speak understandingly when I say that it is a monument of patient toil which reflects the very highest credit on tho diligent laborer who has produced it; and that, as a local history as well as a guide to the more general inquirer concerning the past of New York, no work has preceded this which for minuteness of detail, for precision of statement, and for undoubted correctness, may be at all compared with it as a rival or a substitute."

Henry B. Dawson, Esq.

"When I consider the little time you can spare from your attention to business, 'The Market-Book' is at once a monument of your unflinching zeal and untiring industry. Those only know the drudgery required (and this I speak from experience) in searching through musty documents or files of newspapers, to verify or confirm some isolated fact, who have performed that service; your book gives the evidence of this most irresistibly. The pages teem with a freshness of historic matter that ought to gladden the heart of every New Yorker, but more especially your own profession.

"The interest of the subject grows as we progress in the perusal; there is a fund of humor, of anecdote, and of personal history which incites the reader onward in his agreeable task. The arrangement of the book is admirable, and precludes the possibility of confusion.

"I hope the old market-place of New Amsterdam will ever be secure from innovation or desecration, and so long as the Bowling Green remains, it will be. And old 'Fly Market,' although among the things of the past, how many pleasing memories it must call up from the storehouse of the past to those among us who remember its noticeable features! What visions of juicy steaks! — the fat and luscious rib-pieces, and the inviting leg of lamb, must be theirs. And there were also those famous old fellows of the cleaver, viz: Astor, Pesinger, Gibbons, Seaman, etc., the remembrance of whom calls up a secret wish for the enjoyment again of those 'good old times.'

"To your craft you have rendered an essential service, in rescuing from oblivion the many good deeds of your forefathers, who were among the first to volunteer to meet the foe, — to face the pestilence which wasteth at noonday, or extend the hand of charity to the needy.

"I have no doubt but that your book will be fully appreciated, so that you will have no cause to regret the labor and time bestowed on its production; and I heartily wish your success in every particular will be adequate to its merits.

Late William J. Davis, Esq.

"I beg to express to you the pleasure I have had in reading your historical account of the Markets of our city. Having been aware of your persevering labors in searching our records and procuring information from every source which could throw light on your subject, I anticipated an interesting and reliable work. My expectations have been more than realized, and those who feel an interest in our city history will feel grateful for the pleasure they must derive from the result of your labors." — *David T. Valentine, Esq.*

"The items of the history of the city of New York contained in this volume of yours, if not the most important in a political aspect, yet is exceedingly valuable in its civil and domestic relations. The domestic habitudes of any community controls most other interests, and is a pretty true indication of its state of civilization." — *Dr. Horace Webster.*

"The patient labor which you have bestowed in the collection of the materials to form so complete a history of the rise and progress of Markets in New York, entitles you to the thanks of the community. You have given to the world not only a history of the rise and progress of Markets, but have also collected and given a vast amount of valuable information relating to the transitions through which societies and colonies have passed since their first landing among the Indian tribes. Valuable lessons may be learned from the sufferings of the colonists, brought on, as a natural consequence, by the falsehood, fraud, and violence practiced by them in dealing with these Indian tribes. It is lamentable to find how slow mankind is to learn that every act of cruelty brings wretchedness in its train.

"It is also encouraging to know — as you have shown — how the fair dealing of Gov. Stuyvesant, a single individual, could restore peace and a prosperous trade to a whole colony." — *Peter Cooper, Esq.*

"You have given to a special department of local history one of the most remarkable contributions which it has fallen within my experience to hear or read of. I could hardly have thought of a topic less likely to reward literary labor; and after looking with care at what you have done, I confess myself unable to understand by what powers for minute observation, or by what process of labor, you have assembled so vast an amount of information relative to a subject in which almost the whole world considers that the chief business is "consumption;" and which we would suppose in general treasured so few records for the pen of History.

"Your volume, past doubt, is encouraging to every investigation into local history; for it shows that nothing in the material world which concerns men at all, is without memorials, quite its own, which require but the man and the hour to collect and bring them forth for the instruction of every order of society. As I laid down your volume, I recalled the declaration of Cicero: '*Etenim omnes artes qua ad humanitatem pertinent, habent quoddam commune vinculum: et quasi cognatione quadam, inter se continentur.*'

"The Philadelphia Markets have had, in the estimation of our own people, at least, some agreeable distinctions; and I am happy to hear that you purpose to devote some of your efforts to teaching us a little about ourselves." — *John William Wallace, Esq.*

"My father has just finished the reading of your work. I need not say how much the book gratified him. He expresses a wish that some Philadelphian may have the leisure and inclination to write a history of the market-houses in Philadelphia. There is ample material for such a history, and I presume such a volume would be acceptable to all our citizens, except a few of the aristocracy, who might not wish to have their families traced back to the ancient and honorable society of victualers." — *John A. McAllister, Esq.*

"The subject is one which none better understand than yourself, and you have handled it at once in a luminous and agreeable manner; and when I say so, I beg you will acquit me of any desire to flatter, unless the strict truth may be called so." — *Ferd. J. Dreer, Esq.*

"Its style is clear and vigorous, it is fraught with useful information, and abounds in pleasing anecdote. To me, as an old New Yorker (having lived in the city nearly half a century), it has been exceedingly interesting.

"Many of the facts you state, and scenes you describe, had passed from my memory, but you have revived them in all their freshness; and many of the actors in these scenes, whom you name, were, in their day, my personal friends, and some of them members of the church to which I minister; so that, in reading your book, I have been thrown once more into communion with many old friends, and lived life over again.

"There is also in this volume much historical matter (some of it connected with our Revolutionary struggle) that is both interesting and important; and the proceedings of our city authorities from time to time, which you narrate, it appears to me renders your book a *necessity*, or at all events, *desideratum*, to our authorities now — the *present* ought to learn wisdom from the *past*, even from its errors. I will only add that I cannot but admire the indomitable patience and perseverance displayed in your researches. How, with the active business life which you lead, you ever found time to collect from various and varied sources such an amount of useful information as you have condensed in this volume, I cannot conceive." — *Rev. D. J. McElroy.*

"I have read portions of it, and found them highly interesting and instructive. The index is of great value. The more I read of the book, the greater is my surprise at the diligence and thoroughness and extent of your researches. It seems as if but little more could be gleaned on the topics which you have taken up; and a great amount of incidental information respecting the city and its inhabitants has been saved by you from oblivion." — *Rev. John Langdon Sibley.*

"It is certainly a book of merit, and much more interesting than its title would at first suggest. The manner it was received by the New York Historical Society was, in my opinion, but a just appreciation of what the book deserves, and my acknowledgments would add very little to the compliments of a body so distinguished." — *Rev. Aug. J. Thebaud.*

"I have begun its perusal, and have already become much interested in its historic details. It is a *unique* work, — as satisfactorily filling a blank hitherto unfilled; — and when completed, it will certainly be most creditable to its author, as bearing evidence of very careful research, and much literary toil on his part." — *Rev. Thomas Lyle.*

"But now what shall I say of the book itself? It really surprises me, and I hardly know whether most to admire its multiplicity and range of subject, the perseverance and energy which has collected so vast an amount of material from sources not easily accessible, or the judgment and correct taste shown in their arrangement and connecting remarks. All is admirable.

"I will now confess, that when you first mentioned the intended work several years ago, and hinted that some day it might be in print, I feared it would not be possible to invest so dry a subject (seemingly) with sufficient interest to make the book readable, and that disappointment would be the result.

"Your lecture removed that fear, and begat a strong hope of its success among a certain class. But really, your Market is so superabundantly supplied with 'tit bits' of every kind, and suited to the craving of every appetite, that only a *nondescript* can fail to find what pleases his palate!

"The book is a feast of fat things to men of antiquarian tastes; and while reveling in the lusciousness of such a repast they cannot but admire the industry which prepared, and the public spirit that has placed it before them. In this view, it is a valuable contribution to the history of New York.

"The intelligent man of leisure will value it as a collection of those rare and curious incidents which enter so largely into the history of a people, and so clearly serve to illustrate their progress.

"In this respect you have spoken of every thing, from the 'Cedars of Lebanon to the Hyssop on the Wall.' From 'Mars on a market-day smiling at Mrs. Mingay's call, to old Johnny Day's gratitude to his benefactress'; with many others quite as interesting but far more ludicrous. In fact, yours is a book for the *million*, and if that million only have sense enough to buy and appreciate it, it will be a pleasing proof of healthy intelligence." — *Late Rev. Jesse Pound.*

"A book full of curious research and information upon a subject that concerns us all, and hitherto unexplored.

"It could not be better done." — *Late Lt.-Gen. Winfield Scott.*

"I have read with much interest your very pleasant and agreeable book upon the Markets of New York.

"It exhibits much research, and presents a great number of incidents of the early history of New York which I have never before seen in print, although familiar to me as one of the older residents.

"It is, as far as my own memory extends, perfectly reliable in all its leading facts, and I hope you will continue your labors in this department of local history so interesting to us, who have grown with the growth of this great city and who can remember when it was a small one." — *Major-Gen. Charles W. Sandford.*

"I regret I lack the ability fully to describe the enjoyment I experienced in looking over its pages, and what I think of your great industry, devotion, and untiring research and perseverance in bringing together so many and such various subjects and incidents in connection with the history of the markets. I find related with great truthfulness many circumstances of which I myself in my younger days was cognizant, — many incidents of the *olden times* which I have received as traditions from older persons, — many names of distinguished individuals, some of whom I have known personally, and others with whose positions and actions I have been familiar In my estimation, it is a book the perusal of which cannot fail to greatly interest those who take pleasure in whatever relates to the days gone by, and the unexampled growth and prosperity of our goodly city, not only in its markets, but in every thing else which adds to our comfort and enjoyment." — *Major-Gen. Henry T. Kiersted.*

"I think you have done good service to the public in carefully collecting the facts that you have brought together and presenting them in a form both interesting and statistical.

"It is a literary virtue that you have not attempted to go outside of your subject; and the step by step progress that has brought our city from a wilderness to its present greatness is well and interestingly shown in your book of markets.

"I esteem the subject of good markets and market regulations of the first importance to the health and comfort of a great city, and any thing that directs the public mind in the right channel is a public benefit.

"After devoting so much time to this subject and presenting it in so able a form, I hope you will go still further and give the city the benefit of your experience and practical knowledge of how to bring the producer and consumer nearer together, and to supply our markets abundantly with wholesome food.

"I believe every citizen owes you thanks for your labors thus far; and rich and poor will alike be indebted to you for much needed reform that may follow your further investigation of the subject." — *Brig.-Gen. William Hall.*

"I have read the history of the Markets written by you, and have done so with a great deal of pleasure, as it has brought back to my memory youthful days and recollections of more than fifty years ago, and traditionary a great many more on the back of that, — the many remarkable events and incidents which occurred around the old market-places, — Peck Slip, Exchange, Oswego, Catherine, Bear, and the old Fly Market, all of which have been most faithfully portrayed by you. It also calls back to my knowledge and associations the names of Thomas Gibbons, David Marsh, David Seaman, Mathew Vogel, and many other old butchers whose lives are examples worthy of being recorded on the brightest pages of history. To me this is a valuable book, and what pleases me more than all is that its author is one of the profession, who I think ought to be promptly encouraged, not only by all belonging to it, but by every New Yorker." — *Col. William Appleby.*

"My time has been so much occupied as to prevent my making as yet more than a hasty examination of the volume; but even that has disclosed enough to warrant my hearty commendation of the work. It evinces most industrious and successful research, the results of which are admirably arranged. Its historical fullness will afford valuable aid to our city authorities in the matter of market legislation. The high literary excellence which characterizes the style of the book adds much to the interest of the narrative, and must render it not only interesting and instructive to the antiquarian, but inviting to the general reader." — *Hon. George Opdyke.*

"I have just finished the perusal of your work entitled 'The Market-Book,' and certainly found it far more interesting than I had expected.

"Had you confined yourself simply to the subject indicated by the title of the work, it would still have possessed great interest, as showing the early modes of supplying the city with the means of daily subsistence and the almost patriarchal control of the Common Council in reference to the establishment of public markets; their supply of country produce; and the system of licensing butchers and others to occupy stands, and dispose of provisions thereon. But you have done much more than this.

You have for the first time collected the scattered and curious materials of the city's early domestic history in a volume of ample proportions, and have superadded various legends, from living witnesses who still linger on the verge of time, and which would have been forever lost, had not your industry and perseverance thus rescued them from oblivion.

"In my course of reading in ancient and even in modern history, I have often regretted that the limits of the historian did not permit him to unfold more of the social habits and occupations of the people, and that little appears in history but its more salient points, such as national wars, revolutions, and the change of dynasties. It is true Hallam has done more, and so has Macaulay, and a few others of our recent historians; but in the matter of social history, which is after all the great exponent of human happiness, little has been or perhaps could have been accomplished.

"In view of the above, it has been gratifying to me to find that you left the tented field, with garments rolled in blood, (I mean human blood,) and all the pomp and circumstance of glorious war, to take care of themselves, and that you have become the less ambitious chronicler of the plain, every-day lives of the honest, sturdy burghers of the past, telling our present degenerate boys and girls that the colossal fortunes of many of our citizens commenced in the simple, persevering industry of their ancestors; thus showing that while labor may appear antiquated to many, it is the only sure foundation and precursor of enduring prosperity.

"So too you have told us that Pope was not mistaken when he said that

"'Honor and shame from no condition rise;
Act well your part, there all the honor lies.'

"The unpretending man who retails meat, and the woman who did the same by vegetables, were found, when the emergencies required it, among the ranks of the patriot and philanthropist; facing death in the battle-field or at the bed of the sufferer from malignant disease, and leading or following in all that was calculated to elevate humanity, or enlarge the boundaries of human happiness.

"Your work contains also much of the facetious and joyous, for at those early periods business did not make such heavy drafts on leisure; there was more time, as the proverb has it, 'to laugh and grow fat;' and the butcher who drove fat oxen enjoyed his laugh, and did not leave all the fat to the oxen. In a word, those who suppose that your work (from its title) is limited in its range, or dry and uninteresting in its details, had better be disabused at once by reading it, and they will assuredly become convinced, as I have, that no genuine *New Yorker* should be without it."

Hon. Thomas Jeremiah.

"I have read the work with pleasure and interest. The great labor and research you have bestowed upon it makes it a valuable addition to the history of our city. Although the work ostensibly treats of the public markets and market-places of the city of New York, yet it contains a vast fund of information and personal history very difficult to be obtained. I trust you will receive such patronage for this work that the second volume you are preparing may be placed at an early day in our hands." — *John W. Chambers, Esq.*

"The author of this book subscribes his modest preface, 'Thomas F. De Voe, *Butcher*,' a title which, in connection with that which graces his title-page, gives assurance of the solid character of his book. He is an author in spite of himself. Having been led to make some researches in the archives of the New York Historical Society to gratify his own curiosity as to the antiquities of his profession, he was induced to prepare a paper on this subject, and to read it before the Society in acknowledgment of its services to him. His labors were so warmly received that the expanding of his paper into a book was simply a development in the order of Nature. The book itself is best described by the following sentence from its second title-page: 'This volume contains a history of the public markets of the city of New York, from its first settlement to the present time, with numerous curious and remarkable incidents connected therewith, the introduction of cattle, supplies, trading, prices, and laws; sketches of the old burgher butchers, and the licensed butchers of modern times; together with a compilation of facts of every sort and character relating to the subject.'

"Not the least edifying portions of this book are those in which the chronicle runs parallel with that of Diedrich Knickerbocker; it is sometimes hard to say whether the literal record of the days of Van Twiller and Kieft or the mock-heroic history is the more grotesque. Some idea of the relative value of commodities of the market and the loom in 1638 may be formed from a legal transaction of that date, described as follows: 'Cornelius Petersen appeared before the Secretary Van Tienhoven, and declared with true Christian affirmation, in lieu of a solemn oath, that it was true that he had purchased a hog from Ann Jackson, in payment of which she took from his store so much of purpled cloth as was sufficient for a petticoat.' It is easy enough, as every one knows, by mere excerpts such as this from antique records and documents to insure a certain kind and measure of interest for a book treating of local habits, customs, and institutions; but our author succeeds not less in giving entertainment to his readers as he approaches our own times, and narrates the results of his own observation and experience within familiar precincts.

"The book is really a curious one, and to be commended to the student of manners and customs. We trust Mr. De Voe will not disappoint us of a second volume. Some of the material which he collects and preserves is of a kind to amuse and entertain, if not greatly to instruct, posterity." — *North American Review.*

"The first volume of 'The Market-Book,' by Thomas F. De Voe, is in the market. As you can generally judge of a man by his face, so you can of a book by its preface. The preface of this is dated from Jefferson Market, and signed 'Thomas F. De Voe, Butcher.' There is an honesty about this opening especially commendable. The author of a very recent publication dated from the Fifth Avenue Hotel — he probably wished to have the world know that he lived there. Mr. De Voe also wishes his friends to know where he is to be found, and, accordingly, dates from his place of business. He is a butcher by trade, — a good one, we will guarantee, — and he writes himself so. He considers his profession quite as honorable as those of banker, broker, lawyer, or physician. And he is right. Why should we accord a respect to that man who mixes us pills and prescribes draughts, which we refuse to give to him who furnishes us with palatable steaks and juicy joints? And so on through the list. It is customary to bow to the man who discounts a bill for us at an enormous 'shave,' and to exchange cards with one who loses or gains for us a lawsuit that proves the ruin of all parties concerned, while we speak rather condescendingly, or nod patronizingly, to our butchers and bakers. Much of this sort of thing will be changed some time before the Millennium commences.

"In giving us this history of the markets, Mr. De Voe very nearly furnishes us with a history of our city. In all manner of queer recesses and out-of-the-way receptacles, he seems to have dived and delved for the material of his book; and as facts generally lie in clusters, like oysters or potatoes, the consequence is, that he has fished up many that are of interest to even those who care little about market reform and the steady progress and gradual development of the butcher's art. Commencing with the reign of Wouter Van Twiller, Mr. De Voe brings his history down to that of

Wood. Interesting as it always is to watch the progress of the professions — to follow the feeble footsteps of their infancy until the field comes to ring with the firm, assured tread of their virility — it is especially so to follow the progress of those that pertain to killing, to mark the dawn of the art, the gradual development, and the slow but sure degrees by which it has been brought to perfection. In military science, from the club of Abel to the columbiad of the present day is a step, somewhat long, but instructive and amusing to take. In the medical profession, between the first rude appliances of the art to the perfected prescriptions and deftly constructed instruments which now lie ready to the chirurgeon's hand, lies a path of progress that it is pleasant to trace. And all the foregoing remarks apply to the butcher's trade.

"We are willing to stake our reputation that this first cut of Mr. De Voe's in the literary line will please even that most fastidious of customers — the reading public." *New York Times.*

"Of all the curious works which a spirit of antiquarian research has yet produced in the United States, this book is the most remarkable. History, when devoted to the recital of noble actions and great events, is sufficiently interesting to attract intelligent readers of all classes. It is a more confined sphere which limits the local chronicler to a tedious and industrious unearthing and narration of the comparatively petty events which have occurred in the progress of a county or township. Nothing but a strong enthusiasm can repay the annalist for his labor in reviving the memory of events that seem but trivial in comparison to the more solemn transactions which mark the progress of communities. The investigator of family history may indulge a hereditary pride in gathering the personal reminiscences which preserve the memory of good and useful actions, and which reflect credit upon the descendants of the worthy. But who would have thought that a handsome and interesting book could be made out of the dry records of the markets of a large city? Evidently it would require for such a task a gentleman whose connection with the business of buying and selling produce was carried on under a feeling of the dignity and importance of his vocation. Such a man the writer of this singular and highly interesting volume seems to be. Claiming fraternity with the important guild of butchers, having for years carried on the business with honor and profit, having also distinguished himself as a good citizen, useful in many local enterprises, Colonel Thomas F. De Voe has made of this work a labor of love and pride. It is, in fact, a minute and faithful history of the New York markets from the earliest times, embracing therein matter of local interest and reminiscences of the progress of the great city, which very fitly illustrate the character of a people with whom good eating is a prime necessity. It is quaint, and in many particulars strange, illustrating the character of the people who bought at the markets as much as it does the characters of farmers, truckmen, fishermen, and butchers, who supplied the wants of a large population. There are many persons of antiquarian tastes to whom this singular book will be attractive. We recommend it to them as an oddity in history, original in the design, curious in particulars, and evidently exhausting in its treatment of the topics chosen. The second volume, which is now in preparation, will be devoted to the history of the markets in other cities than New York, including our own. From the industry and assiduity displayed in volume first we can confidently promise that very much of our market history long since forgotten will be brought to light and placed in such a permanent form that it will in all time to come prove a permanent and enduring record for preservation and instruction." — *Philadelphia Sunday Dispatch.*

"Tom Quick says: 'We have many items of great interest to the old and new butchers that we have, in the kindest manner, been allowed to take from the notes of an Old Sport who has not spent his days nor nights in idleness, but to the end that he might serve up a rich feast of facts concerning the butchers of Gotham, from the year 1656 to the present day; his searches among bygone carcasses have enabled him to give one great work on our Markets, which is now before the public as "The Market-Book," by Thomas F. De Voe, Butcher; and also caused him to declare his intentions of adding another volume on the same subject up to the present time. I shall freely, by his permission, use portions of the rich cream the book is so full of. No butcher, or butcher's family, should be without this great work of a "boss" upon their reading-table.'" — *New York Leader.*

"'The Market-Book,' containing a historical account of the Public Markets in the cities of New York, Boston, Philadelphia, and Brooklyn, with a brief description of every article of human food sold therein, the introduction of cattle into America, and notices of many remarkable specimens, by Thomas F. De Voe, member of the New York Historical Society, in 2 vols., Vol. I. (New York: printed for the author, 1862,) is a very notable and meritorious work. The author, a self-made man, long engaged in the State militia of New York, and himself practically conversant with and moving in the sphere of the market, has amassed here an amount of curious and interesting information truly prodigious. The first volume is occupied with a minute sketch of each of the many New York markets, from the earliest period of the settlement of the country to the present time. Mr. De Voe has evidently been at an infinite amount of pains to sift and winnow the early records, the journals of courts, the city newspapers, the law reports, private letters and collections, public libraries and archives, histories, books, tracts, petitions, and legislative proceedings; but it is clearly a work of love. We presume no history of New York has been written which contains so much entertaining knowledge about early manners and customs; the style of living; the kinds of food used; public and private entertainments; price of provisions; the local changes of streets, buildings, and markets; the food, drink, and clothing of the people; anecdotes of the colonial era; history of the wars, panics, taxes, laws, morals, crimes, punishments of different eras. The journal of Winthrop, the local histories of Wood, and other English chroniclers, are the things one is reminded of in reading Mr. De Voe. Every page has on it something worth knowing and worth remembering. A careful index of the butchers whose names occur in the work, and a general index, add much to the practical utility of the book. We commend 'The Market-Book' (Vol. I.) to our local readers in New York and the vicinity. Some of the *novi homines* may wince under the publication of the fact that their ancestors held the very necessary and respectable post of the Fulton, Washington, or Tompkin's commissariats of the city: but those who measure family renown by use, and who believe that

> 'Honor and shame from no condition rise;
> Act well your part, there all the honor lies,'

will not be ashamed to be descended from the honorable and benevolent butchers of New York, among whom are as fine men as any in this world. Mr. De Voe's work will have a wide and interested circulation. Thousands in each of the great cities, whose annals, in this respect, he proposes to record, will wish to see such a mass of valuable and curious information." — *Christian Inquirer.*

"The first volume is a history of the public markets of New York, with sketches of many of the principal butchers, from the earliest time down to some now living. Statements and descriptions are introduced, interspersed with anecdotes, so that one gains a very clear idea of the habits of the people, the laws of the city, and the location of the markets; and in whatever has any connection with the sale of human food, the book is particularly full and clear. The history of public buildings, streets, squares, ferries, of the origin of now prominent and wealthy families, of the Revolutionary War, and of important civil and military events as successively they had a bearing on the craft, give to the work ever-varying interest. We have perused it with very great pleasure and instruction, and find everywhere evidence of great discrimination and accuracy. It has especial interest to the agriculturist, because not only the first introduction of neat cattle and small cattle into New Netherlands is recorded, but changes in the character of market stock are noted, as well as record made of the most notable animals; and in a subsequent volume, in which histories of the markets of other cities also will be given, Mr. De Voe purposes to discuss the ways in which various kinds of meat, and other produce, are brought to market, and to describe every article of food sold in the public market, the manner of its production, and how it is prepared for sale." — *American Agriculturist.*

" Volume I. of this work has lately been published, and is in many respects a remarkable production. Going back to the earliest period of the settlement of this city, it gives the origin and progress of all the market-places, together with a detailed account of the manner of doing business, the habits, customs, and laws of the people through many generations, historical reminiscences of all the prominent market people and dealers, and a full and faithful history of all events and places in any manner relating to markets or market business. As a part of the history of the city of New York, it deserves more than usual attention, covering, as it does, a field hitherto unexplored; and the fund of biographical lore and anecdote, with which it is liberally interspersed, makes it one of the most readable books of the times. To the old New Yorker it must be of great value and interest, and many of the aristocratic leaders of the present generation can not fail to trace back their lineage to some of the many hundred names among the honored class of butchers. As a historian, Mr. De Voe is accurate and truthful, and the whole work shows a labored research; undoubtedly a labor of love, yet one that has required close application and a deal of hard work. We shall welcome with pleasure the appearance of the second volume, but sincerely hope that it will not end the historical writings of such an agreeable and instructive writer." — *The Horticulturist.*

" The butchers of New York are and have always been a most respectable and flourishing class in society. Generally honest, intelligent, independent men, with proverbially robust health and remarkable physical development, the 'butcher boys' have never failed to exert a weighty influence in the community. It is not strange, then, that they should have their historian, and that he should be a prominent member of their own order. To be a good butcher is a good thing; but to be a good butcher and a good author at the same time does not often happen, even in New York. Col. Thos. F. De Voe, of Jefferson Market, is well known as a prince among the butchers. He has also made his mark as a military man, having won himself a good name by the excellent state of discipline and drill to which he brought a regiment of militia mostly composed of stalwart butchers. Once or twice he has appeared at the Historical Society as a reader of a paper on the great men among the butchers in past days. But now he comes before the public as a full-fledged author in an entertaining volume of 621 pages, giving a historical account of the public markets in this city from the earliest record to the present time, with personal notices of many remarkable men in his line of business.

" This is only the first volume of the work. In a second, Col. De Voe proposes at some future time to give similar accounts of the markets of Boston, Philadelphia, and Brooklyn, and of every article of human food sold therein. In the volume at present issued, the Colonel has done himself infinite credit, and has managed to invest with interest a naturally rather dry subject to any but the antiquarian. From piles of musty old documents, family memoranda, society archives, etc., he has extracted notices of over twelve hundred butchers, from Wm. Clasen, Gerit Jansen Roos, and Jan Van Haerlan, who were the first sworn butchers, appointed in November, 1656, to the Hardenbrooks, who were the lessees of Harlem Market in 1857. Many of these butchers were notable men in their day, and some of them rose to high public positions. Not a few of them furnish Col. De Voe with material for interesting anecdotes, and all seem worthy of being dragged from the obscurity in which they have so long been hidden from public notice.

"With indefatigable industry and perseverance, Col. De Voe appears to have collected almost every particular in regard to the public markets and market-places of this city. His book is a feast for the lover of quaint accounts of the way things were done two hundred years ago, and is a capital illustration of the gradual progress of this city from the crude matter-of-fact simplicity of the days of 'the Company's store,' to the polish of the present day. It abounds in extracts from documents, and many of the transactions of its characters are told in their own language, with faithful adherence to grammar, orthography, and style." — *Evening Express.*

"'The Market-Book,' giving a historical account of the markets of our city, from their foundation; that is, altogether covering a period from 1625 to 1861. This survey is not barrenly rendered; it is constantly enlivened by quaint extracts from the ancient records, anecdotes of the trade, stories of the olden days of the town, mad-cap frolics, and exploits of heroes of the stall. With these, however, we have the solid history carefully prepared, for Mr. De Voe is a most diligent collector, who traces up every fact and incident to their utmost source. He writes without affectation or attempt at finery; and has really furnished one of the most agreeable, useful, and instructive of all our volumes of local history; and has inseparably connected his name with the future renown of his native city." — *The New-Yorker.*

"This is a most curious contribution to local history; but when the history of the New York markets affords matter for a volume of over six hundred pages, it was well worth the writing, and the task could not have fallen into better hands than those of the painstaking, industrious, and discriminating author of this work, who proudly styles himself 'Butcher,' in his preface to his literary labor. The matter is purely history of New York city; and in treating of the various markets, the author gives, to a considerable extent, the history of the city itself, especially of its social life." — *Historical Magazine.*

"It is not often that bullocks and books share pretty equally the attention of one man. The slaughtering of beeves and the writing of books are not generally regarded as congenial occupations, albeit authors in the main have no antipathy to beef, and are often indebted to 'sheepskin' for a covering. But this is an age of progress, and the same hand that profitably wields the cleaver now gracefully guides the pen. There lies before us a very handsomely printed octavo volume of some six hundred and twenty pages, bearing the title 'The Market-Book, containing a historical account of the public markets in the cities of New York, Boston, Philadelphia, and Brooklyn, with a brief description of every article of human food sold therein; the introduction of cattle in America, and notices of many remarkable specimens.' The author is Thomas F. De Voe, who signs himself 'Butcher,' is a member of the

New York Historical Society, and holds also the military rank of Colonel. All hail to the cleaver and the pen! Who will deny that the world moves, and that butchers keep it moving? Hurra for the union of butchering and book making! Success to the man who slaughters cattle, but gives life to history.

"Nay, stop, Mr. Cynic. We do *not* mean that 'The Market-Book' is a specimen of butchery in book-making. Far from it. That Col. De Voe — a modest claim to descent from De Foe, doubtless — lacks Addison's purity and Junius's classic force of diction we will admit. That the supervision of some one practiced in the art of composition would have in some respects improved our author's style, we will not deny. But then the work would have been no longer the sole production of 'Thomas F. De Voe, Butcher,' which mades it as unique as it is meritorious. Very quaintly and pleasantly does the Colonel tell us how the author grew up side by side with the butcher, giving him pleasant thoughts and occupations in return for savory steaks and juicy roasting pieces; for as it ever happens in this mundane sphere, the latter has the larger share of the good things of this life. The butcher became rich and plethoric; the author would only have nibbled his pen in the vain search for nutritious juices. But with a well-filled larder at all times accessible, the author set himself cheerfully and industriously to work, and the result is this 'first' of we know not how many volumes of a really valuable and interesting 'historical account' of an institution to which we are all immensely indebted." — *Commercial Advertiser.*

"This work is in two volumes, and Vol. No. I. is before us. It is a very singular volume. In the first place the title-page has no punctuation marks at all; in the second place the preface is as full of them as if they had been sprinkled from a pepper-box. As for the literary contents of the volume, we may justly say that they are written in a plain, unpretending, very intelligible style, and narrate in an interesting manner the history of various markets. The narration is rendered the more entertaining because the author indulges in a multitude of amusing episodes, and when carried away by an incidental suggestion elaborates it to its fullest extent, returning subsequently to his original starting-point. Thus the 'Markets' become a series of pegs on which are hung a world of curious old facts and singular reminiscences. Mr. De Voe has made a useful and agreeable volume, and we trust that No. II. will possess the same elements of value and popularity." — *The Times and Messenger.*

"The leisure hours of the author during the intervals of business as a practical market-man in Jefferson Market have been devoted to the preparation of this work. He has sought his materials in the collections of the New York Historical Society, and numerous other authentic sources, and with the genuine enthusiasm of the antiquary, has spared neither time nor labor in the prosecution of his researches. The volume abounds in curious details of the olden time, and places the manners and customs of the early settlers of Manhattan in a clear and interesting light, besides giving a complete historical view of the specific subject to which it is devoted." — *Daily Tribune.*

"The work will consist of two volumes, and the first, which is just issued, is devoted to the markets of this city, from its settlement to the present time. One of the most interesting features of the book is the personal sketches of the old burgher butchers, who occupied stalls in the Old Slip and Fly Market in the early part of the last century. The entire contents, indeed, possess great interest, and are valuable additions to our local history. Colonel De Voe has executed his work in a successful manner, and given a plain, concise, and reliable account of his subject. The work is worthy of a place in the library of every Knickerbocker in the land. We cordially commend the book to our readers. The worthy author has several times read papers on the subject before the New York Historical Society, which have elicited much attention. He is another instance of what may be accomplished by industry, perseverance, and talents." — *Home Journal.*

"The following communication, which will be read with interest, is from an erudite and able pen, and treats upon a subject both unique and piquant. We are no believers in the aristocracy of wealth, and conceive that no affluent or eminent man ought to be ashamed of his ancestors because they earned an honest living by their industry. 'Honor and shame from no condition rise,' says the poet; and we agree with him. There *are* people, though, who go into agonies over their recollections of the social *status* of their grandfathers, and no doubt all such will deem our correspondent very just in his quaint observations:

"*To the Editors of the Sunday Times:*

"GENTLEMEN, — I have just arisen from the perusal of a very singular sort of book lately published by one Thomas F. De Voe, 'member of the New York Historical Society, etc.,' as he signs himself on the title-page, and 'Butcher,' as he writes after his signature to the preface. The work in question is called 'The Market-Book,' and professes to contain 'a historical account of the public markets in the cities of New York, Boston, Philadelphia, and Brooklyn, &c., &c., &c.' The author appears to have taken a great deal of pains to gather facts and dates, and I have no doubt that his book will be treasured up as a valuable contribution to local history. His researches have led him into many interesting fields of knowledge, and occasionally he digresses from the main subject in a most agreeable manner and with very entertaining results.

"It seems to me, however, that he might have spared the feelings of several of the first families in New York by omitting to mention some disagreeable and humiliating facts. He treats genealogy as he would an ox. He bleeds, cuts, dissects, and flays without remorse. Without the slightest regard for the sensitive feelings of the present generation, he publishes to the world — and gives names and dates, too! — that many of our wealthiest citizens, residing in the Fifth Avenue, or living in luxury abroad, are descended from butchers!

"Now, you will allow, Messrs. Editors, that a man is not responsible, morally, socially, or otherwise, for the conduct of his grandfather. If my grandfather chose the trade of a butcher, why should I be blamed for it? This is my case exactly. My father's father *was* a butcher, and, just as my family had almost outlived the disagreeable memory, along comes this 'member of the New York Historical Society — Thomas F. De Voe, *Butcher*,' and blurts out the whole thing before the world. He deliberately puts upon record a fact which I have always endeavored to keep from my children, and of which my very wife was ignorant until she saw my grandfather's name conspicuously paraded in the book.

"There may be no remedy for this outrage. The book may not be libelous. The law may give me no relief. If I were to sue Mr. De Voe, he might admit the publication, and *justify*, as the lawyers call it, by *proving* my paternal ancestor's trade, which would only give greater notoriety to a circumstance I had hoped might pass out of human recollection. Besides, there might be two or three butchers on the jury, and then my chance for damages would be small indeed.

"All I can do, therefore, is to denounce the author of 'The Market-Book' as a reckless disturber of family pride. In behalf of many proud and wealthy families of New York, I denounce him. He might have told the world all about Bear Market and Vlie Market, when they were built, where they stood, &c.; but he should have kept to himself the names of the men who sold meat there. He had no right to remind us that our grandfathers trundled mutton to market in a wheelbarrow, and then carried it to their customers on a wooden tray. The cause of historical truth, for which Mr. De Voe affects so much veneration, would have been quite as well served had he omitted names and disagreeable details. It is to be hoped that these suggestions will, in the next edition of his book, receive the attention to which they are entitled. Should they be disregarded, I now give him due notice and timely warning that I shall not be responsible for the consequences. Your obedient servant,

"An Indignant Gentleman.

"Gramercy Park, March 11, 1862."

—*The Times and Messenger.*

www.ingramcontent.com/pod-product-compliance
Lightning Source LLC
Chambersburg PA
CBHW031819270326
41932CB00008B/470

* 9 7 8 3 7 4 4 7 3 6 4 4 2 *